DISABILITY

A DIVERSITY MODEL APPROACH IN HUMAN SERVICE PRACTICE

DISABILITY

A DIVERSITY MODEL APPROACH IN HUMAN SERVICE PRACTICE

Romel W Mackelprang
Eastern Washington University

Richard O. Salsgiver
California State University, Fresno

Brooks/Cole Publishing Company
I(T)P® *An International Thomson Publishing Company*

Pacific Grove • Albany • Belmont • Bonn • Boston • Cincinnati • Detroit
Johannesburg • London • Madrid • Melbourne • Mexico City • New York • Paris
Singapore • Tokyo • Toronto • Washington

Sponsoring Editor: *Lisa I. Gebo*
Marketing Team: *Steve Catalano, Aaron Eden*
Marketing Representative: *Mickey Morris*
Editorial Assistant: *Susan Wilson*
Advertising Communications: *Margaret Parks*
Production Editors: *Karen Ralling, Janet Hill*
Manuscript Editor: *Jennifer McClain*

Interior Design: *John Edeen*
Cover Design: *Terri Wright*
Cover Illustration: *Diana Ong/SuperScript*
Design Coordinator: *Kelly Shoemaker*
Typesetting: *The Cowans*
Cover Printing: *Webcom*
Printing and Binding: *Webcom*

Copyright © 1999 by Brooks/Cole Publishing Company
A division of International Thomson Publishing, Inc.
I(T)P   The ITP logo is a registered trademark used herein under license.

For more information contact:

BROOKS/COLE PUBLISHING COMPANY
10 Davis Drive
Belmont, CA 94002
USA

International Thomson Editores
Seneca 53
Col. Polanco
11560 México, D.F., México

International Thomson Publishing Europe
Berkshire House 168-173
High Holborn
London WC1V 7AA
England

International Thomson Publishing GmbH
Königswinterer Strasse 418
53227 Bonn
Germany

Thomas Nelson Australia
102 Dodds Street
South Melbourne, 3205
Victoria, Australia

International Thomson Publishing Asia
60 Albert Street
#15-01 Albert Complex
Singapore 189969

Nelson Canada
1120 Birchmount Road
Scarborough, Ontario
Canada M1K 5G4

International Thomson Publishing Japan
Hirakawacho Kyowa Building, 3F
2-2-1 Hirakawacho
Chiyoda-ku, Tokyo 102
Japan

Printed in Canada

10   9   8   7

Library of Congress Cataloging-in-Publication Data
Mackelprang, Romel W, [date]
   Disability : a diversity model approach in human service practice
/ Romel, W Mackelprang, Richard O. Salsgiver.
      p.   cm.
   Includes bibliographical references and index.
   ISBN 0-534-34494-1 (paperbound)
   1. Handicapped—Care—United States.   2. Handicapped—Services
for—United States.   I. Salsgiver, Richard O., [date]
II. Title.
HV1553.M33   1998
362.4'048'0973—dc21   98–22619
                                                                        CIP

I owe a debt of gratitude to my friends, colleagues, and mentors with disabilities who have helped me begin to appreciate the lives of persons with disabilities. I am also deeply appreciative of my parents, who instilled a thirst for knowledge, and of Susan and our children for their support and encouragement.

Romel W Mackelprang

I would like to dedicate my efforts in the book to Janet McClure, my librarian at Blairsville High School, who was my first role model as a professional educator with a disability. I am also deeply appreciative of Pamela, my partner and closest friend.

Richard O. Salsgiver

ABOUT THE AUTHORS

 **Romel W Mackelprang** is an associate professor with the School of Social Work and Human Services, Eastern Washington University. He has worked as a rehabilitation social worker. He is a cofounder and former chair of the Council on Social Work Education Task Force on Persons with Disabilities, and is currently a member of the CSWE Commission on Disability and Persons with Disabilities. He has been involved in the independent living movement for more than a decade.

 **Richard O. Salsgiver,** Doctor of Arts, MSW, is currently professor of social work education at California State University, Fresno. Dr. Salsgiver is a person with a disability, having cerebral palsy since birth. He has taught at both the high school and college levels. In addition, he has served in various administrative positions in social welfare and higher education, including executive director of the California Association of the Physically Handicapped Independent Living Center in Fresno, California, and director of diversity programs in the California State University, Office of the Chancellor. He currently serves on various disability-related boards and committees, including the CWSE Commission on Disability and Persons with Disabilities.

CONTENTS

Chapter 6
DEAF AND HARD-OF-HEARING PEOPLE   104

Chapter 7
PERSONS WITH VISUAL DISABILITIES AND BLINDNESS   124

PREFACE

Disability: A Diversity Model Approach in Human Service Practice is written primarily for preparing students for human service careers that are directly related to working with persons with disabilities. Human service careers can include social work, psychology, rehabilitation counseling, family counseling, school counseling, and so on.

The authors first met in Kansas City at a Council on Social Work Education Annual Program Meeting in the spring of 1992. Each writer came from a different background. One had been a clinician in a rehabilitation environment and had served on the board of directors of an independent living center. The other had directly participated in the independent living movement, being an administrator in two centers of independent living since the middle '80s. One was a person with a disability; the other was not. Both taught social work education at the university level, both talked the same language when it came to issues of disability, and within their professional circles, both felt pretty much isolated in their perspective.

The language that we speak is one of disability being a condition of diversity and of oppression rather than a condition of psychological or physical dysfunction. Our language centers on the theme that the origin of the vast majority of the problems of persons with disabilities does not reside with "distorted ego function" or "crooked limbs," but with the way society views disability, and how it reacts to and treats persons with disabilities in light of its limited vision. Our language acknowledges a disability culture and a disability history. It asserts that persons with disabilities as a group have more commonalities than dissimilarities. It proposes that the answers to the "disability problem" lie with interventions not only with individuals but primarily with society. It is a language that exudes empowering persons with disabilities in the economic and political arena. It is a language that celebrates disability as an important piece of the great mosaic of diversity that makes up our society. Our language calls upon professionals to cast aside old models of conceptualizing disability and to embrace a model of difference rather than dysfunction.

This textbook invites controversy and discussion. We seek to probe old ideas and ways of looking at both human service practice and persons with disabilities. We ask students to grab hold of the lion's tail and get ready for a wild and different ride. We urge students to reach deep within and examine their beliefs and attitudes about disabilities. We encourage students to examine old ways of categorizing disabilities and persons with disabilities. We challenge students to view persons with disabilities from their strengths rather than their "dysfunctions." And we call upon students to become politically involved in the struggle. Politics is the biggest game in town!

We also wish to challenge instructors and other professionals. Many of the concepts presented in this book are controversial at best and downright heresy at worst. Some professionals may have trouble seeing disability as a social construct rather than primarily as a function of people's biological and psychological problems. Some may find it difficult to accept that we focus on disabled people's commonalities rather than focusing on classifications of disabilities. Some may continue to see proponents of the independent living movement as "paraprofessionals." And some may continue to believe that those with disabilities need to be taken care of by professionals. However, the text truly reflects the winds of change, as demonstrated by visionaries in the human services and as reflected in the changing ethical standards of many professions.

This book is divided into three sections. The first section establishes a nontraditional context of disability. We invite readers to move away from the perspective that persons with disabilities are sick, passive, and deviant. We create a context that acknowledges the devaluation and oppression of persons with disabilities, that recognizes the development of a culture built upon that oppressive experience, and that suggests the need for an aggressive political struggle to remove that oppression.

The second section looks at groupings of disabilities placed within the context of the social definition of disability. Each chapter discusses the implications of various disabilities on people's lives. Each also contains a personal account from someone living with these disabilities. Readers will find many common themes in the lives of people with different disabilities.

The third section discusses human service practice with persons with disabilities using the frames of reference presented in the first and second sections. Chapters 11 and 12 in this section approach practice from a strengths and diversity perspective. Chapter 13 lists six guiding principles of practice that we believe practitioners should use when working with people with disabilities. They represent our guiding principles in the textbook as a whole and in our professional lives. We introduce them here.

1. People with disabilities are capable and have potential.
2. Devaluation and the lack of resources, not individual pathology, are the primary obstacles facing persons with disabilities.
3. Disability, like race and gender, is a social construct, and a primary emphasis of intervention with people with disabilities must be political in nature.
4. There is a disability culture and history that professionals should be aware of in order to facilitate the empowerment of persons with disabilities.
5. There is joy and vitality to be found in disability.
6. Persons with disabilities have the right to self-determination and the right to guide professionals' involvement in their lives.

ACKNOWLEDGMENTS

So many people deserve to be recognized in the endeavor of writing this book. There are the many theorists and writers from whom we have borrowed. We would be remiss if we did not specifically mention Paul Longmore, now teaching at San Francisco State University. All the people who participated in the personal narratives deserve special recognition: Resa Hayes, Judy Heumann, Bill Hyatt, Abby Kovalsky, Donna Orrin, Karen Pendleton, Brenda Premo, Kevin Shirey, and Martha Sheridan. Their stories remind us of people's value and potential. Their insights are invaluable.

We would like to thank the many colleagues who reviewed the book at various levels. Among those are Liz DePoy, University of Maine, who spent much time and offered many suggestions for strengthening the book. We'd also like to thank Michael Lynch, M.D., who reviewed the chapter on mobility, and Fred Childers, who reviewed the chapter on cognitive disorders. We appreciate the efforts of Martha Sheridan and Janet Pray, Gallaudet University, who provided valuable input for the chapter on deaf and hard-of-hearing people. Thanks go also to Tom Bucaro, College of Staten Island, and Kris Tower, University of Nevada, Reno, who reviewed the entire manuscript, and to B. J. Bryson, East Tennessee State University; Linda Shaw, University of Florida; Diane Strock-Lynskey, Siena College; and Matthew Westra, Longview Community College. We are grateful to Eastern Washington University and California State University, Fresno, as well, for their support in terms of grants and graduate assistants. Finally, thanks to Mike Burpkee for helping with many tasks during the writing of this book.

Part One

CONTEXT FOR PRACTICE

One of the most important elements of knowledge possessed by the effective human service practitioner is that which comes from knowing your personal values. This particularly holds true for those who work with or plan to work with persons with disabilities. Our internalized values and beliefs come from a variety of places, including the aggregate culture, various subcultures, family teaching, life experiences, educational experiences, and so on. Values and beliefs concerning disability impact the work that you will be doing with one of the largest minority groups in the world—persons with disabilities.

To understand personal views regarding persons with disabilities, it is necessary to explore the various ways society and the cultures of society see persons with disabilities. This understanding is also extremely important in determining an approach to intervention and the types of intervention that will facilitate the development of enfranchised, empowered, and independent human beings.

How does society view disability and where do these views come from? What is your view of disability and how is it connected to history, culture, and society? A current cultural perspective on disability includes the idea that persons with disabilities are objects of pity who exist to be taken care of. Some fear persons with disabilities either because they may tear the very fabric of society or because they remind these able-bodied folks of their vulnerability and mortality. Others see persons with disabilities as sick. Some see them as perpetual children, sexless and in need of care. Still others see persons with disabilities as incompetent. Some see them as freaks. Others see them as either a gift or curse from god. And some see persons with disabilities merely as people who are, in superficial ways, different from people without disabilities. They recognize that persons with disabilities are, like everyone else, striving to get by, to live, to have good jobs, to have nice homes, to have fun, to lead fulfilling lives.

The etiology of these various beliefs and viewpoints can be traced to a myriad of sources. They stem from various religious beliefs and ideologies. They stem from the idea that humans should be, and are capable of, perfection. And they can stem from creative thinking, research, and political action.

The origins of these beliefs, their impact on society, and their impact on the human service professions influence each of us as professionals. How we assess persons with disabilities depends on how we view disability. If we see disability as a

1

curse from god, our assessment will look for unchangeable immorality. If we see persons with disabilities as incompetent or as perpetual children, they will be categorized as being helpless. If we perceive persons with disabilities as competent and having potential for success, we will find strengths on which to build bridges to empowerment.

Our values and beliefs about disability also guide our work with persons with disabilities. If we see persons with disabilities as sick or incapable, we will take care of them. If we see them as a menace, we will lock them away in institutions and in their homes. If we see them as a minority group that has been stereotyped and subjected to discrimination, we will seek the changes in society, economics, and politics that will empower them.

The first four chapters of this text provide a context for human service practice with persons with disabilities. We explore historical and current societal values and beliefs about disability. We examine the effects of these beliefs on persons with disabilities. We also explore how societal values influence human service practice.

Chapter 1 examines, in depth, the various stereotypes applied to persons with disabilities. It addresses the influences of various professions on how practitioners approach practice with persons with disabilities. It also offers ways you can begin to examine your own values and beliefs about disability. Chapter 2 introduces the unique view that, out of their minority status, persons with disabilities have created a culture of disability with a characteristic history, language, and values concerning disability. This chapter draws parallels between persons with disabilities and other devalued groups in society. Chapter 3 reviews the history of disability, including the origins and impacts of models used to define disability. It also presents readers with an overview of important legislative milestones. Chapter 4 explores ideas concerning developmental theory and persons with disabilities. It reviews traditional theories of psychosocial development and discusses their limitations as they apply to disability. It then addresses developmental issues for persons with disabilities through the life span.

Chapter 1

SOCIETAL AND PROFESSIONAL STEREOTYPES

*Don't make us angels and don't make us devils. There are
stupid, angry people with disabilities. Among us are people who
are very capable. Professionals need to understand that. Do
not stereotype us.*

—Brenda Premo, Director, California Department of Rehabilitation, Sacramento, California

Student Learning Objectives:

1. To understand that human service practitioners can bring prejudices and stereotypes concerning persons with disabilities into their practices that need to be addressed and discussed.
2. To understand common stereotypes about persons with disabilities. These include perceptions of persons with disabilities as objects of pity, as menaces to society, as sick, as incompetent, as curses from god, as gifts from god, as tests from god, and as freaks.
3. To understand role expectations of various professions for persons with disabilities.
4. To understand how identifying with specific professions influences human service practitioners' relationships with persons with disabilities.

◆ STEREOTYPES AND HUMAN SERVICE PRACTITIONERS

Human service practitioners who work with persons with disabilities and their families are often forced to face their own attitudes and values about the meaning of disability and their feelings about those who have disabilities. These values and feelings may run deep and are often unconsciously held. Bryan (1996) observes that

> *Although rooted in superstition and ignorance, the bias against persons with disabilities is generally not meant to be malicious or segregate the population into a caste system. Regardless of the intentions, many "nondisabled" persons exhibit feelings of frustration, uncertainty, and bigotry when encountering a person with a disability, especially if the disability is severe. . . .*

> *The care and concern of persons with disabilities were generally considered the responsibility of the family. The family could not expect to receive much, if any, support from*

3

*the community. . . . These attitudes served to separate the "nondisabled" from the
"disabled," which further disenfranchised persons with disabilities. (pp. 6–7)*

Societal attitudes have tended to separate people with disabilities, denying them full societal participation. Isolation and unfamiliarity have, in turn, led to stereotypical attitudes toward persons with disabilities. We use the term *ableism* to describe the belief that people with disabilities are inferior to nondisabled people because of their differences. Ableism is similar to other "isms" such as racism and sexism, wherein the dominant segment of society defines minority or nondominant segments of society in stereotypical and/or negative ways. Ableism devalues people with disabilities and results in segregation, social isolation, and social policies that limit their opportunities for full societal participation. Unfortunately, persons with disabilities are also susceptible to internalizing stereotypes and negative beliefs. This process, which we call *internalized ableism,* is similar to internalized racism and sexism of other devalued people. The concept of ableism was developed in the disabled community and is slowly becoming recognized by scholars and researchers.

Human service workers are susceptible to adopting society's ableist attitudes without conscious awareness. Ableism can lead workers to underestimate the capabilities and to restrict the self-determination of people with disabilities with whom they work. Therefore, professional awareness about our attitudes pertaining to disability is the first critical component of professional practice.

◆ COMMON STEREOTYPICAL ATTITUDES TOWARD PERSONS WITH DISABILITIES

A quarter century ago, Wolfensberger (1972) illuminated common attitudes held toward persons with disabilities. He contended that people with disabilities are frequently labeled as deviant and assigned societal role expectations based on these stereotypes. He also observed that people internalize these societally imposed roles. Wolfensberger states

When a person is perceived as deviant, he is cast into a role that carries with it powerful expectancies. Strangely enough, these expectancies not only take hold of the mind of the perceiver, but of the perceived person as well. It is a well-established fact that a person's behavior tends to be profoundly affected by the role expectations that are placed upon him. . . . Unfortunately, role-appropriate behavior will then often be interpreted to be a person's "natural" mode of acting, rather than a mode elicited by environmental events and circumstances. (pp. 16–17)

Because of ableism, persons with disabilities have been perceived as deficient or deviant and have been expected to fill roles foisted on them by a larger society. For example, persons with intellectual and psychiatric disabilities have routinely been institutionalized. When their behavior has displayed signs of institutionalization, it has reinforced stereotypes, thus reinforcing the perception that they need to be institutionalized. Thus, society creates the environment that reinforces its expectations—in these instances, dysfunctional behaviors and limited social functioning. With limited opportunities, persons with disabilities have little choice for anything else. We outline some samples of societal stereotypes in the following paragraphs.

Persons with disabilities may be perceived as *objects of pity* (Wolfensberger, 1972). This attitude is displayed in a variety of ways. Promoting public pity has been consistently used as an effective fund-raiser for human service organizations serving people with disabilities. Posters, billboards, and telethons depict brave but pitiable people. Shapiro (1993) revealed the feelings of Evan Kemp, Jr., regarding telethons. An advisor to George Bush, a prime mover of the Americans with Disabilities Act (ADA), and a person with a disability himself, Kemp believes that "by arousing the public's fear of the handicap itself, the telethon makes viewers more afraid of handicapped people." Kemp goes on to say, "Playing to pity may raise money, but it raises walls of fear between the public and us" (Shapiro, 1993, p. 22).

Pity is born out of ignorance and stereotypes. Even when intentions are altruistic, fund-raisers such as telethons have repeatedly created pity and exploited guilt to achieve their purposes. The result is that human service professionals involved in these kinds of fund-raising events inadvertently reinforce negative stereotypes. Bogdan and Biklen (1993) state

> *Thus, the crippled child becomes a poor soul whose disability evokes pity and guilt and the spirit of giving, but also lessens the possibility that disabled people can be regarded as people with personalities, with individual aspirations, and with an interest in being perceived as ordinary people.* (p. 74)

This pity is manifested in other ways. In the 1981 film *Whose Life Is It Anyway?*, pity is dramatically displayed when Richard Dreyfuss's character begs for the right to end his life after an automobile accident leaves him with quadriplegia and in need of renal dialysis. The film intended for the audience to be relieved when this likable, charismatic character was granted his wish. His life with a disability was portrayed as worse than death, a message that was loud and clear to the audience. As another example, Morris (1991) recalls that opposing forces debating the abortion issue could often find agreement that abortion is acceptable when a fetus has a severe disability. Prior to acquiring a disability herself, Morris, like many others, was unaware of the imbedded societal assumption that disability is worse than death. Human service professionals who support assisted suicide for persons because they have disabilities give the ultimate reinforcement to the false perception that disability is a horrible fate.

Another perception of persons with disabilities is that they are a *menace* (Wolfensberger, 1972) or *threat to society*. One of the authors found these attitudes strongly displayed in his personal life when, on separate occasions, he was asked to become involved in community efforts to keep two group homes out of his neighborhood. One of the group homes was to serve persons with developmental/intellectual disabilities; the other was for people with psychiatric disabilities. The rationales expressed for keeping them out were similar for both groups. There was a strong plea to "protect our children." People were terrified that their children would be sexually molested and physically attacked by "retarded" and "crazy" people.

Neighborhood activists believed group home residents would prey on the community. The rhetoric expressed in door-to-door contact and community meetings included calls for violence, if necessary, to protect the community from these people. The group homes were eventually located in the neighborhood. However, even though problems failed to materialize, some community residents continued to shun people living in the group homes.

The perception that people with disabilities are a menace to society has been documented by Rhodes (1993) in recounting how societal fears have led to institutional segregation, marriage restrictions, and sterilization. Draconian measures have been taken to prevent contamination of the gene pool and to protect persons without disabilities.

People with disabilities are often portrayed as *sick*. Society expects them to fill sick roles even when they are perfectly healthy. In the sick role, they are not expected to be productive and are denied opportunities to be productive and economically self-sufficient (Bryan, 1996). They are to be cared and provided for. Their responsibility is to be grateful for the help provided them, even though that same system makes it difficult for them to be independent and to exercise self-determination (Devore and Schlesinger, 1987; Mackelprang and Salsgiver, 1996).

People with physical disabilities who need attendant care are often forced into the sick role. Rather than having the opportunity to manage their own care, they are forced to rely on physicians to write "orders" and on nurses to provide care. Instead of directing their own care, they are forced to rely on home health agencies that control purse strings and personnel.

A language of sickness is endemic in popular and professional language relative to people with disabilities. People with disabilities are "confined" to wheelchairs or "wheelchair bound," just as sick people are confined to bed. Language such as "afflicted with cerebral palsy" and "mental illness" convey widely accepted attitudes that persons with disabilities are sick.

Making sickness synonymous with disability maintains a power imbalance that can victimize persons with disabilities. Care providers maintain status and professional worth by exercising control over those who are forced to rely on them for services. Professional control creates a conflict of interest in which increased client or patient autonomy would reduce the need for professionals and threaten the status and need for human service professionals. For example, status is maintained when people must rely on physicians to obtain medications, durable medical equipment, therapy, or attendant care. Consumer autonomy in obtaining these needs would decrease the need for, reduce the role of, and reduce the income of physicians.

People with disabilities are sometimes portrayed as *perpetual children*. For example, the Muscular Dystrophy Association's annual Labor Day telethon consistently portrays people with disabilities as "Jerry's kids," whether their age is one day or one hundred years. Wolfensberger labels this the role of the "eternal child." Rather than expecting the person to go through developmental processes, perpetual children have few expectations placed on them; thus, few opportunities for growth and development are provided for them. Low expectations result in expenditure of fewer resources to help them reach their potential.

Another common stereotype is that of *incompetence*. Innumerable wheelchair users have felt the sting of this stereotype in restaurants (or other establishments) when they have been with companions who do not use wheelchairs. Rather than servers taking the wheelchair user's order, servers ask their companions what the wheelchair user wants to eat, the assumption being that the user is incapable of ordering and needs the help of someone else. One of the authors, who uses a wheelchair, attended a conference in Washington, D.C., with a colleague who did not. At the airport while both were together, the ticket agent asked his colleague whether or not he needed to be pushed to the airplane. The ticket agent assumed that, because the author used a wheelchair, he also could not talk or respond intelligently to questions. After the author's quick and articulate response, the ticket agent became very much aware of the intellectual ability and verbal skills of someone with a disability.

The perception of incompetence is manifested in various ways and to various degrees. In health settings, these assumptions may be covert, but the meaning can still be clear, as recounted one person who had experienced a spinal cord injury:

> [In rehabilitation] they really blew it. They told me when to get up, when to go to bed, when and what to eat. They told me when I had to take my medications and didn't always bother to tell me why I was taking them. I had to go to therapy at 9:00 A.M. It didn't matter that I've always been a late sleeper. They even told me when I could and couldn't take a crap. Then after three months of this, I was told that I was ready to go home and live completely independently. Hell, what a joke.
> (Mackelprang, 1986, p. 43)

Stubbins (1988) discusses the impact of this particular stereotype on rehabilitation services. The revival of social Darwinism and its ideology of the survival of the fittest and the menace of the imperfect are manifested in rehabilitation not only in the cutback of programs but in the emphasis on assessment and medical model diagnosis as a means of solving the "problem of disability" by determining who can compete and who cannot. Proponents of this perspective argue that those who cannot function in competitive employment should not receive rehabilitation services.

Assumptions of incompetence are often displayed when professionals take control over the lives of persons with disabilities. When professionals wrest control over life from persons with disabilities, these assumptions can be proven correct because people do not develop the skills to manage their lives. In the preceding situation, for example, the individual was ill prepared to manage his medications because he was uninformed as to their uses and side effects. His capabilities were limited because of a dearth of opportunity.

Another stereotype is that disabilities are the result of a *curse from god*. This attitude is displayed in the New Testament when the disciples of Jesus assumed that a man was born blind because either he or his parents had sinned. By logical extension, people with disabilities are less worthy and have less favor in god's eyes than people without disabilities.

Individuals with disabilities and their families have experienced much guilt and shame as a result of this perception. Parents blame themselves and each other. Internalized ableism can lead people with disabilities to believe that god views them with disfavor. An example of this occurred with an individual with whom one of the authors worked for several years. Upon learning of his diagnosis of a progressive neuromuscular disorder, he sought religious help. He received a blessing that he would be healed if he had "faith and live[d] a worthy life." Initially, he refused to believe his condition was permanent, even refusing all treatment. However, his condition steadily progressed. Three years later, he was depressed and maintained little self-worth. He could not understand what he had done in his life to deserve this "curse from god." He blamed himself for his unsuccessful faith healing. He knew god was punishing him and held him in disfavor. He stated that the only reason he did not commit suicide was that suicide led to "eternal damnation, not just the damnation on this earth" caused by his disability. Parenthetically, members of his religious community also questioned his worthiness and openly wondered what he had done to deserve god's curse.

Conversely, disability can sometimes be perceived as a *gift* or *test from god*. Some individuals and families find divine purpose when events, including disabilities, enter their lives. Religious and spiritual beliefs should be respected and can be great sources of strength. However, divine explanations can also lead people to ignore the larger picture. As Condeluci (1995) states,

> *If raising a child with cerebral palsy is seen as being more difficult than raising any other child then we need to look, not at God, but at people and society. Why is it harder for a family with a child with a disability? One reason is that people have not understood, nor accepted. Another is because our society has not adjusted to welcome someone who might move, talk, or think differently. These don't seem to be God's problems but ours.* (p. 22)

We acknowledge the value of people finding spiritual meaning to events in their lives. However, there is danger in establishing an identity primarily based on speculations about god's interventions or intentions.

People with disabilities have often been treated as *freaks*. Circuses have exploited this belief through freak sideshows in which people pay to gawk at people with unusual appearances, many with disabilities. Similarly, "grand rounds" presentations in which naked or nearly naked people have been paraded in front of large groups of professionals may have some educational value, but the practice dehumanizes people with disabilities. Quasimodo, Victor Hugo's 1831 mythical hunchback of Notre Dame (Hugo, 1996), illustrates the long-term perception of people with disabilities as freaks. Pregnant women were cautioned not to look upon him out of fear for their unborn children. His "ugliness" was equated with evil, and he was mocked without mercy. As a freak, Quasimodo was dehumanized; his life and feelings were unimportant.

Stereotypical attitudes are pervasive in society, and human service professionals are as susceptible to them as anyone. Close monitoring of personal reactions to people with disabilities can help professionals identify and deal with their personal attitudes based on stereotypical beliefs. It is important to acknowledge that stereotypes are not always borne of negative presuppositions. Some are borne of compassion and sympathy. However, even these stereotypes have negative results. French (1996) points out the consequences of negative attitudes on the part of human service professionals. Negative attitudes and stereotypes may adversely influence the self-image and future independence of newly disabled individuals. Human service professionals have a direct effect on the general public's view of disability. Their attitudes are also perpetuated as they influence their students, the future human service professionals. They can reinforce the perception that problems rest exclusively with individuals and small systems, ignoring meso and macro impacts on people's lives.

Based on his own experience both in teaching about disability and being a person with a disability, one of the authors developed the following values questionnaire, which he uses when he trains professionals on issues surrounding persons with disabilities. The questionnaire helps participants explore underlying stereotypes and values they hold regarding persons with disabilities. It focuses on subjective feelings and thoughts rather than attempting to objectively ascertain individual or group values around disability. The questionnaire uses a four-point Likert-type scale (1 = strongly agree, 2 = agree, 3 = disagree, 4 = strongly disagree) to ascertain the extent to which participants agree or disagree with the following statements:

1. It is more beneficial to teach a wheelchair user to jump curbs   1   2   3   4
   rather than to convince the city to install curb cuts.
2. Walking, if possible, is better than using a wheelchair.   1   2   3   4
3. People with histories of drug and alcohol abuse should be   1   2   3   4
   considered as persons with disabilities.
4. A severely physically disabled person in a restaurant makes   1   2   3   4
   other diners uncomfortable when the person's eating is sloppy
   and is perceived as disgusting.
5. Persons with severe disabilities should not be expected to work.   1   2   3   4
6. Persons with an amputated limb should wear their prostheses   1   2   3   4
   in social situations, including work.
7. The biggest factor in preventing persons with disabilities from   1   2   3   4
   accomplishing their goals is the fact that they do not take risks.
8. Few persons with disabilities are ashamed of their disabilities.   1   2   3   4
9. In spite of all the publicity and activism, persons with severe   1   2   3   4
   disabilities can never *really* live on their own, independently.
10. It is a tragedy for parents to have a child with a disability,   1   2   3   4
    either at birth or in childhood.
11. It is common for persons with disabilities to be angry and   1   2   3   4
    resentful toward nondisabled people.

12. People with severe developmental disabilities should be   · 1 2 3 4
    prevented from marrying.
13. Severely developmentally disabled individuals will not benefit   1 2 3 4
    from job clubs.
14. Given the choice, nondisabled persons would declare them-   1 2 3 4
    selves disabled to get out of work and collect the benefits.
15. For a person to acquire a disability from an injury is a   1 2 3 4
    tragic event.
16. Persons with disabilities are usually friendly and receptive to   1 2 3 4
    being helped.
17. The new "inclusion" movement in primary and secondary   1 2 3 4
    education causes more harm than good to both the disabled
    student and the nondisabled student.
18. Reasonable accommodation under the ADA gives special   1 2 3 4
    privileges to workers with disabilities.
19. The biggest factor in preventing persons with disabilities   1 2 3 4
    from accomplishing their goals is their lack of hard work.
20. Persons with disabilities cannot produce as much in the work   1 2 3 4
    environment as a nondisabled person.
21. Only persons with disabilities should provide human services   1 2 3 4
    to other persons with disabilities.
22. Persons with severe developmental disabilities should be   1 2 3 4
    prevented from having children.
23. Civil rights laws like the ADA take away rights from productive 1 2 3 4
    productive nondisabled workers.

Statements 1 and 21 explore the question of the nature of disability and how it should be addressed. For example, are solutions to problems best addressed individually or societally? Who should deliver services and what kind of services should be delivered to persons with disabilities? Statements 2, 4, 6, and 16 address the issue of difference. Many professionals push persons with disabilities to look and act as "normal" as possible in the name of job acceptance or social acceptance (Sheafor, Horejsi, and Horejsi, 1991). For example, they believe that, among other things, persons with disabilities should never show their anger. What values and beliefs lie behind these objectives? Statements 3 and 8 explore the belief that persons with disabilities, including drug and alcohol abusers, are sinful and immoral and should be ashamed of themselves. They invite a discussion of looking at disability as a curse and its impact on the services or lack of services to persons with disabilities. Statements 5, 9, 13, 17, and 20 probe the stereotype of incompetence. Can persons with disabilities really compete? Can they really be productive? Statements 7, 14, and 19 help professionals examine the issue of the social definition of disability and issues of dependency. They probe the idea, as purported by Stone (1984), that people seek to be defined as disabled to get out of work and receive benefits. Statements 10 and 15 explore underlying attitudes and fears of disability by professionals and how these might manifest in family practice situations. Statements 11, 12, 18, 22, and 23 address the nature of disability and the social Darwinist ideology of persons with disabilities being a menace to humanity, either directly in terms of violence or indirectly in terms of an adverse effect on the genetic pool. Students of human service delivery can use this questionnaire as a beginning point for looking internally into values and beliefs and discussing with other students these issues around stereotyping and prejudice.

Human service practitioners need to help persons with disabilities understand the prejudice and discrimination that exist around disability and the impact these have on the individual's self-concept. French (1996) states

> *Disabled people are, of course, members of society and the prejudices which are held against them may become part of their own self-identity and view of the world leading to a "self-fulfilling prophecy."* (pp. 152–153)

Human service professionals must be aware of societal stereotypes in order to evaluate their preconceived notions of persons with disabilities. This self-awareness will help them move away from stereotypes and embrace people with disabilities as unique individuals.

◆ PROFESSIONAL DEFINITIONS OF DISABILITY

In addition to societal roles and expectations, various professions label persons with disabilities in distinct ways. The professions are involved as a result of problems or needs they have identified with persons with disabilities. Role definitions as well as personal and professional expectations are created in the context of the particular profession. Professional goals help define professional roles and place expectations on the people they serve. For example, special education has a function of educating people who are identified with learning, education, or behavioral problems. People with disabilities are expected to fill the role of student while professionals fill the roles of teacher, educator, and remediator. Table 1.1 briefly outlines the roles and expectations associated with the professions frequently involved with persons with disabilities. These are defined as a result of the functions of the professions and the perceived problems and needs of the people served.

Often, professionals may be unaware of the definitions and role expectations used by those in other professions, which can inhibit multidisciplinary collaboration. For example, physicians who view people as patients work in a context that is different from vocational counselors who work in a context in which people are students or clients. Lack of recognition of these differences in approach limits the effectiveness of interdisciplinary collaboration.

A universal problem among traditional professional models of defining disability is that these definitions are individual and pathology based. Roles and expectations can be valuable when they provide a context in which people are able to decide from whom they will receive the most valuable services. Generally,

Table 1.1 ◆ PROFESSIONAL MODELS OF DISABILITY

Model	Problems	Role Definitions of the Person	Professions	Controls	Expectations of the Person
Medical	Illness, sickness	Patient	Medicine, nursing, physical therapy	Physician with consultation of allied health professionals	Passive recipient of treatment
Mental health	Mental illness, personality deficits	Patient, client	Psychiatry, psychology, mental health, social work	Psychiatrist, clinical psychologist with consultation of other professionals	Passive recipient of treatment, compliance with treatment plans
Vocational	Unemploy-ability due to personal problems	Client, student	Educational psychology, vocational rehabilitation, rehabilitation psychology	Rehabilitation counselor, job coach	Follow vocational plans
Educational	Learning, attention, and/or behavioral deficits	Student	Special education, behavioral therapy, educational psychology	Resource/special education counselors, educational psychologists	Remedial learning and improving behavior
Social service	Social worker, social service worker, financial worker	Client	Social work, social services	Social worker, financial worker, eligibility worker	Being compliant and remaining eligible

people use human service providers to help with problems or needs. However, when professional definitions of disability focus primarily on individual problems, the focus is placed on fixing problems in the individual, not acknowledging the social elements of disabilities. Thus, there is a danger that professional role expectations can be extremely constraining and oppressive to the people the professions are supposed to help. As Brzuzy (1997) states,

> *[The] definitions and categorizations of people with disabilities reveals how the view of disability in our society perpetuates inequality. When attempts are not made to change structures to accommodate the variations in people's abilities, responsibility for adaptation is placed entirely on the individual with an impairment. The focus on individual responsibility rather than social awareness and accommodation is perpetuated by the way we define disability. The result is that the civil rights and liberties of people with impairments are ignored and blocked. Challenging the social construction of disability is an effective way to enhance the rights and opportunities for people with impairments.* (p. 82)

Professional definitions and, thus, approaches to disability generally place the responsibility for change on individuals. They are based on traditional social constructions of disability and ignore the need to change the social structures that limit individual rights and opportunities. When professions adopt approaches based on traditional societal values, professionals unwittingly contribute to the devaluation and oppression of those people who come to them for assistance.

Alternatively, human service professionals can adopt a social model of disability and acknowledge that society has created social structures that limit opportunities and access to resources for people with disabilities. They can also adopt a goal to work toward a society that strives for universal access and opportunity (Brzuzy, 1997) as well as helping individuals solve personal problems and grow personally. These are tenets of empowerment-based human service practice.

Such an approach requires professionals to understand the connection between oppression and personal problems. Solomon (1976) recognized this connection and applied it to address the empowerment of African Americans; however, her work can be applied to those working with all oppressed people, including persons with disabilities. Solomon recognized the importance of the human service professional exploring stereotypes and negative attitudes to help the consumer gain an understanding of internalized stereotypes and negative attitudes:

> *Overwhelming environmental and interpersonal conditions are the hard facts of life for many people who live in black communities. The negative valuations from the larger society are expanded and reinforced in the primary relational systems. Self-knowledge under such circumstances is likely to have to begin at a point of such unbearably low self-esteem that only a deep and abiding relationship in which the "other" is willing to experience with the client incredibly painful emotions can free the client to move toward effective self-knowledge. Effective self-knowledge is defined here as understanding the manner in which one's own attitudes, emotions, and behavior patterns influence a problem situation.* (p. 350)

The process of understanding and overcoming internalized stereotypes and negative attitudes can be difficult for persons with disabilities and for human service professionals who help them. Professionals must be aware of these negative attitudes, eschew them, and develop empowerment-based strategies for personal growth and social empowerment. The consumer as service provider role moves from the personal to the political realms of actions. Consumers become providers for themselves and minimize the need for professional intervention. In addition, persons with disabilities become resources for others with disabilities through informal support networks and peer counseling and by assuming roles of human service practitioners.

Professionals begin by assisting consumers in dealing with the personal implications of societal attitudes and stereotypes. However, personal awareness is only the beginning. Empowering human service practice focuses on teaching consumers effective methods of dealing with these stereotypes, both on a personal level and on societal and political levels. Understanding the dynamics of oppression involves recognizing that people with disabilities are

1. denied the privilege associated with not being disabled
2. exploring and understanding internalized forms of devaluation and self-hatred
3. understanding the "prevalence of stereotypes and beliefs which make it difficult for people with disabilities . . . to form alliances with each other and with other minority groups" (Onken and Mackelprang, 1997, p. 5)

We believe that consumer understanding of the social and political issues empowers persons with disabilities to address inequities and redress wrongs individually and as groups. It empowers them to reject dominant society stereotypes and enables them to grasp and maintain control over their lives and to advocate for others. Finally, it helps them to recognize shared experiences and develop a positive disability identity.

◆ Summary

Human service practitioners who work with persons with disabilities and their families are often forced to face their own attitudes and values about the meaning of disability and their feelings about those who have disabilities. Professional self-awareness of our attitudes about disability is the first critical component of professional practice.

Common societal stereotypes that practitioners bring to their experiences with persons with disabilities include perceiving persons with disabilities as objects of pity, as menaces to society, as sick, as incompetent, as curses from god, as gifts from god, as tests from god, and as freaks. Human service practitioners need to help persons with disabilities understand the prejudice and discrimination that exists around disability and the impact this has on the individual's self-concept. Human service professionals who are unaware or in denial about their own stereotypes have difficulty admitting such stereotypes exist in the larger society and certainly cannot help persons with disabilities move away from them.

In addition to societal roles and expectations, various professions label persons with disabilities in varying ways that are usually related to the functions the professions fulfill. These definitions may hinder the self-development and independence of a person with a disability.

◆ ◆ ◆   *Personal Narrative: Abby Kovalsky*   ◆ ◆ ◆

Abby Kovalsky LCSW, is Disabilities Project Coordinator for the Jewish Family and Children Services, San Francisco, California. Abby has been very active in the independent living movement for several years. She has myasthenia gravis, a neuromuscular disability that produces symptoms such as weakness of the voluntary muscles, including facial muscles and muscles that affect speech and swallowing.

My disability is myasthenia gravis (MG). I was diagnosed with MG at age 16. Before my disability, I did not know any children who were disabled, but I did know a few adults. One had a developmental disability. All the children in the neighborhood made fun of her, including me. But a part of me felt sorry for her. There was a store owner in the neighborhood who had an adult daughter with severe cerebral palsy. She was on the telethon every year and was kind of a celebrity. She was always dressed beautifully, with makeup and a lovely hairdo. Other than that, I don't remember much about her.

Becoming disabled in adolescence was devastating. I had never heard of myasthenia gravis and could barely pronounce it. I thought that if I got proper medical care it would go away. Because it affected my speech, facial muscles, eyes, and limbs, I was very limited in physical activity. It progressed rapidly and I spent a lot of time in the hospital. We had to move to New York from Connecticut during my senior year in high school because I needed specialized medical care. I didn't want to see my friends. I was embarrassed because I couldn't smile or speak clearly. Slowly, they stopped calling and visiting. I don't think they knew how to react around me either. Over time, I became more and more isolated.

My mother became overprotective after I became disabled. The doctor told her I couldn't be emotionally upset or I could get worse. So she walked on eggshells around me. My mother was also ashamed of my disability. I can remember being in line at the market with my mother. We knew the people who worked there because it was a neighborhood store. The man at the cash register, who we both knew well, asked my mother what was wrong with my voice. She told him that I had a cold. Later, when I asked her why she said that, she said my condition was none of his business. I knew then how she felt about me.

I didn't date much—I was too embarrassed. Only once did a friend ever introduce me to a date. I can recall being on a date with someone I met at a disco. We were having dinner after spending the day together. I was supposed to take my medication every three hours. I was embarrassed to take it in front of my date so I waited hours past the scheduled time and snuck into the bathroom to take my pills. Unfortunately, the water in the bathroom sink wasn't running, and I had to try to swallow the pills dry. Swallowing was one of my weakest areas. I spent what felt like an eternity in the bathroom choking on every pill. I thought I was going to have to go to the hospital.

For years, I considered myself sick. I spent much time in the hospital and was always concerned about staying alive. I met a couple of friends in college. I felt I had to keep up with them, rather than admit that, because of my disability, I couldn't do it all. I felt very different and uncomfortable telling anyone, especially my family. I really didn't have "role models" to help me accept myself, disability and all.

When I was an undergraduate in 1972, the California Department of Vocational Rehabilitation told my brother they wouldn't fund my education because they thought my prognosis was poor. Even though their job was to help people with disabilities become employed, I wasn't assertive enough to get them to change their minds.

I had always wanted to be a nurse, so I wanted to attend nursing school in college. I was not allowed to do so because people told me it was too physically demanding.

My college career was interrupted due to hospitalizations. When I was able to return to college, I decided to go into medical research. Everyone told me the load was too much. All my classes had laboratories with them; it was like taking a double load. In a sense, I was my own role model. The more people told me I shouldn't go into medical research, the more determined I was to prove them wrong. As a result, I entered a Ph.D. program in medical microbiology and immunology.

I was in my third year of the Ph.D. program when I decided to take a leave of absence from the program to rethink my goals. I had just completed a peer counseling course at the local center for independent living (CIL), and I was going to volunteer there. Synchronistically, when I left my graduate program, a job opened at the CIL for an information and referral counselor. I was hired. I was 29 years old, and after 13 years of living with MG, this was the first time I identified as a person with a disability, not a sickness. It was a major transition.

I had a real role model at the CIL—my supervisor, a licensed clinical social worker. Since that time, there has never been a doubt in my mind that I am a person with a disability. It is so much a part of who I am today. It feels liberating. I swore to myself that I would never again hide anything about my disability.

There is no generalized way in which I see others with disabilities. As people with disabilities, we are as varied as any other group of people in the community. I can tell you I see all of us as people, with whatever baggage we have.

I definitely think there is a disability culture. For me, any group that has been so totally discriminated against for unsubstantial reasons has a commonality that is unique to that group. There is a history, a language, and a rich montage of art forms relating to disability.

My supervisor at the CIL encouraged me to apply to social work school. I did, got accepted, and formally left my Ph.D. program for an MSW program. By then, I was more assertive when I applied for vocational rehabilitation services in social work school: they paid half of my tuition at a private institution. Unfortunately, social work has not been as accepting as I had hoped.

When I was in social work school, I was railroaded into my placements because the field placement person decided that the only agency that would accept me was a rehabilitation hospital. She never bothered to send my packet of practicum materials to any other agencies, and I had no interviews. I was enraged. I wanted my social work education to be in the health track, but if my first-year placement was in a hospital, I wanted a different placement in my second year. Instead of planning my second-year placement to meet my needs, I was placed in a setting otherwise used for first-year placements because the supervisor had no problem with my disability. Again, I was not given an opportunity to interview with other agencies or determine my placement—I had little choice in the matter.

Upon graduation, after getting straight A's and having excellent references from my placement supervisors, I spent two years looking for work. I had lots of interviews. One person had the audacity to say to me, "I had to meet you, you look so good on paper, but we don't have any openings." This statement was not true because I had answered an ad in the paper and knew the agency was looking for a social worker. I had directors of hospital social work departments tell me I should go into administration. Again, there was this concern that doctors wouldn't understand me. I offered to work two weeks for free at one hospital just to prove I could do the work. I was angry. Here I was in a profession where I thought people are supposed to be caring and sensitive. Was I wrong!

From the school personnel (who had an obligation once they accepted me in the program to do all they could for me) to social workers in practice (who are some of the most prejudiced people I have met), I learned the hard way about outright discrimination. I have also experienced rude questions and comments from doctors with whom I have worked. (Interestingly, these doctors were older women.)

Social work was not the first place I experienced discrimination. For example, when I first graduated from college, I wanted to apply to a training program in laboratory technology. Yet I was blatantly told by most schools that I shouldn't even bother applying because the doctors would have a hard time understanding me. Since this was a very competitive field that paid quite well, I didn't waste my time applying. Even though educational and employment discrimination were not new to me, I guess I expected social workers to be different. That made my treatment in the social work profession especially hard to deal with.

The biggest obstacle people with disabilities face is discrimination, pure and simple. I experience discrimination and stereotyping in my everyday life. People assume that because I have a speech impairment I must also be deaf or "mentally retarded." The ADA was too little, too late for me. Perhaps I have been helped by 504 [section 504 of the Rehabilitation Act of 1973] in some ways.

The major issue around disability continues to be unabated discrimination. This one issue has serious consequences in every aspect of a disabled person's life, from employment to housing to dating to raising a family. It's the age–old dilemma, learning to tolerate people who are different. The difference between other minority groups and the disabled is that anyone can become disabled at any time. I think this touches a vulnerable place in all of us that we don't want to acknowledge. The paradox, as I see it, is that, until people with disabilities are a solid part of the work force, with earning power and voting power, it will be slow going. However, it is hard to develop earning power when we are shut out of the job market. The flip side is that, for people who are not able to work, society needs to acknowledge their value as human beings even though they are not part of the Puritan work ethic.

On a personal level, I joined a dating service a year and a half ago. All I hear from the agency is that everyone who reads my profile and then sees my photo is basically not willing to meet someone with my disability.

As we all know, we cannot legislate attitude. What must happen is education of the masses, constant and persistent, and, in every way possible, creation of opportunities for people to experience people with disabilities. The agency at which I work sponsors an educational program for nondisabled children under the auspices of the program I coordinate, where speakers with disabilities go into the classroom to talk about living with a disability. It is a powerful experience for these children. They ask questions and learn about advocacy, rights, and prejudice. People with disabilities become more human and less frightening to them.

People have many differences; disability is just another way people are different. I have always felt different from others in many ways, and my disability is one of those ways. However, before I developed an identity as a person with a disability, I thought it was terrible to be a person who was disabled. I never asked anyone with a disability if it was terrible, I just assumed so because that is what I heard from others.

The older I get, the more comfortable I become with the way I am, although there are still times when I am struck in a vulnerable way by something someone might say or the stares I still get. I have been discriminated against most definitely; the most traumatic area has been in employment. However, I have also been successful. What helped me to be successful was sheer determination. I do get tired sometimes of having to fight for everything, but I continue to move on.

As for my mother, she has grown. It was recently that she said to me, "I am very proud of you. You could have just spent your life as a vegetable."

◆   ◆   ◆

Discussion Questions

1. Now that you have read the chapter, go back to the values questionnaire and answer the questions as honestly as you can. Write a two–page essay on the questions with which you have the most difficulty. How might these issues impact your future practice? How can you develop strategies to lessen their impact on future work with persons with disabilities?

2. Interview a person with a disability that you know or have seen on campus. Ask them about the stereotypes and prejudices they have experienced. Do they fit into the ones discussed in this chapter? What additional ones did they relate to you?

3. Have there been times when you have been temporarily disabled? Maybe you broke an arm or a leg or badly sprained an ankle in sports. What was that experience like? Did you experience any stereotypes during the time you were using crutches or limping?

Suggested Readings

Bryan, W.V. (1996). *In search of freedom: How people with disabilities have been disenfranchised from the mainstream of American society.* Springfield, IL: Charles C Thomas.

Condeluci, A. (1995). *Interdependence: The route to community* (2nd ed.). Winter Park, FL: GR Press.

Mackelprang, R.W, and Salsgiver, R.O. (1996). People with disabilities and social work: Historical and contemporary issues. *Social Work, 41*(1), 7–14.

Morris, J. (1991). *Pride against prejudice: Transforming attitudes to disability.* Philadelphia: New Society Publishers.

Shapiro, J. P. (1993). *No pity: People with disabilities, forging a new civil rights movement.* New York: Times Books.

References

Bogdan, R., and Biklen, D. (1993). Handicapism. In M. Nagler (Ed.), *Perspectives on disability* (pp. 69–76). Palo Alto, CA: Health Markets Research.

Bryan, W. V. (1996). *In search of freedom: How people with disabilities have been disenfranchised from the mainstream of American society.* Springfield, IL: Charles C Thomas.

Brzuzy, S. (1997). Deconstructing disability: The impact of definition. *Journal of Poverty, 1*(1), 81–91.

Condeluci, A. (1995). *Interdependence: The route to community* (2nd ed.). Winter Park, FL: GR Press.

Devore, W., and Schlesinger, E. G. (1987). *Ethnic-sensitive social work practice* (3rd ed.). Columbus, OH: Merrill.

French, S. (1996). The attitudes of health professionals towards disabled people. In G. Hales (Ed.), *Beyond disability: Towards an enabling society* (pp. 151–162). London: Sage.

Hugo, V. (1996). *Hunchback of Notre Dame.* New York: Bantam Doubleday.

Mackelprang, R. W (1986). *Social and emotional adjustment following spinal cord injury.* Unpublished doctoral dissertation. Salt Lake City: University of Utah.

Mackelprang, R. W, Salsgiver, R. O. (1996). People with disabilities and social work: Historical and contemporary issues. *Social Work, 41*(1), 7–14.

Morris, J. (1991). *Pride against prejudice: Transforming attitudes to disability.* Philadelphia: New Society Publishers.

Onken, S. J., and Mackelprang, R. W (1997). Building on shared experiences: Teaching disability and sexual minority content and practice. Presented at the annual program meeting, Council on Social Work Education, Chicago, IL.

Rhodes, R. (1993). Mental retardation and sexual expression: An historical perspective. In R. W Mackelprang and D. Valentine (Eds.), *Sexuality and disabilities: A guide for human service practitioners* (pp. 1-27). Binghamton, NY: Haworth Press.

Shapiro, J. P. (1993). *No pity: People with disabilities, forging a new civil rights movement.* New York: Times Books.

Sheafor, B. W., Horejsi, C. R., and Horejsi, G. A. (1991). *Techniques and guidelines for social work practice* (2nd ed.). Boston: Allyn & Bacon.

Solomon, B. B. (1976). *Black empowerment: Social work in oppressed communities.* New York: Columbia University Press.

Stone, D. (1984). *The disabled state.* Philadelphia: Temple University Press.

Stubbins, J. (1988). The politics of disability. In H. F. Yuker (Ed.), *Attitudes toward persons with disabilities.* New York: Springer.

Wolfensberger, W. (1972). *The principle of normalization in human services.* Toronto: National Institute on Mental Retardation.

Chapter 2
DISABILITY CULTURE

I have developed an identity as a Deaf person. I went from being a child in a hearing school who "had trouble hearing," felt I was different, and just couldn't seem to succeed in school and not understanding what being deaf meant or even that I was in fact "deaf," to readily identifying myself as Deaf, understanding what that means to me and others; and I embrace it comfortably.

—Martha Sheridan, Assistant Professor, Gallaudet University, Washington, D.C.

Student Learning Objectives:

1. To identify how culture is developed and transmitted.
2. To understand the development of a culture of disability.
3. To compare and contrast disability culture and racial/ethnic culture.
4. To identify elements of cultural development and maintenance of devalued groups.

A culture of spinal cord injury? Deaf heritage? Blindness as diversity? Even 20 years ago, questions like these were unheard of. Persons with disabilities have been defined by their differences, and their differences have always been perceived as pathological. Franklin D. Roosevelt went to great measures to hide his wheelchair from the public. Why? Because his wheelchair was a sign of weakness, a cause for shame. Roosevelt reacted to this ableism by seeking to hide the fact that polio made the use of a wheelchair necessary for mobility. A man without two good legs for walking was not a whole man. If an FDR were to run for president in this era of mass television coverage, would he have a chance to be elected as president? Arguably, probably not. Even today controversy rages about whether the FDR memorial in Washington, D.C., should acknowledge his disability and use of a wheelchair.

After an automobile accident left Tim Johnston (pseudonym) with paraplegia in 1986, he felt the same way Roosevelt seems to have felt. His wheelchair was a cause of shame. An avid recreational athlete before his injury, he saw no way that he would participate in sports again. He told his wife to divorce him and find a "whole" man. He was mortified at the thought of being seen in public with others in wheelchairs. He internalized all the ableist messages he had received throughout his life and accepted his lot as "half a man, looking like some freak." Like Roosevelt, Johnston's disability was a cause for shame and self-doubt. Unlike Roosevelt, however, Johnston lives in an era in which people with disabilities are beginning to take pride in their whole selves, disability and all.

◆ Culture

To discover the culture of disability, we must first understand some of the elements of culture in general. Historically, T. S. Eliot (1949) discussed three important conditions for culture that embrace the ways culture has been viewed for much of this century. First, he contended there must be an organic structure to foster the transmission of culture; in other words, the culture must have a way of being passed along to others. Eliot believed the family to be the primary means by which culture is transmitted, but others could perform this function as well. Second, he believed in the existence of local cultures within larger cultures. These cultures have been largely geographically determined, although with modern technology, geographical boundaries are becoming less important. Finally, Eliot recognized the existence of unity and diversity within cultures. Both the diversity and the strength of commonalities within each culture led him to conclude that culture is "not merely the sum of several activities, but a way of life" (p. 40).

Eagleton (1978) suggests that culture can mean "a society's 'structure of feeling,' its lived manners, habits, morals, values, the learned atmosphere of its learnt behavior and belief." In the societal context, Eagleton continues, it can mean "a society's whole way of life in an institutional sense, the totality of interacting artistic, economic, social, political, ideological elements which composes its total lived experience" (pp. 4–5). Thompson, Ellis, and Wildavsky (1990) suggest two ways of defining culture: "One views culture as composed of values, beliefs, norms, rationalizations, symbols, ideologies, i.e., mental products. The other sees culture as referring to a total way of life of people, their interpersonal relations as well as their attitudes" (p. 1).

Storey (1993) discusses meanings of "popular" culture. Popular culture can be defined as culture that is widely accepted or favored. Storey separates "high" culture, which comes from the upper classes, from "popular" culture, which comes from the people or the masses.

By combining all these perspectives, we can conclude that culture is a way of thinking, feeling, and believing—a stored knowledge that guides people's lives. In part, culture is developed as a social legacy, learned as a result of belonging to a group. Forged by constant conscious and unconscious influences as well as social and political forces, culture affects its members from birth to death. On an individual level, feelings, reactions, and behaviors become second nature in the context of cultural experiences and identities (Epstein, 1973; Milner, 1992; Storey, 1993).

Culture influences society's expectations about how people should act. Rules that govern interpersonal and social interactions are developed within cultural contexts. Social and political structures and organizations are reflections of the cultures in which they are developed. Conversely, power structures and the dominant classes of society do not merely rule but lead society morally and intellectually (Milner, 1992; Storey, 1993).

In great measure, culture provides people with a meaning to life. It is transmitted through a number of means. Families are usually the first context in which the meanings and rules of life are developed. The meanings and values of attributes such as gender, religion, sexuality, education, socioeconomic status, and disability are conveyed within families beginning at birth and continuing throughout life. Family therapists Minuchin and Fishman (1981) describe one way Puerto Rican families and communities transmit life meaning to their children as they simultaneously search for that meaning.

> *In a playground in Central Park, a Puerto Rican mother watches her three-year-old son playing in the sand box. An older woman tells her in Spanish that her son has a very nice* cuadro *(picture or image). She says that he will grow up to become a teacher. The prediction obviously pleases the mother. . . . A child's cuadro floats above his head, for everybody who is knowledgeable to see and transmit. Puerto Rican parents search for a child's cuadro, unaware that they are contributing to its construction.* (p.73)

The Puerto Rican *cuadro* embodies a search for individual meaning and identity. Others may not call the image a cuadro, but their search for identity is similar. Families and communities are the immediate transmitters of meanings that are strongly influenced by their cultures (Epstein, 1973). Reciprocally, over time, individuals and groups influence their cultures. For example, in traditional European American culture, the roles of men and women were sharply defined. In marriage, men were expected to work outside the home and be the financial providers for families while women were expected to be "homemakers" and primary caregivers for children. These strictly defined cuadros for men and women have been evolving dramatically in recent generations to the point where most women now work outside the home and where the roles ascribed to people because of gender have expanded significantly.

For Susan, born in 1933 to European American parents, life was mapped out clearly. Her father worked outside the home, and her mother's job was to raise children. She always assumed her life would be the same. Finding a profession or developing a career never crossed her mind. From her earliest memories, she learned from her family, friends, school, church, and community that marriage and motherhood were her destiny. Susan graduated from high school, married at age 18, and bore and raised six children. "I never considered doing anything else. That's what women were supposed to do." However, her daughter Rachel, born in 1956, was born as times were changing. Rachel saw female role models who worked outside the home. Unlike her mother, she was encouraged to take math and science courses in high school. When she told her minister she wanted to be a nurse, he envisioned her as "volunteering" her talents, a vision she rejected. During Rachel's 20-year marriage and raising of four children, she has worked in a nursing career. Earning and parenting responsibilities are not as tightly defined by gender as in her mother's marriage. Now the culture has evolved even further for Rachel's children. Her daughters have recreational and sports opportunities in school never provided their mother or grandmother. Her son can take courses in home economics, and her daughters can take auto mechanics courses, unheard of in previous generations.

Though changes have occurred over the last 50 years, many elements in their lives have remained the same. Their European American heritage continues to be a source of identity. Stories of ancestors have been passed through the generations. For the most part, political beliefs have been passed from generation to generation. Individuals may differ on political issues; however, the commitment of family members to the U.S. system of government is abiding. The religious and spiritual heritage of the family has been conveyed through several generations. Susan, Rachel, and their families are a sample of evolution with constancy that has occurred in a culture over the last 60 years. Family and gender roles have evolved while many sociopolitical values have remained relatively unchanged.

It is important to recognize that families like Susan's have had the advantage of being part of the dominant culture of North America. However, when people belong to groups that are in the minority or without power, their experiences can be very different. Their cultures are in danger of devaluation and oppression. Marxism suggests that power differentials have been based on economics and production. Historically, dominant/subservient classes have included master/slave, lord/peasant, and bourgeois/proletariat relationships. Similarly, feminism has viewed culture and the causes and effects of oppression from a gender context, in which women and their place in society have been devalued (Storey, 1993). Persons from racial and cultural minorities have also been subjected to pogroms and attempts to destroy their cultures. The next section presents examples of attempts to eradicate racial and ethnic peoples and/or cultures.

◆ CULTURE AND OPPRESSION

In Alex Haley's *Roots,* a historical novel of Haley's ancestors, the reader is made painfully aware of the implications of being wrested from family, community, and land. Haley presents the life story of Kunte Kinte who, as a lad, was abducted by slave traders, forcibly shipped to America, and sold into slavery. Kinte maintained his strength by continuing to assert his identity; a pride in who he was. He was proud of his tribe, his culture, and himself. His fierce determination to maintain his identity and assert himself as a person of worth caused him much grief. However, his identity also gave him the determination to continue. Kinte's roots were so firmly planted in the pride of his culture that he never lost his personal and tribal identity. At the same time, however, he was deeply influenced by his new environment.

Subsequent generations of slaves lost much of their unique cultural identity. One of the ways slavers kept slaves subjugated was to strip them of a collective identity. Holloway (1990) observes that slaves, especially those who labored in close proximity to European Americans, "were forced to give up their cultural identities to reflect their masters' control and capacity to 'civilize' the Africans" (p. 16). Families and friends were always at risk of forced separation. "Masters" forbade the observance of African traditions by slaves. Slaves who attempted to escape were beaten or killed with impunity. Stripping slaves of individual pride and collective identity helped keep them subjugated. However, though some of the unique

African cultural identities could not be preserved undefiled, they were replaced with the beginning elements of African American culture. As Holloway points out, traditions and elements of various African cultures were incorporated in a new and developing American environment.

The history of the United States and Native Americans is another example of attempts to strip culture and identity. As European Americans encroached on Native lands and conflicts arose, Native Americans were forced off their lands. The lives and traditions that had sustained them for millennia were wrested from them and replaced by reservations, geographic limitations, and government control. As Berthrong (1976) states, "It was the policy of the United States government to grind the Cheyenne into cultural submission and remold them into replicas of white, Christian farmer–citizens with red skins" (p. viii). Attempts to impose a white brand of "self-sufficiency" proved to be formidable and met with failure as Natives struggled to maintain themselves as unique peoples. For more than a century, Native American nations have sought to reclaim and maintain their cultural identities.

Jewish tenacity in maintaining identity during the Holocaust is an example of the importance of culture and heritage. Elie Wiesel, a survivor of the Holocaust, provides an example of the importance of cultural identity. Even while incarcerated at Auschwitz, he recounts, "we practiced religion even in a death camp. I said my prayers every day. On Saturday I hummed Shabbat songs at work, in part, no doubt, to please my father, to show him *I was determined to remain a Jew* even in the accursed kingdom" (Wiesel, 1995, p. 82). Even as Jews were being humiliated, tortured, and murdered by the millions, they clung to their identity as a people. Years later in 1992, the Dalai Lama asked Wiesel "about the secret of Jewish survival, wondering how it could be applied to his own people, also exiled, its religion also threatened: 'Despite the persecution and hatred that surrounded you, you managed to keep your culture and memory alive. Show us how. . . . We Tibetans have much to learn from our Jewish brothers and sisters' " (Wiesel, 1995, p. 226–227).

Although Jewish survivors maintained their Jewish identity, the Holocaust also changed them, individually and as a group. Upon liberation, many Jewish youths were housed and schooled together in supervised group settings. Jewish counselors were employed to help survivors readjust to life in a post-Holocaust world. Wiesel recounts his experiences as follows:

> *Poor counselors, did they think they could educate us? . . . The youngest among us had a fount of experiences more vast than the oldest of them . . . imperceptibly the roles were reversed, and we became their counselors, feigning docile submission to their authority only because ours was superior.* (p. 111)

These youth and other survivors had developed an identity of their own, a culture not transmitted by biological families but through common experiences. Though they were orphans, they shared a deep and abiding identity. They came from different countries and survived different camps, but they shared bonds forged and solidified from similar experiences.

Persons with disabilities share a history of devaluation and oppression with racial and ethnic minorities such as African Americans, Native Americans, and European Jews. In Europe and the United States, social Darwinism of the late 19th and early 20th centuries defined persons with disabilities as a major source of social ills. Social workers and others were taught the virtues of eugenics and were encouraged to permanently segregate persons with a variety of disabilities (Devine, 1912). Extant wisdom of the times caricatured people with disabilities as sexually immoral and in need of segregation from the rest of society. Forced sterilizations were common and institutionalization was encouraged. "Feebleminded" women were especially dangerous and were thought to be highly fertile and major transmitters of "venereal disease" (Rhodes, 1993; Adams, 1971).

Nazi Germany produced the ultimate in discrimination against persons with disabilities. Hitler's minions trained exterminators, using persons with disabilities as subjects, before they began mass exterminations of Jews. In "hospitals" like Hartheim, "those deemed mentally, morally, or physically unfit to participate" (Levy, 1993, p. 267) in society were euthanized while their murderers kept detailed records of their executions to perfect their killing techniques.

Unlike ethnic and racial groups, persons with disabilities have not had centuries of collective identity and history to aid them in rejecting stereotypes and overcoming discrimination. It has only been recently that collective disability identity has been developed and fostered (Hallahan and Kauffman, 1994). This identity has been manifested in organizations like People First and Paralyzed Veterans of America and in the independent living movement. Like Jews, African Americans, and Native Americans, persons with disabilities are acknowledging and rejecting societal devaluation and oppression. Previously, isolation produced powerlessness and resulted in internalized societal ableism. Now, people with disabilities have begun to claim their identities and their power.

◆ Minorities and Culture

The meaning of disability has been heavily influenced by society and by human service professionals. Disability has often been a cause for grieving and loss rather than joy and celebration for families (Featherstone, 1980). The focus of attention "ordered" by physicians has been cure at best, improvement at worst. Until recently, children with disabilities were segregated from the community and sometimes from their families. People with psychiatric disabilities were kept in institutions, often under subhuman conditions. Children with intellectual disabilities were often removed from their families and placed in large facilities. For example, one of the authors has a family member who lived his entire life in a facility with several hundred beds that was labeled as a "training school for the mentally retarded." His family placed him there because they were strongly advised that it was the best place for him. Had he been born 40 years later, he could have grown up in his family's home and attended public schools. The facility in which he lived and died is closed, and residents have been moved to the community. One of the authors spent most of his childhood separated from his family in a rehabilitation institution where professionals worked, unsuccessfully, for years to make him walk normally.

Devalued populations such as ethnic minorities and persons with disabilities are often forced to transmit culture primarily in untraditional ways. Eliot's view (1949) of family as the primary cultural transmitter is not always available. For example, families of early African Americans were often unable to transmit culture because of forced separations. When families of persons with disabilities adopt the negative attitudes and stereotypes of the aggregate culture, they avoid association with others with disabilities. At best, they are a neutral influence and can become deterrents to the transmission of disability culture. Persons with disabilities living in families in which they are the only person with a disability may be forced to rely on nonfamily to convey culture. The community of persons with disabilities, therefore, is critical in developing and sharing identity and life meaning.

Historically, isolation has been a major obstacle for persons with disabilities in developing culture. Isolated from others with disabilities, people with disabilities have been given little opportunity for shared development. Society has labeled them as hopeless and has treated them accordingly. Further, the energy it has taken to survive has contributed to isolation. Lack of access to employment, education, transportation, and housing has produced poverty and has restricted access to society. For some people with physical disabilities, the lack of attendant care to assist with basic activities of daily living has created overwhelming physical demands. Communication barriers have isolated deaf and hard-of-hearing people. People with visual disabilities have faced environmental barriers. Thus, many people with disabilities are isolated and forced to expend so much energy on basic survival that participation in society is limited.

However, although people with disabilities have been isolated from each other, they have shared many common experiences that have allowed the rapid growth of a collective identity. Since the early 1960s, social and political activism to create civil rights legislation has facilitated the coming together of persons with disabilities to share and develop collective identities. Increasingly, a pool of educated persons with disabilities is spreading its cultural stories, using literature, the arts, oral traditions, and educational institutions to raise awareness of the lives and contributions of people with disabilities. Culture, developed in isolation, is being enriched and further developed in groups, creating a new and evolving heritage, and perceptions of culture as a "way of life" are evolving rapidly in the disability community.

The existence of local cultures within larger cultures is manifested in unique ways within minority communities. Different Native American nations, for example, have diverse cultures. However, they share many commonalities because of their backgrounds and their similar experiences with the United States government, Christian missionaries, and other outsiders. Similarly, persons with different disabilities have different life experiences but shared identities as well. For example, persons with blindness experience the world differently than persons with psychiatric disabilities. However, both groups have much in common. Both live in a society that perceives them as different, deficient, and pitiable. Historically, both groups have lacked civil rights protections and have experienced discrimination in education, employment, socialization, and entertainment. These experiences have provided a common ground and culture within the larger disability community. However, each group still maintains its uniqueness.

Because of the isolation and powerlessness experienced by persons with disabilities, the nondisabled world has historically assigned labels, roles, and identities to them. Unlike racial and ethnic minorities, however, persons with disabilities have not always had families and communities to reject or insulate them from ableist identities ascribed by the dominant culture. Rather than celebrating the uniqueness and capabilities of their children who have disabilities, families, guided by the medical profession, have been susceptible to experiences of loss, grief, and shame (Ziolko, 1993) and to transmitting their negative feelings and beliefs to their children.

A burgeoning culture of disability is filling the void of cultural poverty. This development is strongly reflected in the language of disability. Increasingly, life with a disability is being perceived as different, not deficient (Gerber, Ginsberg, and Reiff, 1992). People are not "confined" to wheelchairs; instead, they use wheelchairs for mobility. The *Disability Rag,* a militant disability newspaper, portrays persons with disabilities as having "disability cool." As societal barriers are eradicated, the opportunities for persons with disabilities are expanding. The *cuadro* for persons with disabilities is, increasingly, being defined *by* persons with disabilities. Ed Roberts defined himself on national television when he corrected Larry King's reference to him as a victim of polio. He acknowledged his disability but refuted the victim label applied by King, a label readily accepted in an ableist society. *Disability Rag* editor Mary Johnson embraces the term *disability* and rejects terms such as *differently abled* and *physically, emotionally,* or *mentally challenged,* stating, "These euphemisms come from nondisabled 'do-gooders' who wouldn't understand disability culture if we ran over their toes with a wheelchair. These words have no soul and no power. They're all like vanilla custard" (Shapiro, 1993).

Actress Marlee Matlin won an Academy Award portraying a student at a school for deaf people in *Children of a Lesser God.* Since then, her television roles in such series as *Reasonable Doubts* and *Picket Fences* have established her as a solid actress in which her disability has influenced but has not defined her roles. Author and cartoonist John Callahan's book *Don't Worry, He Won't Get Far on Foot* (1989) chronicles his life with quadriplegia and is full of cartoons and experiences with which people with mobility disabilities readily identify. Callahan scoffs at the notion that life with quadriplegia is a tragedy, and he yearns for the day that people with disabilities will be able to thrive in a society "based on incentive and encouragement. They will be free to develop their talents without guilt or fear—or just hold a good steady job" (p. 187).

One manifestation of the collective development of culture is the 1988 uprising at Gallaudet University in which the first deaf president in the school's history was installed. For more than a century, schools for the deaf have been used as a means of educating deaf people. Historically, these schools have been run and operated by hearing professionals to help those who are deaf and hard of hearing. Such schools have isolated and kept deaf people subservient; however, they have also given them a sense of community and shared identity, thus contributing to the development of a strong deaf culture. The Gallaudet uprising was a manifestation of this culture in which the alumni, students, and faculty rejected the appointment of a hearing president in favor of its first deaf president, Dr. I. King Jordan, in more than a century of existence. This protest demonstrated Deaf cultural awareness and Deaf pride, resulting in a determination that leadership for the group should come from one of its own members.

In spite of tremendous opposition, people from diverse backgrounds have developed and clung to their cultural identities with tenacity. In so doing, they have had to surmount personal, physical, social, and societal barriers. Culture has provided them with an identity, a reason for living, and meaning to life. Persons with disabilities have learned from other minorities the importance of culture in developing personal identity and strength, including social and political action. Majority groups may define minority groups by their differences and perceived deficiencies. However, a strong sense of identity empowers people to preserve their cultures in the face of great opposition (Hallahan and Kauffman, 1994; Spekman, Goldberg, and Herman, 1992).

◆ DEVELOPMENT OF DISABILITY CULTURE

Disability culture requires a nontraditional way of viewing people with disabilities. Historically, a focus on functional limitations has predominated research and practice with persons with disabilities (Hahn, 1991). This focus assumes that the major problems facing persons with disabilities reside within the person. Hahn states

> From this viewpoint, disability resided exclusively within the individual; and emphasis was centered on a clinical assessment of a person's remaining skills. Little interest was devoted to external restrictions in the individual's social and work environment. (p. 17)

This emphasis on functional limitations is often expressed in a medical model approach in which persons with disabilities are defined based on individual deficiencies and biology, definitions used to justify denying people their rights to full participation in society (Mackelprang and Salsgiver, 1996; Meyerson, 1988).

Traditional views of persons with disabilities relegate them to the roles of patients and clients in need of social aid and professional services. Traditional approaches also make them more vulnerable to devaluation and discrimination. Jews and persons with disabilities shared this way of being perceived during the Holocaust. The Nazis perfected their genocidal methods on persons with disabilities before ever trying them out on Jews. The view that both groups were inferior and deficient enabled their murderers to justify their actions. Present-day policy in

China mandates forced abortions of fetuses with disabilities and forced sterilization of women known to be at risk of having children with disabilities. Though the United States has not instituted policies such as those in China, it is important to recognize that it was legal to discriminate against persons with disabilities in most areas of nonfederally funded public life until passage of the Americans with Disabilities Act in 1990. In addition, our history is replete with forced sterilizations and laws prohibiting marriages of people with disabilities.

The cultural perspective for viewing the lives of persons with disabilities requires a dramatic change of focus. Disability culture strikes against the "naming activity that erases diversity and wants homogeneity above all else" (Noble, 1993, p. 52). Life with a disability becomes something to celebrate rather than an existence to be mourned. Disability is seen as diversity, not deficiency. People with disabilities are viewed as individuals and citizens rather than clients and patients. The problems facing persons with disabilities are recognized as environmental rather than residing exclusively within the individual. Because people with disabilities have been denied basic rights as a group, the focus of intervention becomes one of civil rights rather than individual treatment. Access to full societal participation is seen as allowing persons with disabilities to integrate into society rather than struggle to merely survive (Hirsch, 1995; Johnson, 1996).

Important to this alternate perception of disability is the view of persons with disabilities as having interrelated, shared customs and traditions. By viewing the origins of the problems that persons with disabilities face as coming primarily from the environment rather than from individual pathology, it becomes possible to think of a culture of disability. Just as survivors of the Holocaust developed culture, persons with disabilities have much in common. When Tim Johnston was first injured, he shared the dominant cultural perspective; to have a disability was a cause of shame and embarrassment. However, within weeks, Tim had begun to meet others with spinal cord injuries (SCI). Like Tim, they had all gone through the shock of losing the ability to walk. They had all known the embarrassment of losing volitional control of their bladders and of having bladder accidents. They shared the common experience of having nondisabled people assume they were unable to speak for themselves because they used wheelchairs for mobility.

Even those whose SCI occurred thousands of miles apart had commonalities. Whether injured in California or Florida, their experiences were similar. Soon Tim found himself sharing a language and a culture of SCI. When Tim called himself a "T-12 para" (a spinal cord injury at the 12th thoracic level), everyone in his newfound culture understood. When Tim talked about his "Quickie," friends knew he was talking about his wheelchair. When a nonwheelchair user walked by, and someone called her a "TAB," all knew she was being called "temporarily able bodied." Conversely, it was a sign of solidarity of their shared experience when he and his friends referred to each other as "gimp" or "crip." An outsider using those labels, on the other hand, would have been considered offensive.

Even as an adult, Tim's disability provided an opportunity to become part of a new culture. Though Tim had to make many adjustments to his disability, paraplegia gradually lost its negative meaning. He resumed his athletic life, participating in activities such as wheelchair basketball, adapted track and field, and waterskiing. Tim was able to eschew society's view of him and others like him.

Though born with a disability, it was in adulthood that Jennie Marsh (pseudonym), a friend of one of the authors, found disability culture. The third of five children, Jennie was born with spina bifida in 1963. Her eagerly anticipated birth turned out to be extremely traumatic for her parents. She had surgeries to close the neural tube in her thoracic spine and to place a shunt to drain fluid from her brain. The family pediatrician told Jennie's parents she would likely not live to adulthood and that she would never be independent from them. As some of her earliest memories, Jennie remembers numerous doctor visits. Physical touch, as a child and adolescent, was either painful or part of the process of caregiving. She learned to accept the way people treated her as an object rather than as a complete human being, such as when, at age 14, she was paraded half naked in front of several physicians. Entering puberty and dressed only in panties, she was forced to walk across a stage so they could observe her gait.

The devotion of Jennie's parents' to her led them to treat her as their "special" child. Her family was protective of her, relating that they wanted to shield her from the cruelty of others. All of Jennie's siblings grew up, moved out of the home, and married. Jennie, however, never considered independence from her family or marriage as possibilities in her life.

Jennie attended special classes in public school, eventually graduating from high school. She found part-time work as a secretary, using paratransit to get to work. Though capable of driving with hand controls, she had never considered acquiring a driver's license. She had experienced crushes on men but had never considered the possibility that a man might be interested in her romantically.

When she was 25 years old, Jennie was still living with her parents. Because her parents were aging and she was frightened about her future, it was at this point that Jennie entered counseling. She wanted to be independent of her family but felt unsure of herself. She was also fearful of being disloyal by leaving the family home but was afraid of burdening her parents by living with them.

In working with Jennie, it became clear that she had the intellectual and physical capabilities to live independently. However, she felt incapable of living independent of her family. She was terrified of driving, thus had never attempted to obtain a driver's license. Living in an apartment of her own seemed impossible. Though her siblings grew up and went through regular life transitions of leaving home, developing financial independence, and starting families, Jennie's family had never considered these as possibilities for her. She continued to be juvenilized. Her family had relied on the extant advice of the best professionals. Jennie had internalized the ableism that defined her as dependent, fragile, and incompetent—a definition that had been conveyed by family, professionals, and society as a whole.

An integral part of counseling and growth for Jennie was to connect her with others who had similar life experiences. The first time she met Marnie, another woman with a disability, there was an immediate connection. Though they had never met before, they developed an immediate sisterhood forged from shared circumstances. Both remembered wondering why their families never talked to them about growing up, getting married, and moving away as they had with their siblings. Both remembered shunt revision surgeries and hospital experiences that were strikingly similar. Both mourned the fact that they had always experienced their bodies as painful and as objects of probing and invasion, not as pleasant and as the means for pleasure and competence. Both had experienced objectification by health care providers and isolation from peers. As a result, their self-concepts and the meanings they had ascribed to their disabilities were similar.

Though unbeknownst to each other, Jennie and Marnie had shared a cultural identity. As persons with disabilities, they shared many commonalities but were isolated from others like themselves. Unfortunately, because of their isolation, the cultural transmission was relayed by persons without disabilities who ascribed negative and limiting meanings, roles, and identities to their disabilities. With few or no role models with disabilities, their disabilities were defined as negative, shameful, and a cause for mourning. Their treatment was similar to the treatment experienced by racial and ethnic minorities; however, they did not have families and communities to buffer and correct the ableist identities ascribed by the dominant culture.

As Jennie and Marnie became involved in their local independent living center, they found others who took pride in their disabilities. They met the director of the ILC, a woman with quadriplegia who lived independently with the aid of attendants. They were impressed by an independent living specialist with blindness, who was a strong disability advocate. They saw a group of people with intellectual disabilities who were moving from an institution to supported apartments. Others with psychiatric disabilities were active in advocating for themselves. Though their disabilities were varied, they shared bonds forged from a determination to overcome devaluation. In numbers, they rejected the societal views of them as powerless and invalid.

As Jennie and Marnie got to know each other and as they began to network with other people with disabilities, a transformation occurred. As Jennie stated, "I got so mad when Marnie told me about what people had done to her. She was smart, attractive, and a lot of fun. All of those people were so wrong to tell her [that she was incompetent]. It was wrong that she couldn't go to school with the other kids." As Jennie saw the prejudice and discrimination directed against Marnie, something happened to her. "Gradually, I began to realize all those things they did to Marnie they did to me too! And it was just as wrong. I got mad." Jennie began to reject the limitations and stereotypes she had passively accepted for years. Instead of psychotherapy to correct her personal deficiencies, Jennie began to realize that she needed skill development and independent living counseling to help her gain confidence and competence.

◆ ADVOCACY AND CULTURAL DEVELOPMENT

Political activism has resulted in environmental change, and it has reinforced a sense of unity and pride among persons with disabilities. Every culture has its stories from which its myths are garnered. Every culture has its heroes and icons, and disability culture is no exception. The 1988 Gallaudet uprising announced to the country that people with hearing disabilities are a force to be heard. In 1980, Patrisha Wright, a woman with a visual disability, set up shop in Washington, D.C., representing the Disability Rights Education and Defense Fund (DREDF) to advocate for the civil rights of persons with disabilities. Mentored by Judy Heumann, a prominent leader in the disability movement, Wright had repeatedly seen the discrimination and patronization people with disabilities experience. Wright's work was instrumental in preserving section 504 and in facilitating passage of the ADA (Shapiro, 1993).

With leaders like Bob Kafka, members of the militant American Disabled for Accessible Public Transit (ADAPT) have fought for the rights of people with disabilities, especially for accessible transportation. ADAPT has led protests throughout the country for persons with disabilities, using tactics such as bus stoppage and sit-ins. In 1986, one of the authors engaged in a protest against a local transit authority whose board repeatedly denied accessible transportation services to persons with disabilities while offering a "free fare" zone geared to serve affluent businesspeople. Several local members of ADAPT pleaded with the board to make basic transportation available to people with disabilities for doctor's visits, work, and entertainment. When that did not work, several members descended on the free fare zone to take advantage of the free bus rides. Members of ADAPT with severe physical disabilities were helped to transfer from their wheelchairs to the first step of the bus, where they slowly wriggled up the stairs on their backs to lie on the floor for their free rides. In the meantime, other protesters ran with their wheelchairs to the next bus stop, where the riders would disembark. In this way, members of ADAPT brought attention to the discrimination they faced daily. At the same time, their sense of empowerment and unity was a source of great pride. While the transit authority board, comprised exclusively of nondisabled people, expected them to be thankful for the minimal, expensive service they received, they knew they were citizens who were being denied access because they were different. They had no reason to feel "thankful" and much reason to feel outraged.

Persons with disabilities are indebted to disability rights leaders and advocates like Judy Heumann, Ed Roberts, Patrisha Wright, I. King Jordan, Justin Dart, and Evan Kemp, Jr. These pioneers have helped usher in a new era in which persons with disabilities are afforded human rights that nondisabled persons take for granted. They have also served as role models for young and newly disabled persons who have protections and opportunities unimagined a generation ago. These leaders and others on national, regional, state, and local levels are creating and developing a new disability culture (Shapiro, 1993).

In addition, culture is being developed through other means (Holcomb, 1996). Places like Gallaudet University are breeding grounds for deaf and hard-of-hearing people to nurture their culture. Places like summer camps for youth with disabilities have allowed people to share hopes, desires, experiences, and fears they cannot share with people without disabilities—who would not understand them anyway. Performers like Marlee Matlin and Chris Burke, who has Down syndrome, provide examples that invalidate traditional views of persons with disabilities. Movies such as *Gaby, Passion Fish, Water Dance, Coming Home,* and *Children of a Lesser God* portray people with disabilities as loving, competent, and vibrant human beings, in contrast to movies such as *A Fish Called Wanda* and *It's a Wonderful Life* that portray them as evil or incompetent. People like John Callahan provide disability humor. Academic organizations such as the Society for Disability Studies are affording scholars and educators opportunities to develop and transmit knowledge about disabilities. Some colleges and universities are developing disability curricula and creating disability studies programs.

This generation is ushering in a new disability era. Increasingly, people with disabilities are defining their lives rather than accepting pathology-laden roles and labels placed on them by the dominant society. People who are acquiring and being born with disabilities have role models who are forging new vistas of civil rights and societal participation. Out of adversity, a disability culture is being created, as are many disability-specific subcultures. Increasingly, disability is becoming defined as different, not bad; persons with disabilities are thriving, not just surviving. New generations of persons with disabilities can continue to build a rich heritage and to transmit positive disability culture, thereby becoming a social and political force in society.

◆   ## SUMMARY

Culture is a way of thinking, feeling, and believing—a stored knowledge that guides people's lives. In part, culture is developed as a social legacy, learned as a result of belonging to a group. Forged by constant conscious and unconscious influences as well as social and political forces, culture affects its members from birth to death. On an individual level, feelings, reactions, and behaviors become second nature in the context of these cultural experiences.

When people belong to groups that are in the minority or without power, their experiences can be negative and their cultures in danger of devaluation and oppression. Persons with disabilities have been defined by their differences, and their differences have always been perceived as pathological. Persons with disabilities share a history of devaluation and oppression with racial and ethnic minorities such as African Americans, Native Americans, and European Jews. In Europe and the United States, social Darwinism of the late 19th and 20th centuries defined persons with disabilities as a major source of social ills. Social workers and others were taught the virtues of eugenics and were encouraged to permanently segregate persons with a variety of disabilities. Forced sterilization was common and institutionalization was encouraged.

Unlike ethnic and racial groups, persons with disabilities have not had centuries of collective identity and history to aid them in rejecting stereotypes and overcoming discrimination. It has only been recently that collective disability identity has been developed and fostered. Perceptions of culture as "a way of life" are evolving rapidly in the disability community. Because of isolation and powerlessness, persons with disabilities have been assigned labels, roles, and identities by the nondisabled world. A burgeoning culture of disability is filling this void of cultural poverty. This development is strongly reflected in the language of disability. Increasingly, life with a disability is being perceived as different, not deficient.

In spite of tremendous opposition, people from diverse backgrounds have developed and clung to their cultural identities with tenacity. In so doing, they have had to surmount personal, physical, social, and societal barriers. Culture has provided them with an identity, a reason for living, and meaning to life. Persons with disabilities have learned from other minorities the importance of culture in developing personal identity and strength, including social and political action.

Human service practitioners must be knowledgeable of the language and history that make up this culture. They must be aware of the resources of this culture and be able to facilitate the person with a disability in establishing links with this culture.

Discussion Questions

1. What is culture? What is the culture of disability?

2. What are some of the ways culture is conveyed?

3. What are some similarities and differences between ethnic culture and disability culture?

4. Many persons with disabilities have led lives isolated from others with similar disabilities. How do their combined experiences contribute to disability culture?

5. What are some ways to promote and enrich disability culture?

6. Why is knowledge of disability culture important to practitioners?

Suggested Readings

Callahan, J. (1989). *Don't worry, he won't get far on foot: The autobiography of a dangerous man.* New York: William Morrow.

Hahn, H. (1991). Alternate views of empowerment: Social services and civil rights. *The Journal of Rehabilitation, 57,* 17–19.

Hallahan, D. P., and Kauffman, J. M. (1994). Toward a culture of disability in the aftermath of Dino and Dunn. *The Journal of Special Education, 27*(4), 496–508.

Holcomb, T. K. (1996). Development of deaf bicultural identity. *American Annals of the Deaf, 142*(2), 89–93.

Noble, M. (1993). *Down is up for Aaron Eagle: A mother's spiritual journey with Down syndrome.* San Francisco: Harper.

Storey, J. (1993). *An introductory guide to cultural theory and popular culture.* Athens, GA: University of Georgia Press.

References

Adams, M. (1971). *Mental retardation and its social dimensions.* Columbia: New York.

Berthrong, D. J. (1976). *The Cheyenne and Arapaho ordeal.* Norman: University of Oklahoma Press.

Callahan, J. (1989). *Don't worry, he won't get far on foot: The autobiography of a dangerous man.* New York: William Morrow.

Devine, E. (1912). *The family and social work.* New York: Survey Associates.

Eagleton, T. (1978). The common idea of culture. In P. Davison, R. Meyersohn, and E. Shils (Eds.), *Literary taste, culture and mass communication, (Volume 1), Culture and mass culture* (pp. 3–25). Cambridge, England: Chadwyck-Healey.

Eliot, T. S. (1949). *Notes towards a definition of culture.* New York: Harcourt Brace.

Epstein, S. (1973). The self-concept revisited. *American Psychologist, 28,* 404–416.

Featherstone, H. (1980). *A difference in the family.* New York: Basic Books.

Gerber, P. J., Ginsberg, R., and Reiff, H. B. (1992). Identifying alterable patterns in employment success for highly successful adults with learning disabilities. *Journal of Learning Disabilities, 25,* 475–487.

Hahn, H. (1991). Alternate views of empowerment: Social services and civil rights. *The Journal of Rehabilitation, 57,* 17–19.

Hallahan, D. P., and Kauffman, J. M. (1994). Toward a culture of disability in the aftermath of Dino and Dunn. *The Journal of Special Education, 27,* (4), 496–508.

Hirsch, K. (1995). Culture and disability: The role of oral history. *Oral history review, 22*(1), 1–27.

Holcomb, T. K. (1996). Development of deaf bicultural identity. *American Annals of the Deaf, 142*(2), 89–93.

Holloway, J. E. (1990). The origins of African-American culture. In J. E. Holloway (Ed.), *Africanisms in American culture.* (pp. 1–18). Bloomington, IL: Indiana University Press.

Johnson, J. D. (1996). Critical missing ingredients: The expertise and valued roles of people with disabilities. *NAMI Advocate, 19*(5), 10.

Levy, A. (1993). *The Wiesenthal file.* Grand Rapids, MI: William B. Eerdmans.

Mackelprang, R. W, and Salsgiver, R. O. (1996). Persons with disabilities and social work: Historical and contemporary issues. *Social Work: Journal of the National Association of Social Workers, 41*(1) 7–14.

Meyerson, L. (1988). The social psychology of physical disability: 1948 and 1988. In M. Nagler (Ed.), *Perspectives on disability* (pp. 13–23). Palo Alto, CA: Health Markets Research.

Milner, A. (1992). *Contemporary cultural theory: An introduction.* St. Leonards, NSW, Australia: Allen & Unwin.

Minuchin, S., and Fishman, H. C. (1981). *Family therapy techniques.* Cambridge, MA: Harvard University Press.

Noble, M. (1993). *Down is up for Aaron Eagle: A mother's spiritual journey with Down syndrome.* San Francisco: Harper.

Rhodes, R. (1993). Mental retardation and sexual expression: An historical perspective. In R. W Mackelprang and D. Valentine (Eds.), *Sexuality and disabilities: A guide for human service practitioners* (pp. 1–27). Binghamton, NY: Haworth Press.

Shapiro, J. P. (1993). *No pity: People with disabilities, forging a new civil rights movement.* New York: Times Books.

Spekman, N. J., Goldberg, R. J., and Herman, K. L. (1992). Learning disabled children grow up: A search for factors related to success in the young adult years. *Learning Disabilities Research & Practice, 7*(3), 161–170.

Storey, J. (1993). *An introductory guide to cultural theory and popular culture.* Athens, GA: University of Georgia Press.

Thompson, M., Ellis, R., and Wildavsky, A. (1990). *Cultural theory.* Boulder, CO: Westview Press.

Wiesel, E. (1995). *All rivers run to the sea.* New York: Alfred A. Knopf.

Ziolko, M. E. (1993). Counseling parents of children with disabilities: A review of the literature and implications for practice. In M. Nagler (Ed.), *Perspectives on disability* (pp. 185–193). Palo Alto, CA: Health Markets Research.

Chapter 3

DISABILITY HISTORY IN THE UNITED STATES

I think we're certainly moving ahead on implementing laws like the Individuals with Disabilities Education Act, section 504 of the Rehabilitation Act, and the Americans with Disabilities Act. We're seeing some major structural changes in this country as far as physical barriers are concerned, and I think those changes are quite remarkable and are having a profound effect on both disabled and nondisabled people.

—Judy Heumann, Assistant Secretary for the Office of Special Education and Rehabilitation Services, Washington, D.C.

Student Learning Objectives:

1. To understand the complex history of persons with disabilities.
2. To understand the various historical origins of how society looks at disability, including the moral, medical, and social models of disability.
3. To understand the historical origins of professional treatment of persons with disabilities.
4. To understand the history of the minority/diversity approach to perceiving disability.
5. To understand the key pieces of legislation that impact the lives of persons with disabilities.

◆ THE MORAL MODEL

Like all cultures, the culture of disability is built upon a history. The history of disability is dominated by three overall models of conceptualizing disability: the moral model, the medical model, and the social/minority model. In the United States, the two models that dominate the way society views disability historically and currently are the moral model and the medical model. The most ancient of these is the moral model. Simply stated, the moral model is the view that disability is directly linked to sin and evil. The moral paradigm of understanding disability views persons with disabilities at "odds with the moral order and the spiritual power that is the heart of the universe" (Longmore, 1993). Paul Longmore, in an address to a disability leadership conference in Anaheim, California, stated

The cause of disability is then not just wrong doing but wrong living; more deeply still, wrong being. In other words, disability like all forms of social deviance is explained within a cosmic, moral context. (Longmore, 1993)

Digging even further into the moral model, Longmore presented the deep, underlying perception of disability within the moral model:

Disability is perceived as embodying, as expressing, a preexisting loss of control at the very moral center of the person; that out-of-control behavior stems from a disabled spirit and a disordered heart.

This "moral" view of disability sprang forth from early human cultures and continued to dominate thinking until the end of the Middle Ages. As discussed in Chapter 1, vestiges certainly continue to exist today in attitudes such as the "sin" of drinking, viewing persons who are alcoholics or substance abusers as morally abject. Perceiving disability as a moral consequence probably originated with the Neolithic tribes, who perceived persons with disabilities as possessed by spirits with negative consequences if the spirits were evil (Albrecht, 1992). The Spartans, with their rugged individualism, abandoned persons with disabilities—both young and old—to die in the countryside. Plato, to whom we owe much of our ethical framework, saw persons with disabilities as standing in the way of a perfect world. He wrote in Book V of *The Republic* that "the offspring of the inferior, or of the better when they chance to be deformed, will be put away in some mysterious, unknown place, as they should be" (Plato, 1991, p. 183). The Romans, who borrowed the concept of reciprocity from the Greeks, gave assistance to adult persons with disabilities with the expectation of their thanks in the form of social complacency (Morris, 1986). But like the Greeks, they also at times abandoned disabled or deformed children to die.

Judeo-Christian tradition was prevalent among Europeans during the Middle Ages and beyond, wherein persons with disabilities were thought to be expressions of god's displeasure (Livneh, 1982). Although Judeo-Christian philosophy did not advocate killing, people with disabilities were ostracized and stereotyped. Biblical history is full of references linking disability to sin and evil. Disability signified "sinner" to the ancient Hebrews, and people with disabilities were thought to be possessed by demons. The Bible prohibited people who were deformed, "crippled," or of short stature from the possibility of becoming priests. The Old Testament forbade the blind or lame from entering the houses of believers (Wright, 1960). In the New Testament, people with mental disorders were believed to be possessed. It was thought that people had blindness and other disabilities as a result of their sins or the sins of their parents.

Judeo-Christian thought, upon which much of Western culture is based, has also taught that humans are made in God's image and are different from and superior to the rest of the animal kingdom. Livneh (1980) contends that persons with disabilities remind those without disabilities of humankind's link with the rest of the animal kingdom and bring to consciousness their fallibility. Thus, disabilities suggest to people humankind's imperfections and dissimilarities to god while illuminating humankind's relationship to the imperfect animal kingdom.

As astonishing as it may sound, the link between moral degradation and disability remains a part of contemporary society. Persons with disabilities can be ostracized because of their link with evil. Discrimination in all arenas, including employment, can be traced in part to the moral paradigm of understanding disability. Some individuals still believe that people are disabled because of their evil or the evil of their parents. While one of the authors worked as an administrator for a university system, he gave a presentation on prejudice and disability. After the presentation, one of his colleagues called him into his office. The colleague explained, "You know, you are wrong about the link between sin and disability causing prejudice. It's true. People who are disabled are disabled because they have sinned against God. This is particularly true of alcoholics and drug addicts." Even persons with disabilities themselves continue to seek out the answer to the question, "Why me?" through understanding their own imagined sin (Salsgiver, 1995).

◆   THE MEDICAL MODEL

The second model of conceptualizing disability, which plays the most prominent role today, is the medical model. By the mid-1700s, a new perspective on the human situation, the Enlightenment, was making its impact upon Europeans and, eventually, Americans. Out of the tenets of the Enlightenment era came the idea that perhaps humans could be perfected. A paradigm of understanding began to emerge that defined persons with disabilities by their biological inadequacies—their pathology, so to speak. Within this environment, the medical model emerged (Mackelprang and Salsgiver, 1996). In America, institutions dedicated to perfecting the imperfect sprang up (Rothman, 1971) with the hope that these inadequacies could be cured by professional intervention. When cure was not possible, persons with disabilities could, at least, be trained to become functional enough to "conduct themselves in a socially acceptable manner" (Longmore, 1987b).

But the medical model of perceiving disability, while benevolent on the surface, is in reality insidious. Longmore(1993) emphasized the following:

I think it's obvious that this very definition of how people with disabilities should be regarded and dealt with by society presents us with an impossible dilemma because being made over after the model of nondisabled people is exactly by definition what people with disabilities can never do; can never achieve. I think also this medical model displays a considerable degree of social ambivalence toward people with disabilities. In fact, the medical model in practice has much of the time been the institutionalized expression of anxieties in society about those who look different and those who function differently.

In many respects, the rhetoric of the medical model has been paternalistic. Now this word paternalism, *since it comes from the root word for* father, *sounds benign. But in*

practice, it's often been oppressive because fundamentally, this model of disability re-
gards people with disabilities as repulsive; as incompetent to manage their own lives;
and at times even as dangerous to society. Therefore, historically in the modern era,
they have needed to be supervised by professionals in various medical and social service
fields; regulated by them perhaps throughout their lives.

Jennie Marsh, whose life was discussed in the previous chapter, illustrated Long-more's assertions as she recalled her relationships with health care professionals as an adolescent:

I was barely human. One time, as a 14-year-old, I was paraded in front of a whole
class of doctors so they could see my "abnormal gait." I was wearing only my panties.
They would never have done that to a nondisabled girl but it was OK to parade me
almost naked. And the crazy thing is, it wasn't until years later that I realized they
had dehumanized me.

◆ SOCIAL DARWINISM AND EUGENICS

The 1800s began with a continuing belief that humans could change. The optimism of the Enlightenment existed, but so did a fear of those who were different. Professionals held great hope that "deviants," which included persons with disabilities, could be molded into assimilated, less threatening, more acceptable people (Rothman, 1971); however, by the end of the 19th century, the ominous philosophy of social Darwinism and eugenics came to prominence. Eugenics sought the development of socially beneficial persons and the prohibition of reproduction of the "nonproductive," undesirable components of society (Rhodes, 1993). Linked both with the moral model and the failures of the medical model, eugenics became a convenient explanation for the ills of society and stereotyped persons with disabilities as dangerous and degraded, making them extremely vulnerable. Professionals lost confidence in their ability to perfect persons with disabilities, concluding that they were innately unproductive and thus endemically without worth. Treating them with the hope of changing them into "normal" human beings was against the laws of nature. No intervention could bring about that change because the laws of nature deemed them unfit (Longmore, 1987a). People with disabilities were to be prevented from marrying or having children for fear of propagating their imperfections. As the 19th century progressed, the number of institutions to deal with the threat and nuisance of persons with disabilities increased dramatically; people with disabilities were increasingly isolated and institutionalized, sometimes under subhuman conditions.

The beginnings of the 20th century in the United States offered little attitudinal progress concerning disability. Both the moral model and the medical model were tightly entrenched in American thought. Persons with disabilities were objects of shame and disgrace. Parents, often on the advice of professionals, hid their children with disabilities from society in their homes or consigned them to institutions (Mackelprang and Salsgiver, 1996). Gallagher (1985) offers insight into the regressive 20th-century mind-set concerning persons with disabilities. He recounts the experiences of President Franklin D. Roosevelt as a person with a disability and relates these experiences to the prevailing attitudes of the time. Roosevelt was continually forced to compensate for these attitudes and to hide his disability from the American public. World War I and World War II marked superficial advancement for persons with disabilities in the sense that federal rehabilitation legislation produced money for treatment of veterans disabled by war. However, the stereotype of persons with disabilities as nonproductive and socially abject was prominent through the 1950s (Longmore, 1987b).

Within the academic community in the mid-1940s, research was beginning to be presented that would pave the way for the pragmatic political action of the '60s, '70s, '80s, and '90s. Researchers such as Roger Barker and Beatrice Wright, using the theoretical frameworks of Kurt Lewin, began to bring forth findings that demonstrated similarities between the experiences of persons with disabilities and disenfranchised minority groups. They presented the idea that the lowered status of persons with disabilities may be crucial in understanding the behavior of persons with disabilities. They planted the seed that the locus of the problems related to disability may not lie exclusively with the disabled person but with society and how it defines disability (Meyerson, 1990).

◆ THE SOCIAL/MINORITY MODEL AND THE INDEPENDENT LIVING MOVEMENT

In contrast to the medical and moral models, the social/minority model of disability views persons with disabilities as a minority group within a dominant nondisabled society. It sees the phenomenon of disability as a social construct much like race or gender. The limitations of disability, widely known as handicaps, come about because of society's definition of disability rather than any innate characteristic of disability. Therefore, intervention is not necessarily with the person who has the disability, but with the society that creates and harbors the definition. The independent living movement rested on this philosophical/political view.

The birth of the independent living movement arose out of the turbulence of the 1960s. The youth of the 1960s led the nation in a process of reexamination, challenge, analysis, and change. Turmoil commanded center stage, and youth found comfort in their differences, often rejecting traditional values. Authority was challenged as never before, and diversity was embraced. The same atmosphere that gave rise to the women's and African American movements also gave birth to the disability movement. For the first time in American history, significant numbers of persons with disabilities demanded access to and were allowed to participate in the mainstream of society (Mackelprang and Salsgiver, 1996).

As with every movement, there were leaders. Among many others, Judy Heumann and Ed Roberts served this role in the initial phase of the movement.

Models of Leadership

Judy Heumann, currently the Assistant Secretary for the Office of Special Education and Rehabilitative Services, was born in Brooklyn to German-Jewish immi-
grant parents. At 18 months, she contracted polio. Shapiro (1993) points out that
doctors urged her parents to institutionalize her. Relatives expressed to her parents that she must have caught polio because of "some horrible sin on their part"
(p. 56). When she was denied access to regular school, her parents fought to have
her admitted. Heumann (1994) recounts

> *My parents were immigrants, and so as the first child, my mother very proudly took*
> *me to enroll me in public school. She never thought she would be told to take me*
> *home. They said, "Your daughter isn't welcome; she's a fire hazard because our school*
> *has a few steps." They could have said, "Welcome," but they didn't.*

After continuing battles in grade school, middle school, and high school,
Heumann graduated from high school to once again face battles in her quest to be
educated. At college, she had to fight to live in the dorm and to gain access into
buildings that had only steps. Initially denied her teaching certificate for physical
reasons, she fought and got it—only to be denied teaching job after teaching job.

In 1970, Heumann started the Disabled in Action, a disability rights group
whose sole function was political action and protest. On several occasions, she
organized demonstrations against the educational and welfare policies of the
Nixon administration. In 1975, she went to Berkeley to work for another fighter
for burgeoning disability rights, Ed Roberts (Shapiro, 1993).

Unlike Heumann, who had known the effects of polio since being a very
young child, Ed Roberts contracted polio at the age of 14. Shapiro (1993) paints a
morbid picture of this adolescent, newly stricken and negatively impressed by
medical professionals:

> *Roberts saw himself as a "helpless cripple" overwhelmed by depression, powerlessness,*
> *and self-hatred. He asked his parents if he would ever go to college, marry, or hold a*
> *job. The answer, based on what doctors, nurses, and counselors had said, was always*
> *no. It would have been more humane, a doctor had told his mother, if the high fever of*
> *the polio had killed him quickly.* (p. 42)

Through acts of rebellion and victories of school access, Roberts began to view his
life certainly as different but not powerless.

Perhaps it was his tenaciousness as a "playground rat" before he was disabled
or perhaps it is what each of us as a person with a disability must do to grab life at
its fullest, but Roberts met each barrier he encountered with a fight. He fought to
get his high school diploma when school officials said he could not graduate
because he had not completed driver's education and physical education. He
fought to get into UC Berkeley when his rehabilitation counselor, also a person
with a disability, ruled that money spent on Roberts's education would be wasted

because he would not be able to work. He fought to live on campus when no dorm could accommodate his special needs (Shapiro, 1993).

His fighting experience propelled him naturally into the political arena. From a small informal disabled student group (called the Rolling Quads) evolved the Physically Disabled Student's Program, which offered advocacy and services to disabled students at the Berkeley campus. This group expanded to work with persons with disabilities beyond campus in the form of the first independent living center in the United States: the Center of Independent Living located in Berkeley, California.

Shapiro (1993) offers a succinct description of Roberts's vision of the Center of Independent Living:

> *It would be run by disabled people; approach their problems as social issues; work with a broad range of disabilities; and make integration into the community its chief goal. Independence was measured by an individual's ability to make his own decisions and the availability of the assistance necessary—from attendants to accessible housing—to have such control.* (pp. 53–54)

Today, there are more than 28 of these centers in California, over 400 in the United States, and a movement to create centers in Europe and Japan.

Roberts's most important political nexus arrived when Governor Jerry Brown appointed him in 1975 as director of the California State Department of Rehabilitation. Roberts was ecstatic. He headed the very agency that had once declared him unemployable. Ed Roberts remained until his death in 1995 an important leader in the independent living movement. He spoke regularly in educational settings and at political functions of the importance of persons with disabilities taking control of their lives and working toward the dissipation of social and environmental barriers that prevent them from doing so (Shapiro, 1993).

Prejudice, Discrimination, and Work

The independent living movement applied the social/minority model of conceptualizing disability as the foundation of the political process of gaining the civil rights of persons with disabilities (Berkowitz, 1987). Whereas the traditional moral and medical models focused on individual pathology (Weich, Rapp, Sullivan, and Kisthardt, 1989), the independent living movement focused on societal responses and discrimination based on deep-seated prejudices.

The social/minority model conceptualized and utilized by the independent living movement asserts that discrimination against persons with disabilities is rooted in prejudicial values of the culture. The most fundamental of these cultural beliefs is that persons with disabilities cannot and really should not work or be otherwise productive, in spite of slogans such as "hire the handicapped." The cultural value that persons with disabilities should be taken care of stems from the origins of the current welfare system in the Elizabethan Poor Laws of 1601. The poor laws were the legal attempt in early industrial England to control the rabble and at the same time maintain competition of labor by classifying the poor as deserving and nondeserving. The orphaned, blind, and disabled were deserving in nature and thus could receive charity in a more legitimate way than the so-called nondeserving poor (Trattner, 1989). Categorizing people with disabilities as deserving poor creates a dubious benefit wherein they qualify for an ever-eroding baseline of services while being relegated to subsistence-level living. Because of its history, America's social welfare system creates pervasive work disincentives and reinforces the belief that persons with disabilities really do not need to work. The independent living movement views this underlying value as repressive and decries the resulting discrimination that prohibits people with disabilities from working, keeping them dependent on the power structure.

The Independent Living Frame of Reference

Traditional medical paradigms define the nature of disability in terms of the individual deficiencies and the biology of the disability. For example, customary justifications for keeping disabled children out of regular public schools have centered on their impairments. By contrast, the social/minority model approach focuses on society, its beliefs, and resulting discrimination. Traditional justifications for denying children with disabilities access to education are rejected by independent living proponents. The social/minority model approach contends that children with disabilities have not been enrolled in regular schools because they have not been allowed in. As a group, as a minority, they have been denied their rights to education (Meyerson, 1990).

The social/minority perspective fundamental to the independent living movement offers a constructive alternative to traditional ways of viewing persons with disabilities. The paradigm shift from individual incapacity to environmental discrimination is in itself empowering. The behavior, the self-concept, the educational achievement, and the economic success of persons with disabilities can only be understood by looking at people with disabilities as a minority group that is subjected to discrimination found in the social environment (Fine and Asch, 1988). Rather than remain objects of pity, this perspective encourages persons with disabilities to begin to assert their capabilities, personally and politically. It encourages persons with disabilities to see themselves as part of the great diversity mosaic that makes up our society. Independent living has provided role models of personal independence and political power. Rather than remaining passive objects of service and service providers, people with disabilities become active and capable consumers. Rather than organizing their lives around their deficits and problems, they begin to acknowledge and build upon their strengths and take control of their lives. Personal decision making replaces passivity; empowerment replaces powerlessness. This awareness of strength and control has resulted in significant social and political change.

◆ Disability and the Law

Several key pieces of legislation are important in understanding disability. These include the National Defense Act of 1916, the National Rehabilitation Act of 1920, the Social Security Act of 1935, social security disability insurance, supplemental security income, the Rehabilitation Act of 1973, the Equal Education for All Handicapped Children Act of 1975 and its various updates and amendments, and the Americans with Disabilities Act of 1990.

The National Defense Act of 1916 and the National Rehabilitation Act of 1920

The beginnings of any concerted effort in dealing with services directed toward persons with disabilities were found in the *National Defense Act of 1916*. The focus of the service components of this act centered on the training of soldiers disabled in World War I so that they could compete for jobs in civilian life. Four years later, the concept of vocational rehabilitation expanded from focusing on soldiers to the public in general in the form of the *National Rehabilitation Act of 1920*. Funds were provided for job training, job counseling, job adjustment, job placement, and accommodation such as prosthetics. The National Rehabilitation Act of 1920 created a cost-sharing program between the states and the federal government. The federal government picked up half the costs of rehabilitation in return for the development of a state plan, an annual report on costs and services, the creation of a comprehensive state program, and assurances that the federal funds would not be used for buildings and equipment (Albrecht, 1992).

The Social Security Act of 1935

The *Social Security Act of 1935,* the product of a long and arduous battle by FDR, has become the cornerstone of social welfare related to disability. Permanent public assistance was provided for the elderly, blind persons, and children with disabilities (Albrecht, 1992). In 1956, Congress enacted *social security disability insurance* (SSDI). Based upon the individual's prior payments into social security, SSDI expanded coverage to all persons with disabilities. SSDI defines physical or mental disability in terms of the inability to hold any employment at any geographic location in the country (Berkowitz, 1987). Albrecht (1992) states that three general categories of persons with disabilities qualify for receiving benefits under SSDI. These include (1) insured workers who become disabled for a year or more and who are under 65 years of age, (2) widows, widowers, or divorced wives between the ages of 50 and 59 who are persons with disabilities and meet the qualifications for widows' or widowers' benefits, and (3) the disabled sons and daughters of an entitled worker.

In 1974, Congress implemented *supplemental security income* (SSI), which provides an income floor for persons with disabilities and the elderly. SSI, which replaced state-run programs, is paid from the general revenues of the federal government. Some states supplement this minimum income from state funds. Generally, to qualify for SSI, an individual must have little or no income or resources and must be considered medically disabled. In addition, to become eligible for SSI, people must be unemployed or if employed, their earnings must be less than limits set each year by the Social Security Administration (SSA). These limits are called "substantial gainful activity" (Social Security Administration, 1994). Eligibility for SSI is determined at the state level, and payments are administered by the federal SSA. SSI eligibility is especially important because most SSI recipients qualify for Medicaid coverage and services.

Medicaid, made a part of the Social Security Act in 1965, provides health care for people who are poor, aged, or disabled. Persons with disabilities who qualify for SSI automatically qualify for Medicaid, which provides physician and hospital services, including inpatient and outpatient hospital care, laboratory, and X-ray services. Medical services are administered by states using a combination of state and federal funds.

Persons with disabilities who have a work history may qualify for Medicare. Medicare, also enacted in 1965, is a hospital and medical insurance plan. The hospital insurance is compulsory and the medical insurance is voluntary. Benefits under the hospital insurance include hospital services and limited skilled nursing home care and home health care services. The supplemental medical insurance provides physician services and outpatient hospital care (DiNitto, 1991).

Persons with disabilities who receive either SSDI or SSI benefits qualify for the Plan for Achieving Self-Sufficiency (PASS). PASS allows persons with disabilities to return to work by setting aside moneys earned to achieve a specific vocational goal in a time-limited period so they maintain medical benefits through SSDI and SSI. The primary goal of the PASS program is to facilitate persons with disabilities in moving to employment. Recent changes in the Social Security Administration's policy on PASS appear to be discouraging this innovative program (Ervin, 1997).

The Rehabilitation Act of 1973

The *Rehabilitation Act of 1973* was the culmination of many years of struggle on the part of a variety of political forces, including persons with disabilities involved in the independent living movement. The Rehabilitation Act of 1973 established several significant components that mandated services and civil rights for persons with disabilities involved in federally funded programs. The act established the Rehabilitation Services Administration within the Department of Health and Human Services. It established the policy that the most severely disabled persons should receive priority in rehabilitation services. This emphasis was in direct opposition to the historic approach to rehabilitation called "creaming," a procedure of accepting the least disabled person for rehabilitation services in order to quickly close the case (DiNitto, 1991). The Rehabilitation Act of 1973 established the rule that all consumers receiving rehabilitation services must have an individualized written rehabilitation program (IWRP) to ensure they have input into their services. The act also created the Architectural and Transportation Barriers Compliance Board to facilitate the elimination of architectural barriers in public places to persons with disabilities. The act funded a national center for the deaf-blind and increased funding to rehabilitation research. The 1978 amendments to the Rehabilitation Act of 1973 established the National Institute of Handicapped Research (now called the National Institute on Disability and Rehabilitation Research) as well as funding for independent living centers and for employer incentives to train and hire persons with disabilities (Albrecht, 1992).

Section 503 of the Rehabilitation Act of 1973 requires entities contracting with the federal government in excess of $2,500 to establish affirmative action plans for persons with disabilities. Recently updated to contracts of $150,000 with firms of 150 or more employees, section 503 requires an employer to initiate affirmative action for all employment openings, including administration. Affirmative action applies to promotion and upgrading as well as layoff and termination. The affirmative action program must include outreach practices to agencies and organizations that have a likelihood of access to qualified persons with disabilities. The employer must periodically review job qualifications to determine if they adequately reflect the essential functions of the job and do not systematically screen out persons with disabilities. Employers need to consider known job applicants who are persons with disabilities for other positions in the company for which they may qualify. Employers must develop internal practices and procedures to insure management's cooperation in affirmative action for persons with disabilities (Department of Labor, 1992).

Section 504 of the Rehabilitation Act of 1973 guarantees that employers contracting with the federal government cannot discriminate against persons with disabilities. Since section 504 provides the legal foundation for the Americans with Disabilities Act of 1990, the discussion of its components is included under the ADA discussion that follows.

The Equal Education for All Handicapped Children Act of 1975

The *Equal Education for All Handicapped Children Act of 1975* is one of the few pieces of legislation known well by professionals in human services and education by its original number, *PL 94-142*. The Equal Education for All Handicapped Children Act of 1975 went through several levels of evolution and was finally renamed the *Individuals with Disabilities Education Act (PL 101-467),* or IDEA, in 1990. Congress last modified this historic law in March of 1996. IDEA stipulates that education be provided at public expense for all children, including children with disabilities. The age range of those covered under IDEA is 3 through 21. It calls for the education of children with disabilities to be provided in the most open and "normal" (least restrictive) environment possible. When children need to be diagnosed, evaluated, and prescribed for, the diagnosis, evaluation, and prescription should not produce stigmatization and discrimination. The parents and the child need to be primary players in any remedial or pedagogical plan established for the child's education (Albrecht, 1992).

The original legislation provided for the establishment of the Individual Education Program (IEP). IDEA maintains the IEP as the central process in the education of a child with a disability. These plans should include the current level of education of the child, the goals and objectives of the child's educational process, specific services needed and when they need to be provided, and the method by which the plan will be evaluated. The educational environment in which the child is to be educated—that is, whether or not the child is placed in a regular classroom or special education—is established in the IEP. A key determinant in this educational environmental placement is the degree of benefit to the student with a disability in interacting with nondisabled students and the potential disruption of other students, which, in effect, would make it impossible to meet the educational needs of the student with the disability (*NEA Today*, 1995).

The interactive component of IDEA with the central position of the child and parent is characterized in the IEP process (Van Reusen and Bos, 1994). The IEP must include the child, the parents, other individuals at the parents' request, the student's teacher, a school district representative, and other individuals at the school district's request. If the school, student, or parent is considering the placement of the student with a disability in a regular classroom, the teacher of the classroom in which the student seeks placement should be part of the process (*NEA Today*, 1995).

Part H of IDEA mandates participating states to provide early intervention services to children with developmental disabilities from birth to their third birthday. State participation is not mandatory, but strong financial incentives for state participation are offered by the federal government. The objective of part H is to provide early intervention in the context of the child's environment with maximum family involvement in the total care of the child with a disability. Crucial to this objective is the individualized family service plan (IFSP). The IFSP is developed in a similar manner as the IEP. The child's parents and family play a crucial role. The IFSP team may include an advocate or person outside the family at the parent's request. Other team members should include a service coordinator, the evaluations and assessment professional, and the service provider. Since the focus of the IFSP is both the child and the family, the IFSP may include services to the family that will facilitate growth on the part of the child with a disability. As the child with a disability moves closer to the age of 3, a plan of transition to part B of IDEA or other preschool services should be included in the IFSP. Each participating state should have an agency in place to administer part H, utilizing an advisory council (Bernstein, Steitner-Eaton, and Ellis, 1995).

The Americans with Disabilities Act of 1990

The *Americans with Disabilities Act of 1990 (PL 101-336)*, or ADA, was a civil rights landmark for persons with disabilities. With the passage of the ADA, Congress acknowledged that 43 million Americans with disabilities have been subjected to serious and pervasive discrimination. Congress also acknowledged that, unlike other populations who have experienced discrimination, persons with disabilities have had no recourse within the law to deal with this discrimination. Thus, the ADA was enacted to prevent further discrimination and to promote the rights of persons with disabilities.

The Americans with Disabilities Act of 1990 is considered one of the most comprehensive pieces of civil rights legislation in the history of the United States. The ADA has five parts. Title I addresses issues of discrimination in employment of persons with disabilities. It deals with the definition of disability, outlines reasonable accommodation in the workplace, identifies what is considered undue hardship in not providing accommodation, and defines essential functions of the job. Title II applies the ADA to public entities, including public transportation. There are no funding limitations, as with section 504 of the 1973 Rehabilitation Act; all government activity is covered. Government agencies were required by the ADA to develop transition plans that assess physical barriers in a public entity's facilities and to create a detailed plan to make the facilities accessible. Government agencies were also required to complete a self-evaluation that analyzed all services, policies, and practices to determine whether or not they complied with the ADA. Then a plan was to be formulated for bringing those things that did not comply with the ADA into compliance. Title III brings the Civil Rights Act of 1964 and the Rehabilitation Act of 1973 into the private sector for persons with disabilities. Basically, it makes discrimination against persons with disabilities illegal in public accommodations and in commercial facilities. If services are provided, services must be made available to persons with disabilities. Title IV mandates the establishment of telecommunications relay services. Title V contains several miscellaneous provisions and exclusions, including alternate access to phone services (Jarrow, 1992). We will address titles I through III here.

The Americans with Disabilities Act defines disability based upon the definitions established under the Rehabilitation Act of 1973. Disability means "(1) a physical or mental impairment that substantially limits one or more of the major life activities of such an individual; (2) a record of such an impairment; (3) being regarded as having such an impairment" (EEOC, 1991, p. I-25). One significance of this definition is that it encompasses the individual who is considered disabled out of prejudice or bias. Individuals encountering stereotyping as a person with a disability can be defined as disabled under the ADA. They are legally entitled to reasonable accommodation. The ADA defines physical or mental impairment as

> *(1) Any physiological disorder or condition, cosmetic disfigurement, or anatomical loss affecting one or more of the following body systems: neurological, musculoskeletal, special sense organs, respiratory (including speech organs), cardiovascular, reproductive, digestive, genito-urinary, hemic and lymphatic, skin, and endocrine; or (2) Any mental or psychological disorder, such as mental retardation, organic brain syndrome, emotional or mental illness, and specific learning disabilities.* (EEOC, 1991, p. I-26)

Finally, major life activities are defined by the ADA as "caring for oneself, performing manual tasks, walking, seeing, hearing, speaking, breathing, learning, and working" (EEOC, 1991, p. I–27). Although the definitions appear at first glance to be fairly clear–cut, many conditions fall into gray areas, such as extreme overweight and infertility. Each of these conditions are settled in individual legal cases to determine if, in fact, the condition can be defined as a disability under the ADA, thus entitling persons to the protections of the law.

Title I of the ADA defines reasonable accommodation as a modification or adjustment to a job, the work environment, or the way things usually are done that enables a qualified individual with a disability to enjoy an equal employment opportunity. An employer cannot deny an employment opportunity to a qualified applicant or employee because of the accommodating process. The obligation to provide a reasonable accommodation applies to all aspects of employment; it is ongoing and may arise any time that a person's disability or job changes. Potential employees with disabilities must be accommodated in the job application process to enable a qualified applicant to have an equal opportunity to be considered for the job. Reasonable accommodation must be provided to enable an applicant or a current employee to perform the essential functions of a job. An employee with a disability must not only be accommodated around the task performance but also with regard to the benefits and privileges of employment, such as training, social events, health programs, and so on (EEOC, 1991).

The following are examples of reasonable accommodation. In *recruitment,* an employer sends notices of jobs to various organizations where persons with disabilities are likely to be found, such as independent living centers. In the *application process,* the employer provides assistance in filling out an application form or provides the application in a form (e.g., braille) that is accessible to a person with a visual disability or a person who lacks manual dexterity (Johnson, 1992). In the actual *job performance,* the employer can reassign an employee with a disability to a job with essential functions that the person can perform, or the employer can restructure a job by redistributing nonessential functions to other employees. Most of the time, reasonable accommodation means obtaining assistive equipment or devices, providing qualified readers and interpreters, modifying examinations, training materials, or policies, offering job reassignment to a vacant position, permitting use of accrued paid leave or unpaid leave for necessary treatment, providing reserved parking for a person with a mobility impairment, and allowing an employee to provide equipment or devices that an employer is not required to provide. In *benefits,* the employer assures that the office picnics or other social activity events are held in an accessible place (EEOC, 1991).

Title I of the ADA defines the concept of essential functions as the basic tasks that a person must be able to perform in order to carry out the purpose of the position. They focus on the purpose and intended results of a position rather than on how the job is typically performed. Essential functions do not include marginal functions (EEOC, 1991) and include functions that the position exists to perform. For example, if a person is hired to enter data into a computer, an essential function of that job is data entry. It is not the ability to type or even to see. If a person is hired to teach math, the essential function of that job is to transmit knowledge to students. It is not the ability to stand in front of a class or to write on the chalkboard. If a person is hired to unload a truck, the essential function is moving the material inside the truck to a designated place. The essential job function is not lifting *x* number of pounds. Essential functions may include a wide span of functions when there are a limited number of other employees to perform the necessary job tasks. For example, it may be an essential function for a file clerk in a very small and busy office to answer the telephone, greet arrivals to the office, and process incoming and outgoing mail.

Finally, essential functions are highly specialized functions in a job or position. For example, a company may want to expand its market into Mexico. For a new sales position, in addition to sales experience, it may require a person to communicate in Spanish. As another example, a school of social work may hire a professor to teach industrial social work, in which the essential function requires knowledge of EAP programs. In each of these examples, the essential job functions of speaking Spanish and knowledge of EAP programs focus on the purpose and intended results of the positions.

Title I of the ADA also deals with the concept of undue hardship, which refers to significant difficulty or expense on the part of the employer. This is determined generally by evaluating the cost of an accommodation in relationship to the overall fiscal resources of the employment organization and the total number of employees hired by the company. The EEOC, in looking at comparative resources to determine whether or not an employer is compliant with the ADA, seeks data that substantiate that an employer has sought outside sources for reasonable accommodation (EEOC, 1991). Finally, it is an undue hardship for an employer when an accommodation would negatively impact the basic nature and operation of the business.

Title II applies the ADA to public entities, including those that supply public transportation. All activity of government is covered whether or not the public entity has a contractual agreement with the federal government. The ADA mandates the following:

1. Agencies must make information on the ADA, including the rights of persons with disabilities, available to applicants, employees, and consumers of the agency's services.
2. At least one employee must be designated to coordinate efforts to comply with the ADA and carry out the responsibilities under the ADA.
3. Agencies must have published and available procedures for dealing with complaints.
4. Government agencies are required by the ADA to complete a transition plan and self-evaluation. The self-evaluation is a self-analysis of all services, policies, and practices to determine whether or not they comply with the ADA.
5. A transition plan involves accessing physical barriers in the public entity's facilities and detailing the plan to make the facilities accessible. (Jarrow, 1992)

Title III of the ADA provides basic civil rights to persons with disabilities in the private public-service sector. Persons with disabilities have the right to equal enjoyment of goods, services, facilities, advantages, or accommodations of any place of public accommodation. This also applies to services or establishments that are leased by commercial enterprises. Public accommodations cannot circumvent the law by providing goods or services that are different or separate from those offered to the general population unless they equalize accommodations; for example, special rest rooms may be provided separate from regular rest rooms. Goods and services must be offered in the most integrated setting appropriate to the needs of the individual. Service providers such as liability or health insurance companies cannot offer policies that discriminate against persons with disabilities. Commercial facilities may not refuse to serve individuals who associate with people known to have disabilities (EEOC, 1991).

◆   SUMMARY

The history of persons with disabilities is rich and varied. History has brought forth three models of how society conceptualizes disability: the moral model, the medical model, and the social/minority model. Evidence of the existence of persons with disabilities dates back to the Neolithic period. Judeo-Christian thought of the early Middle Ages viewed disability as a result of sin. The Enlightenment in Europe established the idea that persons with disabilities could be perfected, made "normal." The United States adopted these perspectives up until the independent living movement of the 1960s. This civil rights movement for persons with disabilities championed the view that nonaccess in society resulted from architectural and attitudinal barriers rather than the dysfunction of the individual person with a disability. Much of the legislation that impacts persons with disabilities is the result of the political work of persons with disabilities themselves. It is extremely important for practitioners working with persons with disabilities to be aware of these laws.

◆   ◆   ◆   *Personal Narrative: Judy Heumann*

Judy Heumann is Assistant Secretary for the Office of Special Education and Rehabilitation Services; she acquired a disability from polio in 1949 when she was a young girl. She has been a leader in the disability civil rights movement since its early years in the '60s.

As far as disabled people are concerned, I didn't have a lot of role models as I was growing up. That was part of the problem. There weren't a lot of disabled role models out there; we didn't know them. The truth of the matter is from elementary to high school and even through college, I had one teacher with a disability. She was an elementary school teacher, and she had one leg that was four or five inches different in length from the other. Outside of that, I don't remember any disabled people in special positions.

I had one teacher, Mrs. Malikoff, she was a speech pathologist in my elementary school. She didn't have a disability, but she was the only professional who ever really talked to me about a career. I remember her very vividly, saying, "You can be a speech therapist."

President Roosevelt was an important person in my life because I knew that he was disabled and my parents always made sure that I knew that he was. You couldn't get a higher role model than at that level.

As I was growing up, I realized a lot of people influenced my life in different ways. Many were nondisabled civil rights leaders and women's leaders. They were challenging themselves and challenging the system. They had beliefs that they fought for. These role models have ranged from local people in the community to more famous people known at the national and international levels.

As far as disabled people are concerned, I have learned a lot over the years from people like MaryLou Breslan and Ed Roberts and Kitty Cone and Denise McQuade and Justin Dart. In my lifetime, there has been a very strong emerging movement of disabled individuals who feel common problems and common solutions and feel an identity among each other as a group of disabled people. We have a common agenda, a common vision for what we hope to accomplish, and I think that's been critically important.

When you consider the 49 million disabled people in the United States, I do not know how many of them identify with disability culture. For those of us who have felt the need to come together and work together, we definitely feel this is a very important part of our lives that has really helped us to improve our individual lives as well as the collective lives of disabled people.

Problems still exist in the United States, and they are many and varied. We don't have a national health care policy, which would guarantee that all individuals, disabled or not, can get health care. Work disincentives exist in policy that result in disabled individuals who are capable and who wish to work being unable to do so. Various policies also make it more difficult for children to be integrated into schools. For example, I personally wish personal attendant services were much easier for people to obtain and that people could get money directly to hire their own personal attendants. I wish personal attendant services were available on a 24-hour-a-day basis. I wish the government would provide easy and direct assistance for things like technology at school and in the workplace. Those types of barriers still limit opportunities for too many people.

I think we're certainly moving ahead on implementing laws like the Individuals with Disabilities Education Act, section 504 of the Rehabilitation Act, and the Americans with Disabilities Act. We're seeing some major structural changes in this country as far as physical barriers are concerned, and I think those changes are quite remarkable and are having a profound effect on both disabled and nondisabled people.

As disabled people, we have to become more involved in identifying problems and working toward solutions to those problems. We need to be doing much more organizing at the local, state, and national levels, both with disabled individuals and through alliances with other civil rights and women's organizations. We need to be doing a better job of educating the general public and Congress about problems and solutions to those problems. We could all do a better job if we were more organized—organized in a political sense.

Some of the challenges we are continually facing include (1) identifying our personal barriers, (2) recognizing the barriers of other disabled individuals, (3) prioritizing how we're going to work to remove those barriers, and (4) as those barriers begin to fall, figuring out how we're going to benefit from the new opportunities that have been created.

It is important to recognize where we are today versus where we were 10, 20, 30, or 40 years ago. We are definitely making important strides. But far too many individuals with disabilities are not benefiting to the degree to which they should from existing legislation. There are many ongoing needs, which, if not addressed, are really going to continue to hold back the opportunities of disabled kids and adults.

Our lack of ability to get universal health care is not only a disability issue. It's a national issue. Right now, we are getting incremental health care reform, which is important. I think the president has been vigilant in working with certain members of Congress on making changes slowly but surely in health care. But, ultimately, it is a fact that people in this country haven't had a right to health care, whereas individuals in many European countries just take health care as a right.

Barriers in the environment certainly cause a lot of limitations. Barriers that exist within the community make it more difficult for people psychologically as well. Those of us who had disabilities years ago and fought for changes have seen them beginning to happen. With those changes, we have to learn how to live in a new reality in which people go from having a very restricted environment to an environment that is becoming more and more open. This forces people to learn how to participate in that more open environment, something that is sometimes difficult to do.

Our image of who we are and what we are able to do is, in part, created by the environment in which we exist. When the environment is made accessible, people have to start going out and becoming more independent, doing things they never did before. A simple example of this occurred in a synagogue that I attended when I lived in Berkeley. The bema, an area where people go to do readings and worship, was not accessible. One day I told the rabbi, "The bema is not accessible." Two weeks later it was accessible. The rabbi said, "OK, now it's accessible and you have to come up and do some of the things that other people do." I thought, "Oh my god, I've never been trained!" I didn't even know how to participate because I hadn't learned the things that a person needs to learn in order to participate. When it was made accessible, I had to learn how to participate and be unafraid of getting up in front of people.

I have been able to develop a strong inner self. Somehow, in the middle of everything going on in my life, I believed in myself and others; I still do. My disability was all-encompassing because so many barriers were placed before me. I was able to accept the fact that I wasn't going to allow society to limit me. In order for me to really make life meaningful, I had to find an inner strength and verbalize it in a way that could help make change. I needed to be able to make changes, not just for myself but in conjunction with other people. Many of us who had disabilities as children had so many negative experiences when we were growing up that it had a cumulative negative effect. At the same time, however, my family was trying to have positive input. They would tell me, "You can do this, and you can do that," in spite of the fact that everyone and everything around us were saying that I couldn't.

If professionals don't believe that disabled people can achieve, they should get out of the way. They need to learn as much as they can to help ensure that disabled people are given the tools we need in order to move ahead in our lives. Professionals who work with kids need to give their parents positive images of their children's abilities and possibilities. They should not limit people's thinking; they should help expand people's horizons. They need to understand the implications of discrimination and bias in order to allow people to remedy those problems. They need to be part of the solution, not part of the problem.

I think professionals play different roles. People who are working with newly disabled people need to make sure that those newly disabled people find role models. Disabled kids and adults need role models; role models are critically important. Help them get broad-based role models, people doing lots of different types of things. Being involved in social movements is very important. Professionals who work with disabled people should work with them on making changes at the local, state, and national levels. Professionals must have positive images of disabled people; they have to be willing to learn. They have to reach out. They have to continually explore and learn.

◆ ◆ ◆

Discussion Questions

1. How do the ways in which persons with disabilities are perceived and treated directly connect to individual human service practice?

2. How does the current welfare system reinforce the oppression of persons with disabilities?

3. How have the ideas of the Enlightenment influenced the treatment received by persons with disabilities in the modern rehabilitation and medical industry?

4. How can the value that people can be made "normal" lead to their increased oppression and disenfranchisement?

5. How does the independent living movement view "treatment" for persons with disabilities?

6. If the independent living movement views the locus of the problem of disability with society rather than the individual, what is the impact on the psychological treatment of persons with disabilities?

7. What were you raised to believe about persons with disabilities? Can you trace some of these beliefs to their historical roots? How will these beliefs impact your practice?

8. If you plan to work with children with disabilities, how will knowledge of IDEA help make you a better advocate for both the children and their parents?

9. How does the ADA impact the total human social service industry in both employment and service provision?

Suggested Readings

De Jong, G. (1979). *The movement for independent living: Origins, ideology and implications for disability research.* East Lansing: University Center for International Rehabilitation, Michigan State University.

Gallagher, H. G. (1985). *FDR's splendid deception.* New York: Dodd, Mead.

Jarrow, J. E. (1992). *Title by title: The ADA's impact on postsecondary education.* Columbus, OH: Association on Higher Education and Disability.

Johnson, M. (Ed.). (1992). *People with disabilities explain it all for you: Your guide to the public accommodations requirements of the Americans with Disabilities Act.* Louisville, KY: Advocado Press.

Nagler, M. (Ed.). (1993). *Perspectives in disability* (2nd ed.). Palo Alto, CA: Health Markets Research.

Shapiro, J. P. (1993). *No pity: People with disabilities, forging a new civil rights movement.* New York: Times Books.

References

Albrecht, G. (1992). *The disability business: Rehabilitation in America.* London: Sage.

Berkowitz, E. D. (1987). *Disabled policy: America's programs for the handicapped.* London: Cambridge University Press.

Bernstein, H. K., Steitner-Eaton, B., and Ellis, M. (1995). Individuals with Disabilities Education Act: Early intervention by family physicians. *American Family Physician, 52*(1), 71–76.

De Jong, G. (1979). *The movement for independent living: Origins, ideology, and implications for disability research.* East Lansing: University Center for International Rehabilitation, Michigan State University.

Department of Labor. (1992). 41 CFR Part 60–741. Affirmative action and nondiscrimination obligations of contractors and subcontractors regarding individuals with disabilities, proposed rule. *Federal Register, 57*(204), October 21, 48084–48122.

Devore W., and Schlesinger, E. G. (1987). *Ethnic-sensitive social work practice* (3rd ed.). Columbus, OH: Merrill.

DiNitto, D. M. (1991). *Social welfare: Politics and public policy.* Englewood Cliffs, NJ: Prentice Hall.

Ervin, M. (1997). Social security passes the buck. *One Step Ahead, 1*(5), July, 1–9.

Equal Employment Opportunity Commission (EEOC) and the U.S. Department of Justice. (1991). *American with Disabilities Act handbook.* Washington, DC: U.S. Government Printing Office.

Fine, M., and Asch, A. (1990). Disability beyond stigma: Social interaction, discrimination, and activism. In M. Nagler (Ed.), *Perspectives on disability* (pp. 61–74). Palo Alto, CA: Health Markets Research.

Gallagher, H. G. (1985). *FDR's splendid deception.* New York: Dodd, Mead & Company.

Heumann, J. E. (1994). *New connections for the 21st century.* Unpublished address to the Assumption College's 14th Mary E. Switzer Lecture Series, April 15, Worcester, MA.

Jarrow, J. E. (1992). *Title by title: The ADA's impact on postsecondary education.* Columbus, OH: Association on Higher Education and Disability.

Johnson, M. (Ed.). (1992). *People with disabilities explain it all for you: Your guide to the public accommodations requirements of the Americans with Disabilities Act.* Louisville, KY: Advocado Press.

Livneh, H. (1980). Disability and monstrosity: Further comments. *Rehabilitation Literature, 41,* November/December, 280–283.

Livneh, H. (1982). On the origins of negative attitudes toward people with disabilities. *Rehabilitation Literature, 43,* November/December, 338–347.

Longmore, P. K. (1987a). Elizabeth Bouvia, assisted suicide and social prejudice. *Issues in Law & Medicine, 3*(2), 141–168.

Longmore, P. K. (1987b). Uncovering the hidden history of people with disabilities. *Reviews in American History, 15,* 355–364.

Longmore, P. K. (1993). *History of the disability rights movement and disability culture.* Unpublished address to the California Disability Leadership Summit, October 11, Anaheim, CA.

Mackelprang, R. W, and Salsgiver, R.O. (1996). People with disabilities and social work: Historical and contemporary issues. *Social Work, 41*(1), 7–14.

Meyerson, L. (1990). The social psychology of physical disability: 1948 and 1988. In M. Nagler (Ed.), *Perspectives on disability* (pp. 13–23). Palo Alto, CA: Health Markets Research.

Morris, R. (1986). *Rethinking social welfare: Why care for the stranger?* New York: Longman.

NEA Today (1995). Inclusion: What does the law require? *NEA Today. 13*(7), March 10–12.

Plato. (1991). *The republic: The complete and unabridged Jowett translation.* New York: Vintage Books.

Public Law 101–336. (1990). The Americans with Disabilities Act of 1990.

Rhodes, R. (1993). Mental retardation and sexual expression: An historical perspective. In R. W Mackelprang and D. Valentine (Eds.), *Sexuality and disabilities: A guide for human service practitioners* (pp. 1–27). Binghamton, NY: Haworth Press.

Rothman, D. (1971). *The discovery of the asylum: Social order and disorder in the new republic.* Boston: Little, Brown.

Salsgiver, R. O. (1995). *Persons with disabilities and empowerment: Building a future of independent living.* Unpublished invitational speech to the Council on Social Work Education Annual Program Meeting, March 4, San Diego, CA.

Shapiro, J. P. (1993). *No pity: People with disabilities, forging a new civil rights movement.* New York: Times Books.

Social Security Administration. (1994). *Red book on work incentives: A summary guide to social security and supplemental security income work incentives for people with disabilities.* Washington, DC: U.S. Department of Health and Human Services.

Trattner, W. *From poor law to welfare state: A history of social welfare in America* (4th ed.). New York: Free Press.

Van Reusen, A. K., and Bos, C. (1994). Facilitating student participation in individualized education programs through motivation strategy instruction. *Exceptional Children, 60*(5), 466–476.

Weich, A., Rapp, C., Sullivan, P., and Kisthardt, W. (1989). A strengths perspective for social work practice. *Social Work, 34*(4), 350–354.

Wright, B. (1960). *Physical disability—a psychological approach.* New York: Harper & Row.

Chapter 4

LIFE STAGE DEVELOPMENT

I discovered that there was a difference between me and most boys that I was around when I was about 8 or 9 years old. I figured out that I wasn't going to be a policeman or a fireman. It was around that age that I began to see some differences between me and the other kids at the special school. In a lot of ways, I seemed like a fish out of water because I didn't fit in totally with the kids at the special school and I didn't fit in totally with the kids at the regular school. I feel that way even today.

—Bill Hyatt, Resource Developer, Central Valley Regional Center, Fresno, California

Student Learning Objectives:

1. To understand prominent theories of human development.
2. To be able to compare common themes in the "adaptation to disability" literature.
3. To identify general tasks of human development through the life span.
4. To understand some of the implications of disabilities on human development through the life span.

All persons develop as they go through life. Disabilities, whether present from birth or acquired later in life, strongly influence people's lives. In this chapter, we briefly review major developmental theories. Then we discuss theories of how people adjust to disabilities. To this point, disability adjustment theories have focused on the personal problems people face in coping with disabilities. Finally, we discuss human development in the context of disability. Our emphasis in this chapter is on the individual life development with disability as a part of development. We do not assume that disabilities are innately problematic; rather, we assume that disabilities are a part of the broader human fabric of society. Discussion of social and structural elements of disabilities are reserved for Chapters 11 and 12.

◆ TRADITIONAL DEVELOPMENTAL THEORIES

Since the time of Freud, developmental theorists have articulated theories of developmental stages relative to age. Freud believed all development was sexual and tension reducing in nature and focused on the intrapsychic elements of human development (Freud, 1964). He outlined six stages of development. The *oral* phase occurs during the first year, wherein the mouth is the primary source of pleasure.

He believed sucking is a primary source of sustenance and satisfaction. For Freud, the mother's breast, sucking, and oral pleasure and exploration were the major libidinal foci in this stage. During the second year, the *anal* phase, control becomes important with retention and expulsion of feces a focus. Toilet training and regulating reflexive bowel impulses are libidinal foci as the child learns to control the bowel in order to receive parental approval. From years three through six, in the *phallic* phase, the focus switches to the genitals. The child learns that stimulation of the genitals produces pleasure. Freud believed that female feelings of inferiority to males and penis envy originate in this stage as females learn males have a penis. During this stage, Oedipus and Electra complexes, castration anxiety, and the development of the superego or conscience are key elements. In Freud's fourth phase, *latency,* occurring in the preadolescent years, the child is seemingly uninterested in sexual matters. Sexual energy is sublimated and directed toward socially acceptable activities. The final stage of development, the *genital* phase, begins at the onset of puberty as libido dramatically rises. Oedipus and Electra conflicts resurface, and the person directs sexual impulses toward persons of the opposite sex. The person needs to develop new defenses and may become rebellious and withdraw from family to meet psychosexual needs (Newman and Newman, 1995; Rappaport, 1972).

Freud's psychoanalytic theory accents the tensions between intrapsychic and interpersonal worlds and the ways in which people cope with these conflicts (Newman and Newman, 1995); it emphasizes biological processes and internal conflicts. It has been criticized because of its gender bias and devaluation of women (Alpert, 1986; Ellenberger, 1970; Fast, 1984).

Psychoanalytic theory uses persons without disabilities as templates for development. If persons with disabilities are addressed in the context of developmental tasks, they are viewed as the consequence of abnormal development. For example, those whose disability delays bowel and bladder control will experience arrested development. Similarly, persons whose parents provide physical care during the genital phase are susceptible to serious Oedipus and Electra complexes.

Jean Piaget's focus on human development lay within the cognitive realm. He believed people develop cognitive schemas that guide them in organizing their lives and perceiving the world (Piaget, 1985). People are always striving for equilibrium, which allows them to interact effectively with the environment. Adaptation occurs as individuals' thinking evolves in response to new experiences. Piaget viewed cognitive development as occurring in four progressive stages, in which children develop new thought structures and integrate them with old competencies. Critical to development are *cognitive schemes,* out of which people develop life meanings and organize their worlds. Schemes evolve through assimilation and accommodation. *Assimilation* occurs when problems are solved by utilizing existing schemes. For example, an infant that cries because it is cold is employing a preexisting schema used to signal hunger. *Accommodation* is the process of developing new schemes out of old ones in response to new problems. Walking, tricycle riding, and bicycle riding are progressive schemes in which new schemes develop and elaborate on preexisting schemes (Rappaport, 1972).

Like Freud, Piaget's stages of development were confined primarily to the childhood years. In Piaget's first stage, *sensorimotor intelligence,* which lasts until about 1½ years, infants learn to organize and control elements of their environment as they develop increasingly complex sensor and motor schemes. This is manifested in the hungry infant who learns to spit out a rubber pacifier when it is hungry because it has learned that nourishment will not be forthcoming. Stage two, *preoperational thought,* begins with language development and continues until about age 6. The use of symbolic schemes such as language and make-believe play are important elements as the child organizes its world. Concrete thinking is prominent at this stage, in which children view things arbitrarily and immediately. For example, "This toy is mine because I have it and I want it." Children are self-oriented and lack the ability to analyze their thinking processes. Stage three, *concrete operational thought,* begins at about age 6 and continues to early adolescence. Increased understanding of causal relationships leads to improved problem solving; problem solving is concrete rather than abstract and hypothetically related. Stage four, *formal operational thought,* begins in adolescence, continuing into adulthood. The ability to understand interconnected variables allows people to develop complex rules and laws to use in problem solving (Newman and Newman, 1995; Rappaport, 1972).

Complementing and building on Piaget, Vygotsky emphasized the social, contextual, and interactional nature of development. In particular, he emphasized the importance of culture and language in shaping thought and ideas. A critical cultural element in shaping cognition, according to Vygotsky, is the development and use of tools of human invention. Physical tools include advances such as automobiles and weapons. Psychological tools include languages, alphabets, and coding systems (Miller, 1993; Vygotsky, 1978). Although Vygotsky's work does not specifically focus on disability, the concepts of culture elucidated in this framework are especially important as persons with disabilities establish language and symbols to enhance culture. Tools are especially important, as technological advances such as wheelchairs, telecommunication devices, and drugs change the context in which persons with disabilities live and interact with their environment.

In ego psychological theory, development occurs in psychosocial stages. Erik Erickson (1963) describes eight stages of psychosocial development and ego tasks. Occurring in the first year, the infant develops a sense of *trust versus mistrust.* Trust is developed when parents provide a safe and nurturing environment. From 1 to 3 years is *autonomy versus shame and doubt.* Children begin to forge individual identity and control. The third stage, *initiative versus guilt,* occurs at ages 4 to 5 years. In this stage, children exercise increased environmental control. *Industry versus inferiority* occurs from ages 6 to 11. School, peers, and an expanding world are important elements of this stage. *Identity versus role confusion* occurs during adolescence. Dramatic physical and emotional changes take place as people attempt to find meaningful identities and begin to separate from family. Beginning at about ages 18 to 20 years is stage six, *intimacy versus isolation,* which lasts until about age 25. Successfully developing strong intimate relationships is important in this life stage. *Generativity versus stagnation* comprises the adulthood years from ages 25 to 65. Success in raising children and developing satisfying work and community activities and rela-tionships are important at this stage. Stage eight, *ego integrity versus despair,* comprises the years from age 65 and older. In this stage of life, people review their lives and strive for meaning in their retirement years. Erickson believed that stages follow an epigenetic or biological pattern and that development is progressive as people tran-sition from one stage to the next.

In recent years, others have expanded on Erickson's work. For example, Newman and Newman (1995) added three stages to Erickson's eight: a *prenatal* stage occurring from conception to birth, a *very old* stage from 75 years to death, and a division of the adolescent stage into *early* and *late.*

The stages of development outlined by Erickson and other psychosocial the-orists have been influenced heavily by Western culture and lifestyle. For example, Erickson's stage eight, *ego integrity versus despair,* was developed in the context of Western, first-world environment, life expectancy, and retirement age. The roles of women and men have also been based on traditional European American practices. Ego psychological developmental theorists have also viewed development only in a nondisabled context. The healthy development of persons with disabilities has been neglected. Instead, persons with disabilities have been portrayed in the context of missed or unresolved stages of development.

Henry Maas developed the contextual-developmental-interactional approach to human development throughout the life span. Though influenced by Erickson's ego psychological approach, Maas (1984) focuses on the "interaction between per-sonal social development and contexts" (p. 4). Maas's nine stages of development are cumulative and additive. They are concerned with the interaction of environments that foster successful personal social development. In stage one, *birth,* prenatal influ-ences, ongoing society, and living place influence neonatal responses and the ways the infant influences the environment. During stage two, *infancy,* caring social net-works are conducive to the infant's developing attachments to those with whom interaction is frequent and satisfying. In *toddlerhood,* a foundation of reciprocal attachments developed in infancy, combined with new and explorable arenas, pro-motes curiosity and exploration of an expanding surrounding world. During stage four, *nursery and primary school age,* in response to responsive environments, the child develops competence by learning to explore and manipulate the immediate world. Competence is interactive and dependent on a malleable environment that also provides structure. Maas believes that, by about age 9, children develop the cogni-tive abilities to engage in reciprocity and collaborative behavior that are the major goals of the *preadolescence* stage. A cultural milieu that promotes sharing in a caring community is a critical environmental factor at this stage. The ability to collaborate and reciprocate prepares children for the *youth* stage, in which physical and emo-tional changes combined with the environment lead to a new sense of self-worth. The search for productive workplaces and intimate relationships occurs within this context. In stage seven, *young adulthood,* parenting partnerships are heavily influ-enced by the social and community supports available to them. Strong informal and supportive resources negate the need for formal or remediative services and minimize the possibility that young families will be forced to break up. Maas considers *middle age* to be more diversified in terms of contexts and lifestyles than any earlier stage. As children mature and leave home, people's concerns and options expand beyond family. Individual options are generally broadened, and a sense of community responsibility may also increase. People may become more involved in civic and community activities or may accelerate self-seeking activities. In *old age,* arising during the 60s and later, personal competence may decline significantly. The ability to manage and control the environment is important. The variety of contexts and availability of supports determine options. In addition, the sequence of development throughout the life span continues to influence people at this stage.

Maas's emphases on the environment, contexts, and social development are critical in understanding the development of people of difference. Maas acknowledges the impact of discrimination and devaluation on individual and social development. For example, he states that the basic problem of high unemployment rates for black and Latino/Hispanic youth is societal and structural. He cites racism, discrimination, segregation, and lack of community resources as major factors. Personal demoralization and lowered self-esteem result, and, because of their inability to find legitimate employment, some "slide into illegal work" (p. 156). Maas discusses disabilities but has a tendency to refer to people with disabilities in the context of patients and lost competencies. However, Maas also discusses the need for supportive environments to maximize the capabilities of persons with disabilities.

◆ THEORIES OF ADAPTATION TO DISABILITIES

When considering development and life adjustment for persons with disabilities, we must also consider the perception and meaning of having a disability in contemporary society. In reviewing the literature, adaptation to disability has almost universally focused on the negative aspects of having a disability. One of the first to write on the subject, Crate (1965), outlines five stages of adaptation to an acquired chronic illness or disability. In stage one, *disbelief,* the person denies the disability or minimizes its effects. Stage two, *developing awareness,* begins as denial cannot be maintained. Anger and depression are common reactions. In stage three, *reorganization,* the person further accepts limitations and begins to modify relationships with loved ones. Stage four, *resolution,* occurs as the individual comes to grips with loss of function, grieves, and begins to identify with others with the same disability. In stage five, *identity change,* the person accepts the disability and modifies behavior accordingly. Subsequent writers have elucidated stages of adjustment that are similar to Crate's (Lawrence and Lawrence, 1979; Bray, 1978). These articles were written to help professionals deal with the trauma of disabilities and focus on psychosocial problems in adjusting.

Stewart and Rossier (1978) discuss seven dominant personality types that can guide interventions with persons with disabilities, specifically spinal cord injuries. The *dependent, overdemanding patient* needs boundless care and attention. The *orderly controlled patient* uses much self-discipline but needs extensive explanations of his or her condition. The *dramatic and emotionally engaging patient* is warm and well liked but easily slighted by lack of attention. The *long-suffering and self-sacrificing patient* derives self-worth and comfort from suffering. The belief of the *paranoid patient* that others are out to get him or her is validated by the disability. The *patient with feelings of superiority* is self-centered and feels all-powerful. The *unloved and aloof patient* needs an isolated lifestyle. Human service professionals using this typology would expect problems in adjustment and personality with all patients, as all are defined by their pathology.

Other authors have focused on different aspects of working with persons with disabilities. Rolland (1988, 1989) places chronic illness and disability in three categories: progressive (e.g., diabetes, arthritis), constant (e.g., spinal cord injury, blindness, deafness), and relapsing or episodic (e.g., multiple sclerosis, systemic lupus erythematosis). He also discusses three time phases to which individuals with illness and disabilities and their families must adjust: the initial *crisis* phase, the *chronic* phase, and the *terminal* phase. Rolland focuses on losses, incapacities, and family struggles that people experience with illness and disabilities. Again, his focus is on the struggles of life with a disability. Patterson (1988) articulates many difficulties experienced by the family members of children with illness and disability. She also discusses the hardships that disabilities produce in the contexts of Piaget's cognitive stages and Erickson's psychosocial stages of development. Though Patterson's focus is primarily on the negative aspects of illness and disability, she concludes that far more is known "about the hardships and demands in families of chronically ill children and how they develop problems than we know about how they successfully adapt. . . . This focus on successful adaptation is clearly needed" (p. 106).

The preponderance of literature directed to professionals working with people with disabilities focuses on the incapacities and adjustment problems facing persons with disabilities and their families. Although it is important for human service workers to understand individual, social, and family dynamics of disabilities, a strong pathological focus creates a number of problems.

First, professionals automatically expect that disability and pathology are synonymous. People with disabilities and their families are expected to experience emotional problems such as depression and anxiety. If they do not manifest these psychological problems, they are perceived as not adjusting well. In other words, if emotional difficulties are absent, the person has psychological difficulties. Trieschmann (1980) asks and observes

> *Have professionals in clinical interactions placed disabled persons in a "Catch 22" position? If you have a disability, you must have psychological problems; if you state you have no psychological problems, then this is denial and that is a psychological problem.* (p. 46)

Second, when human service workers focus on problems and incapacities, they are unable to acknowledge and cultivate strengths inherent in the people with whom they work. In addition, if persons with disabilities and their loved ones do not adopt the views of professionals, they are at risk of being labeled as problematic, "in denial," or resistant. To be acceptable, they are pressured to internalize pathological views of themselves. When everyone around them views their situation as a tragedy, it is difficult to view their situation any differently.

Third, in the tradition of the medical model, most authors view chronic illness and disability as synonymous. Therefore, people with disabilities are sick. Sickness implies a need for professional guidance and control, a lack of health. People who are sick deserve sympathy and pity (Mackelprang and Salsgiver, 1996).

Although we do not want to minimize the impact of disability on the lives of individuals and families, we approach disability and adjustment from a different perspective. First, we recognize that illness and injury often cause disabilities. However, rather than defining the disability in terms of illness or disease, we define disability by the meaning the disability carries for the individual. People with disabilities are people in which a disability is part of their lives—not the definition of their lives. Having a disability means difference, not tragedy. Given the opportunity and the resources to perceive disability as difference, families can provide nurturing and validating environments for children with disabilities (Affleck, Tennen, and Gershman, 1985; Summers, Behr, and Turnbull, 1989).

Therefore, as we discuss disability through the life span, we approach the processes without assuming that there are problems. In presenting developmental processes we discuss the psychological-emotional, cognitive, and social tasks and implications of development. Although having a disability influences these processes, it does not define the processes.

◆ Human Development in the Context of Disability

In developing a framework for development through the life span for persons with disabilities, we must account for the social and cultural context in which they live. Historically, persons with disabilities have been neglected in the developmental literature. When they have been included, their inclusion has typically been from an ableist perspective, in that the focus is on the problems that disabilities bring to people and their families (Gaylord-Ross and Browder, 1991). We will focus on the implications of disabilities in the social context; that is, the implications of acquiring and/or living with a disability at different times in life. Rather than proposing our own set of ages and stages, we draw on the works of other developmental theorists and apply those concepts to people who are living with disabilities at various times in their lives.

Birth to 3 Years of Age

Many disabilities are acquired at birth or soon thereafter. Children who acquire disabilities in infancy or toddlerhood experience lives different from persons who acquire disabilities later in life.

One of the major implications of disabilities acquired early in life is that the disability is present before individuals have the cognitive skills to be aware of their disability. Their first experiences are from a disability perspective. Families are aware of the disability from infancy and integrate infants as children with disabilities. The family and community cuadro for the child is a disability cuadro. Identity is forged as loved ones search for the child's identity and life meaning (Minuchin and Fishman, 1981). The child's earliest memories will be of being treated and perceived as a child with a disability. Families who are heavily influenced by a medical model approach to caring for their children are likely to treat a child with a disability differently from a nondisabled child.

Some children grow up in families and communities in which they are treated similarly to children without disabilities rather than as special or deficient. When these children are supported in developmental tasks, they may not perceive their differences as they develop cognitively (Wright, 1960). For these children, increased awareness of disability may come later when their world expands. Some may be surprised by societal ableism in school and community.

Children with early onset disabilities may experience more protectiveness than children without disabilities. In infancy, there may be increased contact with parents and other nurturers because of increased needs (Affleck et al., 1985). Using Erickson's framework, this may lead to a strong sense of trust in the environment. On the other hand, if contact with the infant is painful, such as may occur with physical disabilities requiring therapeutic physical touch or surgeries, contact with parents and others may be perceived as unsafe. Mistrust can be especially problematic when separations from family occur because of hospitalization or institutionalization.

Children with sensory disabilities such as deafness and blindness need nurturing that accounts for their disabilities. For example, a deaf child may require visual nurturing cues, such as placing a playpen in easy view of the parent to compensate for the lack of auditory cues that let the child know that a nurturer is nearby. Children with blindness may benefit from increased auditory and verbal stimuli in the environment.

An early developmental task common to all theorists is infants' need to gain increasing physical and cognitive control over their environments. Infants with disabilities may have greater difficulty in learning to manipulate and control their environments than youngsters without disabilities. Physical limitations may hamper the efforts of some, such as a child with cerebral palsy who has difficulty shaking a rattle or holding a bottle. Children with intellectual disabilities may have cognitive delays that constrain development of language abilities. Maas's emphasis (1984) on context and supportive environments can be helpful in understanding the development of infants with disabilities. For example, children with intellectual or cognitive disabilities who receive early educational opportunities in their first three years are showing far greater capabilities than professionals of the past thought possible. Vygotsy's emphasis (1978) on tools is important to understand the development of young children with disabilities. Wheelchairs, TTYs, and other adaptive devices are critical tools for children with disabilities as they learn to control their environments at this stage.

Persons with early onset disabilities and their families are susceptible to environmental problems not faced by children without disabilities (Gallagher, Beckman, and Cross, 1983; Valentine, 1993). First, some parents become protective, sometimes to the extent that their children are unable to successfully meet cognitive and physical developmental tasks expected at their ages. Born of good intentions and with the advice of professionals, children may have things done for them to the extent that they are not allowed to struggle and learn from failure and success in controlling their environments. Parents may lack knowledge and skills. It is critical that parents learn the developmental needs of their children with disabilities, develop skills, and obtain the tools to help those children successfully meet developmental tasks and learn to control their immediate environments (Davis, 1993).

Second, children with disabilities are at greater risk for experiencing their environment in unpleasant ways. Surgeries, injections, physical therapy, and medications are examples. The touch of others can become frightening and unpleasant. Parents may be forced to restrain their children while undergoing procedures. Separations from family for hospitalizations may be required. Therefore, efforts to compensate for aversive procedures may be needed. Parents may need education and support in making sure their children receive additional, safe, and nurturing contact with others. Environments can be modified to minimize children's fears and treatments limited to those with maximal value.

Third, children with disabilities may have higher susceptibility to being mistreated and abused than those without disabilities (Garbarino, Brookhouser, and Authier, 1987). Several factors contribute to this. Some children require higher levels of physical contact from others who may exploit them. Some may be less capable of understanding abuse or explaining it when it occurs. Still others may not be believed or valued when abuse occurs.

Fourth, low expectations have traditionally limited children significantly. For example, in the past, parents of children with Down syndrome were routinely advised to institutionalize their children in such institutions as training schools where they were segregated and warehoused. Even the most caring professionals could not compensate for the lack of individual attention and nurturing of home environments. Today, more children with Down syndrome are reared from birth in family homes.

Increased expectations and opportunities have resulted in vastly improved lives. In homes and living with families, there are more opportunities for bonding and for environmental stimulation and control that assist children with disabilities in developmental tasks. It is critical that parents and caregivers understand legal protections and opportunities that are available to their children with disabilities. Federal legislation such as the Equal Education for All Handicapped Children Act (PL 94-142) of 1975 and the 1990 Individuals with Disabilities Education Act (PL 101-467) have made services available from birth to children with disabilities, and families can use these resources to access technology, interventions, and supports to aid them in helping their infants and toddlers with disabilities in the development process.

Three to 6 Years of Age

By age 3, children's understanding of their symbolic world is increasing rapidly. Words are primary symbols in their lives as language development expands their understanding of the world. Language provides a cognitive scheme for vastly increased communication with others and for increased cognitive sophistication (Lenneberg, 1967; Nelson, 1973). Children begin to develop a sense of right and wrong and begin to shape behaviors in response to others' expectations and needs. Nonverbal language such as voice tone, facial expressions, and gestures, which are meaningful from birth, continue to be important. The scope of relationships expands to friends and others, beyond parents, family, and caregivers.

Disabilities can significantly impact this time of development. For example, language development is often different with disabilities. Children with intellectual disabilities may experience delays in verbal language skills. They may rely on alternate ways of communicating, such as gestures, nonverbal vocalization, and pictures, developing verbal mastery later than children without intellectual disabilities. Deaf children are responsive to language but not the verbal language predominant in hearing culture. Visual communication and early attention to sign language are critical to language development for these children (Spencer, Bodner-Johnson, and Gutfreund, 1992). Language comprehension develops visually rather than auditorily; language articulation is manual rather than vocal. Thus, although language development is different for children with disabilities, supportive environments, sometimes including technological aids, can help them gain skills in the symbolic scheme development that Piaget considered important. Their sense of industry in relationship to their environment is enhanced as they learn that their world responds to their efforts to control their lives. Though traditional developmentalists focus on "speech" development as the critical task at this age, in reality it is language and communication that are important, not this one form of expression.

Expanding the environment for children with disabilities is as important as it is for other children. It is critical that they have the opportunity to interact with others with and without disabilities. To experience their expanding world at this age, children with physical disabilities may require technology such as wheelchairs and physical assistance. Because of the reactions of others, they may also be compelled to learn how to cope with "being different." Successfully doing so, however, permits them to control their lives. Contact with others who have disabilities provides them with the chance to be with others who have similar social experiences and physical perspectives on the world. For example, children who use wheelchairs for mobility share commonalities that those without disabilities cannot understand. Exposure to peers and role models with disabilities can permit the sharing and cultural development upon which they can build throughout their lives. Playing and interacting with children and others with and without disabilities can provide a foundation for later in life when disability takes on increased meaning.

Relationships between parents and children at this time of life are changing as children gain independence and an increased cognizance of separateness from others. Children with disabilities may be forced into greater physical closeness with caregivers because of physical or other needs; however, they still have these developmental tasks. Therefore, independence and autonomy may be gained in alternate ways. Children needing physical assistance in activities of daily living may develop a sense of separateness by controlling the time and methods of their care. It may be necessary for others to physically assist them, but they can learn about and begin to exercise control and direction of their personal care. They develop a sense of personal separateness as they establish personal, body-space boundaries.

Two common practices involving children with disabilities have severely limited their development. Institutionalizing some children with disabilities has isolated them from the larger world and hampered their abilities to develop the skills to interact with it. Others have been isolated in family homes for protection. These practices have deprived children with disabilities of the environments that allow them to develop skills and have denied them the opportunity to learn how to meet challenges in society. Fortunately, children with disabilities are being segregated less and integrated more (Rhodes, 1993).

Six to 12 Years of Age

For most children, their world expands greatly from ages 6 to 12. Schools and increased numbers of peers broaden their world socially and geographically. Increased concrete problem-solving skills are important to help children deal with new situations. Many children with disabilities are already accustomed to having many people in their lives, especially when they have had ongoing professional involvement. Now, however, their expanding environment is different. With medical and other professional involvements, they are placed in the passive roles of patients and clients who are needful of remediative interventions. As they enter school settings, they encounter the roles of students and learners. The numbers of potential peers expands greatly as they come into contact with other students. Relationships with educators may be a new experience (Galbo, 1983). This is a time for much opportunity as well as for potential problems.

Maas's concept of supportive environments is especially critical at this stage as children take their first major steps away from their families. Educational environments that provide resources to meet the needs of students with disabilities without segregating or stereotyping them are important. Children with learning disabilities may need individualized educational plans that address their specific learning capabilities. Children with physical disabilities may require alternate but equivalent physical education opportunities. It is important to balance the need for integration with other students without sacrificing educational needs.

Whenever possible, meaningful contact with peers with disabilities is important at this age. Traditionally, young school-aged children with disabilities have been inculcated with a culture that views them as deficient. Because thinking at this age is still concrete, children are especially susceptible to internalizing messages that they are bad and undesirable. Opportunities to socialize, interact, and learn as equals of peers without disabilities can help dispel some of these misperceptions and prevent internalized ableism. In addition, increased exposure helps children without disabilities perceive children with disabilities as peers and friends rather than as tragedies or as "special" people.

A common manifestation of internalized ableism that people with physical disabilities experience at this time of development is body images that are not consonant with their reality. Because they have been subjected to pervasive negative messages about disabilities, it is common for children with disabilities to perceive themselves as nondisabled, denying the presence of the disability. For example, one of the authors regularly dreamed about himself without his disability during childhood. He was sometimes surprised to see himself in a wheelchair in full-length mirrors. The negative connotations of disability influenced him to view himself without his disability. Children who use wheelchairs may visualize themselves as great runners. Some experience the shock of body image dissonance when they see reflections of themselves because their self-images are not the images reflected in mirrors. This is a response for these children who may otherwise, with their burgeoning but limited cognitive abilities, be forced to see themselves as undesirable and defective because of society's pervasive attitudes. This phenomenon is similar to children of color who have tried to wash dark skin white to be acceptable. These are healthy responses in ableist or racist environments. These children see themselves as acceptable; however, their characteristics are unacceptable. Therefore, to develop and preserve a positive self-image, they try to mold themselves to approved images.

A challenge for providing supportive environments for children with disabilities at this age is determining the optimal exposure to people from different backgrounds. Contact with others with disabilities can be extremely critical. For example, deaf people have been greatly aided in developing culture and solidarity from contact with each other. For some, early contact occurred in special schools and residential centers for deaf and hard-of-hearing people. These contexts allowed them to experience lives in which hearing disabilities were the norm, not inferior. However, "special" programs can isolate and deny people other opportunities. For example, nursing homes and institutions for people with physical and intellectual disabilities as well as psychiatric disabilities have been closing down in large numbers. Once commonplace, they are now seen as archaic and isolating. More children with disabilities are living in homes and are being educated in regular schools and classrooms. The isolationist wisdom of the past has been replaced by extant wisdom of considerable integration.

An important issue for children with disabilities at this time of development is the age of onset of the disability. Children with early life onset disabilities know nothing else. By the time they reach this age, families have generally organized their lives and adjusted emotionally to the child's disability. However, when the onset of disability occurs at this time of life, it can be especially confusing. For example, some forms of muscular dystrophy may not be diagnosed until this age;

children with muscular dystrophy may face progressive physical limitations and physical restrictions that are distressing. Children become confused and frustrated at changes taking place in their bodies. Families experience the crises of uncertainty during evaluations and diagnostic procedures. Self-concept is modified in response to disability. Family and social relationships are altered. Grief and mourning can be experienced by the child and family. Financial resources can be strained and support systems taxed (Valentine, 1993).

Onset of disability at this age presents children with cognitive, emotional, and social changes that those born with disabilities do not experience. On the other hand, children who acquire disabilities during childhood can have advantages. They have not been limited by discriminatory attitudes and practices from birth. Thus, early personality development and positive self-concepts can be valuable as children cope with changes brought about by disability. For example, Ed Roberts reported that the street skills he developed before becoming disabled by polio provided life skills he drew on after his disability (Shapiro, 1993).

Twelve to 18 Years of Age

The search for personal identity and the meaning of life are major elements in the lives of adolescents. Physical, emotional, and social changes beginning with puberty must be coped with. Sexual development and feelings burgeon during this time of life (Brooks-Gunn and Reiter, 1990; Tanner, 1978/1990).

Adolescents with disabilities experience the same changes as those without disabilities; however, development is sometimes complicated by the social environment. A common adolescent developmental task is the need to separate from family and find one's own sense of unique identity. Individuals whose parents provide physical caregiving can be hampered in this separation. Ambivalence and conflict can result between parent and adolescent when adolescents need parents to assist with activities of daily living but resent the need for parents to provide intimate care. Technological aids and attendants can sometimes alleviate the need for intimate parent-child physical contact, but attendants can complicate family relationships. Their assistance may be appreciated, but they may also usurp traditional family caregiving roles and produce ambivalent responses.

The development of identity for persons with disabilities is sometimes complicated by the problems concomitant to disability. For some, the extra time and effort to get through the day can deplete energy they might otherwise expend in age-appropriate activities. Ongoing relationships with peers and role models with disabilities, nonableist portrayals of persons with disabilities, and an environment that values their disabilities can be critical to developing disability-affirming self-images and rejecting shame-based identities. People in the lives of adolescents, including families, friends, counselors, and teachers, can all be resources in helping adolescents with disabilities reject the images, stereotypes, and limitations of an ableist society. Supports that facilitate future educational, employment, and living options can provide a sense of hope for the future.

Cognitively, adolescents develop an increased understanding of complex and interconnected societal rules and norms. Historically, people have been forced to accept their disabilities as the cause for the limitations imposed on them by society. With supportive environments and positive identities, they can be better equipped to acknowledge that limitations are often externally imposed rather than internally caused. The sense of right and wrong, developed at earlier ages, expands to a fuller understanding of right and wrong, justice and injustice. Positive self-identity can help adolescents with disabilities recognize injustices rather than accept societally imposed ableism.

Developing a positive sexual self-image is an important part of adolescence. As with all youths, this can be problematic for youths with disabilities who do not meet the artificial standards of beauty and physical prowess set in today's media and mainstream culture. Adult role models can help provide more realistic understanding and social opportunities to facilitate normal sexual development. In families without similarly disabled adults, these role models may need to be found outside the family. Adolescents will view themselves as sexual beings when parents and others relate to them in a way that assumes they will marry or develop other long-term relationships as adults. Overprotectiveness and avoidance of sexuality and relationships can lead adolescents to internalize messages that they are asexual. Finally, sexual knowledge is critical—both knowledge about sexuality in general and the specific implications of the disability on sexuality. Adolescents need opportunities for self-exploration. In addition, group and educational programs about sexuality and disability can aid positive psychosexual development.

Some adolescents have intimate physical contact with personal care attendants, physicians, nurses, therapists, and others. Increased intimate contact with others can serve to enhance or hamper adolescent sexual development. Burgeoning sexuality can be influenced by contact with these people, and adolescents may experience romantic and sexual feelings toward caregivers. If their bodies are objectified by others during care, therapy, examinations, and other procedures, they may come to view their bodies as asexual. Adolescents (and others) with disabilities are also more susceptible to sexual abuse by providers and others who may take advantage of their vulnerabilities (Andrews and Veronin, 1993; Rhodes, 1993; Sigler and Mackelprang, 1993). Sexual abuse can occur at any age, and environments that discourage victimization and help adolescents (and others) exercise sexual self-determination are important for personal and sexual growth.

People who acquire disabilities as adolescents face added challenges that those who enter adolescence with disabilities do not have. Commonly, they carry stereotypical ableist attitudes that can hamper acceptance of a disability. Families can be thrown into crisis. Sometimes predisability friendships are lost, and people may be forced to find alternate peers and activities. For example, listening to music may be impossible for people who lose their hearing, and adaptive sports may be required for persons who acquire physical disabilities. Developing an identity with a disability can be difficult and can produce confusion, especially in the months following onset. Therefore, supportive environments that account for adolescent developmental needs and are disability affirming are important. Opportunities to maintain friendships and family relationships as well as to develop new peer and mentored relationships can aid significantly in this process.

Young Adulthood

Disability can present many challenges as people move into adulthood. Families of origin lose legal and often physical control and responsibility. This is a time in which primary intimate relationships shift from families of origin to families and loved ones in the making. Young adults successfully meeting the challenges of this time of life can depend on how well families have prepared them to launch independent lives. Individuals whose disabilities necessitate ongoing care and support find that independence may mean that they take control of who, what, and how care is provided. For some, it means that they become employers of caregivers. Adequate supports are critical to this transition. Too often, adults with disabilities have been relegated to large institutions such as nursing homes because they are unable to meet their needs elsewhere. Social structures and priorities are especially important for adults with disabilities who rely on social supports for independence. Allocating resources to communities rather than institutions provides greater access to a variety of living options. Deprofessionalizing services and redirecting resources to the control of individuals allows people who use attendants to hire and direct their personal attendants rather than being dependent on others to control how and from whom they receive care. Directing resources for people with psychiatric disabilities to isolated, self-contained settings fosters dependence, whereas directing resources to the community provides more options and greater self-determination and community integration.

At this time of life, people search for intimacy with others. Historically, people with disabilities have been denied opportunities for intimate relationships. For example, people with intellectual disabilities have been legally enjoined from marrying (Rhodes, 1993). Some have been forcibly sterilized, sometimes without their knowledge. People with disabilities living in institutions, including persons with psychiatric and physical disabilities, have been denied access to intimate relationships with others. To successfully meet the challenges at this time of life, barriers to intimacy must continue to be removed. Given the opportunity, persons with disabilities are increasingly entering into intimate relationships; partners include people with and without disabilities. Relationships include persons with intellectual disabilities who are marrying and who, with adequate supports, can successfully raise children (Whitman and Accardo, 1993).

To prevent isolation, young adults depend on adequate resources. For persons with disabilities, job and educational opportunities and access to transportation and technology may be especially important (Murphy and Murphy, 1997). Without these resources, dependence and lack of control are likely to result. For example, unemployment among persons with disabilities is rampant, in large measure because of current laws. As an illustration, young people with spinal cord injuries are often unable to work because employment income would terminate federal medical benefits that are critical to their ongoing health. Entering the workforce would raise their income to a level that disqualifies them for benefits such as Medicaid. Thus, if they work, they lose medical coverage for expenses that can cost hundreds of dollars per month. Consequently, they are forced to live on SSI and/or SSD rather than enter the workforce.

Young adulthood is a time in which people with disabilities can continue to use role models to imbue disability culture and pride. At the same time, they are shapers and developers of disability culture for those who follow. In addition, given the opportunity and the right, they can help dispel common myths that perpetuate ableist societal views. This further prepares them for the roles of parents of children with and without disabilities who, in turn, have parents with disabilities capable of providing love and nurturing.

People who acquire disabilities in young adulthood generally have the majority of their lives to live. They have already developed personalities and self-images. A new disability, however, can force a changed self-image and modify intimate relationships. Newly formed intimate relationships such as recent marriages can be especially vulnerable if one of the partners acquires a disability. Community supports such as independent living centers and professional and peer supports can help people who acquire disabilities to successfully integrate changes personally and can assist families who undergo the changes precipitated by an acquired disability. Accepting the disability and embracing the social and cultural elements of their new life situations can help make this time of life successful.

Middle Adulthood

Middle adulthood is a time of expanded interests and options. Persons with disabilities who are in their 40s and 50s continue to invest time and energies with families, but their focus can increasingly extend outward to community and others. Generating legacies and contributing to society are elements of this time of life. As people journey through middle adulthood, they are more likely to have the stability to expand their interests outward than previously (Erickson, 1963; Maas, 1984).

Persons with disabilities in their middle years have been instrumental in developing a burgeoning disability culture and in changing the political and legal landscape for those that follow. Some middle adulthood–aged persons with disabilities are contributing at the local level by influencing entities such as school boards, municipal governments, and community organizations. Others, such as Evan Kemp Jr. and Justin Dart, have contributed on a more sweeping scale by influencing national policies. Whatever the scope of their influence, middle adulthood–aged persons with disabilities can receive personal satisfaction from their accomplishments by acting as role models for future generations of persons with disabilities. In addition, national leaders with disabilities, such as Franklin Roosevelt and Bob Dole, have contributed to enhancing positive perceptions of people with disabilities in society. Finally, disability advocates, especially those with disabilities, have also contributed to society by leading the move for expanded rights and opportunities (Shapiro, 1993).

Middle adulthood is a time of life in which large numbers of people begin to acquire age-related disabilities as a result of conditions such as diabetes or heart disease. Traditionally, people who acquire disabilities at this age usually have not identified with a general culture of disability. Their identities have continued as nondisabled persons who have problems. They can benefit from an accurate understanding that acquiring a disability need not be shameful or tragic. Learning to live with changes and to integrate changes into their lives is important. Finding meaning to and growth from acquiring a disability may be helpful. Networking with others who are successfully living with similar disabilities can be an excellent way to facilitate this growth.

Persons with disabilities, whether newly acquired or long term, can be a great asset to the community. The maturity and stability that come with this time of life provide them greater opportunities to influence communities and society. As the numbers and visibility of middle adulthood–aged persons with disabilities increase, so can their societal contributions and legacies to the disability community.

Older Adulthood

A common label in the disability community for persons without disabilities is TAB, or "temporarily able bodied." By old age, most people acquire disabilities from a variety of conditions. Visual, hearing, and physical disabilities are common. Anyone who lives long enough acquires some type of disability in life. Most who acquire late life disabilities, however, do not identify with disability culture, although resources and supports are important to persons in the later stages of their lives. Ageism as well as ableism can endanger full lives when manifested in attitudes and social policies. Without supports, despair and hopelessness result (Erickson, 1963; Maas, 1984).

Persons who have lived their lives with disabilities can be better prepared for the problems attendant to old age than those who acquire disabilities late in life. Their life experiences may have prepared them to deal with social systems that are important to meeting their needs. However, they may also be more susceptible to a myriad of problems as a result of their long-term disabilities. For example, people who have had polio are susceptible to postpolio syndrome, in which strength and endurance are significantly diminished. Persons who have used wheelchairs for mobility may experience shoulder deterioration from long-term wear and tear as a result of pushing their chairs.

As people enter older adulthood, self-determination and the opportunity to contribute are important. Independence, whether physical or in directing others who provide care, is important to help maintain ego integrity. As with other stages, supportive environments are critical to successful lives in older adulthood.

Social policies can be critical to the well-being of older persons who acquire disabilities and of their families. Policies that allow people who need physical assistance to live in the community rather than being relegated to nursing homes are important. Too many older Americans are institutionalized because resources that could help them live in the community are targeted for high-cost, low-self-control, institutional care. Policies that foster independent living contribute to high-quality lives.

Other social supports that allow people to acquire physical aids such as therapies and durable medical equipment (e.g., wheelchairs and walkers) without impoverishing them are critical in helping maintain independence. Adequate access to tools (Vygotsky, 1978) that promote independence can help change the meaning of older adulthood as older persons with disabilities have access to the tools that allow them to control their lives and exercise self-determination. At no age is this more important than in older adulthood.

End-of-life decisions and policies are especially important for older persons with disabilities. Older persons need to maintain control over decisions; however, there is much controversy in society over these end-of-life decisions. For example, Oregon has legalized physician-assisted aid in dying, with other states considering similar measures. These measures have been advocated to ensure self-determination, but they have been formulated in a society that devalues old age and disability. Supportive environments can help people find value in their lives and make end-of-life decisions, consider health care directives, complete living wills, and so on, based on their needs and not out of any duty to get out of the way or reduce their burden on society.

◆ SUMMARY

Both traditional and contemporary developmental theories, including those of Freud, Piaget, Erickson, Maas, and others, have generally either ignored disability or have conceived of disability from a pathology framework. To affirm lives with disabilities, a shift in perception is needed that includes the implications of living with a disability as a normal part of life. We recognize the fact that acquiring a disability may require many adjustments; however, we eschew focusing exclusively on the problems that disabilities cause for individuals and families. The developmental tasks and needs of persons with disabilities and their families mirror the needs of persons without disabilities. However, as with all diversity, there are considerations and needs that are unique to persons with disabilities. Our discussion of human development with a disability does not depict concrete stages but general, loosely connected life periods that are relatively common to people in Western society. Our hope is that future writers will continue to explore and broaden the understanding of human development with a disability in a changing society.

 ◆ ◆ ◆ *Personal Narrative: Bill Hyatt* ◆ ◆ ◆

Bill Hyatt has lived with a disability since birth. He currently works as a resource developer for the California Central Valley Regional Center in Fresno, California.

I was born with CP. It took my parents a while to figure out that there was something different with me. My family was a migrant working family so they kept going from doctor to doctor, each one giving various diagnoses. It wasn't until I was 3 that there was a correct diagnosis. Since I was the youngest of five and had a disability, my parents tended to be overprotective of me. I think they had lower expectations of me than they did of my other brothers and sister. I think that, in their minds, the scenario was that I was going to grow up and live in a wheelchair forever and ever and they were going to take care of me.

As a child, I went to a "special" school. This school had a wide range of kids. We had a high incidence of people with mental retardation but had people with low IQ, normal IQ, and above normal IQ. Eventually, they started integrating me from special schools to regular schools.

I discovered that there was a difference between me and most boys that I was around when I was about 8 or 9 years old. I figured out that I wasn't going to be a policeman or a fireman. It was around that age that I began to see some differences between me and the other kids at the special school. In a lot of ways, I seemed like a fish out of water because I didn't fit in totally with the kids at the special school and I didn't fit in totally with the kids at the regular school. I feel that way even today.

When they integrated me from the special schools to the regular schools, they did two things. First, they started me off with short periods of time in the regular school and each year increased to longer periods of time. Second—and this is what I don't understand—they put me in remedial classes instead of with kids who were more capable. Academically they assumed that because I had a disability I was best suited for the lower level classes.

When they began integrating me in junior high, it was terrible. Other kids did not accept me; they would call me names and hurl insults and that sort of thing. When it came time to hurl the insults, I would hurl them back and they couldn't catch them because they would just go over their heads. But I still didn't feel accepted.

High school was a little bit better for me in that I didn't have so much of that. When it came time to go to high school, they gave me a choice of staying in the special school or going full-time at the regular one—I chose the regular one. I always wanted to go to my high school. That was where all my brothers went and that was where I wanted to go. It was also pretty accessible.

In high school, I found my niche, which happened to be in journalism. I was a part of that for four years. I got along pretty well with the kids in high school and made some friends there, but I didn't date. I couldn't take behind-the-wheel training in driver's education because they didn't have any cars with handicap equipment. So I adapted a golf cart and took my behind-the-wheel training in that. But it's kind of hard to date in a golf cart. I actually got a driver's license when I had the golf cart.

I attribute a lot of my drive and success to my therapist. My physical therapist was a very big man, about six feet tall. Interestingly, he had a disability himself; he had polio as a child. In some ways he was like a third parent because, growing up in a special school where I had therapy about 70% of the day, he was a very significant adult in my life. While my parents had low expectations of me, he on the other hand had very high expectations. I remember one incident very clearly. When I was just about to graduate from junior high, I started talking about working in a special workshop because that was what we disabled people did back then. He responded that if I did he would "kick my butt." He'd had a lot of experience observing differences in people, and he saw that I had more abilities than others saw.

My first two years at Bakersfield College were a really great time for me. I loved it. Sometimes I wish I could go back. I didn't get a real car until I went to college. I got my first student aid grant for $800 and went right out and bought an $800 car. For the four years I was in high school, I was the only person there with a significant disability, but at Bakersfield there were lots of disabled students from all around. Because I had a car, I got involved with other disabled students. There were a whole lot of interesting things going on in college life.

I also started dating in college. I didn't date a whole lot, but I did date a mix of disabled and nondisabled students. I wound up getting semiserious about one particular young woman who happened to have epilepsy. I remember vividly that whenever she would have a seizure at the mall or elsewhere, she would turn toward a window in order to hide it and she never even remembered doing it. It was her coping mechanism, but she had no consciousness of it after.

The term *disability culture* has particular significance to me. It's a shared experience that people with disabilities have. Not every disability is the same, but the reaction that the greater society has toward us is very similar. So even though I don't have mental retardation or epilepsy or those other things, I've shared experiences with people who do. The commonality I have with other people with disabilities is very important to me. It helps keep me balanced.

I'm on the Internet a lot, and I find it's a great source of strength. It has become a place I can go to connect with others with disabilities. For example, it's one of the few places I can tell a disability joke and they get it.

I grew up in the late '60s and early '70s, so the civil rights movement was very important to me. People like Robert Kennedy and Martin Luther King, Jr., were great role models for me. I don't really recall disabled role models from my youth. When I was growing up, the only one I remember that had a disability was President Roosevelt, and I didn't really have much of a desire to be president. And we know he wasn't too open about having a disability either. But when I was growing up, I remember people were always mentioning Roosevelt's disability to me. I do remember one TV show, *Ironside*. It really wasn't a very good show, but the star was a wheelchair user. So, as for disabled role models, I really didn't have too many.

I think the number one issue facing people with disabilities is a recognition of how people with disabilities are treated. The greater society needs to recognize that people with disabilities have been treated differently and negatively by society. Laws to protect us are in place; now it's a matter of people honoring the law, and understanding why laws are there in the first place.

I have personally experienced discrimination in my life because of my disability. Sometimes, though, discrimination is so subtle or hidden that it's hard to figure out when it's happening. I've applied for jobs that I didn't get because of my disability. At the time it really hurt. Sometimes I have felt like an outsider in work situations too. It's not because other employees were bad people or anything like that, but that's the way it's been. They have felt uncomfortable by my presence or just haven't been accepting of me.

ADA and other laws have been helpful to people with disabilities. Disability laws have prompted people to do things, not because they were the right things to do but because the law said they had to. In spite of the fact that some say people can't be changed legislatively, I think we have to begin somewhere. The laws are getting people's attention.

The issue is important not only for the greater society but among ourselves as people with disabilities. People with disabilities are sometimes slow to identify with a disability, especially in these times when it is not OK to be outside the norm. Too often we believe that we must overcome our disability rather than live with it. Too often people feel shame or embarrassment at being disabled.

I want to be very clear in my own mind about what success means. I'm a success because I have the capability to do the things that I enjoy doing. I feel successful because I have a job I enjoy, but people who don't have jobs can be successful as well. Most people do not have the ability to be happy all the time, but having choices in my life is really important to feeling successful.

One of the biggest obstacles to success, I think, is other people's expectations about me. They don't know me, but they have preconceived ideas about what somebody with CP in a wheelchair can and can't do. That's one of the biggest problems for me. I can deal with the physical barriers, but the other barriers are much harder to contend with. It's people's attitudes, their stereotypes, and their assumptions that create barriers.

We've got to remember that everybody is an individual. Don't make assumptions about people with disabilities. Some people are very good people and some people are jerks—people with and without disabilities. I think if people can begin to see people as people, the rest will follow.

◆ ◆ ◆

Discussion Questions

1. What are the important elements of human development from birth to 3 years of age for people with and without disabilities?

2. What are the important elements of human development from 3 to 6 years of age for people with and without disabilities?

3. What are the important elements of human development from 6 to 12 years of age for people with and without disabilities?

4. What are the important elements of human development during adolescence for people with and without disabilities?

5. What are the important elements of human development during adulthood for people with and without disabilities?

6. What are the strengths and limitations of viewing adaptation to disability from the focus traditionally taken by theorists?

Suggested Readings

Chilman, C. S., Nunnaly, E. W., and Cox, F. M. (1988). *Chronic illness and disability.* Newbury Park, CA: Sage.

Mackelprang, R. W, and Valentine, D. (1993). *Sexuality and disabilities: A guide for human service practitioners.* Binghamton, NY: Haworth Press.

Myer, L. H., Peck, C. A., and Brown, L. (1991). *Critical issues in the lives of people with severe disabilities.* Baltimore: Paul H. Brooks.

Newman, B. M., and Newman, P. R. (1995). *Development through life: A psychosocial approach.* Pacific Grove, CA: Brooks/Cole.

Shapiro, J. P. (1993). *No pity: People with disabilities, forging a new civil rights movement.* New York: Times Books.

References

Affleck, G., Tennen, H., and Gershman, K. (1985). Cognitive adaptations to high risk infants: The search for mastery, meaning, and protection from future harm. *American Journal of Mental Deficiency, 89*(6), 653–656.

Alpert, J. L. (1986). *Psychoanalysis and women: Contemporary reappraisals.* Hillsdale, NJ: Analytic Press.

Andrews, A. B., and Veronin, L. J. (1993). Sexual assault and people with disabilities. In R. W Mackelprang and D. Valentine (Eds.), *Sexuality and disabilities: A guide for human service practitioners* (pp. 137–159). Binghamton, NY: Haworth Press.

Bray, G. P. (1978). Rehabilitation of spinal cord injured: A family approach. *Journal of Applied Rehabilitation Counseling, 19,* 70–78.

Brooks-Gunn, J., and Reiter, E. O. (1990). The role of pubertal processes. In S. S. Feldman and G. R. Elliott (Eds.), *At the threshold: The developing adolescent* (pp. 16–53). Cambridge, MA: Harvard University Press.

Crate, M. A. (1965). Adaptation to chronic illness. *American Journal of Nursing, 65,* 73–76.

Davis, H. (1993). *Counselling parents of children with chronic illness or disability.* Baltimore: Paul H. Brooks.

Ellenberger, H. (1970). *The discovery of the unconscious.* New York: Basic Books.

Erickson, E. (1963). *Childhood and society* (2nd ed.). New York: Norton.

Fast, I. (1984). *Gender identity: A differentiation model.* Hillsdale, NJ: Analytic Press.

Freud, S. (1964). New introductory lectures on psychoanalysis. In J. Strachey (Ed.), *The standard edition of the complete psychological works of Sigmund Freud* (vol. 22). London: Hogarth.

Galbo, J. J. (1983). Adolescents' perceptions of significant adults. *Adolescence, 18,* 417–428.

Gallagher, J. J., Beckman, P., and Cross, A.H. (1983). Families of handicapped children: Sources of stress and its amelioration. *Exceptional Children, 50*(1), 10–19.

Garbarino, J., Brookhouser, P. E., and Authier, K. J. (1987). *Special children, special risks: The maltreatment of children with disabilities.* New York: Aldine de Gruyter.

Gaylord-Ross, R., and Browder, D. (1991). Functional assessment: Dynamic and domain properties. In L. H. Myer, C. A. Peck, and L. Brown (Eds.), *Critical issues in the lives of people with severe disabilities* (pp. 45–66). Baltimore: Paul H. Brooks.

Lawrence, S. A., and Lawrence, R. M. (1979). A model of adaptation of chronic illness. *Nursing Forum, 18,* 33–42.

Lenneberg, E. H. (1967). *Biological foundations of language.* New York: Wiley.

Maas, H. S. (1984). *People in contexts: Social development from birth to old age.* Englewood Cliffs, NJ: Prentice Hall.

Mackelprang, R. W, and Salsgiver, R. O. (1996). People with disabilities and social work: Historical and contemporary issues. *Social Work, 41*(1), 7–14.

Miller, P. H. (1993). *Theories of developmental psychology* (3rd ed.). New York: W. H. Freeman.

Minuchin, S., and Fishman, H. C. (1981). *Family therapy techniques.* Cambridge, MA: Harvard University Press.

Murphy, D. M., and Murphy, J. T. (1997). Enabling disabled students. *Thought & Action: The NEA Higher Education Journal, 13*(1), 41–52.

Nelson, K. (1973). Structure and strategy in learning to talk. *Monographs of the Society for Research in Child Development, 38*(1–2).

Newman, B. M., and Newman, P. R. (1995). *Development through life: A psychosocial approach.* Pacific Grove, CA: Brooks/Cole.

Patterson, J. M. (1988). Chronic illness in children and the impact on families. In C. S. Chilman, E. W. Nunnaly, and F. M. Cox (Eds.), *Chronic illness and disability.* Newbury Park, CA: Sage.

Piaget, J. (1985). *The equilibration of cognitive structures.* Chicago: University of Chicago Press.

Rappaport, L. (1972). *Personality development: A chronology of experience.* Glenview, IL: Scott, Foresman.

Rhodes, R. (1993). Mental retardation and sexual expression: An historical perspective. In R. W Mackelprang and D. Valentine (Eds.), *Sexuality and disabilities: A guide for human service practitioners* (pp. 1–27). Binghamton, NY: Haworth Press.

Rolland, J. S. (1988). A conceptual model of chronic and life threatening illness and its impact on families. In C. S. Chilman, E. W. Nunnaly, and F. M. Cox (Eds.), *Chronic illness and disability.* Newbury Park, CA: Sage.

Rolland, J. S. (1989). Chronic illness and the family life cycle. In E. A. Carter and M. McGoldrick (Eds.), *The changing family life cycle: A framework for family therapy* (2nd ed.). Needham Heights, MA: Allyn & Bacon.

Shapiro, J. P. (1993). *No pity: People with disabilities, forging a new civil rights movement.* New York: Times Books.

Sigler, G., and Mackelprang, R. W (1993). Cognitive impairments: Psychosocial and sexual implications and strategies for social work intervention. In R. W Mackelprang and D. Valentine (Eds.), *Sexuality and disabilities: A guide for human service practitioners* (pp. 89–106). Binghamton, NY: Haworth Press.

Spencer, P. E., Bodner-Johnson, B. A., and Gutfreund, M. K. (1992). Interacting with infants with a hearing loss: What can we learn from mothers who are deaf? *Journal of Early Intervention, 16,* 64–78.

Stewart, T. D., and Rossier, A. B. (1978). Psychological considerations in the adjustment to spinal cord injuries. *Rehabilitation Literature, 39,* 75–80.

Summers, J. A., Behr, S. K., and Turnbull, A. P. (1989). Positive adaptation and coping strengths of families who have children with disabilities. In G. H. S. Singer and L. K. Irvin (Eds.), *Support for caregiving families: Enabling positive adaptation to disabilities* (pp. 27–40). Baltimore: Paul H. Brooks.

Tanner, J. M. (1978/1990). *Fetus into man: Physical growth from conception to maturity.* Cambridge: Harvard University Press.

Trieschmann, R. B. (1980). *Spinal cord injuries: Psychological, social, and vocational adjustment.* New York: Pergamon Press.

Valentine, D. P. (1993). Children with special needs: Sources of support and stress for families. In R. W Mackelprang and D. Valentine (Eds.), *Sexuality and disabilities: A guide for human service practitioners* (pp. 107–129). Binghamton, NY: Haworth Press.

Vygotsky, L. S. (1978). *Mind in society.* Cambridge, MA: Harvard University Press.

Whitman, B. Y., and Accardo, P. J. (1993). The parent with mental retardation: Rights, responsibilities and issues. In R. W Mackelprang and D. Valentine (Eds.), *Sexuality and disabilities: A guide for human service practitioners* (pp. 123–136). Binghamton, NY: Haworth Press.

Wright, B. (1960). *Physical disability—a psychological approach.* New York: Harper & Row.

Part Two

DISABILITY GROUPINGS

One of the guiding tenets of the independent living movement discussed in Chapter 3 centers on the belief that, although there are differences among disabilities, the life experience and culture of disability have more commonality than difference. People with a variety of disabilities share a common experience. This view contrasts sharply with the medical model, which seeks to categorize and classify disability for the sake of treatment, study, and determining qualifications for benefits. To date, no one has come up with a universally accepted system of grouping disabilities. We believe that if you perceive yourself to be a person with a disability, then you are indeed a person with a disability. Grouping then becomes a mechanism of understanding commonalities. This is in line with an ethnographic perspective on cultural classification that relies on self-identification with groups and avoids the pitfalls of stereotyping individuals. Self-declaration also is well within the tenets of the independent living movement. We believe it is important to understand that, because of ableism and discrimination, people with disabilities have remained closeted about their disabilities. Increased acceptance of disability as a social construct reduces the need for persons with disabilities to hide or deny their disabilities and helps them embrace their total selves.

In Chapters 5 through 10, we attempt to satisfy the need to bring understanding to the differences that make up the tapestry of disability without stereotyping people. Not all people will agree with our groupings, nor should they. In fact, the groupings currently used came about after much discussion, debate, and compromise. We offer the groupings as a beginning point of discussion and debate, which ultimately will result in increased understanding and knowledge, and we encourage others to add to the discussion.

Because of the diversity of disability types and because of space limitations, we have made no attempt to be comprehensive in our coverage of the range of disabilities. Instead, we focus on samples of the wide variety of disabilities in human existence. It is our hope that students will generalize the information to disabilities not covered.

Chapter 5 addresses mobility-related disabilities. We include a discussion of several mobility disabilities that are congenital. Typically, people with these disabilities live with them throughout their lives. We also discuss mobility disabilities that are acquired later in life and to which people must adjust after living without disability.

Chapter 6 looks at the diverse world of deaf and hard-of-hearing people. The disability movement owes much to Deaf culture, which has been visible and highly developed for years. It is interesting to note that deaf members of Deaf culture diverge from most people with disabilities by eschewing "people first" language (i.e., "person with a disability"). Because of space considerations, we focus primarily on deaf people, with less emphasis on hard-of-hearing people. We recognize that many more people are hard of hearing than deaf; however, we place emphasis on deaf people and Deaf culture because of their historical contributions to the disability arena.

Chapter 7 explores persons with visual disabilities and blindness. We focus on their capabilities and discuss common misperceptions about their limitations.

Chapter 8 discusses persons with developmental disabilities, including intellectual disability, Down syndrome, autism, and seizure disorders. Grouping disabilities for this chapter was most difficult and controversial. Since disabilities acquired before adulthood are generally considered developmental disabilities, most disabilities found in the text could have been included in this chapter. We selected only a few. Another area of difficulty involves terminology—specifically, use of language relative to people who traditionally have been referred to as having "mental retardation." This term is commonly accepted in governmental and professional circles but rejected by self-advocacy groups such as People First. We use the term *intellectual disabilities* out of respect for people who find the term *mental retardation* pejorative and offensive. We welcome further exploration of this issue.

Chapter 9 reviews psychiatric disabilities, including schizophrenia, major depression, and bipolar conditions. Recognizing the explosion of knowledge relative to psychiatric disabilities, we enlisted the help of Marilyn Wedenoja, who wrote this chapter.

Chapter 10 examines cognitive disabilities, including learning disability, attention deficit hyperactivity disorder, and traumatic head injury. Again, we were able to include only a small sample of disabilities that might be considered cognitive. We also recognize that our label, *cognitive disabilities,* is controversial and could be applied to a variety of other disabilities. Some doubt the existence of some of the cognitive disabilities. We chose to include categories of disabilities in this chapter that have similarities.

Chapter 5

PERSONS WITH MOBILITY DISABILITIES

The doctor never told me I would never walk again. I remember that on about my fifth day in the hospital I said, "So what's the deal here, doctor?" He said, "Let me put it this way, Karen; you and I will both be able to go to McDonald's someday, but it will take you a little bit longer than it will me because you'll either be in a wheelchair or on crutches." Still, I had this totally positive attitude at that time, thinking, "I'm going to walk again!" And each time I would come out with this positive attitude, my doctors or my therapist would say, "Well, that's a really nice attitude, but . . . ." Eventually I got it, like everybody else who's been through this.

—Karen Pendleton, School Counselor, Comprehensive Youth Services, Fresno, California (former Mouseketeer)

Student Learning Objectives:

1. To understand the many varieties of disabilities related to mobility.
2. To have a very basic knowledge of the major mobility disabilities likely to be experienced by clients and consumers.
3. To understand the similarities and differences between those who acquire mobility disabilities at or near birth and those who acquire mobility disabilities later in life.

◆ DEFINING MOBILITY DISABILITY

We are going to assume a definition of physical disability related to mobility based upon our social/minority perspective on disability and its interplay with the variety of worlds that are a part of contemporary society. In light of the social/minority perspective, persons with a mobility disability are those whose physical differences compel them to achieve physical activities in a variety of alternate ways. For example, persons with cerebral palsy may be considered have a mobility disability because they can achieve personal mobility differently than a person without cerebral palsy. We say "may" because, from an ethnographic perspective, people have the right to choose the group they identify with most. Ultimately, disability, no matter what kind, is a phenomenon of social construct (Wright, 1988).

As a matter of convenience, we have divided mobility disability into two categories: physical characteristics impacting mobility acquired before, during, or immediately after birth, known as congenital disabilities, and physical characteristics impacting mobility acquired later in life, usually during or after childhood. Congenital disabilities may include cerebral palsy, spina bifida, congenital osteogenesis, arthrogrypsosis, dwarfism, and amputations. Some of these are included under other categories of disabilities. Physical disabilities impacting mobility acquired later in life may include traumatic brain injury, stroke, amputations, muscular dystrophy, rheumatoid arthritis, multiple sclerosis, myasthenia gravis, spinal cord injury, and poliomyelitis. Conditions such as traumatic brain injury can also fall under other disability categories, such as cognitive or emotional; we deal with traumatic brain injury under cognitive disabilities. Some of these disabilities, such as muscular dystrophy, have a genetic etiology, but their physical characteristics generally do not manifest until months or years after birth. We have attempted in the following to define some of the more common types of physical disability affecting mobility that are encountered by human service practitioners who work with persons with disabilities.

◆ CONGENITAL DISABILITIES

CEREBRAL PALSY   *Cerebral palsy* is one of the better known congenital conditions resulting in mobility disability. More than 700,000 Americans have cerebral palsy. Cerebral palsy is a condition that can be caused by injury to the brain at birth or during fetal development before birth. The injury may result from bleeding into the brain, lack of oxygen at or near birth, or an infection that is shared between the mother and the developing fetus. Infants who are born prematurely are especially susceptible to cerebral palsy. Cerebral palsy also may be considered an acquired disability if the cause occurs postnatally. Head injuries, infections such as meningitis, and other forms of brain damage occurring in the first months or years of life are the main causes of acquired cerebral palsy (National Organization for Rare Disorders, Inc., 1993c).

Cerebral palsy usually results from changes to the areas of the brain that govern motor control. The changes in the brain usually impact voluntary muscle systems. Resulting differences in muscular control vary, depending on the location and degree of the changes in the brain. Spasticity (tense, contracting muscles), athetosis (constant, uncontrolled motion of limbs, head, and eyes), ataxia (poor muscle control, balance, and coordination), tremor, and rigidity can result in increased or decreased muscle tone, muscle contractions, hyperactive reflexes, slow involuntary muscle movement, and jerky movements. These neuromuscular differences can result in subsequent changes in bone structure. The muscle and bone changes result in different and unique methods of mobility and movement. Sometimes in cerebral palsy, in addition to changes in muscular control, changes in mental processes and perception occur as well (Winnick, 1995).

SPINA BIFIDA   *Spina bifida* is a condition that results from the neural tube not closing completely during the first four weeks of fetal development. One in 2,000 babies in the United States are born with spina bifida, 80% with the most severe type. With spina bifida, the vertebrae and usually the spinal cord of the fetus do not develop in the usual manner. In more severe types, there is an opening in the spinal column. Neurological changes may occur because of spina bifida.

Spina bifida is usually classified into three types. *Myelomeningocele* results when the spinal cord and its protective covering, the meninges, protrude from the opening in the spine. Myelomeningocele is usually accompanied by hydrocephalus, where the circulation of the cerebrospinal fluid is blocked in one of the cavities of the brain. If not treated, the cavity becomes enlarged because fluid cannot drain appropriately. Brain pressure, head enlargement, and intellectual disabilities can result. *Spina bifida meningocele* is characterized by spinal cord development in the usual manner but the meninges protrude from the opening in the column. *Spina bifida occulta* occurs when vertebral development is incomplete but the meninges are closed around the spinal cord. In this form, there are usually no changes in neurological development compared to other children (National Organization for Rare Disorders, Inc., 1993h).

Children with spina bifida demonstrate several unique characteristics. Some alternative mobility techniques are usually required. These may include the use of braces, crutches, and wheelchairs. Usually, some alternative bowel and bladder alleviation methods must be developed and used. These may include special diets for bowel control and intermittent catheterization for urination. Finally, because of the use of the wheelchair and a lack of physical exercise opportunities, children with spina bifida have a tendency to be obese (Winnick, 1995).

CONGENITAL OSTEOGENESIS IMPERFECTA   *Congenital osteogenesis imperfecta* is relatively rare. One in 20,000 to one in 50,000 babies in the United States are born with this condition. More popularly known as the "brittle bone disease," osteogenesis imperfecta is characterized by unusually weak bones that break or fracture with minor stress or trauma. There are four levels of severity in this condition. The congenital form, type II, is the most severe; other forms range from mild to severe.

Osteogenesis imperfecta results in a change in the protein matrix of collagen fibers of bones. This change reduces the amount of calcium and phosphorus, which weakens bone structure. Physical characteristics include shortened and bowed bones resulting in bone fractures, increased elasticity of joint tissue, changed skin coloration, and changes in eye coloration (blue tinge of the eyeball) (National Organization for Rare Disorders, Inc., 1993g). Osteogenesis imperfecta can require people to use crutches and/or wheelchairs. Sometimes surgery is necessary to strengthen bones by inserting steel rods lengthwise through the bone shaft (Winnick, 1995).

ARTHROGRYPOSIS   *Arthrogryposis* is a condition in which the range of motion of the joints of all limbs is changed from typical development. In many cases, the shoulders are bent inward and internally rotated. Persons with arthrogryposis usually have

extended elbows and bent wrists and fingers. The hips may form outside their sock-
ets and are usually slightly bent. Many persons with arthrogryposis have extended
knees, heels bent inward from the midline of the leg, and feet bent inward at the
ankle (known as "club foot"). Muscles of persons with arthrogryposis have not
developed in the typical manner (hypoplastic), and their limbs tend to be tubular in
shape and featureless. Fatty, connective tissue is present over the side of fixed joints.

The cause of arthrogryposis is unknown. Most types are not inherited.
Arthrogryposis may be primarily a neurological disorder; it may also be a muscle
disease. About 500 infants a year are born in the United States with arthrogryposis.
Both males and females are affected (National Organization for Rare Disorders,
Inc., 1993b).

Depending on the severity, persons with arthrogryposis may need to use
crutches and/or wheelchairs for mobility. Sometimes braces are used to accommodate mobility. Other manifestations linked to the condition include changes in
heart and lung function and in the strength of facial muscles (Winnick, 1995).

DWARFISM   The Little People of America (LPA) defines *dwarfism* as a male or
female adult with a height of 4′10″ or shorter that is the result of a medical or
genetic condition. The most frequently diagnosed cause of dwarfism or short
stature is *achondroplasia*. Other genetic conditions that result in short stature include
spondylo-epiphyseal dysplasia (SED) and *diastrophic dysplasia* (Kennedy, 1996). Infants
born with achondroplasia typically have an arched skull to accommodate an
enlarged brain that is generally a characteristic in this condition. This results in a
very broad forehead. The child may also develop hydrocephalus. Infants with
achondroplasia typically have a low nasal bridge. Arms and legs are usually very
short and the trunk of the body appears long in comparison. The hands of children
with this condition are generally short and broad. The index and middle finger are
typically close together as are the ring finger and the pinkie, giving the hand a
unique appearance. Changes in the spine may result in an outward curvature of the
upper back, and the legs may be bowed. Most adult males with achondroplasia are
under 4′6″ tall, whereas females are typically 3 inches shorter than males. Children
with achondroplasia may also have an atypical rib cage, including curvature of the
ribs. Achondroplasia does not cause any changes in mental abilities. The life
expectancy of infants over the age of 12 months is normal (National Organization
for Rare Disorders, Inc., 1993a).

Characteristics of spondylo-epiphyseal dysplasia include flat facial features,
myopia (nearsightedness) or retinal detachment, short-trunk dwarfism, and barrel-
chestedness. Also, the knees often tend to be atypical, pointing either outward or
inward, changing the walking pattern. Hands and feet appear typical. Mental and
intellectual capabilities are not altered by spondylo-epiphyseal dysplasia. Adults can
reach a height of 2′9″ to 4′2″. In some cases, the characteristics of the condition
may lead to further changes in physical characteristics. For instance, retinal detachment may result in blindness. Compression of the spinal cord may result in changes
in neuromuscular function (National Organization for Rare Disorders, Inc., 1993i).

Short stature and progressive curvature of the spine are major features of diastrophic dysplasia. An open spine in the neck area occurs in most individuals with

diastrophic dysplasia. The pelvic bones as well as the head of the thigh bone and the tailbone, may also be atypical. Fingers are short, the small bones in the hand tend to grow together, and the thumb is extended. With changes in bone structure in the hips and feet, changes in mobility may occur. Cystlike swellings on the outer ear during early infancy may later develop into cauliflower-like shapes. Generally, a quarter of individuals with diastrophic dysplasia have a cleft palate. Occasionally, persons with diastrophic dysplasia have a broad nasal bridge and a unique-shaped nose, and develop benign tumors made up of blood vessels on their faces. Intelligence is not affected (National Organization for Rare Disorders, Inc., 1993d). In the United States, one baby in 14,000 is born with achondroplasia, one in 95,000 is born with spondylo-epiphyseal dysplasia, and one in 110,000 is born with diastrophic dysplasia. Overall, there are more than 100 diagnosed types of dwarfism (Kennedy, 1996).

In 1957, a group of Little People got together in Reno, Nevada, under the leadership of Billy Barty, a widely acclaimed actor; they formed the organization Little People of America (LPA). Originally developed to provide support to Little People in dealing with the challenges of dwarfism, it expanded its role to include not only personal and family support but also advocacy. Through organizations such as LPA, Little People are coming together socially and politically to challenge stereotypes, provide mutual support, and educate not only themselves but all Americans (Little People of America, Inc., 1998).

AMPUTATION   *Amputation* generally is seen as an acquired mobility disability, but infants born without a limb or with a significantly changed limb number approximately twice the number of those who lose a limb by accident, disease, or violent crime. Over 300,000 individuals in the United States are amputees. More than 66% of these are missing a lower limb (Winnick, 1995). Two types of congenital conditions are associated with an absence of limbs at birth. In the first type, a middle segment of a limb is missing, but the part nearest the body and the end part are intact. For example, the hand or the foot may be directly connected to the shoulder or the hip, respectively, without the middle structures. The second type more closely resembles acquired or surgical amputation where there are no structures beyond the missing part.

In many cases, persons with lower-extremity amputations use some method of alternative mobility, usually a prosthetic device. Prosthetic devices today are designed to accommodate the mobility function altered by the amputation. Devices are designed in relationship to the size, type, and area of limb change. Computer technology and alternative high-tech material are key components in contemporary design of prosthetic devices (Winnick, 1995).

◆ ACQUIRED MOBILITY-RELATED DISABILITIES

STROKE   *Stroke* is also known as a cerebrovascular accident. It occurs when blood vessels to a specific part of the brain rupture (hemorrhagic stroke) or become blocked (ischemic stroke). When oxygen fails to reach a specific part of the brain, the brain cells begin to die. In a hemorrhagic stroke, blood collects in brain tissue and blocks the normal transfer of oxygen and other blood elements. Hemorrhagic strokes are usually the result of burst aneurysms (weakened spots in the blood vessels), or of hypertension that causes constant pressure on arterial walls, eventually leading them to leak (Stanford University Medical Center, 1996).

Strokes generally tend to occur in elderly males and in African Americans more than in the general population. Approximately 80% of persons who experience strokes are over the age of 65. Certain subpopulations within the general population tend to be at high risk for strokes. These include persons with long-term alcohol or drug abuse; persons with arteriosclerosis, diabetes, or high blood pressure; and people who smoke, particularly women who smoke and use birth control pills. People who have had strokes are at a greater risk of reoccurrence (National Organization for Rare Disorders, Inc., 1993j).

Stroke can significantly affect areas of the brain that control vital functions. These functions can include a wide range of physical, cognitive, and emotional components in human existence. Stroke can affect motor ability and control, sensation and perception, communication, psychological state and emotion, and consciousness. The most common type of stroke occurs from blockage of a middle cerebral artery, which usually causes partial or total paralysis on one side of the body. Generally, when the stroke occurs in the left middle cerebral artery (which affects the right side of the body), changes occur with speech and language. Individuals who have experienced a stroke generally approach problems and new situations differently than prior to the stroke, usually with caution. Their organizational skills are usually changed. Generally, when the stroke occurs in the right middle cerebral artery (which affects the left side of the body), individuals experience changes in their spatial perception. Their ability to judge distance, size, position, rate of movement, form, and relationship of parts is diminished. They tend to neglect their left side and show impulsiveness (Winnick, 1995).

MUSCULAR DYSTROPHY   The term *muscular dystrophy* covers over 40 separate neuromuscular conditions, which have in common the progressive and irreversible change of muscle tissue in structure and strength. Some of these conditions are known as *dystrophies,* when the muscles change in mass and strength from within. Others are *atrophies,* where conditions in the nervous system result in the loss of the ability to use muscles.

Duchenne muscular dystrophy is the most common and most severe form of the condition. Duchenne muscular dystrophy is a rare inherited condition that results in progressive muscle weakness. Early symptoms usually begin between the ages of 2 to 5 years. Muscle change is initially limited to the shoulder and pelvic areas. An enlargement of the calf muscles in the legs is the result of the infiltration of fat and connective tissue into the muscles. Within several years, Duchenne muscular dystrophy impacts the muscles of the chest and arms. With further progression of the condition, all the major muscles are affected (National Organization for Rare Disorders, Inc.,1993e).

The early symptoms of Duchenne muscular dystrophy may include changes in mobility and an increased need for mobility-accommodating devices. By age 3 to 5 years, generalized muscle weakness has progressed. A stabilization may occur between 5 and 7 years with some increase in muscle strength. Weakness progresses rapidly after age 8 or 9, resulting in some form of permanent accommodation for mobility such as leg braces, a walker, or a wheelchair. By adolescence, extensive accommodation is usually necessary in the form of a manual or electric wheelchair. In the late stages of Duchenne muscular dystrophy, muscles become shorter and there is a significant loss of muscle tissue. This may result in the inability to move the major joints of the body such that they become fixed in place (fixed contractures). There may be increased changes in the spine, resulting in its curvature (known as scoliosis). Lung capacity may decrease. As the condition progresses, more accommodations may be necessary, including special controls for driving and operating of a vehicle, lifts, and modification to home or apartment (Winnick, 1995). With Duchenne muscular dystrophy, death often occurs by young adulthood. Other forms of MD are not nearly so severe.

RHEUMATOID ARTHRITIS   Two and a half million people in the United States have *rheumatoid arthritis* (RA)—about 1% of the adult population. Three-quarters of the people having rheumatoid arthritis are women. RA usually begins in middle age but can start at any age (Arthritis Foundation, 1987). Approximately 165,000 children in the United States have some form of arthritis. Of these, 71,000 have juvenile rheumatoid arthritis, which is the most severe type (Winnick, 1995).

In rheumatoid arthritis, the immune system attacks parts of the body, especially the joints, because it recognizes them as foreign to the body. Known as an autoimmune condition, RA causes inflammation of the joints, but it can sometimes impact multiple body systems, including the muscles, lungs, skin, blood vessels, nerves, and eyes. In addition to joint inflammation, symptoms may include fatigue and weight loss.

Rheumatoid arthritis manifests differently in each individual. Most people with rheumatoid arthritis experience fatigue, soreness, stiffness, and aching early in the course of the condition. For many, joint stiffness is worse in the mornings and after long periods of physical inactivity. Usually, several joints gradually become painful, swollen, and tender. The joints in the hands and feet are usually the first to become involved and are commonly affected bilaterally. Other characteristics of rheumatoid arthritis include loss of appetite and weight loss, a slight temperature, inflammation of the eyes, and painful breathing (Arthritis Foundation, 1987). Generally, one or more joints are impacted in about half of those with RA. Rheumatoid arthritis, especially the juvenile form, usually progresses in severity with time. Special mobility accommodations may be needed, such as canes, crutches, and walkers. Depending on the degree of change in the joint, the use of a wheelchair may help facilitate mobility (Winnick, 1995).

MULTIPLE SCLEROSIS   *Multiple sclerosis* (MS) is one of the most common diseases of the central nervous system. Up to 350,000 people in the United States have multiple sclerosis. For almost two-thirds of these individuals, onset occurs between the ages of 20 and 40; it is 50% more frequent in women than men (Winnick, 1995). MS is characterized by the inflammation and the eventual total deterioration of the myelin sheath, a fatty material that covers and insulates the nerves. Myelin functions similarly to the plastic covering on electric wiring. Changes in the myelin precipitate disruption in the ability of the nerves to conduct electrical impulses to and from the brain. This disruption results in the various characteristics of MS. The cause of MS is unknown, but researchers are speculating that the condition might be the result of a viral attack, an autoimmune reaction, or a combination of both. In addition, there appears to be some genetic susceptibility to the condition. This is suggested by the fact that a slightly higher risk of multiple sclerosis exists in families where it has already occurred (Tierney, McPhee, and Papadakis, 1994).

Multiple sclerosis is a variable condition; the resulting characteristics depend on which areas of the central nervous system have been impacted. There is no typical MS—no established pattern of development. Everyone with MS has a different set of resulting characteristics that can shift from time to time and change in severity and duration. Generally, persons with MS experience changes in vision, coordination, muscular strength, speech and communication, sexual functioning, bowel and bladder control, and cognitive functioning. One of the most common changes brought about by MS is fatigue that can occur unpredictably and without relationship to physical activity (Tierney et al., 1994). Persons with MS generally have a low tolerance to heat.

Multiple sclerosis is usually progressive with periods of symptom exacerbation and remission. Over several years, the progression of MS symptoms may require accommodation. Many persons with multiple sclerosis require accommodation in mobility, including the use of crutches and eventually the use of a wheelchair. Home or apartment adaptations to accommodate wheelchair use may be necessary. Sexual function changes require various types of accommodation. Changes in bowel and bladder control may require alternative methods in the form of external or internal catheters and bowel management programs (Winnick, 1995).

MYASTHENIA GRAVIS   *Myasthenia gravis* (MG) is a chronic neuromuscular condition characterized by weakness and rapid fatigue of the voluntary muscles (those muscles controlled by will). Myasthenia gravis may involve either a single muscle or a group of muscles. Muscle groups generally most affected control speech, chewing, swallowing, and eye movement. Muscles that control the arms and legs are sometimes impacted. In some persons with myasthenia gravis, the weakness is limited to eye and eyelid muscles, resulting in double vision and sometimes drooping eyelids. Rest and relaxation are extremely important to help people with MG regain strength and endurance.

Approximately 100,000 people in the United States have myasthenia gravis. MG can occur in people of any age and either sex, but its prevalence is highest in young women aged 20 to 35 and in men and women over 60 years of age. Characteristics in males usually appear between age 40 and 70 (National Organization for Rare Disorders, Inc.,1993f).

Muscle weakness makes the activities of daily living difficult for people with MG. Some experience difficulty chewing and swallowing. Some have respiratory weakness. The weakness in the muscles used for breathing may result in shortness of breath and the inability to take deep breaths. Usually, persons under 60 years of age with MG do not require mobility accommodation (Winnick, 1995).

SPINAL CORD INJURY   About 10,000 people in the United States experience *spinal cord injury* (SCI) each year. This type of injury is due to a variety of accidents, including motorcycle, auto, falls, athletic, and bicycle. Various forms of violence, including stabbings and gunshot wounds, result in SCI. A large percentage of those injured are adolescents and young adults. Incidence is greater in males than females (Winnick, 1995).

SCI can cause partial or complete paralysis and sensory loss, depending on the severity of the injury (Tierney et al., 1994). SCI in the back results in lower-body paralysis, called paraplegia, whereas arm and leg paralysis (quadriplegia) occurs in SCI in the neck. The location of the injury determines the function impacted. Generally, four parts of the spine are to be considered in dealing with spinal cord injury: the cervical, the thoracic, the lumbar, and the sacrum. The higher the injury, the greater number of functions that are affected; the more extensive the damage to the cord, the greater the neurological loss. At every level, SCI affects bowel, bladder, and sexual functioning. When the spinal cord is severed or damaged so severely that no messages can be transmitted past the damage, the SCI is *complete*. The discussion below assumes a complete injury to the spinal cord.

The cervical spine consists of the first seven vertebrae and eight spinal cord segments. With SCIs at C1 (first cervical segment of the spinal cord) to C3, nerves that control breathing are damaged, and permanent ventilator or other breathing aid is required to sustain life. The C4 region impacts the neck and diaphragm. Injury to this area of the spinal cord generally results in paralysis from the neck down. Head control, arm and leg movement, and bowel and bladder control are all impacted. Respiratory functioning is compromised, but mechanical ventilation is usually not necessary. Mobility accommodation in the form of an electric wheelchair controlled by the mouth or chin is usually required. Home modifications and attendant care for all activities of daily living are generally necessary for independent living.

A C5 injury impacts some shoulder muscles. Injury at this level usually means that head control is unaffected. There is some use of the arms. Persons with a C5 injury can push a wheelchair with modified rims, but usually an electric wheelchair produces better mobility. Persons with a C5 injury usually require mechanical wheelchair lifts to enter motor vehicles and can sometimes drive using modified steering and hand controls to operate gas and brake pedals.

Persons with C6 quadriplegia generally have function of the major muscles of the shoulders and wrists. They can generally control their arms and wrists and are able to weakly grasp objects. Persons with a C6 injury can usually transfer from the wheelchair without assistance. They can utilize a manual wheelchair with a great deal of precision and may be able to transfer into cars without a lift and drive with hand controls and no modified steering. A person with C7 or C8 quadriplegia may have slightly weakened muscles in the shoulders and arms and still retain some finger and hand function. They are capable of self-sufficiency in activities of daily living, utilizing a wheelchair, and managing bowel and bladder functions.

Persons with T1 (first thoracic segment) paraplegia have complete hand and finger function, which allows them to engage in activities requiring fine motor skills such as piano playing and handcrafts. People with injuries to the mid-thoracic area (T6–8) have better balance because back and chest muscles are innervated. In the absence of other problems, complete independence is assured when the environment is accommodating. People with T12 paraplegia have full innervation of back and abdominal muscles. Some hip function is present. Long leg braces combined with crutches allow people to walk short distances; however, community mobility is still with a manual wheelchair. People with injuries to the L1–5 (lumbar) segments of the spinal cord have increased function in their legs as the level of injury descends. Community mobility may be possible for people with low lumbar injuries; however, mobility is still primarily by wheelchair. Lower leg, knee, and foot stability are affected in people with injuries to the S1-5 (sacral) segments of the spinal cord. People with paraplegia at these levels may ambulate with short leg braces, though wheelchairs are usually used for long distances to conserve energy. Bowel, bladder, and genital functioning are also affected at the sacral segments of the spinal cord; therefore, anyone with a spinal cord injury is susceptible to alteration of function in these areas.

Persons with a spinal cord injury are prone to a number of secondary health problems. Decubitus ulcers or pressure sores are a primary concern of persons with spinal cord injury. These usually come about at pressure points where bones tend to protrude, as in the buttocks, pelvis, and ankles. They are caused by reduced blood flow and lack of sensation; they can become infected and heal very slowly (Tierney et al., 1994). Persons with a spinal cord injury must consciously relieve pressure by moving themselves or having an attendant move them at regular time intervals. Extra padding for the buttocks may be necessary, particularly in the wheelchair.

Persons with spinal cord injuries are also susceptible to urinary tract infections (UTIs). UTIs occur when urine is retained in the bladder and becomes infected with microorganisms. People are also susceptible to UTIs when they use an internal catheter over a long period of time. For persons with spinal cord injury, urinary tract infections can be quite serious and can ultimately affect the kidneys. Newer antibiotics are very useful in fighting off urinary tract infections, but bacteria can become resistant to antibiotics (Chamberlain, 1988).

POLIOMYELITIS   Polio is caused by a viral infection of motor neurons in the spinal cord. Since the introduction of vaccines in the early 1950s, *poliomyelitis* has virtually been eradicated from the Western Hemisphere. Since the mid-1980s, only about 86 cases have been reported in the United States. The vast majority of those were vaccine associated (Tierney et al., 1994). Nevertheless, about 250,000 persons in the United States are living with the effects of poliomyelitis contracted before the development of vaccines (American Academy of Neurology, 1995). Polio causes paralysis, which may be slight or severe depending on the number and location of motor neurons affected. Paralysis may be temporary or permanent.

A recent phenomenon has occurred with persons who have developed polio in their pasts, called *post-poliomyelitis syndrome* or *postpolio syndrome*. A fourth to a third of those who have contracted polio will develop new symptoms of weakness, pain, and fatigue many years after recovering from the acute paralytic event. Some persons having contracted polio 30 or 40 years ago are finding increased difficulty in walking, climbing stairs, dressing, bathing, and swallowing. Persons with postpolio syndrome experience weakness and muscle atrophy in previously affected or unaffected muscles. Postpolio syndrome's origins are not infectious but may be related to the premature aging of overworked motor neurons (American Academy of Neurology, 1995).

The type of mobility accommodation depends on the limbs affected and the severity of the paralysis. Mobility accommodation may involve crutches, leg braces, and/or wheelchairs. Hand controls or foot controls may be required in driving.

◆ Common Issues
Prejudice, Stereotyping, and Discrimination

Whether a mobility-related disability is acquired before or at birth or sometime afterward, persons with mobility disabilities experience prejudice, stereotyping, and discrimination. The stereotypes and prejudices in relationship to persons with physical disabilities are numerous and varied. Hahn (1988), using the work of Livneh, points out that persons who have physical disabilities that impact their mobility are considered ugly. Particularly in a culture that defines beauty in a narrow and restricted sense, persons with mobility disabilities are seen as particularly offensive aesthetically, and they create an apprehension of difference—a kind of xenophobia of nonaesthetics. In addition, because of the cultural inculcation of certain mores from the Judeo-Christian heritage, American society has developed an "existential anxiety" toward persons with physical disabilities (Hahn, 1988, p. 39). This feeds the perception that if an individual acquires a physical disability, life ends. This view, along with the stereotype that persons with physical disabilities are sick, promotes the idea that persons with physical disabilities should be and are universally dependent.

Other preassumptions or prejudices feed the discrimination experienced by persons with disabilities in the United States. Fine and Asch (1988) list five assumptions applied by researchers, practitioners, and people in general to persons with disabilities, including those with physical disabilities. First, people generally assume that disability is rooted in biological dysfunction and that biological dysfunction is the primary driving force in their lives; they are "confined" and "victimized" by their disability. For example, Johnny, who has spina bifida, cannot do well in school because of his spina bifida. Sam has trouble making friends because he is "confined" to a wheelchair. Sandra, who seeks counseling for her depression, is depressed because she was a "victim" of polio at the age of 6 and has used crutches ever since.

Second, people generally assume that the mobility disability is the cause of the problems that people face. The human–built world is never viewed as the cause of people's problems—it is always the disability. Third, people assume that persons with disabilities are victims and that they see themselves as such. Persons with disabilities are not in control and can never have a viable, rich life; they are victims of a great and all–encompassing tragedy. Fourth, related to the preceding assumption, people assume that disability is the center of life for a person with a disability. It is central to their self-definition, to their patterns of friends, and to their comparison to others. Persons with disabilities have no other basis to establish a social reference group than other people with disabilities. The fact that they may be male or female, a member of an ethnic group, or part of a professional interest community has little or no bearing on their associations. Only the disability is a factor. And fifth, people assume that the term "person with a disability" and the phrase "I need help" are synonymous. Disability means helplessness. A wheelchair rider needs the door opened for her. A person who is blind needs to be helped across the street. It is the disabled equivalent of the "white man's burden." Help is always given with the expectation of the reward of feeling good and being thanked, much the same as the white colonialist missionary's expectations in 18th- and 19th-century Africa toward native people.

Bogdan and Biklen (1977) discuss the concrete results of stereotypes and pre-assumptions or prejudices for persons with disabilities. Persons with mobility disabilities are generally portrayed in a negative light in the media. Physical differences are associated with crime and horror. Humor is presented at the expense of persons with mobility disabilities. The lives of persons with physical disabilities are depicted as tragic. Telethons present pathetic images of persons with disabilities in order to raise money. Persons with disabilities are portrayed as noble for choosing to live rather than to commit suicide in the wake of such tragedy and pathos. Yet death is portrayed as a natural wish for a person with a disability.

Another major result of stereotyping and prejudice is the discrimination in physical access for persons with mobility-related disabilities. Wheelchair riders are denied access to public toilets, sidewalks, places of commerce, public telephones, housing, parking, parks and recreation, private and public transportation including buses and airplanes, and places of worship.

Persons with mobility disabilities are also denied access to education. Education buildings and classrooms are not designed to accommodate wheelchair users. Libraries are not designed to allow access to wheelchair riders. College campuses are inaccessible, with steps, steep inclines, no parking, broken sidewalks, and so on. In 1986, the International Center for the Disabled commissioned Louis Harris and Associates to poll persons with disabilities across the country. They found that 40% of children with disabilities never completed high school and 69% of persons with disabilities never attended college (Harris, 1986).

Persons with physical disabilities that impact their mobility are denied access to service delivery in both the public and private sectors. An important component to the inaccessibility of service delivery is the segregation of persons with mobility disabilities. In public auditoriums and movie theaters, wheelchair accommodation is separate, usually in the back, and never equal. Wheelchair seating in restaurants is sometimes out of the way, near the kitchen. There are "special education" programs and special sports events for persons with mobility disabilities, rather than integration into professional and amateur athletic events and games.

Casey Martin discovered the extent of this discrimination when he was denied the use of a golf cart in a recent Professional Golfers' Association (PGA) tournament. He sued. Casey has Klippel-Trenaunay-Weber Syndrome, which limits his ability to walk. In commenting on the case, PGA commissioner Tim Finchem revealed the central stereotypes surrounding athletics and disability:

> As we (PGA) have said from the outset of this lawsuit, we believe firmly in the basic premise of any sport, that one set of rules must be applied equally to all competitors. Additionally, we believe strongly in the central role walking plays for all competitors in tournament championship golf at the PGA Tour and Nike Tour levels (Cullity, 1998a).

He fails to mention the sanctioned use of golf carts on the Senior PGA Tour, in the PGA Tour Qualifying Tournament, and at the NCAA level (Cullity, 1998b). U.S. Magistrate Thomas M. Coffin, citing the Americans with Disabilities Act, dismissed the PGA's request to dismiss the lawsuit; he went on to find in Casey's favor. The PGA will appeal.

One of the most significant areas in which persons with mobility-related disabilities are discriminated against is employment. Satcher and Hendren (1992) point out that in 1987, the Bureau of the Census reported that a little over a third of persons with disabilities of working age were employed. Discrimination in hiring was a significant factor in this low employment rate. Balcazar, Bradford, and Fawcett (1988) found that 70% of the disabled population they surveyed experienced major problems in employment. These included no accommodation in the workplace, lack of training and professional development, and work disincentives in social security. Data indicated that 72% of those surveyed felt that persons with disabilities were discriminated against in the workplace and were not given the same employment opportunities as persons without disabilities. As we discussed in Chapter 3, the Americans with Disabilities Act was created and passed to impact discrimination against persons with disabilities. This remains an unachieved objective.

Aging

Most persons with physical disabilities that impact mobility share not only the experience of prejudice and discrimination; they also share the development of secondary physical complications that may be exacerbated in the aging process. Wilkins and Cott (1993) examine the issue of the aging of persons with physical disabilities in detail. Persons with physical disability are living longer and thus aging. A primary factor in this increased longevity is the efficacy of new medical techniques.

Because the aging of persons with long-term physical disabilities is a relatively new phenomenon and because many physical disabilities were considered static and unchanging, little is written on mobility disability and aging. We hope researchers will address this in the future. It suffices to say at this point that persons with congenital and acquired disabilities face a triple whammy. They are already at a social, political, and economic disadvantage. In addition, they not only face the continuing issues of disability but new challenges as well with the biological changes that occur in the aging process. Lastly, more and more research indicates that disabilities such as polio, which at one time were considered static, may indeed have progressive elements.

◆ UNIQUE CONCERNS

Although persons with disabilities face the common concerns of stereotyping, prejudice, discrimination, and aging, there are points of difference. Wright (1960) discounts drastic identity or personality change as the result of a disability acquired later in life. Wright also sees no distinct advantages and disadvantages to having been born with a disability or acquiring one later in life. But acquiring a disability several years after birth requires a person to adjust to acquired changes and integrate these with old ideas of self. The success of this integration depends on a number of variables, including personality development prior to the disability and the degree to which self-concept is associated with societal constructs of health and beauty. If self-concept has had many years to develop around Hollywood standards of beauty, the integration of a physical disability that affects mobility becomes more demanding.

Zink (1992) concludes through personal experience and observation that the age at which a person acquires a disability impacts how he or she accepts it—how it is integrated into the self-concept. She describes the difference between herself having acquired a disability in her teenage years and someone whom she had just met with a disability acquired in his forties. She viewed disability as the normal state of being, whereas her newfound acquaintance viewed himself in his present state as abnormal. She accepted the accommodations necessary for movement as integral to her success, whereas he held onto an inaccessible house, crawling up and down stairs and refusing to utilize a power chair. It was evident that he did not in-tend to become a person with a disability. Disability would never be a part of him.

Zink (1992) attributes the ability of those who acquire a mobility disability early in life to successfully integrate disability into their self-concepts to the energy of youth. The aging process lessens the vast amount of energy it requires to integrate changes in self-perception and status. Also, more years with a disability increase the opportunities to be exposed to role models, leaders, and cultural and political movements centered on the strength, power, and beauty of disability and difference.

◆   SUMMARY

We believe that human service practitioners need to be aware of the different kinds of physical disability related to mobility. Each of these kinds of disability manifests in different ways and may require different approaches to life processes, including accommodation in mobility, in activities of daily living, and in certain basic biological functions.

Human service practitioners need to know that all persons with physical disabilities have faced and experienced stereotyping, prejudice, and discrimination. While this needs to be acknowledged with the person being provided a service, the main intervention in eradicating this barrier centers on advocacy and political action. (More about this will be explored later.)

Finally, the human service practitioner needs to be aware that a physical disability acquired later in life may impact a person differently than one acquired before or at birth. *May* is the important word here. Practitioners cannot assume anything—they must seek knowledge from the consumer. It is the responsibility of human service practitioners to be aware of possibilities but not to presuppose them.

◆ ◆ ◆   *Personal Narrative: Karen Pendleton*   ◆ ◆ ◆

Karen Pendleton was a mainstay in the homes of millions of children during the 1960s as an original member of the Mickey Mouse Club. At age 36, she acquired a spinal cord injury when she was in an automobile accident. Since then, she has become very involved in the disability movement. Currently, she is president of the board of directors for the Center for Independent Living in Fresno, California. She is also a school counselor for Comprehensive Youth Services.

When I was 8, I was chosen to be one of the original Mouseketeers at the Walt Disney Fan Club. It was an absolutely fantastic experience. It was fun when I was doing it. I was so young I didn't realize how important it was and how special it was going to be. I don't think anybody realized it was going to take off like it did.

It was a healthy show. They taught nice things and it was morally a good show. None of us were very professional, so kids watching could identify with us. I had never done anything professional in my life before that. I always capitalized on my mistakes on the show; I was the youngest, people thought I was cute because I was always screwing up.

The Mouseketeers ended when I was 12. I had to go back to being a "regular person," and life got tough. I went right back into junior high school and other kids were really mean to me. For four years, I hadn't had a lot of contact with anybody but the Mouseketeers and had no idea that so many people knew who I was.

My first week in junior high was horrible. Kids would group around me every day at lunchtime and do things like ask me for my autograph and then tear it up. They would say, "Mickey Mouse, wiggle your ears and I'll give you some cheese." I was very shy and insecure. I thought nobody liked me. My self-esteem went down to the floor. From that time on, I really had a hard time thinking I had any value at all. I thought everybody hated me. I went through junior high and high school like that.

In my early adult years, I really wasn't into the Mouseketeers at all. The only contact I had with Disney until after I had my accident was in 1980 when we did a reunion, and that was really fun. But by that time I was married and had my daughter, Stacey. The Mouseketeers didn't have any contact with the public. We just went to the studio and did the reunion show, and then I headed back home.

When I was 36, I became disabled in an automobile accident. I have T-2 paraplegia, which is pretty high up. I feel very lucky I've got my arms. Ha, God knew that if I didn't have my arms I couldn't put my makeup on and I would be miserable. He knows how much I can take.

When I got in the accident, I must have gone into shock because I didn't realize that there was anything wrong with me. As I think back now, when I first got out of the car I could sit up, which is something I can't do anymore. I should never have done that, but I didn't know what a spinal cord injury was then. It seems ridiculous now that, as a grown adult, I had no idea what a spinal cord injury was. My husband picked me up, put me in the car, and drove me to the hospital, which he should never have done. I even told him to take me home; I'd be fine in the morning. I was probably in shock. I think that if I hadn't done those two things, my injury wouldn't have been as severe as it is.

The doctor never told me I would never walk again. I remember that on about my fifth day in the hospital I said, "So what's the deal here, doctor?" He said, "Let me put it this way, Karen; you and I will both be able to go to McDonald's someday, but it will take you a little bit longer than it will me because you'll either be in a wheelchair or on crutches." Still, I had this totally positive attitude at that time, thinking, "I'm going to walk again!" And each time I would come out with this positive attitude my doctors or my therapist would say, "Well, that's a really nice attitude BUT . . . ." Eventually I got it, like everybody else who's been through this.

Before my accident, my husband and I were having problems. He had an affair, so my self-esteem was really low, and I was trying to keep the marriage together. Sex was a very important part of our relationship; because it was important to my husband, I placed a lot of my self-esteem in my sexuality. After my accident, I felt like, "OK, that went right out the window." I basically said to my husband, "Well, I'm worthless to you, so whatever you want to do, you do it." Well, he took me up on my offer. He said, "There's no way I can take care of you." He dropped me right then and there. He was afraid to drop me publicly because he didn't want to look like the bad guy, so eventually I had to file for divorce.

The way I saw my life then was, "I've lost my marriage, my home, and my ability to walk. Everything has gone right out the window." It was really tough.

Since my marriage was ending, I went from the hospital right to my mom and dad's home. Oh boy, did things get interesting. For my parents, I had been an independent married woman with a child. All of a sudden I was their baby again. I let them take care of me because it was much easier on me. I felt guilty about that. If I had gone home with my husband, I would have been independent a lot faster.

But everything happens for a reason. After a year with my parents, I moved out. I finally decided living with them was not good for me, and I started becoming independent. Finally, Stacey and I moved out by ourselves. That was the very first time in my life that I had ever been on my own.

Stacey was only 9 when I became disabled. On the night of my accident, Stacey overheard my mother say, "They took Karen away," when they were taking me to the operating room. When Stacey overheard my mom say that, she interpreted it to mean that I had died. She was so relieved when she found I wasn't dead I think she concluded that whatever was wrong with me was unimportant as long as I was still around.

Stacey was absolutely my rock. She was the only one that didn't treat me any different. She would still get mad or frustrated with me when she didn't get her way. I was still her mommy. It didn't matter that mommy had a disability. She didn't pamper me, and that was comforting.

Stacey would stand on the wheelchair and she would sit on my lap. The wheelchair didn't bother her like it did my mom and dad. She and I did just great together. One of the best things this disability has done for me is give me the opportunity to be with and watch my daughter grow up. I have been at home for her and could give her advice; we have an absolutely great relationship because of that. I could never have been there for her like that had I not been able to be home. Our closeness was a very positive outcome from all this.

Because I was already having problems with my husband, one of the first things I asked for when I was in the hospital was to see a psychologist. With therapy, I started to see my husband differently, and I started to change myself, but I wouldn't admit it to myself. After three years, I stopped therapy, believing I hadn't changed at all. Now I realize I had really gotten a lot out of it but didn't know it at the time.

Over time, I figured out that old Karen was no more. It's like I had to bury her and get to know the Karen that was left here. I found that I liked the new Karen a lot better than the old one! The old Karen had been a big phony. I tried to be everything I thought other people expected me to be. I was what my husband wanted me to be. I was what my parents wanted me to be. I was what my friends at the country club wanted me to be. I wasn't me.

Now all I have left is me. And I like me a whole lot better than I did that other me. That's where my self-confidence came from. It's not being conceited because I believe conceited people have no self-esteem. This disability helped me become more assertive. I've had to take risks. I've had to ask for help, which I never would have done before. Like, when I'm at the grocery store, I will ask strangers, "Excuse me, could you reach that for me?" I would have never done that before and, believe me, at 4'10", I needed help in reaching things. I'm willing to take risks that I would never have taken before my disability. I like it, and I keep trying to teach the same thing to my clients.

I didn't even consider myself disabled for a long time. When I would see the shadow of my wheelchair, I would think it was creepy. I remember once going to a presentation on the electric stimulation of muscles. I was sitting in this roomful of people and all of a sudden I realized these were all people with disabilities. And I thought to myself, "I do not belong here."

For the most part, I had never hung out with anybody with a disability and I didn't even know anybody with a disability. I tried to gracefully embrace people with disabilities, but it was hard. I thought, "I don't know anything about you. I only know about my disability."

It seems weird now, but it took me a while to become really accepting of others with disabilities. A really good eye-opener for me was a college course I took on the psychological aspects of disability. I took the class thinking I would know everything and get an easy A. But I really learned a lot in the class about other disabilities. Since then, I've learned a lot from other people with disabilities. I'm much more accepting of people with disabilities and of myself with a disability.

Some really neat things have happened to me only since I've been disabled. It wasn't until after I was disabled that I actually went out into the public as a Mouseketeer again. I was shocked when I saw how much people loved me after all those years. One time I did a Miss Wheelchair pageant. I'll never forget a young woman from Arizona. She said to me, "When I was growing up, you were the one thing that made me have some kind of happiness in my life. My parents abused me, and the only thing I ever had to look forward to was at five o'clock I could watch the Mickey Mouse Club." It profoundly affected me when she told me that story. All of a sudden I started to realize I had the ability to get some messages out, that people might be listening to me.

I am very grateful for some of my role models after I had my disability. One was Richard, who worked at the independent living center. He talked me into going back to school. I remember him telling me that I had three choices: I could get into commercials; I could start doing wheelchair pageants and make a job for myself doing that; or I could go back to college. I would never have gone back to college before that.

I remember doing a Barrier Awareness Day in Washington, D.C., that was a really neat event. The woman who put that together was phenomenal. She had severe muscular dystrophy. She was probably in her early 20s when she put this thing together. She got President Reagan to sign a National Barrier Awareness Day proclamation. She had half of Congress there. She had Jim Brady there and all the movie stars she could get. It was great. She was a really neat person, and that day was an eye-opening experience for a lot of people.

Disability is a subject that people don't want to talk or hear about. Some people have drawn an analogy between the disability movement and the civil rights movement. There were a lot of white people that went out and supported the civil rights movement knowing that they would never be black. Still, they supported that movement. It's really hard, though, to get people involved in disabilities. Since anybody can become disabled, it's very scary for people to think about. I think disability is an unpleasant subject because people know it could possibly happen to them or to someone they care about. I think it makes some people hesitant to support disability rights.

As a child, I remember being extremely put off by people with disabilities. I was never exposed to them. I didn't understand it. I was made to think disability was bad. I was taught, "Oh, don't look at that poor person," and "How sad that she has a disability." It was a totally negative thing. That's why I think mainstreaming is so great. One way to change attitudes is for nondisabled kids to grow up alongside people with disabilities. That way people won't be afraid of them or think of them as being different. I think we are becoming more mainstream, and that's good. Every time I go to the mall I run into six or seven people in wheelchairs, whereas I never saw people in wheelchairs when I was young.

With exposure, children handle disabilities well. Kids at work love me. I'm down at their level in my wheelchair. Kids like that. They jump up on my lap and they ask me all kinds of questions. Sometimes I joke with them and I say I'm just really lazy so I don't want to stand up and walk. Sometimes it's hard for a four-year-old to understand that my legs don't work, but I explain it anyway. I find that if I treat kids well, they're not going to think twice when they talk to someone else with a disability. They're just going to be totally comfortable with that person. I try to be really good to kids. I love to teach them about disability.

When I was first in a wheelchair, I was terrified that people were going to stare at me. I found people reacted in a completely opposite manner. People turn their eyes away from me; they won't look at me. It sounds strange, but I've gotten to the point now where I'll stare someone down to make them look at me. It's like I'm saying, "I'm here, I'm a person, I'm alive!" People seem so afraid that they don't want to look.

I think familiarity is really important. My nondisabled friends include me in everything, and they sometimes forget that I'm disabled. However, they are also very sensitive to the fact that I am in a wheelchair and plan accordingly. I like to be able to open people's eyes about disabilities. Unfortunately, there are those who will never ever have their eyes opened, no matter what.

When I wake up in the morning, I have to roll around in bed for 45 minutes just to get dressed. Because of my injury, I sometimes get all sweaty and I can't get cool. By the time I get to work in the morning, my hair is combed and my makeup is on and I'm dressed nicely, and people have no idea what it took to get ready. At my former job, some people complained, "Karen's been getting here five minutes late every day." I thought, "I'd like to strap your feet together, young lady, and have you get dressed. Then we'll see what time you get here." Ha, but I don't say those things because I'm too nice.

I'd like some people to sit in a wheelchair for a day and try to park the car in the driveway. I get really angry at that. For example, at my former job, I spoke to the entire staff at work about disability awareness. But I got really frustrated when people still parked in the driveway and I had to go on the grass. It's dangerous; I almost fell several times. I called and left notes for people, asking them, "Please do not park in the driveway," but sometimes people still parked there. I think that's extremely rude. They knew that was the only way I had to get into the building.

I've had other experiences too. Lots of people use disabled parking stalls. Sometimes people park so close to my car door that I can't get into the car because of my wheelchair. Sometimes people leave the parking space open but they park over the ramp. I've got a place to park but I can't get into the building anyway because I don't do well hopping curbs. I'll never forget the time I got out of an upstairs class late and someone had turned the elevator off. I was almost stuck in the building all night. Fortunately, some other students carried me down the stairs. (I think I gave somebody serious back problems.) I hate to think what would have happened if I used an electric wheelchair.

Most people don't think about those things because they don't know any better. It's just a lack of awareness. When I'm with another person with a disability, there's an understanding that goes beyond what someone without a disability would ever know. There's a lot more to disability than what the general public sees. We just share that understanding.

I feel like I became disabled at a good time because things are starting to change. We still have a long way to go, but things are a lot better than when I was a child. I believe things are different for people with disabilities now than they were back then. We have laws and are getting more opportunities.

If I were to offer advice to nondisabled people, I would say to treat a disabled person like a person, first. Second, try to learn as much about a person's disability as you can. For example, if they're in a wheelchair, sit down in a wheelchair and see what it feels like. Experience the wheelchair to some extent. People without disabilities have no idea what it's like with a disability.

Truly, having a disability has not been the horrible experience that people might think. There's some negative stuff that goes along with it like daily living skills, which are a pain. I also get nervous about getting older because things are not going to get easier. But I would not be where I am right now, personally or professionally, had it not been for this disability. I've got to say a lot of positive things have come from it. Because I had no place else to go, I had to get to know the real me.

I would never have met so many important people in my life had I not been disabled. There are so many great people with disabilities, yet a lot of people without disabilities don't even give them the time of day. But it's changing, I think. We're coming out of our closet.

Discussion Questions

1. What are some of the major issues in defining persons with physical disabilities?

2. How does a medical model orientation influence the definition and discussion of disability?

3. What are some of the advantages of defining a physical disability from a social model perspective?

4. Discuss in detail some of the primary issues facing all persons with physical disabilities.

5. What are some of the primary differences between those acquiring disabilities early in life and those who have acquired disabilities later in life?

6. Would knowledge of when a person with a physical disability acquired that disability influence professional assessment and plan of intervention?

Suggested Readings

Berger, L., Lithwick, D., and Campers, S. (1992). *I will sing life: Voices from the hole in the wall gang camp.* Boston: Little, Brown.

Crewe, N. M., and Zola, I. K. (1983). *Independent living for physically disabled people.* San Francisco: Jossey-Bass.

Nagler, M. (Ed.). (1993). *Perspectives on disability* (2nd ed.). Palo Alto, CA: Health Markets Research.

Noble, V. (1993). *Down is up for Aaron Eagle: A mother's spiritual journey with Down syndrome.* New York: HarperColllins.

Shapiro, J. P. (1993). *No pity: People with disabilities, forging a new civil rights movement.* New York: Times Books.

Wright, B. (1960). *Physical disability—a psychological approach.* New York: Harper & Row.

References

American Academy of Neurology. (1995). *Poliomyelitis and post polio syndrome* [www.aan.com]. Synapse Publishing.

Arthritis Foundation. (1987). *Rheumatoid arthritis* (2nd ed.). [www.vh.org]. Electric Differential Multimedia Lab.

Balcazar, Y., Bradford, B., and Fawcett, S. (1988). Common concerns of disabled Americans: Issues and options. In M. Nagler (Ed.), *Perspectives on disability* (pp. 3–12). Palo Alto, CA: Health Markets Research.

Bogdan, R., and Biklen, D. (1977). Handicapism. *Social Policy,* March/April, 14–19.

Chamberlain, J. (1988). *Understanding urinary tract infection.* Bethesda, MD: National Institute of Diabetes and Digestive and Kidney Diseases.

Cullity, M. (1998a). Judge gives Martin his ticket to ride. *Golfweek, 24*(7), 31.

Cullity, M. (1998b). Ruling sets up additional drama: Impact to be felt on tour, on other sports and in legal circles. *Golfweek, 24*(7), 31–35.

Fine, M., and Asch, A. (1988). Disability beyond stigma: Social interaction, discrimination, and activism. *Journal of Social Issues, 44*(1), 3–21.

Hahn, H. (1988). The politics of physical differences: Disability and discrimination. *Journal of Social Issues, 44*(1), 39–47.

Harris, L. (1986). *The ICD survey of disabled Americans: Bringing disabled Americans into the mainstream.* New York: Louis Harris and Associates.

Kennedy, D. (1996). *Dwarfism: Frequently asked questions* [www2.shore.net/~dkennedy/dwarfism_faq.html]. Little People of America.

Little People of America, Inc. (1998). *Introduction* [wwwbfs.ucsd.edu/dwarfism/intro.html].

National Organization for Rare Disorders, Inc. (1993a). *Achondroplasia.* In A. H. Bruckheim (Ed.), *The family doctor.* [CD-ROM]. Portland, OR: Creative Multimedia.

National Organization for Rare Disorders, Inc. (1993b). *Arthrogryposis multiplex congenita.* In A. H. Bruckheim (Ed.), *The family doctor.* [CD-ROM]. Portland, OR: Creative Multimedia.

National Organization for Rare Disorders, Inc. (1993c). *Cerebral palsy.* In A. H. Bruckheim (Ed.), *The family doctor.* [CD-ROM]. Portland, OR: Creative Multimedia.

National Organization for Rare Disorders, Inc. (1993d). *Diastrophic dysplasia.* In A. H. Bruckheim (Ed.), *The family doctor.* [CD-ROM]. Portland, OR: Creative Multimedia.

National Organization for Rare Disorders, Inc. (1993e). *Muscular dystrophy, Duchenne.* In A. H. Bruckheim (Ed.), *The family doctor.* [CD-ROM]. Portland, OR: Creative Multimedia.

National Organization for Rare Disorders, Inc. (1993f). *Myasthenia gravis.* In A. H. Bruckheim (Ed.), *The family doctor.* [CD-ROM]. Portland, OR: Creative Multimedia.

National Organization for Rare Disorders, Inc. (1993g). *Osteogenesis imperfecta.* In A. H. Bruckheim (Ed.), *The family doctor.* [CD-ROM]. Portland, OR: Creative Multimedia.

National Organization for Rare Disorders, Inc. (1993h). *Spina bifida.* In A. H. Bruckheim (Ed.), *The family doctor.* [CD-ROM]. Portland, OR: Creative Multimedia.

National Organization for Rare Disorders, Inc. (1993i). *Spondylo-epiphyseal dysplasia, congenital.* In A. H. Bruckheim (Ed.), *The family doctor.* [CD-ROM]. Portland, OR: Creative Multimedia.

National Organization for Rare Disorders, Inc. (1993j). *Stroke.* In A. H. Bruckheim (Ed.), *The family doctor.* [CD-ROM]. Portland, OR: Creative Multimedia.

Satcher, J., and Hendren, G. R. (1992). Employer agreement with the Americans with Disabilities Act of 1990: Implications for rehabilitation counseling. *Journal of Rehabilitation, 58*(3), 13–17.

Stanford University Medical Center. (1996). *Stroke awareness: Information for patients* [World Wide Web, Med Net].

Tierney, L. M., Jr., McPhee, S. J., and Papadakis, M. A. (Eds.). (1994). *Current medical diagnosis and treatment.* Norwalk, CT: Appleton & Lange.

Wilkins, S., and Cott, C. (1993). Aging, chronic illness and disability. In M. Nagler (Ed.), *Perspectives on disability* (2nd ed.) (pp. 363–376). Palo Alto, CA: Health Markets Research.

Winnick, J. P. (1995). *Adapted physical education and sport* (2nd ed.). Champaign, IL: Human Kinetics.

Wright, B. A. (1960). *Physical disability—A psychological approach.* New York: Harper & Row.

Wright, B. A. (1988). Attitudes and the fundamental negative bias: Conditions and corrections. In H. E. Yuker (Ed.), *Attitudes toward persons with disabilities* (pp. 3–21). New York: Springer.

Zink, J. (1992). Adjusting to early-and-late-onset disability: A personal perspective. *Generations, 16*(1), 59–61.

Chapter 6

DEAF AND HARD-OF-HEARING PEOPLE

When my parents and siblings saw what an important and positive transition I had made and how much signing had opened up for me, they all learned to sign, and communication in our family became much more effective and easier for all of us. I believe my parents were greatly relieved when they saw how much signing and my acculturation into the Deaf community had done for me.

—Martha Sheridan, Assistant Professor, Gallaudet University

Student Learning Objectives:

1. To be able to understand and contrast medical, social, and political definitions of being deaf and hard of hearing.
2. To compare how using different definitions of hearing loss leads people to reach different conclusions about the meaning of hearing loss in people's lives.
3. To identify elements of Deaf culture and how Deaf culture contrasts with mainstream American culture.
4. To identify the implications of being Deaf, deaf, and hard of hearing.
5. To understand the implications of prelingual and late onset hearing loss.

There are approximately 21 million deaf and hard-of-hearing people in the United States, constituting about 8.5% of the population. Of these, about 1.35 million are deaf. About 190,000 persons have prelingual deafness. Another 113,000 people became postlingually deaf as children and 1.05 million became deaf as adults (Reis, 1994; Schein, 1996). Hearing loss can be categorized into three types: conductive, sensorineural, and central. Mixed hearing loss has a combination of sensorineural and conductive components. Each of these can result in hearing disabilities ranging from mild hearing loss to profound deafness. Most deaf people have some residual hearing.

Conductive deafness occurs as a result of changes in the middle ear mechanisms that conduct sound. Middle ear infections and injury to the small bones of the middle ear are common causes. Hearing aids are used by people with conductive hearing loss and deafness who desire to enhance their ability to hear sounds and discriminate speech (Friedlander, 1996; Guyton, 1971; Jackler and Kaplan, 1990). *Sensorineural* deafness results from damage to the inner ear, specifically, the cochlea or auditory nerve. Many adults have sensorineural deafness as a result of congenital rubella. Infections and exposure to loud noises are other common causes. In addition, several genetic conditions lead to sensorineural hearing loss and account for deafness in most of the 10% of deaf children born to deaf parents. Hearing aids are generally ineffective in enhancing intelligible hearing for sensorineural deafness since they enhance sound but generally not speech discrimination. In recent years, cochlear implants have been used to enhance hearing for people with sensorineural deafness. Cochlear implants require surgery and have been extremely controversial in the deaf community because of surgical risks, disputed effectiveness, and concerns of people who are part of Deaf culture that cochlear implants fit the clinical, corrective view of deafness (Friedlander, 1996; Guyton, 1971; Jackler and Kaplan, 1990). *Central* deafness is relatively rare and occurs as a result of conditions involving the brain, such as multiple sclerosis, cerebrovascular disease, or tumors.

The age of onset of hearing disability is important. Prelingual and postlingual hearing loss are age-based terms, based on the acquisition of spoken language and coined before the acceptance of American Sign Language (ASL) as a language. *Prelingual* deafness is deafness that occurs prior to 3 years of age, the usual age of language acquisition. Prelingually deafened individuals do not become fluent in auditory language prior to their deafness. *Postlingually* deafened individuals experience hearing loss after acquiring spoken language, usually at 3 years of age or later. Spoken language is the first language for most persons with postlingual deafness. The later the onset of deafness, the greater the integration of spoken language. Visual/manual language that may be learned after the onset of deafness becomes a second language. Prelingually deafened individuals, especially those who are profoundly deaf, are likely to experience language visually and manually. The native language for many deaf individuals is ASL, which is unique and different from verbal languages. Even English and other vocal languages (e.g., Spanish, Japanese) are learned visually and manually by people who are deaf.

Zak (1996) suggests using two other terms in discussing language and deafness. *Nonlingual* deafness occurs when a deaf child does not acquire language (manual or spoken) at a normal developmental age. *Lingual* deafness occurs when a person, whether prelingually or postlingually deafened, develops language at a normal age. The important distinction is the timely development of language, whether spoken or manual.

The criteria used to define deafness and hearing disabilities are guided by the assumptions and beliefs of those so defining. Though deaf and hard-of-hearing people have traditionally been defined from an individual deficiency perspective, other more recent models have focused on cultural and political realities. Foster (1996) describes three models of understanding deafness. The *medical* model assumes deafness is caused by the failure of a critical sensory system, resulting in personal deficiencies. According to the medical model, people who are deaf need professionals to help them cope with their problems. The *social/cultural* model of deafness "can be best understood as a function of interaction between the individual and society" (p. 5). Barriers experienced by deaf persons result from social, language, and cultural differences between majority and minority groups. The *political* model of deafness focuses on the power differences between hearing and deaf persons. Sociopolitical institutions are controlled by hearing persons who impose their definitions of the meaning of deafness on deaf persons. As a result, deaf people must fight for their civil rights to overcome devaluation and oppression imposed by the dominant society.

In keeping with the emphasis of the book, this chapter focuses on the social and political conceptualizations of deafness. Certainly, hearing loss affects the roles of sound, hearing, and speech in people's lives; however, the sociocultural and political context in which people with hearing disabilities live greatly influences their quality of life. In addition, the chapter is primarily devoted to discussions of deafness and Deaf culture. We do this knowing that the hard of hearing outnumber those who are deaf. However, because the Deaf identity and civil rights movement has been so revolutionary, we believe this focus is essential to understanding the identity and civil rights movement for all people with disabilities.

◆ THE USE OF TERMINOLOGY

Terminology is an important ingredient in discussions on hearing disabilities. Whereas many persons with disabilities embrace "people first" language, many deaf people do not. Martha Sheridan (1997), a deaf social worker, articulates this view.

> *Using this language puts deafness and deaf people in a disability framework. Deaf people do not see themselves in that context and do not advocate that language for themselves. "People with deafness" is not an acceptable phrase. "Deaf people," "deaf" and "hard of hearing" are all acceptable. Deaf people view phrases such as "people with deafness" and people first language as a reflection of society's lack of acceptance of deafness. "I'm deaf, say it, there's nothing wrong with being deaf, I'm not some hot potato you have to be careful with."*

Janet Pray (1997), director of the social work program at Gallaudet University, echoes Sheridan's uneasiness with terms such as *hearing disabilities.* She also prefers the term *hearing loss* rather than *hearing impairment,* though she acknowledges controversy over its use. Language relative to deaf and hard-of-hearing people (as well as other devalued groups) is constantly evolving and potentially controversial. The language we use in this chapter, however, is an attempt to reflect terminology that is acceptable within the deaf and hard-of-hearing community.

Hard-of-hearing individuals are people with reduced hearing ability but who are not deaf. Schein (1996) defines *deafness* as "the common outcome of diverse causes resulting in an inability to hear *and* understand speech through the ear alone" (p. 22). Some people who are deaf can hear, but they do not understand speech through the ear alone. Some people with hearing loss choose to identify as deaf, whereas others with less hearing loss identify themselves as hard of hearing. Thus, *deaf* and *hard of hearing* are defined as much by how individuals define themselves as by the amount of their hearing loss.

◆ **Deaf Culture**

In 1965, Stokoe, Croneberg, and Casterline offered, in print, a unique view of deafness by emphasizing social and cultural characteristics of deaf people, particularly those who use ASL. In the generation since, Deaf people have redefined deafness in a number of ways. As we have noted, the traditional definition of deafness relates to a person who has an audiological impairment. In the generation since 1965, *deaf* and *Deaf* have taken on different meanings. In an anthology edited by Wilcox (1989), contributing authors differentiate between deaf and Deaf. The uppercase, Deaf, is used to describe Deaf people as a cultural group. The lowercase, deaf, refers to noncultural elements of deafness, such as medical conditions or proximity of residence. For example, Padden (1989) discusses the "deaf community" as consisting of hearing and deaf people as well as culturally Deaf people. Deaf communities, like other communities, experience frequent interactions and have common concerns. In contrast to *community,* members of the Deaf *culture* "behave as Deaf people do, use the language of Deaf people, and share the beliefs of Deaf people toward themselves and other people who are not deaf" (Padden, 1989, p. 5). People who may be part of a deaf community are hearing family and acquaintances of Deaf people and people who become deaf later in life but do not participate in Deaf culture.

The definition of who comprises Deaf culture varies. In the broadest definition (Pray, 1997), Deaf culture includes "all those who embrace ASL and other characteristics of Deaf culture, including hearing children of Deaf parents for whom ASL is the first language and others who use ASL as their primary language." Pray also states that the most narrow view of Deaf culture is "those who say the only 'true' members of Deaf culture are the 10% of Deaf who are from Deaf families." We use a broad view of Deaf culture in this book. This definition includes people who have become acculturated into Deaf culture.

Stokoe (1989) uses a 100-cell "map of culture" to present elements of culture and to contrast "mainstream American culture" (MAC) with "Deaf American culture" (DAC). He states that "the use of vision instead of hearing for getting vital and incidental information is the fundamental difference between MAC and DAC, and it shows up in every cell" of the cultural map (p. 55). Stokoe discusses how MAC has attempted to force Deaf people to act as if they hear. He discusses how deaf people who try to "pass" as hearing in an attempt to gain full membership in MAC often fail to achieve full membership in either MAC or DAC. He cites the fact that more than 90% of deaf people marry other deaf people. He acknowledges the sociopolitical discrepancies between Deaf and hearing, noting

> *Deaf Americans who marry one another, who form their own clubs and associations, and who interact largely with their own kind, are seen erroneously by some sociologists as Americans with a physical impairment, a disability, a handicap, who have not been able to achieve the full status accorded to hearing persons.* (p. 56)

Stokoe describes ways that Deaf Americans cope with life, using strategies common to all cultures. He asserts that the culture and lives of Deaf Americans are different but not inferior to mainstream Americans. Deaf Americans may be affected by societal actions and policies that define them as disabled (e.g., ADA, IDEA); however, they reject the disability label. This view is different from other disability advocates who embrace disability language and identity.

◆ LANGUAGE

Language development is a critical task for young children, which, in turn, leads to increasingly sophisticated cognitive skills. The use of language continues to produce significant controversy for deaf people. A primary conflict has been the use of oral versus manual language. One school of language acquisition for deaf people is the "oral" school. Oralists believe that the primary language to be learned by deaf people should be through lip reading (speechreading) and speech. Much emphasis is placed on learning oral English and pronouncing words verbally. Signed language is discouraged (or forbidden) while mastery of English is strongly emphasized. Proponents of oral language as a first language argue that deaf people need to function in a hearing world and, therefore, need to learn the language of the hearing population. One problem with deaf people relying on oral communication is that even the best speechreaders understand only about 40–60% of what is spoken. Therefore, people who rely on oral language can have significant difficulty becoming fluent with their primary language. This is especially critical in the first three to four years of life when people are most capable of learning language.

Some language methods use a combination of English-based oral language combined with facilitative signing. One such method, cued speech, relies primarily on oral language but uses hand shapes around the face to represent sounds not easily distinguished visually (e.g., "t" and "d"). People using cued speech rely on lip shapes and hand cues to send and receive oral messages.

Other language methods are signed English, pidgin signed English, signed essential English, and signed exact English. These methods rely on English; however, they primarily use manual rather than verbal communication. Signing English in its various forms is time consuming and can take about twice the time to communicate as oral English. These forms are not discrete languages but modifications of English; thus, people who learn these methods gain familiarity with the English language. However, they are not strictly English. For example, they may use components of American Sign Language and grammatical shortcuts. Since these communication methods are not languages, some claim they do not provide complete linguistic access (Zak, 1996). Some critics advocate that children learn ASL as a first language and variations of signed English as a second language.

Within American Deaf culture, American Sign Language is the language of choice. Unlike other signing systems, which are based on English, ASL is a discrete language, relying exclusively on visual and manual expression. ASL has unique syntax and structure separate from English. As a unique language, ASL is not understood by the vast majority of mainstream American culture (MAC); therefore, people who use ASL exclusively are limited in their ability to communicate with those who speak English or other verbal languages. Oftentimes, those for whom ASL is their native language will become competent in written and/or oral languages such as English as a second language. Within Deaf culture, however, ASL is *the* language of choice.

It is important to note that ASL is more than a way to communicate words. As a language, it is an influential component of Deaf culture and in shaping a Deaf world view. Humor expressed in Deaf culture using ASL can be incomprehensible to English speakers (Rutherford, 1989). The ways in which Deaf people greet each other, engage in conversations, and depart are different from those in MAC. For example, Hall (1989) states that in Deaf American culture (DAC), people are often very direct in "getting to the point" when talking with others, which can be interpreted by people from MAC as rude and abrupt. On the other hand, in MAC, saying good-bye is often done quickly, whereas in DAC, lingering good-byes are common. In MAC, when large groups of people are in a room, private conversations are common, with people speaking softly to one another. In DAC, private conversations are difficult to have because signed language is visual; thus, cloistered discussions can be considered rude.

Language development is extremely crucial for deaf and hard-of-hearing people, just as it is for hearing people. Language is essential as children develop cognitively and as they interact with the world. Many language acquisition methods have been developed for people with severe hearing loss. It is critical that people develop fluency in at least one language. Therefore, if the hearing loss is severe enough that fluency in English is not viable, it is prudent to provide children with a manual/visual language such as ASL over which they can develop mastery. Then, as a second or supplemental language, English or other verbally based languages can be learned to allow people to function well within the dominant hearing culture.

◆ FAMILY RELATIONSHIPS

Deaf and hard-of-hearing children experience the world differently than hearing children. For example, deaf infants do not rely on environmental sounds that signify the presence of another. They do not hear sounds of comfort from parents. Deaf infants respond to nonvocal parental behaviors rather than their verbalizations. They do not recognize or learn to listen to parents' voices. Hard-of-hearing children may respond inconsistently to parental and other environmental auditory stimuli, depending on the nature and severity of the hearing loss. The lack of auditory responsiveness characteristic of hearing infants and toddlers alerts many hearing parents of deaf and hard-of-hearing children that something is amiss (Marschark, 1993). Unsuspecting parents can experience distress and rejection due to the child's lack of reciprocity (Harris, 1978), prompting them to seek help that can result in the discovery of their child's hearing loss.

Families into which deaf children are born have much bearing on their early life experiences. For deaf children born to Deaf parents, deafness is the norm. The birth of a deaf or hard-of-hearing child is not a shock, as it is when deaf children are born to hearing parents who are usually ignorant of the needs of their child. Deaf parents are likely to communicate easily using visual language. They socialize their children based on their knowledge and personal experiences as Deaf people. They are aware of opportunities and obstacles their children face. Deaf parents are likely to have circles of friends who are deaf and may participate in communities comprised largely of other deaf people (Meadow-Orlans, 1996). Access to Deaf culture is common and deafness is the norm.

For some deaf parents, the birth of a deaf child is a cause for celebration. Some have even sought genetic counseling to ascertain their "risk" of having a hearing child. Other deaf parents, concerned with the societal barriers that severely limit opportunities for deaf children, prefer to have hearing children. This issue is complex; it is influenced by pride in Deaf culture and by the devaluation of deaf and hard-of-hearing people in society (Pray, 1997).

Only about 10% of deaf children are born to deaf parents. Most deaf and hard-of-hearing children are born into families in which their hearing loss is a shock. On average, children are about 15 to 16 months of age when diagnosed (Mace, Wallace, Whan, and Stelmachowicz, 1991; Meadow-Orlans, 1996). In reviewing research on deaf children, Lederberg (1993) found decreased social knowledge, delayed language acquisition, decreased parent-child interactions, increased family stress, and parental grieving. Family grief over a deaf child derives from the perception that deafness is a tragedy. Thus, chronic parental sorrow can result. Hearing parents most often have little or no experience with deafness or deaf people and can feel inadequate. Meadow-Orlans (1996) suggests that two problems arise for hearing parents when a child's deafness is diagnosed:

> First, they must cope with the shock of the presence of an unexpected handicap. Second, they must face the difficulties of socializing their child in the absence of a common—that is, a spoken—linguistic system. This is the central feature of the socialization of deaf children by hearing parents: the easy, effortless, communication of skills, values, rules, and games, taken for granted by other parents, is not available to these families. (p. 72)

Focusing on the social elements of deafness rather than on personal deficiencies is critical in the development of deaf infants and children. Parents who learn to focus on the social elements of deafness are equipped to raise their deaf children who do not hear. Rather than focusing exclusively on developing oral language so they can be more "normal," parents focusing on social elements find ways to communicate with their children. This may require that they learn a second language that relies on manual/visual communication—such as ASL. Hearing parents need to learn that their deaf children must see them to communicate. They can learn that nurturing and socialization for deaf and hard-of-hearing children is different, not inferior, to nurturing and socialization for hearing children.

There are many drawbacks to the deficiency-based view of deafness. Wood (1989) suggests that parents are more reluctant to give up control of deaf children than hearing children because they expect their children to be less capable of increased autonomy. This, in turn, leads to children's increased passivity and poor self-image. Lederberg (1993) emphasizes that when parents of deaf and hard-of-hearing children do not develop the ability to communicate and socialize with them, the children miss critical understanding of the social world. She also emphasizes that deaf children of hearing parents experience social and cultural deprivation when they are not exposed to Deaf role models and Deaf culture.

Whereas traditional research has focused on the problems and deficits that arise from hearing loss in childhood, attention is increasingly being given to normal parenting of deaf and hard-of-hearing children. Research focusing on children's needs rather than on problems can help parents develop parenting skills. For example, studies of deaf parents of deaf children show that they use touch to reinforce interaction, they make sure their infants are looking at them before interacting, and they use simplified sign language and mold their infants' fingers to form signing shapes (Erting, Prezioso, and Hynes, 1990; Spencer, Bodner-Johnson, and Gutfreund, 1992). Parents who are aware of these strategies can help children develop communication skills very early in life. More strengths-based research is important in understanding the specific needs and skills involved in parenting children with hearing loss.

Research that attends to social issues rather than focusing on individual deficiencies can help parents and others know how to remove social barriers that impede deaf and hard-of-hearing children. Full development of young children can be enhanced in several ways. All children need parents and others who can communicate with them. This often requires parents of deaf and hard-of-hearing children to learn ASL. In addition, parents can be aware of their children's rights and help remove obstacles that limit those rights.

Views of deaf and hard-of-hearing people as less competent than others are stereotypical and inaccurate. Deaf and hard-of-hearing children may develop competence in alternate ways that are not inferior to others. Infants and toddlers may not respond to auditory cues, but they do respond to visual and tactile stimulation. Social development of deaf and hard-of-hearing children and youth is enhanced by exposure to peers, role models, and, for some, Deaf culture. Parents can create environments to help their deaf and hard-of-hearing children fully develop socially, emotionally, and intellectually.

◆ EDUCATION

Schools have had a significant influence on deaf and hard-of-hearing children for generations. Twenty years ago, large numbers of children with hearing disabilities were educated in residential schools for the deaf, sometimes far from home. A 1976 national study by Karchmer and Trybus (1977) of nearly 50,000 school-aged deaf children revealed that 38% were in residential schools, 11% were in day schools for the deaf, 22% used full-time special education classrooms, 19% used resource rooms, and 10% were in other programs. The study's authors found that people with more severe hearing loss tended to reside in residential schools, with 59% of "profoundly deaf" subjects and 41% of "severely deaf" subjects attending these schools. They also noted that the proportion of deaf students who used residential schools had decreased in the years prior to their study. The 1976 passage of PL 94–142, the Equal Education for All Handicapped Children Act, and the 1986 passage of PL 99-457, now known as IDEA (Individuals with Disabilities Education Act), have forced public schools to take responsibility for educating children with disabilities. Subsequently, the proportion of deaf and hard-of-hearing children living at home and being educated in neighborhood schools has increased, and enrollment at residential schools has decreased dramatically (Calderon and Greenberg, 1993; Meadow-Orlans, 1996; Moores, 1987).

For generations of deaf people, residential schools became "home and family" from early childhood. Children in residential schools had two families—their biological families and their school families. Many others were educated in day schools devoted exclusively to deaf people. These special programs have had many effects. Residential programs segregate deaf people from hearing people. Some believe that academic standards are lower in deaf-exclusive programs. Separation from hearing people can hamper speechreading and speech skills. Social isolation from the mainstream also occurs. In addition, residential schools produce long-term separation from biological families (Calderon and Greenberg, 1993; Meadow-Orlans, 1996; Moores, 1987), who have less influence, teaching, and ability to nurture the children from whom they are separated.

Residential schools, on the other hand, have created many opportunities within the deaf community. Students have been raised in school communities of people like themselves, rather than as different and isolated individuals in hearing communities. Deafness is the norm rather than an aberration. Younger deaf children have had role models in deaf adults and older deaf children. They have not had to face the language and communication barriers students face in schools made up of primarily oral English users. Learning environments using ASL can also help students achieve at levels beyond what they do in mainstream inclusion programs (Pray, 1997).

Within programs devoted exclusively to deaf people, a culture of deafness has developed over the years. This culture has been built upon language, shared experiences, and sense of identity. As deaf children have grown up, they have established lifelong friendships and a world of Deaf culture. Deaf clubs have provided opportunities for further Deaf culture, and national associations for Deaf people have given them political voice. Relationships that preserve and enhance Deaf people as a diverse group have flourished.

Ironically, deaf schools have had the exact effect that was most feared by people such as Alexander Graham Bell, who a century ago was touted in hearing society as a champion of deaf people. Bell and other deaf "experts" of the day believed in eugenics. Though we know today that only 10% of deafness is hereditary (Pray, 1997), Bell and his contemporaries advocated that intermarriage of deaf persons be forbidden to prevent the perpetuation of a defective race of people. He had a profound influence on the denigration of signing that has had lasting effects. As Shapiro (1993) states,

> *For ninety years after the 1880 Milan conference the use of sign language was banned from American schools. Students who disobeyed got their hands slapped or tied down. Deaf teachers—who by 1869 totaled 41 percent of instructors of the deaf—were driven from the classroom. By the turn of the century, that percentage had dropped to 25 percent and to only 12 percent by 1960.* (p. 95)

Though Deaf students who learned ASL were as literate as hearing people in the 1850s, Bell's contemporaries insisted on teaching oralism exclusively and eradicating Deaf culture and ASL. However, despite the efforts of the "experts," most of whom were hearing, ASL was not eradicated in favor of oralism. Deaf people preserved language, and in recent years Deaf culture has flourished. In part, this is attributable to residential schools and other programs that have brought Deaf people into intimate contact with each other.

Today, one of the largest social and political controversies in the deaf community and about deaf people is the proper forum for the education of deaf people. Cohen (1994) outlines the influences of public policies and summarizes some of the concerns relative to the diminishing numbers of students attending specialized schools:

> *Confusing equality with sameness, they believe in doing away with special schools and educating all children together. How, then, to explain that their interpretation of the law may sever deaf children from a culture that offers them strength? Deaf people, unlike members of other disabled groups, have their own language. They have their own social clubs, their own theater companies and television programs, their own university, their own periodicals, and their own international Olympics. Unlike members of ethnic minority groups, they do not receive their culture through their parents. Cultural transmission, formally and informally, has been carried out by schools for the deaf.* (p. 55)

Ironically, traditions that can be most oppressive to many groups—segregation, removing people from families, and institutionalization—have been essential components in developing and fostering a rich Deaf culture and heritage. Conversely, civil rights laws for persons with disabilities, while providing increased opportunities for people with disabilities, are also affecting deaf and hard-of-hearing people in ways that many consider destructive to Deaf culture (e.g., educating fewer students in deaf schools).

◆ HEARING FAMILIES OF DEAF CHILDREN

Many factors converge to influence the relationships of deaf children with their families. More and more, deaf children are raised with their hearing families. Increased familial stress, altered parent-child relationships, and other difficulties have been documented when deaf children are born to hearing parents (Calderon and Greenberg, 1993). However, changing attitudes about deafness can mitigate negative consequences. If deafness is not perceived as a tragedy, having a deaf child is not perceived as devastating. Recent research demonstrates that language, cognitive, and educational deficits in deaf children "can most likely be attributed to limitations in the availability for deaf children of learning opportunities that allow fully for their hearing loss" (Nelson, Loncke, and Camarata, 1993, p. 124). Fortunately, past attitudes are being replaced by enlightened knowledge that deaf children are not multiply deficient. Access to manual language such as ASL allows parents to learn a second language and to communicate effectively with their young children. Social and learning strategies are available to meet the needs of deaf children rather than forcing children into hearing modalities that can be extremely limiting.

Though lack of knowledge of children's hearing disabilities for the first months of their lives can negatively affect early development and attachments, research with deaf children of deaf parents indicates that hearing loss itself is not the source of decreased interactions and lack of bonding, language acquisition, and cognitive development. When parents of deaf and hard-of-hearing children are sensitive to their children's needs, attachments and relationships are of high quality. Early intervention programs for parents that include language training, counseling, and contact with other deaf and hard-of-hearing people can be critical to providing parents with the knowledge and skills to communicate with, bond with, and nurture their children (Bonvillian and Folven, 1993; Lederberg, 1993).

With increased numbers of deaf children being raised in family homes rather than residential schools, parents and families are exerting an influence greater than ever on a new generation of deaf children. Parents who become bilingual in signed and spoken language create nurturing atmospheres for their children. Parental involvement in the child's school and community environments can positively influence the child's education and socialization (Sheridan, 1997). Parents may need support and education from deaf people, professionals, and others. This support will help them navigate through bureaucracies and systems to ensure access to opportunities for their children.

Parents and students may become advocates with teachers and school administrators in integrated schools. The responsibility to dispel the myths that deaf people are academically and socially inferior often falls to parents. Parents must also take on the role of advocates for accessible learning environments. Ongoing parental involvement may be critical to ensure a goodness of fit between learning needs and the resources allocated to meet those needs.

Parents have become more involved in the lives of their deaf and hard-of-hearing children than in the past. They have more opportunities to transmit their values and culture to their children. Involvement of the larger deaf community varies with families based on various factors, including proximity and access to other deaf people and family attitudes. Parents must balance the various influences in rearing children and youth. However, parents have better access to positive images of deaf people and deaf role models. Greater opportunities also present the necessity of balancing various family, community, and cultural involvement and identities for their children.

◆ MULTICULTURALISM

In recent years, ASL has gained acceptance as a distinct language and Deaf culture is thriving. Within the deaf community, there are widely differing beliefs about relationships with the hearing world. Some call for Deaf separatism, essentially disengaging from hearing culture. Others advocate for assimilation into the hearing world. A multicultural view seems the most rational approach for Deaf people in American society. Humphries, Martin, and Coye (1989) argue for a bilingual, bicultural approach to teaching English to Deaf people:

> We believe that ASL can and does have, for many deaf people, the same function English has for English speakers: the capacity to transmit a culture, a way of life, and happiness. We know that English can add to this happiness. . . . (p. 123)

A bicultural approach acknowledges the importance of Deaf culture and ASL. This approach may be especially important as deaf people are increasingly involved in MAC. For example, the widespread placement of deaf and hard-of-hearing students in public schools can cause deaf students to experience isolation, especially when there are communication problems (Stinson and Kluwin, 1993). Discrepancies between hearing and deaf people in education, occupational attainment, and income (Barnartt and Christiansen, 1996) may also be reduced with increased biculturalism and bilingualism.

It is a reality that deaf people are a small minority and that societal structures and institutions are controlled by a hearing majority. In order for most Deaf people to gain full access to MAC, knowledge of English and MAC is critical. Conversely, increased access to telecommunications such as TTYs and closed-captioned television programming are providing new opportunities. Passage of the Americans with Disabilities Act has opened opportunities in higher education. Opportunities for integrating deaf and hearing worlds are great.

Multiculturalism honors the roots of an individual's culture while acknowledging the intersections with the larger society. This is true for Deaf people as well as other cultural groups. Being from an ethnic background *and* being deaf can complicate things. In a work edited by Christensen and Delgado (1993), the complications for people who are deaf and from different countries and ethnic backgrounds are discussed. For example, Hispanic deaf people in the United States may be forced to deal with two oral languages, English and Spanish, as well as ASL. Deaf people immigrating from England may need to learn ASL in addition to British Sign Language. As the amount of diversity increases, so do the intricacies of promoting multiculturalism.

◆ Hard-of-Hearing Persons

Much of this chapter has focused on Deaf culture and identity. However, Deaf people are the minority in the total population of deaf and hard-of-hearing people. The majority of people with hearing loss self-identify as hard of hearing rather than deaf. We believe it is important that deaf and hard-of-hearing people be identified based on social rather than audiological definitions. In general, Deaf people identify themselves as deaf; conversely, deaf and hard-of-hearing people who use spoken language or use their hearing in everyday life have a stronger identity with the hearing community. In reality, some people who identify as Deaf have greater hearing capacities than people who identify as hard of hearing.

Hard-of-hearing people function with the hearing world as their primary identity group. They often use hearing aids to facilitate improved hearing. They use telephones, often with enhanced amplification. Spoken languge is the first language for hard-of-hearing people. To communicate, they may rely on a combination of hearing, speechreading, and other visual cues. Their expressed language is also generally spoken. Visual and manual language (e.g., ASL) may be learned to supplement communication but not as a primary language.

Early developmental issues for hard-of-hearing children are similar to deaf infants and children. They are less stimulated by auditory stimuli than hearing children. Parents may need to place emphasis on visual and tactile, more than auditory, stimulation. Mechanical devices such as hearing aids are important to help hard-of-hearing children develop language and interact with hearing parents, peers, and others.

Hard-of-hearing children can find themselves in an "in-between" world in which they do not fit into Deaf culture, yet much of the hearing world is not accessible to them. People who are hard of hearing are more likely to feel socially isolated than hearing peers. They may also find only partial acceptance in the Deaf world. Interestingly, social opportunities and the richness of Deaf identity motivate some hard-of-hearing people to immerse themselves in Deaf culture even though they have the physical hearing capabilities for the hearing world. Achieving fluency in ASL helps them achieve membership. Others—even some with severe hearing loss—prefer to identify primarily in the hearing community.

Hard-of-hearing people are more likely than Deaf people to view deafness as a loss. People immersed in Deaf culture are on an even par with others in their culture, whereas hard-of-hearing people who live in and identify with the hearing community are different and disadvantaged in their community of choice. Technology can be extremely important to provide them with access to education, socialization, and work. For example, hearing aids have been miniaturized, and their quality has greatly increased.

With expanded mainstreaming, more deaf and hard-of-hearing people are being educated in public, mainstream schools than ever before. Residential placement has decreased markedly, and everyday involvement in the hearing community has increased. This may add to the numbers of people who identify as hard of hearing rather than Deaf. Technological advances, greater civil rights, and positive attitudes about people with disabilities are leading to increased opportunities for hard-of-hearing people. Heightened attention to the needs of hard-of-hearing people is critical to understanding them as a diverse group in a pluralistic society.

◆ LATE ONSET DEAFNESS

Late onset or postlingual deafness refers to the occurrence of deafness after spoken language is developed. English or another spoken language is the primary language for postlingually deafened persons. For this population, early childhood language and cognitive orientation is based on spoken language. The earlier the onset of deafness, the more likely people are to assume a deaf identity. Young children with acquired deafness become involved in language training at an early age. Their exposure to other deaf children is increased. Given the chance to learn ASL, they have greater opportunities to become bilingual and bicultural. The greater the exposure to deaf people and culture, the more likely they are to identify strongly with the deaf community.

People who become deaf in adolescence and adulthood are more likely to retain their identity in the hearing community. Spoken language is deeply ingrained in their identities. Their language and cognitive development has occurred in a hearing context. Oral language continues to be the primary language for these people. Signed language based on English may be easier to learn and may be preferable to ASL.

Postlingually deafened individuals experience loss and grieving that people with prelingual deafness who identify with Deaf culture may not experience. They feel a sense of loss of something they once had that now is gone. Though most continue to communicate orally, comprehension is diminished. Although they can no longer hear conversations, hearing people may assume they hear because they can speak.

Environmental sounds such as music, doorbells, and telephone conversations are diminished or lost. The way they organize their world changes significantly. TTYs may replace telephones. Oral conversations are more deliberate and may require written messages. Closed-captioned televisions may become necessary.

People who experience hearing loss later in life may need time and resources to adjust to their loss. Their emphasis in coping may be geared primarily to coping in a hearing world in spite of hearing loss rather than immersing themselves in the deaf community and Deaf culture. They need to learn to compensate and adjust to the change in their lives. Technology and legal protections to promote quality of life are more available than ever before.

◆ SUMMARY

Though a small number of people in the United States are deaf, Deaf people have been a major influence in the civil rights movement for people with disabilities.

The development of Deaf culture and Deaf pride have redefined deafness from a cause for the practice of eugenics to a diverse life condition. Increasingly, deafness is defined according to social and political definitions.

There is great diversity among deaf and hard-of-hearing people. Deaf activists have contributed greatly to a strong Deaf culture; however, large numbers of deaf and hard-of-hearing people do not identify themselves as members of Deaf culture. There are opportunities to participate in society, whether Deaf, hearing, or bicultural. For some, deafness is a great source of pride and identity. For others, it means that they must make adaptations to function as a person with a hearing disability in a hearing world. In understanding people who are deaf and hard of hearing, it is critical to understand what hearing loss means to the individual. In the hearing community, it is important that the meaning of deafness change from a condition of deficiency to an attribute of diversity.

◆ ◆ ◆ *Personal Narrative: Martha Sheridan*

Martha Sheridan, who became deaf as a child, is a social work professor at Gallaudet University. She is an active member of the Deaf community and a mentor to deaf and hard-of-hearing students.

Writing about my childhood experiences as a deaf child in a hearing world is difficult for me to do. This is because it presents certain educational and social truths about my early life that were painful at the time and represented the "clinical" perspective on deafness. As I grew and learned more about myself as a d/Deaf person and about my options, I chose a new path, became acculturated within the Deaf community, and adopted a cultural perspective for myself (progressing from "deaf" to "Deaf"). That journey has been quite transcending and empowering for me. Writing this is also difficult because I tend to want to protect my parents, whom I love, from those earlier truths.

In addition, I don't want to imply that my story is representative of every other d/Deaf or hard-of-hearing person. Each person's story should be viewed in the context of the individual variables that exist in their lives. There is much diversity among people who are d/Deaf and hard of hearing and much to be learned from the variety of life experiences that d/Deaf and hard-of-hearing people have. For example, my life experiences would have been altered greatly had I been profoundly deaf from birth, had a nondeteriorating hearing loss, attended a deaf education program from early childhood on, used ASL as my first language, or had Deaf parents. Not every d/Deaf or hard-of-hearing adult would say their early educational and social experiences were painful. Some may have had the goodness of fit early in their educational experiences that I did not have.

Being the first in my family to be deaf, I began, with my parents, a slow and long winding search that would last from early childhood through adolescence before we found the answers we needed. I grew up from the 1950s through the early 1970s when technology such as closed-captioned television and e-mail, as well as professional and legislative advancements such as the interpreting profession, IDEA, 504, and ADA, did not exist. Hearing aids were bulky, awkward, and very visible devices, and TTYs were just being developed and were not commonly known. Historically speaking, the state of education for deaf children was undergoing a heated debate, and all of the professionals my parents met advised against my learning to sign or transferring to a deaf education program. It was not until I was a sophomore in high school that they were advised to consider a deaf education program for the social benefits.

Another important variable in my story is that while I became deaf in early childhood, the severity of my deafness increased throughout those years from onset at age 3 to profound at age 13 (approximately an 85-decibel loss) to what is now a 120+-decibel hearing loss, and I no longer use or benefit from hearing aids as I did in childhood and young adulthood.

Having a deteriorating hearing loss meant that my communication, social, and educational needs were constantly changing throughout my life. This variable and others (the hearing status of my family members and my upbringing in hearing schools) influenced my constantly changing self-image.

Looking back, I remember the struggles and challenges to achieve academically when I was the only deaf child in a hearing elementary school and had no communication supports (no interpreters, no closed captioning for films, no signing teachers, no special education resource personnel, no note takers). I saw myself fail test after test and did not understand why; no matter how hard I tried, I couldn't seem to get good grades like my classmates.

I remember being in a class of 60 students in the first grade before my hearing loss was officially diagnosed and being punished for not following the instructions I did not hear. I remember being humiliated in front of my peers when a teacher forced me to stand up in front of class until I could understand (through lip reading) what a classmate was saying. I remember not "fitting in" and not understanding why. I remember a feeling of failure.

Things changed a bit when I finally repeated the fifth grade. With this, I began to achieve a much higher GPA. It was then that I discovered I was actually an intelligent person who could enjoy school and high academic achievements. I had known that I was different from my classmates but wrongly attributed this difference to intellectual inability. The lack of educational supports available to me had not only given me a dangerously false perception of myself, it had also contributed to an extended period of educational underachievement.

Yes, I considered myself different from the other children. In truth, we were different, but the unfortunate thing was that I misunderstood that difference, as did my peers and many of my teachers. Having d/Deaf peers and d/Deaf adult role models and communication supports could have prevented that.

Many things changed when I attended Gallaudet University in Washington, D.C. At Gallaudet, I finally learned American Sign Language, which I had wanted to learn since age 11 when I began to wonder if perhaps my "fit" was with other d/Deaf children. At Gallaudet, I met my peers and learned what it means to be deaf in the context of both Deaf and hearing communities. There I also learned about, and had the opportunity to begin using, the various technologies available (TTYs, flashing alarm clocks, door and phone lights) and experienced all of the joys of an accessible environment. At last, I could understand my teachers and peers in a signing environment. Gallaudet and the Deaf community helped me to discover the person I really was and to discard that old image of myself as a failure. At Gallaudet, I discovered the tools I needed to continue to achieve.

When my parents and siblings saw what an important and positive transition I had made and how much signing had opened up for me, they all learned to sign, and communication in our family became much more effective and easier for all of us. I believe my parents were greatly relieved when they saw how much signing and my acculturation into the Deaf community had done for me.

At Gallaudet, I majored in social work and went on to acquire an M.S.W. at the University of Maryland and a Ph.D. in social work from Ohio State University in 1996. My career focus has been generalist social work practice with people who are Deaf, deaf, and hard of hearing and people with disabilities. I believe my career also represents a goodness of fit in that I have never had a problem getting a job.

As a child and now as a mother, my role model was my own mother. In high school, that expanded to include hearing friends of mine who were highly accomplished. Since that time, my role models have included my peers, particularly women, who are also d/Deaf, who are successful in their careers and as mothers. As a child or adolescent, I had no visible role models in women who were d/Deaf.

Yes, I have developed an identity as a Deaf person. I went from being a child in a hearing school who "had trouble hearing," felt I was different, and just couldn't seem to succeed in school and not understanding what being deaf meant or even that I was in fact "deaf," to readily identifying myself as Deaf, understanding what that means to me and others; and I embrace it comfortably.

As an adult, being Deaf has become a central and very positive aspect of my life. Although I still run into barriers, I now know what my rights and responsibilities are and how to use them effectively. I still have to struggle to get hospitals, doctors, and public accommodations to provide interpreters but usually succeed in those efforts. On the spiritual side, I grew up Catholic and have faced many barriers to participation in the church, as I know other people with disabilities have. I would like to see that change. Even though laws against discrimination do not include religious organizations, it is a moral and ethical responsibility that the church has to its members.

The things in life that contributed to my success include having a loving family that encouraged my postsecondary endeavors, attending Gallaudet University, learning to sign, and adopting a Deaf identity. Perhaps the most basic psychological aspects of this were those moments of epiphany and initial academic successes from the fifth grade on when I realized that I was an intelligent person and I discovered I thoroughly enjoyed this newfound academic mastery. I also had successes in nonacademic areas such as dance and athletics, which helped me develop a sense of achievement. My early educational experiences were my biggest obstacle—a huge struggle and painful to recall. I was fortunate to have found my way through that to Gallaudet and beyond. I would not advocate those early experiences in a hearing school without proper communication and education supports for any other deaf child. Once I found my way through that early childhood maze, my later educational achievements became an empowering tool.

Professionally, I have worked as a direct service provider, macro-level change agent, and administrator in a variety of settings, including schools, community mental health agencies, and social service agencies. I've been fortunate to be in positions where I have been able to influence change in service systems and in social work education programs. The current joys in my life are my husband and son and my position on the faculty in the Department of Social Work at Gallaudet University.

On the macro level, I believe that laws such as the Rehabilitation Act of 1973 and the Americans with Disabilities Act have been tools that people with disabilities have been able to use successfully. However, I think we are only beginning to see the positive results of these laws. There is much more to come. As awareness and access increase, people with disabilities will become increasingly visible. These laws would not have come about without the successful self-advocacy efforts of people with disabilities, and they will only continue to effect change in the same manner. Although it is important to know and understand your own disability and rights as a person with a disability, it is also important to know and understand how to effect change on the macro level. Skills in community organizing, grant writing, and research are important for social workers with disabilities or for those who work with people with disabilities to have.

Discussion Questions

1. What are prelingual, postlingual, lingual, and nonlingual deafness?

2. How does a medical definition of deafness compare to and contrast with social and political definitions of deafness?

3. What are the elements of Deaf culture? How does Deaf culture compare to ethnic culture?

4. What are the social, cognitive, and emotional differences between being born deaf and becoming deaf as an adult?

5. What are the positive and negative consequences of disability civil rights legislation of recent years on deaf and hard-of-hearing people?

6. What are the social implications of being hard of hearing or deaf? Of being Deaf?

Suggested Readings

Christensen, K. M., and Delgado, G. L. (1993). *Multicultural issues in deafness.* White Plains, NY: Longman.

Cohen, L. H. (1994). *Train go sorry: Inside a deaf world.* New York: Houghton Mifflin.

Higgins, P. C., and Nash, J. E. (1996). *Understanding deafness socially: Continuities in research and theory.* Springfield, IL: Charles C Thomas.

Marschark, M., and Clark, M. D. (1993). *Psychological perspectives on deafness.* Hillsdale, NJ: Lawrence Erlbaum.

References

Barnartt, S. N., and Christiansen, J. B. (1996). The educational and occupational attainment of prevocationally deaf adults: 1972–1991. In P. C. Higgins and J. E. Nash (Eds.), *Understanding deafness socially: Continuities in research and theory* (pp. 60–70). Springfield, IL: Charles C Thomas.

Bonvillian, J. D., and Folven, R. J. (1993). Sign language acquisition: Developmental aspects. In M. Marschark and M. D. Clark (Eds.), *Psychological perspectives on deafness* (pp. 229–265). Hillsdale, NJ: Lawrence Erlbaum.

Calderon, R., and Greenberg, M. T. (1993). Considerations in the adaptation of families with school-aged children. In M. Marschark and M. D. Clark (Eds.), *Psychological perspectives on deafness* (pp. 27–48). Hillsdale, NJ: Lawrence Erlbaum.

Christensen, K. M., and Delgado, G. L. (1993). *Multicultural issues in deafness.* White Plains, NY: Longman.

Cohen, L. H. (1994). *Train go sorry: Inside a deaf world.* New York: Houghton Mifflin.

Erting, C. J., Prezioso, C., and Hynes, M. O. (1990). The interactional context of deaf mother-infant communication. In V. Volterra and C. J. Erting (Eds.), *From gesture to language in hearing and deaf children* (pp. 97–106). Berlin: Springer-Verlag.

Foster, S. (1996). Doing research in deafness: Some considerations and strategies. In P. C. Higgins and J. E. Nash (Eds.), *Understanding deafness socially: Continuities in research and theory.* Springfield, IL: Charles C Thomas.

Friedlander, E. (1996). *Diseases of the ear* [worldmall.com/erf/lectures/earpath.html].

Guyton, A. C. (1971). *Textbook of medical physiology* (4th ed.). Philadelphia: W. B. Saunders.

Hall, S. (1989). Train-gone-sorry: The etiquette of social conversations in American Sign Language. In S. Wilcox (Ed.), *American deaf culture: An anthology* (pp. 89–102). Burtonsville, MD: Linstock.

Harris, R. Y. (1978). Impulse control in deaf children: Research and clinical issues. In L. S. Liven (Ed.), *Deaf children: Developmental perspectives* (pp. 137–156). New York: Columbia University Press.

Humphries, T., Martin, B., and Coye, T. (1989). A bilingual, bicultural approach to teaching English (how two hearies and a deafie got together to teach English). In S. Wilcox (Ed.), *American deaf culture: An anthology* (pp. 121–143). Burtonsville, MD: Linstock.

Jackler, R. K., and Kaplan, M. J. (1990). Ear, nose and throat. In S. A. Schroeder, M. A. Krupp, L. M Tierney, and S. J. McPhee (Eds.), *Current medical diagnosis and treatment* (pp. 124–150). Englewood Cliffs, NJ: Prentice Hall.

Karchmer, M. A., and Trybus, R. J. (1977). *Who are the deaf children in "mainstream" programs?* Washington, DC: Gallaudet College Press.

Lederberg, A. R. (1993). The impact of deafness on mother-child and peer relationships. In M. Marschark and M. D. Clark (Eds.), *Psychological perspectives on deafness.* Hillsdale, NJ: Lawrence Erlbaum.

Mace, A. L., Wallace, K. L., Whan, M. Q., and Stelmachowicz, P. G. (1991). Relevant factors in the identification of hearing loss. *Ear and Hearing, 12,* 287–293.

Marschark, M. (1993). Origins and interactions in social, cognitive, and language development of deaf children. In M. Marschark and M. D. Clark (Eds.), *Psychological perspectives on deafness* (pp. 7–26). Hillsdale, NJ: Lawrence Erlbaum.

Meadow-Orlans, K. P. (1996). Socialization of deaf children and youth. In P. C. Higgins and J. E. Nash (Eds.), *Understanding deafness socially: Continuities in research and theory* (pp. 60–70). Springfield, IL: Charles C Thomas.

Moores, D. F. (1987). *Educating the deaf: Psychology, principles and practices.* Boston: Houghton Mifflin.

Nelson, K. E., Loncke, F., and Camarata, S. (1993). Implications of research on deaf and hearing children's language learning. In M. Marschark and M. D. Clark (Eds.), *Psychological perspectives on deafness* (pp. 123–151). Hillsdale, NJ: Lawrence Erlbaum.

Padden, C. (1989). The deaf community and the culture of deaf people. In S. Wilcox (Ed.), *American deaf culture: An anthology* (pp. 1–16). Burtonsville, MD: Linstock.

Pray, J. L. (1997). Personal correspondence. March 16.

Reis, P. W. (1994). Prevalence and characteristics of persons with hearing trouble: United States, 1990–91. *Vital and Health Statistics*, Series 10, No. 188.

Rutherford, S. D. (1989). Funny in deaf—not in hearing. In S. Wilcox (Ed.), *American deaf culture: An anthology* (pp. 65–81). Burtonsville, MD: Linstock.

Schein, J. D. (1996). The demography of deafness. In P. C. Higgins and J. E. Nash (Eds.), *Understanding deafness socially: Continuities in research and theory* (pp. 21–43). Springfield, IL: Charles C Thomas.

Shapiro, J. P. (1993). *No pity: People with disabilities, forging a new civil rights movement.* New York: Times Books.

Sheridan, M. (1997). Personal correspondence. March 22.

Spencer, P. E., Bodner-Johnson, B. A., and Gutfreund, M. K. (1992). Interacting with infants with a hearing loss: What can we learn from mothers who are deaf? *Journal of Early Intervention. 16,* 64–78.

Stinson, M. S., and Kluwin, T. N. (1993). Social orientations toward deaf and hearing peers among deaf adolescents in local public high schools. In M. Marschark and M. D. Clark (Eds.), *Psychological perspectives on deafness* (pp. 113–134). Hillsdale, NJ: Lawrence Erlbaum.

Stokoe, W. (1989). Dimensions of difference: ASL and English based cultures. In S. Wilcox (Ed.), *American deaf culture: An anthology* (pp. 49–59). Burtonsville, MD: Linstock.

Stokoe, W. C., Croneberg, C., and Casterline, D. (1965). *Dictionary of American Sign Language* (2nd ed.). Washington, DC: Gallaudet College Press.

Wilcox, S. (1989) *American deaf culture: An anthology.* Burtonsville, MD: Linstock.

Wood, D. (1989). Social interaction and tutoring. In M. H. Bernstein and J. S. Bruner (Eds.), *Interaction in human development* (pp. 59–80). Hillsdale, NJ: Lawrence Erlbaum.

Zak, O. (1996). Zak's politically incorrect glossary [www.weizmann.ac.il/deaf-info/zpig.html]. July 13.

Chapter 7

PERSONS WITH VISUAL
DISABILITIES AND BLINDNESS

*The first time I remember understanding that my vision was differ-
ent from other people was in the second or third grade when I
realized other students could read the blackboard. Before then, I
couldn't understand why the teacher would bother to write on the
board. When it dawned on me that other kids could read the board
and I couldn't, it was one of those "aha" moments of life. It was a
new discovery. I knew I was different on some level because I was
in special education classes, but I hadn't known that it was because
I saw differently than others.*

—Brenda Premo, Director, California Department of Rehabilitation, Sacramento,
California

Student Learning Objectives:

1. To understand issues around defining blind and visually impaired disabilities.

2. To understand the many consequences of social stigma, stereotyping, and prejudice around persons who are blind and visually impaired.

3. To understand that persons who are blind and visually impaired are limited only
by society's preconceptions of their abilities or lack of them.

4. To understand the difference of opinion within the blind community regarding
preferential treatment.

5. To understand some of the unique problems of persons who are both deaf and
blind.

◆ DEFINITION

Stroman (1982) offers insight into the various nuances of the task of defining blindness and visual impairment. Traditionally, the medical model has served as the basis
for defining blindness. The origins of the medical model definition go back to at
least 1868. Dr. Herman Snellen developed the "eye-test" chart used today by most
ophthalmologists and optometrists. Based on nine lines of letters, visual acuity is
determined as a fraction based on what a "normal" eye can see at 20 feet. Thus
20/20 is considered "normal." Medically, an individual is considered visually
impaired if vision in the eye with the best sight is 20/80 or less when corrected.
The medical profession defines a person who is legally blind in the United States as

having visual acuity for distant vision of 20/200 or less in the better eye with the best correction. Based on this definition, there are 500,000 legally blind people in the United States, approximately half being over the age of 65 (Tierney, McPhee, and Papadakis, 1997).

According to Stroman (1982), self-reporting and administrative determination are two other methods of defining visual disability. Self-reported definitions of visual disability classify visual acuity based upon visual levels established by a medical authority or a federal agency. A visual problem would be defined, for example, by whether or not a person reported his or her ability to read ordinary newspaper print with glasses. If they could not, they would be self-classified as severely visually impaired. Two problems are associated with this type of definition. One, because of the lack of objective criteria, a great deal of subjectivity in determining the degree of severity of blindness prevails. Second, because of the stigma associated with being blind, people are reluctant to self-disclose regarding the severity of their disability.

The administrative determination of visual impairment classifies visual loss based upon functional categories (Stroman, 1982). Many government agencies and service providers utilize this functional definition to determine eligibility for economic and educational benefits and services. Developed by the American Medical Association, this definition divides visual impairment into five categories. Category one encompasses total blindness, where the individual does not perceive any light at all. This is very rare. The second category centers on the ability to perceive whether or not light is present. Category three, economic blindness, establishes that the individual cannot do any kind of work for which sight is essential. This is the category usually thought of as legally blind. The fourth category, vocational blindness, includes individuals who are unable to do the work for which they have experience or training. The fifth category, educational blindness, is a level of impairment that would make it difficult, dangerous, or impossible to learn by usual and traditional methods of education.

Categories three, four, and five require a word of caution. The essentials of visual acuity required for work and education are relative. With reasonable accommodation, most vocational and educational activities can be mastered by a person with limited visual acuity. Those using the administrative definition of visual impairment should take into account that it is predominantly individuals who are sighted who establish descriptions of the various tasks involved in a position or job. Many times they have difficulty differentiating the essential functions and tasks of a particular job from the nonessential functions. It can be easy to define nonessential functions as essential because of lack of knowledge of the various types of accommodation available. An individual who is sighted may define reading a computer monitor as essential in computer programming. With the use of relatively inexpensive hardware and software, a person who has a visual disability can efficiently utilize a computer for all of its input and output functions without being able to read the monitor. Many times people who are sighted are unaware of simple techniques to accommodate complex tasks that seem to require sight.

◆ CAUSES OF BLINDNESS AND VISUAL IMPAIRMENT

The National Federation of the Blind (1996) found that the most common causes of blindness today are glaucoma, cataracts, and diabetic retinopathy. Diseases such as gonorrhea, retinitis pigmentosa, syphilis, trachoma, smallpox, and rubella may cause blindness. Some people lose their sight through accident or physical abuse. Many older people lose their eyesight through macular degeneration. Less than 2% of blindness is congenital or develops in early childhood.

◆ SOCIAL STIGMA

Stroman (1982) and tenBroek (1993) characterize the specific elements of prejudice regarding persons who are blind and visually impaired. Many people perceive blindness and visual impairment as an impenetrable, terrible fate. This stereotype reinforces the notion that persons who are blind are miserable and innately depressed; that living "in the dark" is almost as bad as being condemned to hell. Because of its negative nature, many in society expound the idea that persons who are blind should be pitied. This view reinforces the notion that persons who are blind are helpless and useless and therefore must be cared for. These views substantiate the misconception that persons who are blind are easily fooled and that, outside of established welfare, the only viable "occupation" for persons who are blind is that of being a beggar.

tenBroek and Matson (1959) demonstrate that many people view being blind as the equivalent to being dead. Directly related to Judeo-Christian heritage, blindness is the symbol of death. In the historical and sacred writings of the Jews, there are many references to the blind man as one who is dead.

As discussed previously throughout this book, there is a societal sense that persons with disabilities are immoral and evil. This belief particularly plagues people who are blind or visually impaired. Again, this stereotype is directly related to the Judeo-Christian tradition that evil and immorality will result in disability and blindness: "The Lord shall smite thee with madness, and blindness, and astonishment of heart" (Deuteronomy 28:28). For persons who are blind or visually impaired, the ramifications of this belief are many. Persons who are blind are feared, at best avoided, and better yet rejected. If they or their families are sinful and immoral in some way, persons who are blind are to be ostracized.

Perhaps one of the more common stereotypes about persons who are blind or visually impaired centers on their maladjustment. Components of this stereotype include the belief that the lack of ability to see has led to maldevelopment of a psychosocial personality, that persons who are blind are envious of sighted persons and exist within the constant turmoil of wishing to be sighted, and that persons who are blind live in constant depression concerning their loss. Many in our society believe that because of the nature of blindness, all persons who are blind are "bored, idle, aloof, self-pitying, paranoid, prone to petty angers, unfriendly and hypersensitive" (Stroman, 1982, p. 95).

◆   THE CONSEQUENCES OF STEREOTYPING

Newberry (1993) indicates that most persons who are blind or visually impaired view themselves as basically normal. To most, blindness or visual impairment is a physical nuisance at worst. As with the population in general, persons who are blind tend to be diverse. Some people who are blind have emotional difficulties such as overdependency, timidity, and depression. For those having emotional difficulties related to being blind, most of those difficulties result directly from the stereotyping and stigma in the socialization process:

> *The various attitudes and patterns of behavior that characterize people who are blind are not inherent in their condition but, rather, are acquired through ordinary processes of social learning. Thus, there is nothing inherent in the condition of blindness that requires a person to be docile, dependent, melancholy, or helpless; nor is there anything about it that should lead him to become independent or assertive. Blind men are made, and by the same processes of socialization that have made us all.* (Scott, 1969, p. 14)

Large (1990) cites studies that indicate some persons who are blind or visually impaired tend to comply with the social stereotypes imposed upon them. Thus, some persons who are blind take on some or all of the psychosocial characteristics of the preceding stereotypes, much in the same way as some African Americans (Solomon, 1976), ethnic minorities, women, and gays and lesbians (Pharr, 1988) respond to their oppression.

Central to the process of inculcating stereotypes of persons who are blind are public and private agencies that "serve" persons who are blind. According to Scott (1969), with as low as 5% of normal vision, a person can function as a fully sighted person in most areas of life. In spite of this fact, Scott (1969) states that "one of the most important, but least recognized, functions performed by organizations of the blindness system is to teach people who have difficulty seeing how to behave like blind people" (p. 71). This happens at two levels. First, when an ophthalmologist diagnoses blindness, the social response is immediate. Prior to the diagnosis, the individual is treated like a person who can see and has difficulty with sight. After the diagnosis, the person is treated like a person who is blind that has some sight. Second, this redefinition of a person is maintained and reinforced upon involvement with an agency dealing with persons who are blind. The training techniques, the mobility strategies, the job training, and the counseling all attempt to socialize the person to take on the stereotypes of persons who are blind:

> *The impaired person is thus under strong pressure to think of himself as blind and to redefine his visual impairment from a medical condition of attenuated vision to a kind*

of welfare problem requiring extensive social services. Accompanying this phenomenon is a strong emphasis on psychological adjustment to blindness and personal acceptance of this condition. The visually impaired person's readiness for the offered services is measured by his willingness to admit to himself the fact of his blindness and to show that he is resigned to the alleged permanence of his condition. (Scott, 1969, p. 74)

Thus, the very agencies designed to empower persons who are blind or visually impaired may in fact further their dependency and disenfranchisement by reinforcing the inculcation of certain psychosocial characteristics. Albrecht (1992) states this paradox well: "Rehabilitation institutions and programs generally perpetuate dependency even though they purport to make people functionally independent" (p. 267).

Scott (1969) points out that human service professionals tend to "treat" blindness from two approaches. The restorative approach seeks to restore persons who are blind to a level of performance that will allow their independence. The process usually involves a period of mourning and bereavement over the loss of sight. Many professionals consider the new blind state as likened to death, where the loss of the old sighted self must be mourned. Rehabilitation is a process of introspection around the loss, counseling, and skills training to establish a new kind of control of the environment as well as an understanding of self. Although much caution should be applied to the idea of blindness being equated to death (since this notion reinforces societal stereotypes), the end product of the restorative approach for the person who becomes blind or visually impaired is usually independent living and perhaps gainful employment.

The second approach, accommodation, also strives for the goal of independence but assumes that only a small percentage of persons who are blind have the capability of becoming truly independent. Professionals who use this approach create an environment free from physical, recreational, and educational barriers. Most job training and job acquisition is within the realm of sheltered workshop environments. Praise is used to reinforce dependency:

The general environment of such agencies is also accommodative in character. Clients are rewarded by trivial things and praised for performing tasks in a mediocre fashion. This superficial and over-generous reward system makes it impossible for most clients to assess their accomplishments accurately. Eventually, since anything they do is praised as outstanding, many of them come to believe that the underlying assumption must be that blindness makes them incompetent. (Scott, 1969, p. 85)

The end result of this approach is, of course, that persons who are blind organize their lives around the "safe" milieu of the agency. They can function effectively only within that agency milieu, thus depending upon it for work, leisure, and education. The larger community and their own independence are lost to them.

The approach we recommend in working with people who are blind or visually impaired is one that lessens the possibility of stereotyping. We believe that the human service professional should see blindness as difference rather than dysfunction and should not assume the need for a grieving process. In fact, the human service professional should assume nothing about the consumer until the consumer lets the professional know. We believe that the human service professional should act merely as a consultant to the blind consumer, who is in total control of the path and direction in which he or she wants to go. Our job as human service professionals is to work with consumers to explore the many paths and alternatives that exist for reaching their goals, and then to provide help, if requested.

One of the most grievous consequences of the stereotypes imposed upon persons who are blind or visually impaired is in employment. As we discussed earlier, many studies, including Harris (1987), estimate that unemployment of persons with disabilities in general is the highest of any other demographic group in the United States. Over 66% of persons with disabilities between the ages of 16 and 64 are unemployed. Of these, over two-thirds want to work. The National Federation of the Blind places the unemployment rate of persons who are blind and visually impaired at 70% of those of working age between the ages of 16 and 64 (L. Rovig, Director of Job Opportunities for the Blind, personal communication, December 11, 1996). Newberry (1993) points out that the stereotypes that persons who are blind and visually impaired are inferior, helpless, dependent, and cannot do physical labor or function in a fast-paced labor market impact their employment:

> *The real problem of blindness is not the loss of eyesight. The real problem is the misunderstanding the general public has about blind people's abilities. We often assume that people who are blind cannot get along without their sight merely because we, with our sight, cannot imagine ourselves doing so.* (p. 11)

◆ WHAT CAN PERSONS WHO ARE BLIND REALLY DO?

It is important for human service practitioners to understand the methods of independence used by persons with visual disabilities. The National Federation of the Blind (1996) has compiled a list of questions addressed to them by sighted children across the United States who were concerned about being blind and visually impaired. From the mouths of children generally comes wisdom. The answers to their questions go a long way in removing the myths and stereotypes concerning blindness and visual impairment.

Mobility

How do persons who are blind and visually impaired get around? There are a variety of techniques for mobility used by persons who are blind. Many use a white cane. This device allows the person to locate steps, curbs, streets, driveways, and most obstacles that may present themselves in everyday living. The cane is a length that allows people to discern potential obstacles about two feet ahead. The length of the cane varies depending on the height of the user.

Some persons who are blind or visually impaired use guide dogs. These are dogs that are specially trained to move around obstacles, go through doorways, and stop at curbs and stairs. The person using the dog is always in control and must tell the dog what to do. When the dog stops at a curb, the person using the dog must listen and determine when it is safe to proceed. Persons who are blind cross a street safely by listening to the sounds of traffic. They listen to ascertain when cars start to slow down and stop at a signal light or a stop sign. When one hears cars to the side start moving, it is time to cross the street. If there is no light, the person listens to hear if any cars are approaching and waits until there are no vehicles or until vehicles stop before crossing streets.

Persons who are blind or visually impaired use a variety of cues to help them locate specific places and addresses. They determine where they are by using pre-described landmarks and directions such as north, south, east, or west. They keep in mind cues, such as a busy street, or a lot that has no house or building, or a noisy school yard. The story of a personal friend of one of the authors (we did not use his real name) illustrates the degree of mobility of most persons who are blind.

Rev. David Williams served as the executive director of Presbyterian House, which served the campus of a small university in western Pennsylvania. David had been blind since birth. He graduated with honors from Harvard, and students, the campus community, and the general community loved him. He had doubled the income of the center, and the place was packed with students every day of the week. There was nowhere in the small college town that David could not go. You could see him anywhere on campus, run into him downtown, or come across him at one of several restaurants in the community. David used neither a cane nor a dog. He had memorized the sounds of the entire town and could go anywhere on his own. For one reason or another, Susan, David's wife, became concerned for his safety in getting about and insisted that he get a guide dog. After much resistance, David gave in and began the process. He went through the training and one day appeared on the campus with a guide dog. The question was, who was guiding whom? David could frequently be seen pulling the dog across the street. Students observed him trying to stop the dog at a curb. On occasion, students would encounter David trying to get the dog to go up a set of stairs. David certainly was in control, but for what purpose? Lack of mobility was never an issue for Rev. Williams, with or without the guide dog.

Reading

How do persons who are blind read? Most people who are blind read either by using transcribed books on audiotape or by using braille. Originally developed by Charles Barbier, an officer in Napoleon's army, as a military code that could be utilized in the dark, braille was refined and made practical by its namesake, Louis Braille, a student at the National Institute for the Blind in Paris in 1829 (Koestler, 1976). Braille simplified the complicated Barbier code into a simple cell consisting of two parallel columns of raised dots of three dots apiece. The dots are numbered

1, 2, 3 from top to bottom on the left side of the cell and 4, 5, 6 from top to bottom on the right side of the cell. The code can be used for letters, numbers, or musical notes, depending on which dots are raised. For example, "a" is the first dot on the left column, "b" is the first and second dots on the left column, and so on.

• o	• o	• •
o o	• o	o o
o o	o o	o o
a	b	c
1	2	3

Braille can be written with a braille writing machine or with a pointed stylus to punch dots down through paper using a braille slate with rows of small cells in it as a guide. There are also braille computer monitors and printers. Braille is read by feeling the different dots in each cell and differentiating combinations of dots in relationship to the letter, number, or note they stand for. There are libraries that provide braille and recorded books and magazines for persons who are blind.

Personal Grooming

How do persons who are blind maintain their personal appearance? How does a man who is blind shave or tie his necktie? Men who are blind or visually impaired shave and tie their neckties by feel. After doing these tasks over and over, they become routine and basically a habit. Many men who are blind prefer to shave in the shower. Generally, men can feel where there is a spot to be shaved and where there is not. Tying ties takes a bit of practice, but again by feel, the man who is blind can determine the length and the nature of the knot. Some men who are blind keep their ties tied when they take them off and hang them up already tied, ready for the next time of use.

How does a woman who is blind apply makeup and do her hair? The first step in this process is to work with someone who can demonstrate the various techniques of makeup artistry and hairstyling. A woman who is blind can feel the different ways of drying, curling, or styling her hair. Women learn to feel when their hair is right or when they have missed a spot. Women who are blind can apply makeup by touch, by feeling the different places where they want different kinds of makeup to be. A woman who is blind can learn the colors that are best for her by asking friends or beauticians whom she trusts. As with sighted people, the decision to wear makeup is a personal choice.

How can persons who are blind know what clothes to wear? Most clothing has some unique characteristic that can be felt. Some shirts and jackets have different shapes of buttons or snaps. Fabric texture may also differ. Dresses or skirts will have different kinds of belts or elastic at the waist. Jackets and shirts may have different sizes of pockets. By matching these different characteristics with colors, persons who are blind can coordinate design and color. For example, the person who is blind knows that the green shirt is the one with the unusually shaped buttons, or the red pants are the ones with straight pockets. The blouse with the wide collar is yellow, which matches the green skirt with the elastic waistband. If similar items feel the same, persons who are blind mark the clothes in order to tell them apart. Special tags are used to sew on braille labels, and specially placed safety pins or buttons can identify articles of a similar texture. Some persons who are blind create a list of their clothing articles that feel similar and match them with others using braille numbers and letters attached to the clothing. Whatever the material, persons with visual disabilities are able to dress with a few accommodations.

Preparing Food

How do persons who are blind shop for groceries? Many kinds of food can be recognized by feel and touch. Different kinds of fruits and vegetables have different shapes and textures. Certain meat items feel different. There is much difference between the feel of a hot dog and that of a chicken. But for wrapped meat items and items in cans or boxes, identifying them by touch is difficult. Many persons who are blind go shopping with someone who can help them identify canned or boxed food items. Blind people often ask store employees to help them find groceries. Many blind people make two lists, one in braille for themselves and one printed for a friend, helper, or store employee.

   How do persons who are blind cook? Persons who are blind can use all the fixtures found in the kitchen. Coded labels using braille or other codes can be affixed to touch buttons and dials on microwaves, stoves, and ovens. Persons who are blind generally use measuring devices such as spoons or cups that stack so the relative size can quickly be determined. The smell, sound, temperature, time of cooking, texture, and consistency can help determine how the foods are cooking.

   How do persons who are blind know which can or package to open in food preparation? Many different foods can be identified by the size and shape of the containers in which they come. Spaghetti boxes, ketchup bottles, tuna cans, bags of beans or rice, flour, sugar, coffee or tea, and butter are just some of the examples of unique sizes and types of containers that can be used to identify the contents. Other items not so unique can be identified by braille labels or other methods of coding. Some braille labels are made in such a way that they can be used over and over again. Some persons who are blind or visually impaired label their foods right at the store. Some food can be readily identified by its smell while in containers.

School and Work

Where do children who are blind go to school? Although most states have "special" schools for children who are blind, the vast majority of children who are blind attend "regular" schools in their communities. Children who are blind or visually impaired participate in regular classrooms and move throughout school using the techniques described previously. Most read and write braille. Resource teachers facilitate the education of students who are blind, receiving textbooks and library books in braille and on tape. Most students type papers using typewriters or computers. Students who are blind have the legal right to accommodation if needed, and technological advances can make accommodation easier than in the past.

Where do persons who are blind work? Persons who are blind work in a vast array of jobs. With necessary training and assistive equipment, people who are blind or visually impaired have the same range of abilities as people who are not. Persons who are blind or visually impaired currently work as artists, boat builders, politicians, computer programmers, lawyers, social workers, teachers, cosmetologists, auto mechanics, fashion models, accountants, and so on.

How do persons who are blind do their jobs? Accommodation on the job for persons who are blind or visually impaired may be relatively simple and low-tech or can include sophisticated computer hardware and software. Accommodation can take many forms. In human services, jobs can be restructured to accommodate transportation issues, particularly in rural settings. If people who are blind or visually impaired cannot make home visits because of lack of public transportation, they can be assigned specialized duties, such as doing new intakes, that involve remaining in the office. In urban areas where mass transit is more available, this particular accommodation would not be necessary. Additional examples of accommodation include using Velcro fasteners on protective clothing. A dot of silicon adhesive on switches or control knobs that need constant monitoring permits a person who is blind or visually impaired to use electronic machines with controls. Enlarged print or braille labels make file folders readable and soft drink selection on the soda machine possible. Striping codes using masking tape can help identify parts on shelves. High-technology accommodation usually involves computers. Hardware and software accommodation can include enlarged print on an enlarged screen, voice synthesizers, and braille tactile boards. An optical scanner along with a voice synthesizer makes reading of regular print possible (Dickson, 1994).

Identifying Money

How do persons who are blind know what money to give when they are purchasing an item? Coins generally have textural difference to the degree that they can be easily differentiated by feel. They vary in size, and quarters and dimes have ridges around them whereas pennies and nickels are smooth. To identify different denominations of paper money, some persons who are blind keep different bills in separate places in their wallets. Most persons who are blind develop a coding system based on folding. They fold different denominations in different ways. One method would be to fold a five-dollar bill in half the short way and a ten-dollar bill in half the long way. A twenty could be folded twice and a one not folded at all. When paper money is exchanged, persons who are blind ask which bill is which and fold it accordingly.

Telling Time

How do persons who are blind know what time it is? Generally, there are two ways persons who are blind tell time. Braille watches open so a person who is blind can feel braille dots at the different hour points. Other watches actually speak the time and have built-in alarms.

Games and Recreation

How do persons who are blind play cards and other games? Most games, including cards, can be easily modified. Braille is put on decks of cards. Word games such as Scrabble can be played with braille letters and a board with raised squares. Playing pieces can be made of different textures and shapes. Dice can be made to have dots that can be felt.

Team sports can be audibly modified so that persons who are blind or visually impaired can play. In baseball, a large ball or a ball with an audible buzzer inside can be used. The first base coach can call to instruct the batter to the base. Playground balls can be modified by cutting them open and placing bells inside and resealing them with bicycle tire patches. Making the playing area brighter through enhanced lighting makes playing easier for persons who are blind or visually impaired. In addition, the use of contrasting colored tape helps in play areas, particularly for gymnastics (Winnick, 1995).

◆ THE ISSUE OF PREFERENTIAL TREATMENT

Berkowitz (1987) discusses the issue of persons who are blind historically receiving preferential treatment in relationship to other disability groups. Persons who are blind have historically held the position of "worthy" poor in the American social welfare system. The original Social Security Act held that only persons who were blind could qualify for welfare. The Randolph–Shepard Act of 1936 allowed for the exclusive operation of snack bars and newsstands in federal buildings by persons who are blind. Many public transit systems have lowered fee rates for persons who are blind. More than thirty states have separate vocational rehabilitation programs for persons who are blind. No other disability group has these privileges.

There are several reasons why persons who are blind are recipients of this targeted treatment. People who are sighted fear blindness perhaps more than other disabling conditions and therefore respond to it with greater zeal. Persons who are blind have been a part of history and seem to have a greater impetus to involve themselves historically in the political process, resulting in legislation and policy favorable to persons who are blind.

Within the blind community, a debate continues on the issue of whether or not persons who are blind should have preferential treatment. tenBroek (1993) argues that there are two kinds of preferential treatment, based upon the motivation of the grantor. Preferential treatment based on irrational motivations, including prejudice or fancy, cannot be supported. There is no argument for giving to blind-related charity out of pity. On the other hand, preferential treatment based upon unique qualities or the particular needs of a group can be supported. The disabling component of the disability of blindness and visual impairment has mainly to do with the misconceptions of persons who are sighted. These misconceptions deny persons who are blind their full membership in society. Reaching full membership means removing the social, environmental, and economic barriers that prevent the full inclusion of persons who are blind. Programs that have these goals and involve preferential treatment certainly can be argued for and supported.

According to tenBroek (1993), programs that have preferential treatment components must have the following characteristics:

1. They must allow persons who are blind or visually impaired to have full autonomy in handling their own affairs.
2. The programs must encourage persons who are blind to develop to their full potential.
3. Programs must direct and encourage persons who are blind to seek opportunities, occupations, and professions.
4. Programs must use a wide range of incentives, including financial remuneration.
5. Programs must encourage the acquisition of private property, not just for consumption's sake but as a means of economic improvement.
6. Programs must reinforce the idea of the individual worth of persons who are blind rather than seeing them as a societal liability.

Other members of the blind community do not agree with tenBroek's position. Shore (1993) questions preferential treatment for persons who are blind or visually impaired. According to Shore, preferential treatment is, by its very nature, demeaning and unnecessary. Preferential treatment prevents persons who are blind from fulfilling the basic desire of financial independence. It reinforces the innate dependency built into the social welfare system and the stereotypes that the blind must be cared for. Preferential treatment substantiates the myth that persons who are blind should be objects of pity and charity, that they are helpless, and that they can only be little more than beggars. As long as preferential programs exist for persons who are blind, they will not have full equality with sighted persons. Persons who are blind must pay their way in full to be seen as equal and viable citizens.

The issues presented by these two perspectives sound very similar to the current debate around affirmative action. Do programs that try to make up for the historical inequities in the cases of gender, ethnicity, and disability have a positive or negative impact on how members of the general society view these groups? Do special programs reinforce negative stereotypes and invite backlash, or do they break down stereotypes by promoting increased interaction and economic parity? Do they compensate for racism, sexism, and ableism, or do they further discrimination? Or do they have little impact one way or the other?

People's answers to these questions depend on their ideological perspectives. Hopefully, continued empirical research and policy analysis will provide increased understanding. However, some cautions must be presented regarding the preceding debate. First, opponents of preferential treatment assume that equal competition exists in both the labor and consumer markets. In our current economic system, preferential treatment for the wealthy in buying goods, acquiring an education, and competing for jobs is standard (DiNitto, 1991). Stigma is not inherent in preferential treatment but, rather, in the negative stereotypes and low status of persons who are visually disabled. Second, the removal of preferential treatment would have little impact on stereotypes, bias, and discrimination that are a part of the lives of persons with visual disabilities. Stereotypes around all disability exist for a variety of reasons. They run deep within the American culture. The avoidance or refusal of preferential treatment by persons who are blind will not significantly impact these negative stereotypes. Third, many persons who are blind and who are in economic or political leadership positions attained their authority in part by using preferential treatment programs. Research that sheds understanding on which policies and what kinds of programs truly add to the economic and social independence of persons who are blind would greatly clarify the preceding issues.

◆   PERSONS WHO ARE BLIND AND DEAF

Shapiro (1993) points out that medical professionals and teachers of persons who are both blind and deaf were the first to realize and act upon the integration of persons with disabilities into society. Samuel Gridley Howe was an educator who opened the Massachusetts Asylum for the Blind in 1832. His most noted success was Laura Bridgman, through whom he brought to the public the knowledge that persons who were blind and deaf could be educated. Laura had been blind and deaf from the age of 2 when she contracted scarlet fever. Howe's success with her brought notables such as Charles Dickens to his school to observe her progress. Perhaps the most famous person who was blind and deaf was Helen Keller. Growing up in the late 1800s, Helen Keller was taught by Anne Sullivan, a graduate of the Perkins School for the Blind. Helen Keller was the first person who was deaf and blind to receive a bachelor's degree from Radcliffe College. She dedicated her life to advocacy for persons with disabilities across the world (Thompson and Freeman, 1995).

    There are four basic categories of deaf-blindness. The first of these includes those who are deaf and blind at birth or those who lose both vision and hearing very early in life. Helen Keller represents this category. The second category includes those who are either born deaf or lose their hearing very early and later lose their vision; the third category includes people who are blind early in life and later lose a significant amount of their hearing; and the fourth category includes adults who later in life, either through disease or accident, lose both their sight and hearing (Cheadle, 1994). Koestler (1976) presents a description of the fourth category given by an English businessman left blind and deaf after being involved in an automobile accident:

> *What is it actually like to be deaf-blind? I can only tell you what it is like for me.*
> *What it's like for a person who has never seen or heard, I do not know. First, it is*
> *neither "dark" nor "silent." If you were to go out into a London fog—one of the thick*

yellow variety—and then close your eyes, you would see what I see. A dull, flesh-colored opacity. So much for literal "darkness . . ."

Nor is my world "silent" (most of us wish it were so!). You have all put a shell to your ear as children and "listened to the waves." You may, at times—when dropping off to sleep perhaps—have "heard" the clang of a bell in your ear, or a sound like the shunting of railway wagons, or a shrill whistle, or the wind moaning round the eaves on Christmas Eve. All these have I perpetually. They have become part of the background. Cracklings, squeakings, rumblings—what I hear is the machinery of my being working. The blood rushing through my veins, and little cracklings of nerves and muscles as they expand and contract. In short, my hearing has "turned inwards." (p. 452)

Persons who are both deaf and blind experience a variety of unique problems. First, if the conditions develop sequentially, the initial diagnosis results in treatment for the earlier condition, generally leaving the later developing condition without consideration. Cheadle (1994) discusses an example. Keri-Ann, attending sixth grade, had been deaf for several years before she began to lose her sight. The educational professionals planned her education based upon her hearing loss and did not take into consideration her visual limitations. As a result, Keri-Ann was doing poorly in school. The problem centered on the unknown fact that Keri-Ann was experiencing tunnel vision. When ASL interpreters signed to her, their signing was very broad, leaving many of the phrasings outside her field of vision. A second problem for those who are both deaf and blind is that services directed to the uniqueness of this condition are very limited. Most services, particularly educational services, are specialized either for persons who are deaf or persons who are blind (Cheadle, 1994). And third, because society views blindness and deafness separately as being overwhelmingly devastating, when they are combined, persons who are both blind and deaf suffer the full force of prejudice and discrimination that is a part of ableism (Koestler, 1976).

The eradication of prejudice and discrimination, resulting in full and rich lives for persons who are both blind and deaf, starts with knowledge and then action. First, Prickett and Welch (1995) point out that total blindness and total deafness are very rare. So most people who are both blind and deaf have either some vision or some hearing or both. The second piece of knowledge that is important is that language formulation exists for persons who are blind and deaf. And for those for whom language development is a difficult alternative, techniques of communication exist (Goode, 1994). As with all disabilities, Goode argues that the disability of deaf-blindness is a social construct. Therefore, with the removal of so-called attitudinal barriers through education and association and of environmental barriers through techniques of accommodation, people who are deaf and blind can lead fulfilling, productive lives.

Prickett and Welch (1995) outline several significant educational modifications for inclusive classrooms, which are also applicable to home, community, and work. Lighting is crucial. Eliminating glare, particularly from the sun, is important.

Seating in relationship to the light and to the source of sound is also important so that persons who are deaf and blind can make use of any residual sight and hearing. In addition, proximity to fellow students or fellow workers is important for using touch as a means of communication. Furthermore, an interpreter using tactile signing or hand signing may help facilitate communication. Used mostly in Canada, intervenors who help persons who are deaf and blind gather information for daily living are becoming more common in the United States. Finally, various pieces of technology, including braille computer equipment, can facilitate independence.

◆ SUMMARY

Traditionally, the medical model has served as the basis for defining blindness. The origins of the medical model definition go back to 1868. Dr. Herman Snellen developed the "eye-test" chart used today by most ophthalmologists and optometrists. Self-reporting and administrative determination are two other methods of defining blindness. Self-reported definitions of blindness classify visual acuity based upon preestablished visual levels. The administrative definition of visual impairment classifies visual loss based upon functional categories.

Many people view blindness and visual impairment as an impenetrable, terrible fate. This stereotype reinforces the notion that persons who are blind are miserable and innately depressed; that living "in the dark" is almost as bad as being condemned to hell. Because of its negative nature, many in society expound the idea that persons who are blind should be pitied and taken care of. By contrast, most persons who are blind or visually impaired view themselves as basically normal. To most, blindness or visual impairment is a physical nuisance at worst.

One of the most grievous consequences of the stereotypes imposed upon persons who are blind or visually impaired is in employment. The National Federation of the Blind places the unemployment rate of persons who are blind and visually impaired at 70% of those of working age between the ages of 16 and 64. The stereotypes that persons who are blind or visually impaired are inferior, helpless, dependent, and cannot do physical labor or function in a fast-paced labor market impact their employment.

Persons who are blind have historically held the position of "worthy" poor in the American social welfare system. Within the blind community, a debate continues on the issue of whether or not persons who are blind should have preferential treatment. Some say that preferential treatment based upon unique qualities or particular needs of a group can be supported. Others say that preferential treatment is by its very nature demeaning and unnecessary. Empirical studies to address the question of what kinds of programs truly add to the economic and social independence of persons who are blind would greatly clarify the issues.

Persons who are both deaf and blind experience a variety of unique problems. Because society views blindness and deafness separately as being overwhelmingly devastating, when they are combined, persons who are both blind and deaf suffer the full force of prejudice and discrimination that is a part of ableism. The eradication of prejudice and discrimination, along with techniques of accommodation, can result in full and rich lives for persons who are both blind and deaf.

◆ ◆ ◆   *Personal Narrative: Brenda Premo*   ◆ ◆ ◆

Brenda Premo is legally blind and has albinism. She has been actively working for persons with disabilities throughout her adult life. Currently, she is the director of the California Department of Rehabilitation.

I have about 10% of my vision, so I am legally blind because of a condition called albinism, which is genetic. I also have no melanin, a chemical that gives people pigmentation and allows them to tan. Thus, I am also very sensitive to the sun.

One early memory that sticks out for me is when I was about 4 years old. There were times I was supposed to be napping but wasn't. My mother would know that I wasn't napping so I started thinking she had ESP. Finally, I asked, "Mom, how do you know that I'm not asleep?" She just said, "Mothers know these things." She didn't tell me, but I eventually figured out that she could see my eyes were open. I couldn't see whether her eyes were open or closed, so I couldn't understand that she would know whether or not my eyes were open. I thought that she had ESP, but the reality was, she could see my eyes.

When I was very young, my mother did not explain that I had a disability. There was no discussion of it. She was a single mother making $1.25 an hour as a waitress, so she couldn't work and keep me. She worked and had to give me up until she met my stepfather, to whom she was married for the rest of her life. So I had to live in foster homes from about age $2\frac{1}{2}$ until about age 5. I did not realize my disability contributed to my having to live in foster homes. I knew that I was different, but I thought I was different then because I was living in homes where people were not my family. The foster families didn't treat me badly, but they didn't treat me like their children either.

As a child, I knew I couldn't go outside much. This was before they had sunblock, which is a very inexpensive way to keep from what I refer to as "having baked albino." I was severely burned on two occasions because of my sensitive skin. Once, I was put in the hospital for three days with third-degree burns because one of my foster parents put me on the beach for three hours.

I don't think I was aware that I was disabled until I was about 5 or 6. Before then, I was conscious of some differences, but I wasn't aware that others saw me differently. My first vivid memory of my disability was when I was in second grade and children chased me and called me names. I had to dive under the playground merry-go-round to escape. I was in a multicultural school in the middle of L.A., and I was, because of the albinism, the only truly white person in the school. There were Caucasian, black, and Hispanic kids and they all chased me. Being taunted by other kids is my first vivid memory of my disability or my difference. It wasn't my vision that caused them to taunt me; it was that I looked different.

The first time I remember understanding that my vision was different from other people was in the second or third grade when I realized other students could read the blackboard. Before then, I couldn't understand why the teacher would bother to write on the board. When it dawned on me that other kids could read the board and I couldn't, it was one of those "aha" moments of life. It was a new discovery. I knew I was different on some level because I was in special education classes, but I hadn't known that it was because I saw differently than others.

As a child, I knew I was different and that people treated me differently than other children. I knew I was perceived as "less than" other children. There were several elements involved in that. At that time, I believe people treated me differently mostly because of my physical difference—the white eyebrows and the white hair, the pink skin, and the squinting. My physical appearance caused lots more reaction than my visual disability. In fact, many people did not even know of my visual difference unless they saw me read. I also felt different because I lived in foster homes.

The fact that I was born with my visual disability has had advantages. I have what my eye doctor calls "compensating skills." My brain has compensated and fills in the pictures of what I cannot see with my eyes. For example, I remember where steps are if I have been on them before. I see the steps because the brain is filling in what the eyes can't see. Sometimes I make mistakes, so I have to be careful, but my brain gives me the picture. It's easier for me than for someone who is blinded later in life.

Most people don't understand my compensating ability. When I was a child, the doctors told my mother and father, "You have a handicapped daughter who'll probably not be able to care for herself." They didn't understand. My mother was proud when we proved them wrong. When she was terminally ill, my dad cared for her physically, but I was responsible for facilitating her required treatments when she was in California. It was with pride that she announced to the family that I was taking care of her.

I began to understand that my difference from other kids was disability related in the fourth or fifth grade. This was before special education laws. I was in a special school, and the school district decided to experiment with letting us be in the regular schools. I was in a pilot project. It was frightening and they didn't think things out too well. For example, they put me in a physical education class and had us playing softball out in the middle of the day in the sun. Softball is not something that a person with 10% vision does really well at. I noticed I was always picked last. It was obvious other people didn't really want me on the team. Early on, I figured out that I didn't really want to be rejected, so I got a teacher to agree to hit for me and then I began to get picked first.

I began to see two things as a result of this school experience. First, I saw that the classes the other kids were in were different from the classes I was in. I was in integrated schools but in separate classes and removed from other kids because they weren't sure if integration was going to work. Second, I noticed that less was expected of me than of other kids. I was expected to do less. I didn't understand it in words, but I knew that I was somehow expected to achieve less, to know less, and to be less than the other kids. It was a standard that people just accepted. I didn't like it. I knew it wasn't right. I don't know why, but I just didn't accept this. I understood I could do more, and I wanted to do more than they would let me.

Finally, in the sixth grade I told my mother that I wanted to go to a regular junior high school. I didn't want to go to special schools or be in special classes. We moved to Orange County, California, which, at that time in the '60s, had superb schools. By then, I had formulated in my mind that I was visually impaired. There were no special education laws at the time, and the school officials just about fainted dead away when I informed them I wanted to go to a regular school.

I remember this bullheaded psychologist who gave me a small-print IQ test and told my mother that I was retarded. What he had really tested was my ability to read small print. Even my mother knew that his diagnosis was not correct. After all, why would someone give me a small-print test when they knew I couldn't read small print very well? Because I was very determined to go to regular school, my mother told the resistant school officials, "You'll have to fight with her. She wants to go here." So this bullheaded psychologist then said to my mother, "Well, we'll let her go here so she can learn about failure." So my mother says, "Yeah, OK." She only had an eighth-grade education, but she understood intuitively that I was brighter than they gave me credit for.

In my first year in junior high, they didn't let me do anything extra. I had a counselor who believed I could actually communicate and reason, but others did not. My sewing teacher almost became a nervous wreck. I had to get so close to see what I was doing she was afraid I would affix my nose to the fabric. One time my mother got called into the principal's office because I wouldn't use big-print books. Instead of just bringing me in and chatting with me, the principal brought my mother in. In the meeting, my mother turned to me and said, "Sweetheart, why don't you want to use big-print books?" I said, "Mom, it's like this; I've got four academic classes and all the teachers assign several chapters to read. In large-print books, chapters are in volumes. So if I have four academic classes and I have to have three volumes each, I need a wagon to take my books home." I told her I needed a magnifier, a $1.50 magnifier, but nobody asked me. So my mother bought me a magnifier and the problem was solved. School helped my dad and me bond a lot because he helped me with lots of projects when I couldn't see well enough to do them alone. The school didn't like it, but my parents stuck up for me.

The second year they let me do everything. In PE, I did track. I didn't do volleyball because I kept getting hit in the face with the ball. We played volleyball outside and when I would see the sun, I'd think the sun was the volleyball. I did basketball and I did a lot of after-school sports and volunteering because my way to achieve recognition was to do volunteer work.

I became a competitive speaker in the seventh and eighth grades. I was on the varsity by the end of seventh grade, and I was one of the leading students on the debate team in spontaneous speaking. I went to the state contest and did very well. I got a lot second- and third-place awards. I think the reason I didn't get first place a lot was because I didn't have skills in eye contact and body language. Those are legitimate skills that I went on to learn in high school, and then I started getting more first places. I had to be taught in a physical way what body language and eye contact are.

I really appreciated the teachers in high school who would accommodate me but who had high expectations. They would ask me, "What can I do that would make this better for you?" but they wouldn't let me slide at all academically. There was a math teacher, an old gruff guy. He would accommodate me, but I had to achieve and I had to earn my grade. I always got B's from him but I respected him, so much more than some other teachers who gave me easy A's. The same thing happened in college. I always appreciated the teachers who expected the most out of me and worked my hardest in their classes. I also got the most out of them.

I didn't have a lot of friends in junior high school and high school. Some teachers liked me, but I never had any other children who saw me as their best friend, with one exception who was a fellow isolate with a disability. I had people who respected me for what I did well, especially in my competitive speech. I even mentored some of them. I did get respect from my peers and I wanted that. But as far as an intimate friendship with any of my peers, I didn't have it.

My family believed that I would always need to be taken care of and struggled with how they would handle that. My uncle expected more of me than anyone else in the family. He was only nine years older than I was, and we became a bonded pair. He would not baby me at all. He was tough on me. The relatives thought he was a mean person but, in fact, he treated me like an equal. He didn't treat me like a disabled child, and that was the difference. It has always been that way between us.

It has always been true for me that it doesn't matter what the bulk of the people think about me. What has mattered are the thoughts of those significant to me. I like to be professional and have the respect of others whom I respect.

An early mentor for me was my junior high speech coach because he saw my talent and he demanded that I fulfill my potential. In high school, it was my psychology teacher who pushed me to achieve. He made me recognize that there were going to be things that were very hard for me to do, but he expected me to do them anyway. He knew I might not be the best at some things, but he wouldn't let me use my disability as an excuse not to learn basic academic skills. He believed I could go to college and helped me get there. He pushed me and I responded. He helped me get into Cal State Long Beach, where I met two women who became my heroes—Norma Gibbs and Kay Goddard. Kay was the assistant dean of student activities. She started by treating me like I was going to be a professional; not a disabled client, but a professional. Disabilities never really came up in our conversations. She knew I was disabled, but we would just talk about things I needed to do to develop. She was a person who I really chose to relate to. Norma is disabled; she had TB. Norma believed in me in even a broader sense, spiritually as well as professionally. She is my picture of a lady, but a lady with no pretense of being anything but what she is. She helped me gain a sense that we should really go out and taste life.

Since those times, Anita Baldwin has become a person I really respect. When issues of blindness come up, I turn to Anita because she has a disability similar to mine. June Kailes has become a role model for me too. June has a disability and has been a leader in the disability movement. June and I are, in fact, role models for each other. We have high expectations of each other and never let up slack on each other. We always try to make each other better. We motivate and set standards for each other. I compare myself to June to make sure I measure up to her respect.

As people with disabilities, we have made progress. In the old days, if we wanted to impact social policy, we were dead before we got to the door. Now we've got people with disabilities in positions to make decisions. But we have a long way to go.

There are some important things to know about policy development. First, policy is developed by individuals, and those individuals have biases that are incorporated in policy. When policy makers have biases about people who have disabilities of some type, whether intellectual, physical, or sensory, those people are discounted. Biases against people with disabilities are usually based on pity. We are viewed as not being capable. That view is then incorporated into policy, which is put into practice. Then the system teaches the persons who are discounted in the policy that they should behave in the way predicted in the policy. We do this to disabled people but also to welfare recipients and others.

If the bias is that disabled people can't work, then systems are set up with workers whose job it is to keep people on disability benefits and away from work. We end up with a self-fulfilling prophecy from the creation of the policy. So a major task for people with disabilities is to modify the biases of policy makers. Policy makers need to recognize that accommodations must be made for people with disabilities. But they must also make the assumption that no class of people is burdened by the characteristic of incompetence. There may be individuals in that class—disabled, poor or other—who will not achieve. But within the class, we must, as a matter of policy, make policy with the assumption that incompetence is an individual characteristic, not a class characteristic. Policy must then be developed with incentives from birth to tell people in society, whoever they are, that they are responsible to achieve to their potential. The tools must then be in place to reinforce that message. We need both public and private polices because the government isn't going to fix it all. The message must be sent early to people with disabilities that we are responsible for ourselves. The message must also be sent that other people are responsible to assist in areas where assistance needs to happen. Finally, we need to accept people's potential, and we need to judge people on what they do with what they are given.

Another side of the issue rests within people. People with disabilities have to step out of the victim role and take on the responsibility for our lives. When we are in bad situations or miserable, we need to take the challenge to get out of it. We need support systems to do that, but it is up to us to do it. We talk about ABs (able-bodied people) and how they have done things to us. But, it is up to us to make things change. People can give 25,000 excuses about why they can't do anything to make things better because they are disabled. I say to them that, as a policy maker, I'm only as powerful in my position as the community that backs me. If I don't have that backing, I have no power in my position at all.

I think it's important for people to get in touch with who they are; who they belong to; their power base. Whether it's women who get in touch with themselves or people with disabilities or whomever, I like to see it happen. Their identity is based on the oneness, something they can be part of. To have empowerment, we need to have something to believe in, something to attach ourselves to.

Going through some of the things my disability has made me go through has given me the character to deal with and achieve what I need to achieve. Having a disability and saying, "I'm not going to let people's opinions or stereotypes hold me down" has created the strength to do what I've done. I can say that if I had a choice between having my disability and having that character or not having the disability and having what I have seen in what are called able-bodied people, I would rather have the disability. It isn't that I'm proud of being blind. It's that I'm pleased that I used what came to me in a constructive way.

What you do with what you get determines whether you succeed or not. Whether it is gender or ethnicity or disability, you get what comes and there's not a second chance. We have to use the tools in our tool kits. My disability was a tool, an opportunity from which I could gain, and it was also a barrier from which I could lose. Every day I confront situations that I can make the choice to use the disability as a gainer or a loser; I choose to use it as a gainer.

In offering advice to professionals, first, I think language is important. There's a reason we say *persons with disabilities*. People with disabilities are members of the pool of humanity who have a characteristic that affects their lives; some more, some less. Disability affects people's personalities and affects them emotionally, but it is one of a whole range of things that affects their lives. Second, don't discount anyone based on their disability. Don't believe that anyone is incapable of any task because of what you see before you. There may be tasks that some people can't perform at this moment but could do if given the support to develop their potential. Some of our greatest inventions have been made by refusing to limit ourselves by what we see today and envisioning what is possible in the future. A prime example is telecommunication devices for the deaf.

I would say that the first thing people should drop from their vocabulary is the word *can't*. Once that word is incorporated, it stops creativity and the potential for development of things that eventually will benefit all of society. For example, speech-activated computers were developed for various disabled people, but pretty soon lawyers, court reporters, and others began using them. And all because someone decided it was possible to solve a problem.

Another thing I would say is that people with disabilities are capable of thinking and doing what anybody else does—good, bad, or indifferent. Don't make us angels and don't make us devils. There are stupid, angry people with disabilities and there are people who are very capable. Professionals need to understand that. Do not stereotype us.

◆　◆　◆

Discussion Questions

1. What are some of the major issues in defining persons who are blind or visually impaired? What cautions must be applied when looking at functional definitions?

2. How might persons who are blind or visually impaired internalize societal stereotypes that would result in feelings of inadequacy and depression?

3. Explain how some social service agencies providing services to persons who are blind or visually impaired might foster oppression rather than empowerment. What kinds of things could social service agencies do to avoid these oppressive processes or characteristics?

4. Prepare a list of jobs that many people in the United States would commonly think a person who is blind or visually impaired could not do. Then discuss what possible accommodations could facilitate a person who is blind or visually impaired in accomplishing each of the jobs on your list.

5. Discuss both sides of the issue of preferential treatment for persons who are blind or visually impaired. Which argument do you think is the stronger and why?

6. What are some of the unique issues concerning persons who are deaf-blind? As a practitioner, how would you accommodate a person who was both blind and deaf?

Suggested Readings

Koestler, F. A. (1976). *The unseen minority: A social history of blindness in America.* New York: David McKay.

Scott, R. (1969). *The making of blind men: A study of adult socialization.* New York: Russell Sage Foundation.

Solomon, B. (1976). *Black empowerment: Social work in oppressed communities.* New York: Columbia University Press.

Stroman, D. F. (1982). *The awakening minorities: The physically handicapped.* Lanham, MD: University Press of America.

tenBroek, J., and Matson, F. W. (1959). *Hope deferred: Public welfare and the blind.* Berkeley, CA: University of California Press.

References

Albrecht, G. (1992). *The disability business: Rehabilitation in America.* London: Sage.

Berkowitz, E. D. (1987). *Disabled policy: America's programs for the handicapped.* London: Cambridge University Press.

Cheadle, B. (Ed.). (1994). Meeting the needs of the deaf-blind child. *Future Reflections, 13*(1), Winter. [http://nfb.org/]

Dickson, M. B. (1994). *Working effectively with people who are blind or visually impaired* [www.ilr. cornell.edu/PED/ADA]. Ithaca, NY: Program on Employment and Disability, New York School of Industrial and Labor Relations, Cornell University.

DiNitto, D. M. (1991). *Social welfare: Politics and public policy.* Englewood Cliffs, NJ: Prentice Hall.

Goode, D. (1994). *A world with words: The social construction of children born deaf and blind.* Philadelphia: Temple University Press.

Harris, L. (1987). *The ICD survey II: Employing disabled Americans.* New York: Louis Harris.

Koestler, F. A. (1976). *The unseen minority: A social history of blindness in America.* New York: David McKay.

Large, T. (1990). The effects of attitudes upon the blind: A reexamination. In M. Nagler (Ed.), *Perspectives on disability* (pp. 165–168). Palo Alto, CA: Health Markets Research.

National Federation of the Blind. (1996). *Questions from kids about blindness* [nfb.org/ftp/nfb/kids/kids.txt].

Newberry, F. (1993). The blind child: Becoming an independent adult. *Future Reflections, 12*(2), 4–11. http://nfb.org/

Pharr, S. (1988). *Homophobia: A weapon of sexism.* Inverness, CA: Chardon Press.

Prickett, J. G., and Welch, T. R. (1995). Adapting environments to support the inclusion of students who are deaf-blind. In N. G. Haring and L. T. Romer (Eds.), *Welcoming students who are deaf-blind into typical classrooms: Facilitating school participation, learning, and friendship* (pp. 171–193). Baltimore: Paul H. Brookes.

Scott, R. (1969). *The making of blind men: A study of adult socialization.* New York: Russell Sage Foundation.

Shapiro, J. P. (1993). *No pity: People with disabilities, forging a new civil rights movement.* New York: Times Books.

Shore, Z. (1993). Free rides for the blind cost us too much. *Future Reflections,* Winter. http://nfb.org/

Solomon, B. (1976). *Black empowerment: Social work in oppressed communities.* New York: Columbia University Press.

Stroman, D. F. (1982). *The awakening minorities: The physically handicapped.* Lanham, MD: University Press of America.

tenBroek, J. (1993). Pros and cons of preferential treatment of blind persons. Address at the AAWB Convention, June 19, 1955, Quebec, Canada. *The Braille Monitor,* Winter. http://nfb.org/

tenBroek, J., and Matson, F. W. (1959). *Hope deferred: Public welfare and the blind.* Berkeley, CA: University of California Press.

Thompson, R. P., and Freeman, C.W. (1995). A history of federal support for students with deaf-blindness. In N. G. Haring and L. T. Romer, (Eds.), *Welcoming students who are deaf-blind into typical classrooms: Facilitating school participation, learning, and friendship* (pp. 17–35). Baltimore: Paul H. Brookes.

Tierney, L. M., Jr., McPhee, S. J., and Papadakis, M. A. (Eds.). (1997). *Current medical diagnosis and treatment* (36th ed.). Stamford, CT: Appleton & Lange.

Winnick, J. P. (1995). *Adapted physical education and sport* (2nd ed.). Champaign, IL: Human Kinetics.

Chapter 8

PERSONS WITH DEVELOPMENTAL DISABILITIES

People First is saying, "Treat people first and everything else is second." Change your low expectations to positive expectations. People's minds are sort of warped about disabilities because they haven't gotten an education. Society's low expectations have said, "If somebody is different than me, let's lock them away." Something's got to change, and I think that change is positive thinking. People First helps people know what they want to do and stand up to people who say, "You can't do that." We can advocate for people. People First can go into the institutions and educate those people to stand up to the staff. We help them get out of institutions.

—Resa Hayes, disability activist, People First of Washington, Spokane, Washington

Student Learning Objectives:

1. To understand issues around defining developmental disabilities.
2. To understand the many varieties of developmental disabilities.
3. To have a very basic knowledge of the major developmental disabilities likely to be experienced by clients and consumers.
4. To understand issues of autonomy regarding persons with developmental disabilities.

◆ GENERAL DEFINITIONS

The first step in seeking a balanced definition of developmental disabilities centers on examining the federal definition. The current revision of the Developmental Disabilities Assistance Bill of Rights Act defines developmental disabilities as disabilities that are severe and chronic in nature. Furthermore, they are caused by either mental or physical impairment, or both; present themselves before the person becomes 22; have a strong probability of continuing for the rest of the person's life; and significantly limit a person's ability to carry on major life activities, including the ability to live independently and earn a living. Developmental disabilities also include disabilities that require some kind of intervention, care, or treatment for a long duration, if not for life. (American Association of University Affiliated Programs for Persons with Developmental Disabilities, 1997).

For all practical purposes, the federal definition of developmental disability encompasses most disabilities acquired before the age of 22. According to the federal definition, if the onset is early and the disability is severe enough to interfere with several major life functions, the condition can be defined as a developmental disability.

A more focused definition is offered by the Association for Persons with Severe Handicaps (TASH), an organization dedicated to the interests of people who have been traditionally labeled as severely mentally retarded (Brown, 1991). TASH facilitates research and policy development for those in the population who are in the lowest 1% of intellectual functioning.

According to TASH, a severe intellectual disability is a disability that requires

> *extensive ongoing support in more than one major life activity in order to participate in integrated community settings and to enjoy a quality of life that is available to citizens with fewer or no disabilities. Support may be required for life activities such as mobility, communication, self-care, and learning as necessary for independent living, employment, and self-sufficiency.* (Brown, 1991, p. 19)

This definition comes closer to reflecting a social perspective on disability because it brings the community into the definition with the goal of independent living. We will apply it to developmental disabilities in general.

No matter which of these definitions we use, several problems occur with a definition of developmental disability that includes intellectual disability. First, Ansello (1992) points out that although service benefits are linked to being classified as developmentally disabled, groups such as persons who are blind, persons who have cerebral palsy, and deaf people resist being identified as developmentally disabled. A primary reason appears to be the connection of the term *developmental disability* with mental retardation. Being categorized as mentally retarded carries with it a significant social stigma. Much of the early legislative and service provisions concerned with developmental disability centered on persons who were diagnosed as mentally retarded. Many states, such as California, limit resources directed to service by making mental retardation the core of their definition of developmental disabilities (California Codes Welfare and Institution Code, Section 4512). Persons who are intellectually disabled have such a low status in our society that few, including many professionals, want to be associated with this group (Hall et al., 1986).

Second, implied by some writers (Smith, 1994) and experienced by many involved in the independent living movement is a kind of dualism: nondisabled reformers use the words of independent living, but the resulting policy and programs leave this ideal far behind. In examining the civil rights quest for persons with developmental disabilities, Shapiro (1993) found extensive parental involvement. Despite great legislative and service provision success, it is still parents doing for their children. This paternalistic value has been translated to some degree into service providers' mentality. Many professionals have an underlying resistance to allowing persons with developmental disabilities to take control of their own lives (Dudley, 1987). This resistance is repulsive to other groups of persons with disabilities having an independent living perspective, and they in no way seek to be connected with this value of dependence.

Most problems with an inclusive definition of developmental disability have to do with stigma and economics. But a broad definition of developmental disability, cemented in a social context, allows the incorporation of the breadth and complexity of these particular types of disabilities. It also fits within the values of the independent living movement—that persons with different disabilities have more characteristics in common than differences.

Much of the literature and several legal statutes agree that intellectual disability (mental retardation), Down syndrome, autism, epilepsy, and cerebral palsy fall under the category of developmental disability. Since we have explored cerebral palsy under mobility disability, we will concentrate here on intellectual disabilities, Down syndrome, autism, and epilepsy.

◆ INTELLECTUAL DISABILITY (MENTAL RETARDATION)

Evans (1991) traces the evolution of the definition of mental retardation. Intelligence quotient (IQ) testing started in Paris as a way to determine which students required special education, and an IQ score of two standard deviations below the mean is still one of the major criteria used to determine mental retardation. However, efforts have been made to replace this simplistic diagnostic method. The American Association on Mental Deficiency (now the American Association on Mental Retardation) first created an adaptive functioning method of classification in response to the limitations of IQ testing. The AAMR used four categories of classification: mild, moderate, severe, and profound. According to this classification system, people who had mild mental retardation could achieve employment on a semiskilled or unskilled level. They functioned independently, owned their own homes and cars, and generally had families. People who had moderate mental retardation might achieve self-maintenance in unskilled or semiskilled work sometimes under accommodated work environments, including sheltered conditions and supported employment. They generally lived with their families or in group home–type situations. People who had severe mental retardation might help in their own maintenance but generally required supervision in work and living environments. People who had profound mental retardation had limited motor and speech skills. They might achieve limited self-care and might need extensive attendant or nursing care.

Recently, the AAMR has revised and simplified its definition of mental retardation. The AAMR now defines mental retardation as a basic difficulty in learning and performing certain daily, personal, and life skills. Specific limitations include those of a conceptual, practical, and social intelligence nature. According to the AAMR, a person with mental retardation has limitations only in conceptual, practical, and social intelligence. Other areas such as health or personality are not included. The one differentiating characteristic of a person with mental retardation is an IQ standard score of 70 to 75 or below assessed from a variety of indicators. Based upon this criteria, a person either is or is not a person with mental retardation. The gradations of mild, moderate, severe, and profound have been removed (AAMR, 1992).

Persons with intellectual disabilities generally learn at a slower rate than most individuals. Learning complex tasks requires breaking up the task into smaller segments and organizing the segments into sequential levels. Persons with intellectual disabilities are slower to generalize information, and they may not learn from past situations. They may not completely process social information and thus may react to social situations differently than most people (Winnick, 1995).

From the mythology perpetuated by films such as *Forrest Gump*, one might assume that life for persons who are intellectually disabled is truly like "a box of chocolates." If people with intellectual disabilities have supportive families and try hard, they will be financially and socially successful and may even meet the President. For most people with intellectual disabilities, however, their lives can be ones of misconception, confinement, and stigma.

Dudley (1987) found that the general public as well as professionals hold several significant misconceptions about persons with intellectual disabilities. The first misconception is that persons with intellectual disabilities have no awareness or understanding of their disability. The reality is that most do and can describe their disability in detail. The second misconception is that persons with intellectual disabilities are passive or indifferent to the pejorative language used to describe them, including the use of the term *mentally retarded*. The reality is that most people with intellectual disabilities do not like the term because of the stigmas attached to it. Further, they do not like the jokes and the negative way they are portrayed in jest. The third misconception is that persons with intellectual disabilities are unaware of the demeaning way they are treated by society in general and professionals in particular. The reality is that most people with intellectual disabilities do not like to be confined in institutions, told what to do with their lives, stared at, joked about, or patronized by professionals.

These misconceptions, if unchallenged and unrecognized by human service professionals, can have dire consequences. Professionals who are unaware that they are guided by these misconceptions may perpetuate them: they may choose to do *for* consumers rather than to facilitate consumers in speaking and doing for themselves. Professionals may bypass the consumer in developing a plan of action rather than making the person with an intellectual disability the most important input in plan development and implementation because the professional may feel the person with the intellectual disability doesn't have the intellectual capability to have the most significant say in their lives. In addition, professionals may relinquish a prime opportunity for change and insight by assuming that individuals don't want to talk about their disability. Professionals may actually tear down self-concept by their unwillingness to discuss the disability, reinforcing the consumer's fear that their disability is too "horrible and undesirable to mention" (Dudley, 1987, p. 81).

By contrast, professionals can help people with intellectual disabilities and their families understand their rights, maximize their potential, and develop resources. For example, DePoy and Werrback (1996) describe a day program in which persons with intellectual disabilities were responsible for developing rules and programming. Participants were cognizant of their strengths and limitations. They enlisted professional support to assist in enforcing rules and managing problems but maintained great programmatic control. The following two cases provide contrasting examples of the effects that professional attitudes and advice have on lives.

From Evan's birth, it was clear he had developmental disabilities. His family was told by health care providers that Evan should be placed in a state institution for the mentally retarded. Evan, who tested to have an IQ of about 65, spent his life in a state training school with 400 others with similar disabilities. The staff who cared for Evan concurrently cared for 10 to 20 other "patients." Individual attention was rare. Though most were caring and devoted, staff members had little time to help Evan become toilet trained, to learn to independently dress, or to become independent in other activities of daily living. It was assumed that Evan had little ability to learn. Scarce time was available for individual nurturing such as reading or cuddling. Evan's social worker maintained contact with Evan's parents, who were encouraged to visit him periodically. She thought Evan was a "sweet boy" but—like Evan's physician, nurses, therapists, and nurse's aides—saw Evan as needing lifelong institutionalized care and treatment. When Evan reached adolescence and developed a crush on another patient, contact between the two was discouraged and prevented. When they kissed, their behavior was labeled "inappropriate sexual conduct." Evan's girlfriend was sterilized.

Evan died in his early 30s, a result of cardiovascular problems present from birth. Evan had received symptomatic treatment throughout his life; however, he had not received aggressive treatments that nondisabled children with similar medical problems received. Although it cannot be stated with certainty, aggressive treatment may have helped Evan live longer. Evan's life was full of caring professionals and caregivers who, nonetheless, reinforced his dependence and low functioning. His life consisted of few choices and no opportunities to live outside a large institution.

By contrast, Myra, with intellectual abilities similar to Evan's, was reared in her family's home. Public health nurses helped educate Myra's parents about her early care needs. A social worker informed the family of early therapeutic and educational opportunities, which they utilized. Myra was enrolled in Head Start and later in public school. By the time Myra began public school, she was independent in toileting, dressing, and grooming. Myra was able to attend public schools throughout childhood. She was socially and academically delayed; however, with resource education and one-on-one attention from classroom aides, she developed skills far in excess of Evan. Myra's parents consulted with an educational psychologist, who helped them negotiate with the school district to ensure they had adequate resources. Myra developed social relationships with classmates and with other children in her neighborhood. She was also involved with school and social groups for children with intellectual disabilities. She had several boyfriends in adolescence. By age 20, Myra wanted to live away from her family. With the help of the local independent living center, she moved into a supported apartment with a room-mate. A social services worker visited to help Myra with finances and other needs. Myra obtained a job bagging groceries, used public transportation independently, and joined in social functions for others with intellectual disabilities. She dates and talks about marriage someday.

The lives of Evan and Myra differ dramatically. In Evan's life, professionals assumed he had few abilities and needed constant care and protection. By contrast, professionals in Myra's life helped her family and provided opportunities for Myra to maximize her potential and independence.

◆ DOWN SYNDROME

Although some professionals view intellectual disability and Down syndrome as synonymous, because of the many components of Down syndrome beyond intel-lectual development, we deal with it separately. Down syndrome is a set of charac-teristics stemming from individuals having 47 chromosomes rather than the usual 46. Twenty-two chromosomes are in pairs; however, there are three 21st chromo-somes. This extra gene material modifies the orderly development of the body and brain. Down syndrome occurs in 1.3 per 1000 births. About 5000 babies a year are born with Down syndrome in the United States. Approximately 80% of those are born to mothers under the age of 35. About 2.5 in 1000 babies born to women over age 35 have Down syndrome (Wilson, 1995).

There are about 250,000 individuals living in the United States with Down syndrome (DS). Although they have differences, people with DS are more similar than not to individuals without DS. There is a wide range of difference within the population in terms of personality, learning style, intelligence, appearance, compli-ance, humor, compassion, congeniality, and attitude. Individuals with DS have a high rate of congenital heart defects (35 to 50%). Some physical characteristics of persons with DS include short stature and a small nose with a flat bridge. Addi-tional characteristics include almond-shaped eyes with white Brushfield spots on the irises, a single palmar crease on one or both hands, and small features. Children with Down syndrome look more like their families than they do one another; they have a full complement of emotions and attitudes and are creative and imaginative in play and pranks (Wilson, 1995).

On standard IQ tests, persons with Down syndrome can score poorly. How-ever, these tests are limited because they do not measure many important areas of intelligence, and persons with Down syndrome often have good memory, insight, creativity, and cleverness. The high rate of learning disabilities in persons with Down syndrome sometimes masks their range of abilities and talents.

There are three major types of Down syndrome, of which trisomy 21 is the most common. Trisomy 21 occurs when an individual carries a third 21st chromo-some rather than the usual pair as a result of the sperm or egg cell failing to divide properly. About 95% of people with Down syndrome have trisomy 21. About 4%

have translocation, which occurs when the extra 21st chromosome breaks off and becomes attached to and exchanges genetic material with another chromosome (Tierney, McPhee, and Papadakis, 1994). And about 1% have mosaicism, where only some of the individual's cells have trisomy 21 (National Organization for Rare Disorders, Inc., 1993b; Wilson, 1995).

◆ AUTISM

The following song expresses the mystery and complexity of autism:

> *Damon, the young dreamer, whose only purpose is in dreaming;*
> *Caught up in a fairy tale, I fear you've been sleeping.*
> *Trusting is so simple in the child-like way you live.*
> *Candle burns in silence; light grows ever dim.*
> *Was your spirit lost and not regained?*
> *Do you suffer some unknown private pain?*
> *Damon, can you reveal the secrets your dark eyes are keeping?*
> *The ghost of the drifter haunts your soul, I fear.*
> *Is there an unknown voice you alone can hear?*
> *Living in the past is so much safer, they all say.*
> *And you have grown secure, accustomed to your ways.*
> *Will you live in silence, all alone;*
> *An island in the sea, so far from home?*
> *Damon, is it true that you exist just for these brief moments?*
> *Damon, do you believe that we all are children;*
> *Drifting aimlessly, too busy to even listen?*
> *My eyes are filled with tears; I do not trust myself to speak.*
> *There's a sadness in your countenance that makes my heart grow weak.*
> *If there were a time to live in chains, will it pass or is it now too late?*
> *Damon, how can you be certain you are not mistaken?*
> (Crevak, 1976)

The song was written by a young therapist, songwriter, and performer to express his disappointment at not being able to reach a young man with autism with whom he regularly worked. The National Information Center for Children and Youth with Disabilities (1995) defines autism and pervasive developmental disorder-NOS (not otherwise specified) as conditions that impact a person's ability to communicate with others, understand language, play, and relate to other individuals. The condition is usually evident by the age of 3. The DSM-IV defines "autistic disorder" using very specific symptoms in the areas of social interaction, communication, and behavior. The diagnosis of pervasive developmental disorder-NOS is used when a child displays similar behaviors to autistic disorder but does not meet the specific criteria (APA, 1994).

Autism and PDD-NOS occur from 5 to 15 times in 10,000 births. Both are four times more common in boys than in girls. Scientists do not know what causes autism. Possibilities include neurological damage and/or biochemical imbalance in the brain (NICCYD, 1995). Genetic factors may play a role in some types of autism because there is a higher incidence rate among siblings. Emerging research indicates that it may be inherited through autosomal recessive genes in some people. Older theories of psychological etiology have been dismissed (National Organization for Rare Disorders, Inc., 1993a).

Treatment and Education of Autistic and Related Communication Handicapped Children (TEACCH, 1996) lists several characteristics of persons with autism. One characteristic is that they sometimes have difficulty with language development. Language may not develop at all, or if it does, it may include the use of words or phrases that don't have standard meanings. Sometimes speech is formal and delivered in a monotone manner. For Grandin (1992), a person with autism, not being able to speak as a child was totally frustrating. If her parents or other adults spoke to her, she could understand them but could not respond. Sometimes the only way she could communicate was to scream.

Persons with autism may also have inconsistent patterns of sensory responses (TEACCH, 1996). At times they may not respond at all to sound. Other times their reaction may be overresponsive. Grandin (1992) states that her hearing was at one extreme or the other. Noises were so loud that she literally had to shut her hearing down. At times her mother thought she was deaf.

The same response swing may occur with pain, heat, cold, or even human touch. Grandin (1995) recounts her approach-avoidance of human touch. She craved human touch but pulled away from its intensity:

From as far back as I can remember, I always hated to be hugged. I wanted to experience the good feeling of being hugged, but it was just too overwhelming. It was like a great, all-engulfing tidal wave of stimulation, and I reacted like a wild animal. Being touched triggered flight; it flipped my circuit breaker. I was overloaded and would have to escape, often by jerking away suddenly. (p. 62)

In addition, persons with autism may exhibit high levels of intellectual functioning in some areas and very low levels in other areas. They may have excellent skills in drawing but may not understand composition balance. They may have perfect pitch but don't understand rhythm. They may have highly developed computational skills in math but don't understand how to use the skill effectively (TEACCH, 1996). Grandin (1992) discusses this inconsistency in herself. She had perfect pitch and could hum a tune, note-for-note, that she had heard just once or twice. But she could not master rhythm. Alone, her rhythm was steady. When she tried to clap along with others, however, she had great difficulty.

Finally, persons with autism may exhibit repetitive body movements or repetitive actions. If the routines or repetitions are changed, they may react in a distressed manner (TEACCH, 1996). One of the authors worked with a 12-year-old boy with autism who, if left alone, would sit on a table cross-legged, methodically tearing a tissue in two, eating half, and stacking the other half neatly to his side. If unsupervised, he would do that continually. When directed toward another task, the youngster would become extremely upset.

Grandin (1992) offers insight for people working with persons with autism. She discusses those who were most helpful to her in facilitating her life goals and those who were not. Generally, people who could help her capitalize on her strengths were most helpful: the governess who kept her and her sister busy with structured activities that had narrowed choices; the science teacher who helped her translate various fixations to actual scientific problems with great practicality, which eventually resulted in her academic career; her mother, who took an active part in her elementary and high school education; the manager of a local firm who supported her interest in the livestock industry while she was in college and who hired her for her first designing job. Grandin's indictment of traditional human service professionals is sobering:

> As I grew older, the people who were of the greatest assistance were always the more creative, unconventional types. Psychiatrists and psychologists were of little help. They were too busy trying to psychoanalyze me and discover my deep dark psychological problems. One psychiatrist thought if he could find my "psychic injury," I would be cured. The high school psychologist wanted to stamp out my fixations on things like doors instead of trying to understand them and use them to stimulate learning. (Grandin, 1995, pp. 98–99)

A most significant skill for anyone in the human service industry working with persons with autism as well as other disabilities is the ability to move out of dogma, ideology, and set ways and to address individuals on their own terms, using their strengths as the beginning points of action.

◆ SEIZURE DISORDERS (EPILEPSY)

Seizure disorder (epilepsy) is a term that defines conditions associated with recurrent seizures. Because of the social stigma tied to the condition, people experiencing this condition generally prefer the term *seizure disorder* rather than epilepsy. In addition, many people with seizure disorder resist being classified as persons with developmental disabilities. We place seizure disorder in this chapter because this classification reflects current state and federal definitions. About 2.5 million people in the United States have conditions resulting in recurrent seizures. A seizure disorder usually impacts children, young adults, and people over the age of 65, although anyone at any age can develop a seizure disorder (Lewis, 1993). The most frequent causes of seizure disorder include head trauma, brain tumors, strokes, substance abuse, severe brain infections, congenital changes, and prenatal injuries (Tierney, McPhee, and Papadakis, 1994).

Seizures are a transient flurry of electrical impulses in the brain that are without order. The result can be anything from a blank stare to convulsions (Lewis, 1993). Tierney, McPhee, and Papadakis (1994) discuss classifications of seizures defined by the International League against Epilepsy. Seizures can be classified into two broad categories: partial and generalized. Partial seizures are restricted to only one part of the cerebral hemisphere. They can be either simple, in which the individual does not lose consciousness, or complex, in which the individual either loses consciousness or consciousness is impaired in some way. Persons experiencing partial seizures of either simple or complex types may have sensory, motor, or autonomic symptoms, such as a tingling feeling, jerking, or sweating. Generalized seizures involve the whole brain, which is suddenly inundated with extra chaotic electrical energy whereby the entire body can be affected. Generalized seizures have five different forms: the absence seizure (petit mal), the atypical absence seizure, the myoclonic seizure, the tonic-clonic seizure (grand mal), and the atonic seizure (Tierney, McPhee, and Papadakis, 1994). The tonic-clonic, or grand mal, seizure is the most dramatic. Lewis (1993) describes a grand mal seizure:

> *An individual having a tonic-clonic seizure may suddenly cry out and then fall unconscious. The body stiffens, and then shakes or jerks uncontrollably. Bladder and bowel control may be lost. Breathing is quite shallow—and may even stop briefly during the seizure—but will return to normal when the shaking movements end. When the seizure ends, usually after a minute or two, the person is often confused and tired.* (p. 20)

Patlak (1992) connects the drama of a grand mal seizure to the supernatural view of epilepsy. The Greeks thought seizures represented visitation from the gods. During the Renaissance period, it was thought that people having seizures were possessed by demons or were themselves demons and that people with seizure disorders received "just" punishment by being burned at the stake.

The dramatic nature of the seizure can result in stereotypes and discrimination. Persons with seizure disorders have trouble finding jobs and advancing in the jobs they do find (Lewis, 1993). Famulari (1992) found that persons with seizure disorders, on the average, have one year less education than people who do not have epilepsy. Males with seizure disorders have much more difficulty in finding a job than individuals who do not have seizure disorders. Finally, the wages paid to persons with seizure disorders who are employed are almost $4.00 per hour less than the wages paid to those workers who do not have seizure disorders.

As with other disabilities, the limitations in education and work placed on persons with seizure disorders stem from myth and stereotyping. The reality is that medication, diet, or, in some cases, surgery can be used to control seizures. Sometimes a combination of all three is used. Three-quarters of all persons with epilepsy can control seizures by drug therapy. Drugs used include carbamazepine, clonazepam, phenytoin, valproic acid, phenobarbital, primidone, and ethosuximide. Sometimes more than one drug is used but this is rare. Drugs can cause side effects, including drowsiness, confusion, clumsiness, nausea, and learning problems. To eliminate side effects, different drugs may be used and dosages manipulated.

Dr. Thomas Young, a friend of one of the authors, is a prime example of how stereotypes of persons with seizure disorders are false. At this writing (October, 1996), Dr. Young is vice president of the California Faculty Association, the union which represents faculty in the California State University system. He is a full professor of communication studies at California State University, Stanislaus, as well as the interim affirmative action officer. He is a member of the systemwide academic senate. And he is a person with a seizure disorder which he identifies proudly and openly. He refers to himself as "a person with a disability" with grace and pride. He has been taking medication such as phenobarbital most of his life to control the seizures. Yet, on occasion, he will experience a seizure.

Dr. Young keeps an unbelievable calendar. He generally works 100-hour weeks. He does not drive. Dr. Young is constantly on a plane going somewhere. His life is a constant stream of activity and pressure. Aside from his family duties, his teaching duties, his affirmative action duties, and his academic senate duties, he has been the prime negotiator for the last three contracts between faculty and the California State University. His life "flies in the face" of stereotypical views of persons with seizure disorders.

If control of seizures cannot be brought about by medication, some persons have been able to control seizures using high-fat diets. The high intake of fat produces ketogens, which seem to prevent seizures, particularly in children. However, blood levels must be continually monitored for reasons of cholesterol and potential organ damage caused by ketogens.

If the seizure activity is limited to a small area of the brain, some persons with seizure disorders can benefit from surgical removal or oblation of the malfunctioning brain cells that cause the seizure. Surgery cannot be used when seizure activity is in the areas of the brain that control speech, language, hearing, or other major functions. Surgery may also be performed to sever the connections between the left and right brain to prevent the spread of the electrical storm (Patlak, 1992). This procedure, however, limits the ability of the brain's hemispheres to communicate with each other.

◆ THE RIGHT TO BE ME

The cornerstone of the civil rights movement of people with disabilities has been the concept of self-determination. Self-determination is usually wrested away at every step of development and leaves persons with disabilities stranded and alone, afraid to enter into the game of chance that is life. Without the experience of independently making decisions that have the chance of failing, persons with disabilities are left without a clue about how to gain economic resources and real power within our society. This has been the case particularly with persons with developmental disabilities. Pfeiffer (1993) demonstrates the deep historical roots of society's fear of persons with developmental disabilities. Pfeiffer describes in detail the thoughts of Havelock Ellis, who was a strong advocate for human rights—particularly women's rights—in the 1920s. Ellis represented the thought of the time that the "feebleminded" were at best a burden to society and a potential threat to the future of human beings. Although Ellis advocated merely sterilization and maintenance, other intellectual leaders of the time advocated extinction.

Controlling people with developmental disabilities has been the driving force of how people with developmental disabilities are treated not only by the aggregate society but also by the "knowledgeable" professional. It is this desire to control that is the focal point of concern for self-advocates. People First is a national self-advocacy organization by and for persons with developmental disabilities. There are over 374 chapters and some 10,000 members (Shapiro, 1993). Quite simply, self-advocates are looking for control over their lives and how they are treated. T. J. Monroe, a self-advocate from Tennessee speaking to the President's Committee on Mental Retardation in 1994, said it most succinctly:

> *I think what we need to do is bring together professionals' knowledge and self-advocates' personal experience. This way, we can build a plan for action that solves the real problems people have. Self-advocates want to become empowered and have a voice in solving the problems they experience. Together with professional and government resources, we can make it work.* (Smith, 1994, p. 22)

Self-advocates question the basic assumptions made about people with developmental disabilities. The first assumption is that persons with disabilities need extensive protections from the myriad of threats and dangers in society. To this false assumption, we need to direct the following questions: How much protection do they need? Who determines the place and nature of the danger? A second assumption is that persons with disabilities cannot make major life decisions because they cannot deal with the risks and the consequences of the decisions. To this misconstrued assumption, we need to ask, How do you experience independence without taking risks? Who benefits from the "protection" from making crucial life decisions? Whose fear is at issue when it comes to decisions about living in an apartment, having a job, having sex, or marrying? The last assumption is that self-advocacy cannot work because parents and professionals provide the "direction," organization, and resources. This misconception is the hardest to challenge. Because of the nature of developmental disabilities, the various skills necessary for gaining civil rights are the skills most difficult for persons with disabilities to acquire. Yet, there are those in the People First movement who strongly believe that the effectiveness of the movement in gaining real independence for persons with developmental disabilities will be compromised as long as persons without disabilities remain in control (Shapiro, 1993).

Spreading the concept of self-advocacy and independence is difficult for a variety of reasons. First, as is the case with most persons with disabilities, a long history of dependency and control exists. As was mentioned previously, there has been particular historic oppression of persons with developmental disabilities. Second, both persons with developmental disabilities and their parents find the idea of independence too frightening. Finally, laws and policies still deter self determination. For example, as late as the 1980s, more than half the states had laws prohibiting persons with developmental disabilities from marrying (Shapiro, 1993).

The nature of developmental disability, particularly when it is intellectually related, challenges the social welfare service provision industry. Human service professionals must remove themselves from the long historic trend of doing for persons with disabilities and lay the foundation of independence. This is no easy task. Teaching self-empowerment at times is work producing and time consuming. Agencies are wanting more for less. Facilitating self-empowerment may produce resistance on the part of the agency, parents and other family members, and other involved professionals. It is far easier to control and dictate. Nevertheless, aside from the long-term benefits empowerment produces for the person with a developmental disability, facilitating independence allows us as a society to experience the richness and joy that the diversity of disability can produce (Schwier, 1994).

◆ SUMMARY

For all practical purposes, the federal definition of developmental disability encompasses most disabilities acquired before the age of 22. According to the federal definition, if the onset is early and the disability is severe enough to interfere with several major life functions, the condition can be defined as a developmental disability. Whereas others offer more succinct definitions, several problems occur with all definitions of developmental disability that include intellectual disability. First, although service benefits are linked to being classified as developmentally disabled, groups such as persons who are blind, persons who have cerebral palsy, and deaf people resist linking with the developmentally disabled banner primarily because of the link between the terms *developmentally disabled* and *mental retardation*. Second, many nondisabled reformers use the words of independent living, but the resulting policy and programs sometimes leave this ideal far behind. Last, many states for economic reasons limit the definition of developmental disability.

Although some may not agree, we have placed intellectual disability (mental retardation), Down syndrome, autism, epilepsy, and cerebral palsy under the category of developmental disability.

Generally speaking, persons with intellectual disabilities learn at a slower rate than most individuals. Learning complex tasks requires breaking up the task into smaller segments and organizing the segments into sequential levels. Persons with intellectual disabilities are slower to generalize information, and they may not learn from past situations. They may not completely process social information and thus may react to social situations differently than most people.

Down syndrome is a set of characteristics stemming from individuals having 47 chromosomes (because of an extra 21st chromosome) rather than the usual 46. On standard IQ tests, persons with Down syndrome can score poorly. However, these tests are limited because they do not measure many important areas of intelligence, and persons with Down syndrome often have good memory, insight, creativity, and cleverness. The high rate of learning disabilities in persons with Down syndrome sometimes masks their range of abilities and talents.

Autism is a condition that impacts a person's ability to communicate with others, understand language, play, and relate to other individuals. The condition is usually evident by the age of 3. Persons with autism sometimes have difficulty with language development and inconsistent patterns of sensory responses. They may exhibit high levels of intellectual functioning in some areas and very low levels in other areas. Persons with autism may also exhibit repetitive body movements or repetitive actions.

Seizure disorder (epilepsy) is a term that defines conditions associated with recurrent seizures. Seizures are a transient flurry of electrical impulses in the brain that are without order. The result can be anything from a blank stare to convulsions. The dramatic nature of the seizure can result in stereotypes and discrimination. Persons with seizure disorders have trouble finding jobs and advancing in the jobs they do find.

Controlling people with developmental disabilities has been the driving force of how people with developmental disabilities are treated not only by the aggregate society but also by the "knowledgeable" professional. The heart of practice with persons with developmental disabilities lies with helping them facilitate their independence and self-determination.

◆   ◆   ◆   *Personal Narrative: Resa Hayes*   ◆   ◆   ◆

Resa Hayes is a 37-year-old disability activist from Spokane, Washington. She works for People First, an organization run by people who have developmental disabilities. In Resa's job, she lectures about herself and about disabilities to parents of developmentally disabled people, professionals, students, and others. The following includes the text she uses when she talks to parents.

I was born in 1960 at Deaconess Hospital in Spokane, Washington. My home was in Davenport, Washington, where I lived on a wheat ranch. I have two brothers and one sister. Their names are John, who is the oldest, Elizabeth, who is the second, and Richard, the third, and I am the youngest. My mom noticed that at six months my arms were slightly stiff. When it was hard to keep my balance while sitting on the floor, my parents took me to a specialist in Spokane. He said that I had cerebral palsy (CP). He demonstrated the way that I would probably walk—he did this several times. Because of the way he did it, my parents were so shocked by his rude and insulting manner that they just wanted to take me and run away from the terrible suggestions of this doctor.

I'd like to tell you about decisions and choices. A decision is the act or process of making a judgment, a determination, or reaching a conclusion. A choice is the option of having the power or right to choose—having the freedom of choice. A choice could be good or bad, constructive or destructive. Some of the early choices my parents made were the product of guessing what would be best for me. We had advice from doctors, which helped some, but a lot of the choices they made came from trial and error. The decision they made to send me to the CP school when I was 8 years old is one they still talk about and wonder if it was the right decision.

My school was good, but to be sent away from my family was very hard on me. My folks took me home every weekend and that helped a lot. My parents struggled to find me a good boarding home to live in. My first place had none of the family feeling of home. I cried every Monday night (after I came back from visiting my parents) for the first two years I was in that boarding house, and this broke my family's heart. Today I am pleased to know that there are more regulations to monitor the care of children now because I was not properly cared for then. The choice to come home and go to high school in Davenport, a small rural farming community, was a good one. It was an uneasy time for a few weeks until the kids got used to me. I made a choice to be the girl's volleyball manager for four years. I was included in nearly all my class activities. At that time was the beginning of when I felt accepted on the part of my peers. At my graduation, I led my class in the procession to our graduation ceremonies. I was so proud.

After graduation I made a choice to move back to Spokane; since it was my choice, I thought to myself, "free at last." I arrived in Spokane with the vision of finding a job and having more opportunities. When I first got there, I was presented with several adult family homes to check into and decide where I wanted to live. The home I picked offered room and board and supervision. I began volunteering at the United CP, and I continued there for five difficult years. But what I really wanted was a real paying job. The agency that was supposed to help me find a job had me doing things I didn't like, such as volunteering at day care centers. This experience told me that people said I had choices, but I really didn't, and I had to rely on the decisions of others even when I was quite capable of making my own individual choices. This happens to us a lot.

I finally got myself a real paying job working for People First of Washington. Since that time, I made the choice to move into my own apartment. I'm still living my full vision even though I have some help with daily living tasks.

In everyone's life there comes a time to think about a relationship. What is a relationship? What do I need out of a relationship? What can I give in a relationship? I am no different than any of you out there today. I have the same heart, I have the same feelings, I have the same aches and pains and the same hopes and dreams that you do. I have suffered disappointment in relationships as have you. I have been hurt too, but through all of this I have grown. I have used these experiences as true learning experiences, not allowing them to turn into bad habits. In summing up, all I am trying to say to all of you is to look within your hearts and accept the disabilities. Your children are people first; their disabilities are secondary. Know when to let go, when your sons and daughters say they want to make choices and decisions for themselves. In closing, I would like to say thank you to God for helping me through my life so far.

It was really difficult growing up. I grew up in the '60s, and people didn't have the information they have today (about CP). So we had to talk to doctors who did different things to me. The Shriner's Hospital helped a lot because I had surgeries done there and therapies and things like that. They (the professionals) said I've got CP. Nobody said that I was mentally retarded, and if I heard that I would punch their nose in because I don't like that word.

I don't think my parents knew what I could do, the potential I had. My mom sheltered me quite a lot. She protected me because I was different and she didn't know how the world was going to treat me. My parents worked with me like they would with any of the other kids to get me to do what I could do for myself. My brothers and sisters treated me no differently. They chased me around with the vacuum cleaner, sucking my hair up with it.

I went to a CP school for eight years, and I was protected from "normal" children. We all had different abilities. We used to tease each other and call each other names, but we didn't think of it like, "He's spastic." We didn't think about (having CP) much, but they didn't prepare us for the outside world and the cruelty of the people when we got into mainstream schools. I was 16 when I went into high school in Davenport and I was 21 when I graduated. I got along better with my younger classmates than my older classmates. They understood me better than the upperclassmen.

In high school, when I came back to Davenport after eight years of living in Spokane, I had about two hours a day in special education classes, and then my other classes were regular. People were mean to me; I remember they used to pinch me and stuff. They used to push my books off my desk in front of the classrooms. They used to put toothpaste on my pictures. They used to jam my walker so I couldn't open it. They would put the sign "kick me" on my back. I laughed, but I didn't like what they did to me. I didn't have the guts like I do today to tell them to knock it off.

I think starting kids out in the regular school system would be best; better than special schools. They could have teacher's aides go into the classroom with them. But they should not be ostracized from the regular class. I didn't have anybody to help me, but my mom did a lot of writing and test taking for me. She was kind of like my right hand when I was in regular school.

I had two brothers and one sister who went to high school ahead of me. I wanted to be just like them because when I came home (from the CP school) every weekend I could see what they were doing. My whole dream was to go to high school like them. When I got into regular high school, I was meeting that dream. But the standards of getting the grades was a big standard too. I wanted to make my dad and mom proud of me. They were proud of me but in their own way. They didn't expect me to do what my brothers and sisters did because they knew I had a learning disability. When I got C's and D's and didn't qualify for the honor roll, I used to lie in bed and cry myself to sleep because it hurt so bad. I guess my dad and mom were just as proud of me as everybody else in the family, but sometimes I wanted to have that academic recognition like all of us do.

My mom was scared for me when I moved back to Spokane. She didn't think that I could use the bus system. Well, once again I showed everyone.

I arrived in Spokane with the vision of finding a job and having more opportunities. When I first arrived I was presented with several adult family homes to check into and decide where I could live. The home I picked offered room and board and supervision. (For recreation,) I did swimming and softball throws. I also did Special Olympics.

I began volunteering at the United CP and I continued there for five difficult years. But, what I really wanted was a real paying job. All these agencies that I went to promised me a job but they didn't know what I could do. They didn't look within me. They thought I could talk good and my hands could work good but my hands did not work as well as the average person's hands. I had to always volunteer because the agencies weren't really meeting my needs by helping me find a job.

I live in my own apartment now. I'm really, really thankful for assisted living because without assisted living I would have to work even harder to do my daily tasks. I have two people that come in twice or three times a week to help me out with daily living tasks and take me to doctor's appointments and grocery shopping. They help me in the community and help me with my personal finances. Without that help I don't know what I would do.

I found a job several years ago working for People First. People First is a non-profit organization for people with developmental disabilities. We have a motto, which says, "We are people first and our disabilities are second." We don't like using the word *disability*. We like to use *different abilities*, because we all are different and we all have abilities. My self-image really grew when I got involved in People First. I was the state president for two years.

When I started with People First, we were working on the Department of Education grant. We went into schools to teach developmentally disabled students about self-determination skills. It was a three-year project. Now I go out to create and support People First chapters in the state.

People First is saying, "Treat people first and everything else is second." Change your low expectations to positive expectations. People's minds are sort of warped about disabilities because they haven't gotten an education. Society's low expectations have said, "If somebody is different than me, let's lock them away." Something's got to change, and I think that change is positive thinking. People First helps people know what they want to do and stand up to people who say, "You can't do that." We can advocate for people. People First can go into the institutions and educate those people to stand up to the staff. We help them get out of institutions.

There is a disability culture. When I was back in the CP school, we had a disability culture in the school. We were safe in the culture we were in. We used to joke and call each other some names because we were safe. In society today, we don't feel safe. People point their fingers at us. But you know something? We found out at a Spokane Transit Authority meeting there was a culture that stuck us together like glue. It was really culturfied. We had lots of disabled people there; old people, young people, people of color. We were voicing our opinions about public transportation and together we felt safe. When they said, "You can't clap," we just clapped louder. Talk about culture—that was a cultural experience for me.

As for role models, I remember my home economics teacher in high school. She treated me like everybody else. I liked the way she acted, the way she ran her class. I would also have to say the Incredible Hulk was a role model. He was deaf but that didn't stop him from acting. It didn't stop him from turning green when he got mad. I often wanted to have him move my bedroom furniture around.

I see other people with disabilities just like I am. When people without disabilities see me, it's shocking for them. They are not accepting and lack education about people with disabilities. I have seen people with disabilities ostracized. People label us. But you don't label people; you label jars. You say, "This is Resa, she's my friend. She has a lot to say." Treat people the way you want to be treated. Our biggest problem is people's low expectations of us. People are in institutions because of that. We've got to get them help and get them educated and say, "Hey, we're going to do our very best jobs to get you out of there." We should educate ourselves by accepting the person and not the disability.

To people with disabilities and their parents, I say talk to your doctors to let the doctors know that you will not accept anything less for your child. Be gutsy, be determined about getting answers. The more guts you have, the better off you are. Treat your children as normally as you can by letting them fall down, letting them experience the pain, letting them know what's right and wrong. Let them fall down on the floor; fall down with other people; share a little hurt because we learn from our falls.

I have been in a relationship. It's been a hurtful relationship but I have grown to understand myself better. I have learned to have high expectations. I haven't found Mr. Right; I am happy with that.

I am proud to be me, but there are days I would love not to have this. I think all people with a disability would like not to have their speaking impairment, or hearing impairment, or visual or other impairment, but I think we are all stronger for it. I do like myself. My disability has made me stronger in my beliefs and in speaking out for other people. It makes me appreciate who I am and what I can do.

To people with disabilities, I say educate yourself, be good to yourself. No matter what, you're a worthwhile person. If people say you aren't a worthwhile person, tell them to get a life!

◆ ◆ ◆

Discussion Questions

1. What are some of the major issues in defining persons with developmental disabilities? How are these issues influenced by the social construct of disability in our society?

2. What are the major misconceptions that practitioners need to address in working with persons with intellectual disabilities?

3. Why are self-advocacy organizations so important, and how will they impact your future work with persons with disabilities?

4. What are some of the specific characteristics of autism, and how would knowledge of these characteristics influence intervention strategy?

5. How can social service agencies and practitioners facilitate the empowerment and independence of persons with developmental disabilities?

Suggested Readings

Grandin, T. (1995). *Thinking in pictures and other reports from my life with autism.* New York: Doubleday.

Meyer, L. H., Peck, C. A., and Brown, L. (Eds.). (1991). *Critical issues in the lives of people with severe disabilities.* Baltimore: Paul H. Brookes.

Noble, V. (1993). *Down is up for Aaron Eagle: A mother's spiritual journey with Down syndrome.* New York: HarperCollins.

Shapiro, J. P. (1993). *No pity: People with disabilities forging a new civil rights movement.* New York: Times Books.

References

American Association on Mental Retardation. (1992). *Mental retardation: Definition, classification, and systems of supports, special 9th edition.* Washington, DC: AAMR.

American Association of University Affiliated Programs for Persons with Developmental Disabilities. (1997). *Definition of developmental disabilities* [www.aauap.org/DD.HTM].

American Psychological Association. (1994). *Diagnostic and statistical manual of mental disorders* (4th ed.). Washington, DC: APA.

Ansello, E. F. (1992). Seeking common ground between aging and developmental disabilities. *Generations, 16*(1), 9–16.

Brown, L. (1991). Who are they and what do they want: An essay on TASH. In L. H. Meyer, C. A. Peck, and L. Brown, (Eds.), *Critical issues in the lives of people with severe disabilities* (pp. xxv–xxvii). Baltimore: Paul H. Brookes.

California Codes Welfare and Institutional Code, Section 4512. www.dds.cahwnet.gov/statutes/4500.htm

Crevak, M. (1976). *Damon.* Unpublished composition performed July 7, 1996, Pittsburgh, PA.

DePoy, E., and Werrbach, G. (1996). Successful living placement for adults with disabilities: Considerations for social work practice. *Social Work in Health Care, 23*(4), 21–34.

Dudley, J. R. (1987). Speaking for themselves: People who are labeled as mentally retarded. *Social Work, 32*(1), 80–82.

Evans, I. M. (1991). Testing and diagnosis: A review and evaluation. In L. H. Meyer, C. A. Peck, and L. Brown (Eds.), *Critical issues in the lives of people with severe disabilities,* (pp. 25–44). Baltimore: Paul H. Brookes.

Famulari, M. (1992). The effects of a disability on labor market performance: The case of epilepsy. *Southern Economic Journal, 58*(4), 1072–1088.

Grandin, T. (1992). An inside view of autism. In E. Schopler and G. B Mesibov (Eds.), *High functioning individuals with autism* (pp. 105–126). New York: Plenum Press.

Grandin, T. (1995). *Thinking in pictures and other reports from my life with autism.* New York: Doubleday.

Hall, J. A., Ford, L. H., Moss, J. A., and Dineen, J. P. (1986). Practice with mentally retarded adults as an adjunct to vocational training. *Social Work, 31*(2), 125–128.

Lewis, S. (1993). Understanding epilepsy. *Current Health, 20*(4), 19–22.

National Information Center for Children and Youth with Disabilities. (1997). *Autism and pervasive development disorder* [gopher://aed.aed.org:70/00/.disability/.nichy/.online/.fact-general/.onlist/.autism]. Fact Sheet Number 1.

National Organization for Rare Disorders, Inc. (1993a). *Autism.* In A. H. Bruckheim (Ed.), *The family doctor.* [CD-ROM]. Portland, OR: Creative Multimedia.

National Organization for Rare Disorders, Inc. (1993b). *Down's syndrome.* In A. H. Bruckheim (Ed.), *The family doctor.* [CD-ROM]. Portland, OR: Creative Multimedia.

Patlak, M. (1992). Controlling epilepsy. *FDA Consumer, 26*(4), 28–32.

Pfeiffer, D. (1993). Overview of the disability movement: History, legislative record, and political implications. *Policy Studies Journal, 21*(4), 724–735.

Schwier, K. M. (1994). Storytelling: The power of listening. *Developmental Disabilities Bulletin, 22*(2), 24–37.

Shapiro, J. P. (1993). *No pity: People with disabilities forging a new civil rights movement.* New York: Times Books.

Smith, B. (1994). PCMR conference report. *Children Today, 23*(1), 20–24.

Tierney, L. M., Jr., McPhee, S. J., and Papadakis, M. A. (Eds.). (1994). *Current medical diagnosis and treatment.* Norwalk, CT: Appleton & Lange.

Treatment and Education of Autistic and Related Communication Handicapped Children. (1996). *Autism primer: Twenty questions and answers.* [www.unc.edu/depts/teacch/20ques.htm]. Chapel Hill: University of North Carolina School of Medicine.

Wilson, P. (1995). *Welcoming babies with Down syndrome.* [nas.com/downsyn/welcome.html].

Winnick, J. P. (1995). *Adapted physical education and sport* (2nd ed.). Champaign, IL: Human Kinetics.

Chapter 9

PERSONS WITH PSYCHIATRIC DISABILITIES

By Marilyn Wedenoja, Ph.D., Eastern Michigan University

I am better off now than I would have been if I had never had
mental illness. . . . The reaction of others is one of the most
difficult parts of mental illness. In a lot of ways, the way we are
treated is worse than the symptoms themselves.

—Donna Orrin, business owner

Student Learning Objectives:

1. To be able to identify and compare the medical, social, and political dimensions of psychiatric disabilities.

2. To know the different types of psychiatric disabilities and variations of onset, course, effects, and needed accommodations.

3. To be aware of the experiences of family members when a loved one has a psychiatric disability.

4. To be familiar with the self-help and advocacy movement composed of mental health consumers and family members.

The needs and experiences of persons with severe and persistent psychiatric disabilities, such as schizophrenia, major depression, and bipolar disorder, are increasingly being included in the movement for improved social awareness, rights, and resources for persons with disabilities (Carling, 1995; Deegan, 1992, 1997; Frank and Kupfer, 1993; Nagler, 1993; Wedenoja and Brown, 1996; Wedenoja and Neal, 1995). In terms of federal rights and benefits, severe mental illness is recognized as a disability. The Americans with Disabilities Act of 1990, for example, includes psychiatric disability as one of the conditions whereby reasonable accommodations are to be made to enable qualified persons to fully participate in employment without being subject to disability-related discrimination or barriers (Mancuso, 1994). With regard to federal benefits, one-fourth of the social security disability payments in this country are awarded to persons with severe psychiatric disabilities (NAMI, 1997). Although the types of needed accommodations and resources may at times differ, there has been a growing recognition among activists, practitioners, and educators that commonalities exist in the struggles, challenges, and strivings for empowerment of persons with a range of disabilities, including psychiatric disabilities.

Much is yet to be discovered about the biochemical dynamics of psychiatric disabilities. Medically significant breakthroughs in research and treatment have been made in recent decades and have brought increased awareness and understanding. Research findings about the etiology of severe psychiatric disabilities point to the significant impact of genetic predisposition, while further theories related to prenatal viruses, exposure to toxic substances, hormonal imbalances, and the effects of severe trauma are also being pursued. We have yet to discover exactly how the brain's information processing system becomes affected to trigger the manifestations of psychiatric disabilities; however, research has been focusing on an imbalance of the brain chemicals (neurotransmitters) that the nervous system utilizes to communicate across the gaps (synapses) between nerve cells (neurons) (Wilson, 1997). Frese (1997), a psychologist with schizophrenia, states that "our disability is one of a biochemical imbalance" (p. 147).

Medical research has thus been helpful in increasing social awareness about the causes of psychiatric disabilities and the resulting effects. Our growing understanding of the intricate workings of the brain, which is now more visible and observable with the assistance of high-technology equipment (e.g., MRI, PET scans), has also served to demystify manifestations of these conditions that were historically thought to be caused by devil possession, weak moral character, or "schizophrenogenic mothering." Such historical beliefs have contributed to the harsh judgments directed toward this population. The social stigma of psychiatric disability has contributed to the resistance of persons with psychiatric disabilities and their families in acknowledging, and identifying with, this disability.

Socially, public education campaigns are beginning to challenge the stigma associated with severe psychiatric disabilities. Mental Illness Awareness Week, held nationally every October, offers an organized effort on the part of numerous national organizations (for example, the National Alliance for the Mentally Ill, American Psychiatric Association, etc.) to increase social awareness on this topic through television and radio public service announcements, programming, and community events. Celebrity self-disclosures have also introduced the public to the stories of persons nationally known and respected who have psychiatric disabilities. For example, the actress Patty Duke (Duke and Hochman, 1992) and psychiatric researcher Dr. Kay Jamison (1995) have published personal accounts of their experiences with manic depression; Mike Wallace and William Styron (1990) have openly shared their struggles with major depression; and Lionel Aldridge became a public speaker after his experience with schizophrenia and homelessness that followed an impressive career as a professional football player and national network sports announcer.

The sharing of these stories has increased awareness of the contributions that can be made by persons with psychiatric disabilities and has challenged the stigma associated with these conditions. Jamison's research on manic depression (1993) further suggests that the cognitive effects of some psychiatric disabilities may for some even enhance creative ability:

Occasionally an exhilarating and powerfully creative force, more often a destructive one, manic-depressive illness gives a touch of fire to many of those who experience it . . . . there is strong scientific and biological evidence linking manic-depressive illness and its related temperaments to artistic imagination and expression. Biographies of eminent poets, artists, and composers attest to the strikingly high rate of mood disorders and suicide—as well as institutionalization in asylums and psychiatric hospitals—in these individuals, and recent psychiatric and psychological studies of living artists and writers have further documented the link. (p. 240)

Although these educational efforts represent an alternative to the stereotypical images in the media of persons with psychiatric disabilities as primarily dangerous "psychotic killers," psychiatric disability nevertheless continues to be a highly stigmatized condition that is often misunderstood, feared, and subject to open social discrimination (Fellin, 1996; Fink and Tasman, 1992; Lefley, 1996; Manning, 1998). Persons with psychiatric disabilities have historically been confined, segregated from society, and treated as subhuman. During the Nazi regime, this population was a targeted group for extinction, together with Jews, gays, lesbians, and persons with developmental and physical disabilities (Nagler, 1993). Within our current society, persons with psychiatric disabilities continue to be shunned by the community, denied basic rights and benefits, and subjected to widespread discrimination and stigma. They consistently have difficulty obtaining or maintaining employment, health insurance, medical treatment, or housing once their condition is revealed. One person described her experience of discrimination as follows:

Life is hard with a diagnosis of schizophrenia. I can talk, but I may not be heard. I can make suggestions, but they may not be taken seriously. I can report my thoughts, but they may be seen as delusions. I can recite experiences, but they may be interpreted as fantasies. To be a patient or even ex-client is to be discounted. Your label is a reality that never leaves you; it gradually shapes an identity that is hard to shed. We must transform public attitudes and current stereotypes. Until we eliminate stigma, we will have prejudice, which will inevitably be expressed as discrimination against persons with mental illness. (Leete, 1997, p. 102)

This discrimination is experienced not only interpersonally but also in terms of the allocation of resources, benefits, and research funding.

Our social neglect toward persons with psychiatric disabilities is also directly visible among those who are homeless on our urban streets (Brown and Fellin, 1988; Fellin, 1996). With the widespread closing of mental institutions on a national basis beginning in the 1960s, our current homeless population includes persons who were displaced from mental health facilities without adequate community services, housing, and social supports. A number of others with psychiatric disabilities are living in the community with poverty-level resources and limited opportunities to participate in work and community activities.

Even the majority of social workers, a profession committed to those most oppressed and disadvantaged, reportedly perceive psychiatric disabilities as the least desirable field of service (Castanuela, 1994; Rubin and Johnson, 1984; Werrbach and DePoy, 1993). Unfortunately, such attitudes tend to be the result of unexamined social biases and lack of direct contact with persons in recovery. Human service workers who are most effective in working in the field of psychiatric rehabilitation have developed a sense of compassion and caring for this population, either from appreciating the struggles and strengths that they have witnessed or based on sensitivities they bring to their work from coping with their own psychiatric condition or that of a loved one.

Politically, it is a time of active change and challenge in the field of mental health services. The National Alliance for the Mentally Ill has become the key organization for advocacy, support, and education, at both the local and national levels. Although a healthy advocacy movement composed of consumers, family members, and concerned professionals has emerged to fight for improved human rights and resources (Deegan, 1992; Fellin, 1996; Lefley, 1996; Watkins and Callicutt, 1997), gains that have been made in improved community services and consumer input are currently at risk with the national trend toward social service reductions, some forms of managed care, and the unpredictable service environment for public mental health agencies. In some states, public not-for-profit community mental health centers must now compete with, or have been replaced by, large for-profit health care corporations.

Self-help organizations composed of consumers and family members have made significant contributions in raising public awareness, articulating the perspective of those directly affected, and in offering innovative empowerment-oriented services and support (Carling, 1995; Kurtz, 1997; Manning, 1998; Segal, Silverman, and Temkin, 1993). Continued advocacy at the legislative level, public education campaigns, and grassroots community organizing are critical to protect hard-fought gains for rights and resources.

◆ ## CHARACTERISTICS OF PSYCHIATRIC DISABILITIES

It has been conservatively estimated by the Center for Mental Health Statistics and the National Institute for Mental Health that from 4 to 5.5 million people in this country have a serious psychiatric disability interfering "with one or more aspects of a person's daily life" (Barker et al., 1992, p. 255). Effects of psychiatric disabilities may include significant functional difficulties in areas such as work, school, self-care, social functioning, concentrating, or coping with daily stress (Lefley, 1996).

Psychiatric disabilities encompass a wide variety of conditions with a complex range of variable effects. Extensive efforts have been made to classify psychiatric conditions according to a universal diagnostic system contained in the DSM-IV manual (APA, 1994). Nevertheless, the diagnosis of these conditions may often be an ambiguous process based on observation over time due to the lack of definitive medical tests (Johnson, 1990). Ruling out other potential causes for the effects (e.g., other medical conditions, substance abuse, head injury, or brain tumor) is a necessary initial step.

Adding to the uncertainty and stress for persons experiencing psychiatric disabilities and their families is the inability to predict the course or severity of symptoms (Biegel, Sales, and Schulz, 1991; Rolland, 1994; Wasow, 1995; Weingarten, 1997). At the time of onset, which may be either gradual or quite sudden, there are few reliable predictors of whether the person will face a future of episodic effects, persistent and/or severe impairments, or no further impairment at all. Beginning signs of psychiatric disability most typically are experienced during late adolescence or early adulthood, although there is increasing recognition of childhood disorders and severe depression among the elderly. Shock and disbelief are not uncommon reactions when a diagnosis of psychiatric disability is made because of the severe social stigma, the lack of apparent cause or warning, and the significant behavioral and personality changes that may occur. Frese (1997) describes the difficulty in accepting the reality of this disability as follows:

> *I cannot tell you how difficult it is for a person to accept the fact that he or she is schizophrenic. Since the time when we were very young we have all been conditioned to accept that if something is crazy or insane, its worth to us is automatically dismissed. . . . The nature of this disorder is that it affects the chemistry that controls your cognitive processes. It affects your belief system. . . . It is exceedingly difficult for you to admit to yourself that your mind does not function properly. It fools you.* (pp. 145–146)

Given the persistent nature of psychiatric disabilities, this acceptance is an important element in deepening the process of recovery and self-acceptance:

> *A California doctor once compared my mental illness to diabetes. "You have a chronic illness," he said. "You will have to take medication for it, probably for the rest of your life. But it will keep your illness manageable and under control." It took me several years and three more hospitalizations before I heeded that doctor's advice. But when I did, I discovered that medication alone was not the only factor that made me feel well, nor was it therapy either. I had to create a life that gave me the structure, support, and meaning I needed to resume normal living.*
>
> *I would like to emphasize that only after I accepted the illness as a chronic one could I really do something about improving my life. I had to learn that I could not "wish" away the illness; I could not "will" it to be so.* (Weingarten, 1997, p. 123)

Psychotic Reactions

Given the complexity of the brain, how a person is affected can be quite variable both across and within different types of psychiatric disabilities. A major distinction involves psychotic compared to nonpsychotic reactions. Occurring by definition at least episodically with schizophrenia and also experienced in severe forms of depression and mania, psychosis involves perceptual and cognitive effects that are outside the realm of ordinary experience. This is commonly described as the person being "out of touch" with reality.

Psychotic reactions include hallucinations, delusions, and disorganized or disordered thinking. Hallucinations may involve either hearing voices, feeling tactile sensations, seeing visual images, or sensing tastes, all of which originate from within the person's brain yet are experienced as quite real. With MRI scans, researchers have been able to observe that the area of the brain that perceives auditory stimuli is similarly active when hearing either an external voice or an auditory hallucination. Delusions, on the other hand, are fixed, irrational beliefs that are not based on fact and tend to be resistant to reason or reflection (e.g., "Any food more than three days old is poison"; "It will not hurt me to jump out of this window because I can fly"; "People with brown hats are following me and trying to kill me").

Hatfield and Lefley (1993) interviewed individuals who had experienced psychotic reactions and reported the following:

> *Disturbed perceptions of the self and the world are the essence of psychosis in mental illness. People with psychotic disorders undergo high levels of stress as they try to accommodate themselves to two realities—that of their inner world and the world as experienced by other people. What is more, their perceived world is often in a state of flux, creating a shifting state of equilibrium to which they are constantly trying to adjust.* (p. 178)

This experience of dual realities has some similarities to the process of adaptation required of persons who are living biculturally and needing to learn how to function in two quite different cultures at the same time.

Misinformed assumptions of the general public tend to include a belief that persons with psychiatric disabilities are always psychotic (Jamison, 1993). Not all persons with severe psychiatric disabilities experience psychotic reactions, and those who do typically experience these effects for periods of time (i.e., psychotic episodes). Only a small percentage of persons with psychiatric disabilities experience ongoing psychotic reactions. In between episodes, people may return to a normal level of functioning or may experience nonpsychotic effects such as low energy, apathy, or difficulties in social functioning. Episodes may be unpredictable and variable in frequency, occurring anywhere from multiple times in a year to periodically over a period of years. For many, antipsychotic and some newer forms of medications have been increasingly effective in ceasing or reducing psychotic reactions, however, in some instances with side effects. One of the most difficult issues to cope with is the "starting over" following an episode—when housing, jobs, and relationships may have been lost or threatened, especially if the person's employers, landlords, and friends have little understanding of psychiatric disabilities.

A supportive, accommodating, and caring social environment and the use of stress management techniques are helpful in managing and preventing psychotic episodes. Donna Orrin (1997), who has a 30-year history of multiple hospitalizations and whose recovery has also included obtaining a graduate social work degree, describes the ways she has learned to respond to psychotic reactions:

> *I start to think squirrels are evil when I begin to become psychotic. Whenever I notice any symptoms, I call my therapist and psychiatrist immediately, so I can "nip my illness in the bud."* . . . *After a few days of increased medication, I have been able to return to my maintenance dosage. I used to decompensate quickly and my symptoms would escalate rapidly and I would land in the hospital.* . . . *I now act quickly enough to prevent that escalation.* . . . *I quickly get to a safe environment that is not overly stimulative and take care of basic needs.* . . . *After all these years of experience, I am now able to easily identify symptoms, and take the appropriate actions quickly.* (pp.142–143)

Such stories point out the increasing ability of consumers to take an active role in managing their lives and the effects of their disability. Such an approach, however, also necessitates a collaborative relationship between consumers and mental health professionals, a supportive and understanding support network, and an attitude of trust and responsiveness to the consumer's self-assessment.

Schizophrenia

Schizophrenia is a complicated condition that affects multiple areas of functioning (e.g., thinking, emotions, perception, judgment, social interaction). Approximately 1% of the population develops this condition (NIMH, 1990). The DSM-IV (APA, 1994) defines schizophrenia as "a disturbance that lasts for at least 6 months" (p. 273) and includes at least one episode of psychotic reactions, such as delusions, hallucinations, and/or highly disorganized speech or behavior. These overtly out-of-the-ordinary, psychotic reactions of schizophrenia are referred to as *positive* symptoms, whereas *negative* symptoms refer to less-than-ordinary functioning, such as apathy, low energy, amotivation, poverty of speech, or social withdrawal. There is a great deal of variation in the course of schizophrenia in terms of the mix of positive and negative symptoms, which researchers have thought might indicate differences in the part of the brain chemistry or structure that might be affected. One person may have episodes of positive symptoms and never have intervening negative symptoms; another may have brief positive symptoms and experience greater impairment from prolonged negative symptoms; another may have a mix of ongoing positive and negative symptoms.

Because of the impact on the information processing system of the brain, persons with schizophrenia often describe feeling highly sensitized to their social and sensory environment. Esso Leete (1997) describes her own experience as follows:

> *Research continues to show that one of the differences between the brain of a "normal" person and one who has schizophrenia is a major difficulty filtering or screening out background noises. I am hyperalert, acutely aware of every sound or movement in my environment. I am often confused by repetitive noises or multiple stimuli and become nervous, impatient, and irritable. To deal with this, I make a deliberate effort to*

reduce distractions as much as possible. . . . I often have difficulty interacting with others socially and tend to withdraw. . . . If I do become overwhelmed in a social situation, I may temporarily withdraw by going into another room to be alone for a while. (p. 99)

One of the reasonable workplace accommodations for an employee with schizophrenia might include providing a work area where distractions and sensory stimuli can be kept to a manageable level. Newer medications (e.g., Clozaril) have significantly improved the management of the effects of psychiatric disabilities, in some situations dramatically. This has meant that an increasing number of persons with schizophrenia are able to experience an improved quality of life; yet they continue to need a social environment that is appropriately supportive, accommodating, and "disability sensitive" (Kopfstein, 1997).

Major Depression

Both major depression and bipolar conditions have effects related to mood and affect. Major depression is the most severe form of depression, characterized by either "depressed mood or the loss of interest or pleasure in nearly all activities" (APA, 1994, p. 320) on a daily basis. Further effects can include persistent insomnia; changes in appetite and weight; daily fatigue; feelings of worthlessness or unreasonable guilt; impairment in the ability to think, concentrate, and make decisions; and suicidal ideation and/or behavior. Women are twice as likely to develop depression compared to men. Theories addressing the high rate of depression for women have tended to focus on the potential effects of women's hormonal systems, low social status, limited life choices due to gender discrimination, and gender differences in verbalizing emotions and asking for help.

A recent international survey by the World Health Organization found that major depression is currently the world's fourth most serious health threat and is predicted to increase to the second most serious health threat by the year 2020. "The top three diseases that shorten life or cause disabilities are still infectious, but fourth is now clinical depression, which will increase as the world's population over age 45 increases in the coming years" (NAMI, 1997). In addition to suicide being a risk of depression, other potentially life-threatening effects can result from a compromised immune system, neglect of necessary self-care and medical attention, increased vulnerability to accidents and victimization, and a general lack of the will to live, which can reduce the ability to respond to potential threats or to take life-saving action.

Bipolar Conditions

Bipolar conditions, commonly referred to as manic depression, incorporate episodes of both depression and mania. The patterns of these episodes may vary by person, with some experiencing predominantly manic episodes and fewer periods of depression and others having more frequent depressive episodes compared to manic episodes. In the most severe form of this condition, the person may face a "rapid cycling" pattern of severe and frequent mood swings or additional psychotic reactions.

Bipolar conditions are most often persistent since "more than 90% of individuals who have a single Manic Episode go on to have future episodes" (APA, 1994, p. 353). The majority of those with this disability, however, can return to normal functioning between episodes (APA, 1994; Jamison, 1993). During an episode, which may last days or months if untreated, effects may include "high" or euphoric feelings, impaired judgment, rapid speech and racing thoughts, sleep disturbance, grandiose and unrealistic thinking, extreme irritability and difficulty concentrating, and behavior that is out of character for the person (e.g., reckless driving, excessive spending, poor decision making, substance abuse) (NIMH, 1989). During a full-blown episode, persons typically have little insight into their own behavior or the changes that are occurring and usually do not see a need for treatment at that time. Suicide is an additional risk, with a 10–15% mortality rate from suicide for persons with this condition (APA, 1994). In contrast to major depression, bipolar conditions affect both men and women in approximately equal numbers (APA, 1994).

The highs and lows associated with bipolar conditions can be quite disruptive to relationships, employment, and day-to-day functioning. Medications in most situations are quite effective in managing or significantly reducing the effects, and many people with this condition have been able to return to high levels of social functioning.

◆ THE EXPERIENCE OF FAMILY MEMBERS

Within the ideology of the mental health system, the family historically has been blamed as the primary cause of the person's psychiatric disability. Remnants of this belief system are still found in some institutional policies and interactions between family members, mental health professionals, and the society at large (Hatfield, 1994; Lefley, 1996; Marsh, 1992). This population of family members have themselves had numerous experiences with the social stigma and discrimination that is associated with psychiatric disability (Lefley, 1996; Spaniol, Zipple, and Lockwood, 1992; Wedenoja, 1991).

In surveys regarding mental health services, family members have expressed dissatisfaction about the quality, availability, and suitability of services for their relatives, and have reported being excluded from information and discussions, being blamed by professionals for their relatives' conditions, and ignored in terms of their observations and concerns (Hatfield, 1994; Solomon, 1994; Solomon and Marcenko, 1992; Tessler, Gamache, and Fisher, 1991). The mental health system, expected to be a resource, has in some instances been experienced by families as a stressor (Lefley, 1987).

An increasing family-oriented focus, however, has been emerging with an emphasis on family empowerment, family education, and building collaborative relationships (Anderson, Reiss, and Hogarty, 1986; Hatfield, 1990; Lefley, 1996;

Lefley and Wasow, 1994; Marsh, 1992; Spaniol, Zipple, and Lockwood, 1992). Family members have reported high levels of satisfaction, for example, when mental health services provided quality services, viewed the family as a resource, and encouraged family participation (Johnson, 1990). This shift has largely been in response to the advocacy, support, and educational efforts of family members within self-help organizations such as the National Alliance for the Mentally Ill, which has chapters in all 50 states.

◆ Creating a Sense of Collective Identity

Reflective of other oppressed groups who have established a cultural identity and self-definition, language and labeling can be significant for either reflecting or transforming the dominant cultural definition of the group (Brzuzy, 1997). This language may change over time, reflecting a dynamic process of self-definition and group identification. Previous terms that have typically been part of the vocabulary of the professional mental health system (e.g., "chronically mentally ill," "the mentally ill," "patients") have been discarded by the self-help and activist community and are "increasingly seen as stigmatizing and connoting hopelessness" (Carling, 1995, p. 71).

Although there is not full consensus, currently the language that is most accepted today and that has been utilized in this chapter includes "consumer," "person with a psychiatric disability," "person with a severe and persistent mental illness," and/or "psychiatric survivor" (Carling, 1995; Chamberlin, 1995; Lefley, 1996). A further suggestion has been "person with a neurobiological disorder" (Francell, 1994). These language preferences tend to signify meaning and identification with a particular philosophy or world view. With the experience of diagnostic labeling and discriminatory labels prevalent in the social environment (e.g., "nut," "psycho," "mental," "crazy"), persons with psychiatric disabilities are acutely sensitized to the power of labels, and self-definition is particularly valued.

The more recent language places emphasis on the concept of "person" (Brzuzy, 1997) rather than having the diagnostic label become the person's total identity. Following this person–centered philosophy, reference would be made to "a person with schizophrenia," rather than "a schizophrenic." Stainsby (1997) elaborates on the reasoning for this:

> *It is difficult to make a statement that indicates I have schizophrenia because of the social stigma attached to the label. Besides that, I do not necessarily identify myself just as a "schizophrenic." No, I "have schizophrenia," an incurable but controllable disease, in much the same way that diabetes is controllable. I also have a dog, a horse, a partner, and just recently earned a second university degree.* (pp. 109–110)

The term *psychiatric survivor* has also been chosen by some for multiple reasons. Similar to the concept of being a survivor of rape or incest, it reflects a sense of "fighting back," actively participating in a process of recovery, self-defining the circumstances, and overcoming the challenges of a disability. For others, the term signifies "their experience in mental health systems that they view as fundamentally oppressive" (Carling, 1995, p. 71).

◆ BUILDING A SENSE OF COMMUNITY AND ACCEPTANCE

Mental health consumers and their families are becoming more active and involved in collective organizing, advocacy, and systems change. They are increasingly joining policy-making boards, initiating new and innovative services and self-help groups, and advocating for significant changes at the local, state, and national levels (Carling, 1995). With this growing activism also comes more visibility as a group and less shame in openly identifying as a consumer or family member.

The self-help movement within this field ranges from peer-run recovery groups (Kurtz, 1988, 1997; Kurtz and Chambron, 1987; Powell, 1990) to consumer-run service centers, advocacy groups, and clearinghouses (Carling, 1995; Chamberlin, 1995; Manning, 1998; Mowbray, Wellwood, and Chamberlain, 1988; Segal, Silverman, and Temkin, 1993) to family support and advocacy groups, such as the Alliance for the Mentally Ill (NAMI). These collective efforts serve as a means of carving out a safe space to be accepted, acknowledged, and affirmed as well as to challenge the status quo of marginalization and lack of accommodation. By taking services, support, and advocacy into their own collective hands, mental health consumers and their families are learning the benefits of self-determination, mutual aid, and organized advocacy.

Advocacy is a critical component of this movement, with consumers and their families seeking social change and social justice. Advocacy focuses on areas such as social discrimination, unjust and inadequate allocation of funding for basic resources (e.g., services, benefits, and research), equal treatment in terms of medical insurance and housing, and reasonable accommodation in order to fully participate in meaningful work and education.

Society at large, and mental health professionals in particular, have tended to approach issues related to psychiatric disabilities with a primary focus on pathology and symptoms. Rather than operating from a deficit model, disability advocates view themselves as fighting for basic human rights and the autonomy to be able to live freely. This perspective reflects the philosophy and values of the independent living movement. First articulated in the late 1970s, this movement begins with the assumption of competence and potential for self-determination while allowing for times when people may be unable to fully self-determine their lives. Efforts focus on how lack of responsiveness, reasonable accommodation, and social acceptance can be major impairments to self-determination (Segal, Silverman, and Temkin, 1993). Howie the Harp, a consumer who was active in the mental health consumer movement, put it this way:

The progressive collective minds of our mental health system have slowly, by degrees, crept toward the realization that what is good for everyone—what Americans have fought and died for—what civil rights movements have struggled for—is also good for mental health consumers. I remember a sign at one of our rallies: "Freedom is the Best Therapy." Freedom of choice, independence, self-determination, and empowerment are what's best for us. (Carling, 1995, pp. xv–xvi)

In contrast to traditional rehabilitation, which has focused narrowly on employment as a successful outcome, this movement views the ultimate goal to be an improved, self-defined quality of life that comes from the increased autonomy to make life choices as an adult. These life choices include the ability to make decisions about work, leisure time, relationships, where and how to live, life goals, financial choices, and psychiatric and/or medical treatment options.

Because of the episodic impairments in the realm of thinking and judgment that may occur with psychiatric disabilities, inherent tensions and conflicts exist within this field of service regarding freedom of choice and self-determination. This becomes a difficult moral and ethical dilemma when a person's choices are influenced by delusions or appear to be self-destructive or harmful toward others. What seems more typically the case, however, is the situation of persons with psychiatric disabilities being treated routinely as if they have impaired judgment, whether currently symptomatic or not.

Since self-help movements have developed outside the realm of professional services, many human service professionals have little familiarity with self-help groups and organizations (Kurtz, 1997; Powell, 1990). When adopting an empowerment practice perspective, self-help activities can complement empowerment practice approaches and may be critical for improving quality of life (Manning, 1998). Caution must be taken, however, that self-help is not exploited to fill in the gaps of a mental health service system experiencing cutbacks or used to justify service cuts under the pretense of self-determination. Just as clients were released from hospitals without the resources following them into the community under the guise of deinstitutionalization, we must be concerned about routine plans to discharge clients to self-help groups without additional supports or funding.

Since the philosophy of self-help is based on the concept of mutual aid, relationships among group members and with others outside the group are viewed as collaborative and peer oriented rather than hierarchical. For stigmatized populations, self-help groups and organizations function as a safe place for persons who are experiencing a hostile social environment. Interactions with those outside of the group may involve an assessment of whether this person or group is 1) "safe," supportive, and can be trusted, 2) "one of us," 3) hostile or insensitive, or 4) uninformed and unaware. Based on an acute emotional sensitivity and the repeated social experiences of being treated as members of a stigmatized group, consumers and family members often develop a finely tuned "radar," highly attuned to the authenticity of the emotional responses of mental health professionals. Efforts to mask contempt, discomfort, or patronizing attitudes are usually detected, and genuine acceptance, supportiveness, and nonjudgmental attitudes are also recognized (Frese, 1997).

◆ Summary

Through the efforts of disability activists and the passage of the Americans with Disabilities Act (ADA), "disability is evolving into a positive term" (Nagler, 1993, p. 1). This term is now serving to build a collective identity among persons with a range of physical, developmental, and psychiatric disabilities (Brzuzy, 1997; Mackelprang and Salsgiver, 1996). By building coalitions and recognizing the common issues related to disability status, such a collective can exert greater influence together rather than individually, as evidenced by the successful passage of this national legislation. Much work is yet to be done, however, in changing social attitudes, implementing the protection of rights, gaining necessary resources, and reducing social stigma.

◆ ◆ ◆ *Personal Narrative: Donna Orrin* ◆ ◆ ◆

Donna Orrin, M.S.W., lives with bipolar disorder. She has worked as a psychiatric social worker. Currently, she is president of her own business, Creative Connections, and provides extensive training to consumers with psychiatric disabilities and their family members. She also provides training for mental health professionals.

The first 18 years of my life were not very happy because I always had negative, self-critical thoughts. However, I didn't tell anyone about them. My mom always had an enthusiastic, happy sense about her and I was always very active.

In high school, I was an honor student. I won an award as the most active senior of the year. I also won humanitarian awards and was always involved in activities. I would put a smile on my face and act happy and people really thought that I was happy. Yet my attention was always riveted on negative, self-critical thoughts; criticizing everything I did as I did it. I never told anyone because I didn't think anybody could help. I had a lot of friends, and they didn't know how poorly I was doing. However, when I started feeling really bad they tended to shy away.

At 18 I left home to go to college, and the real trouble began. My depression really accelerated. I started skipping classes and didn't get involved in any extracurricular activities at all. I ended up not showing up for exams and getting incompletes. I began to feel suicidal.

My twin brother, Dale, was living in the dorm across the street from my dorm. I would contact him when I was suicidal. I reached out to him and he really helped. My God, what a heavy burden to put on an 18-, 19-, or 20-year-old. I feel sorry about how much I relied on him because I didn't realize the impact it had on him. Because of all the problems, I ended up dropping out of college after only two years.

It was then, in 1972, that my psychotic and manic symptoms started. I heard voices and thought I could talk to people who were more than 100 years old and to others who were no longer alive. I could see things that weren't there. I could stare at a Christmas tree, mesmerized by its lights. I don't remember quite clearly what my symptoms were at that point, but my friends and family were concerned and suggested I needed inpatient hospitalization. But I was in denial and I didn't think that what they saw were "symptoms." I just thought I was having wonderful experiences.

Let me say here that a real problem with mental illness is how denial is often a symptom. There is nothing we have discovered yet to solve the problem of denial. I was finally convinced to seek help by a professor because he told me to think of hospitalization as going to a "human potential seminar." He said to think of it like I was going to be there for a couple of weeks with a bunch of other people who were there for the same reason. He said I would be kind of isolated and I would have time to work on my human potential growth. So he drove me to Kingswood Hospital, where they diagnosed me with bipolar disorder with psychotic symptoms. They prescribed lithium. That was the beginning of the recovery path of my mental illness. But the road was a long one. I had over 30 hospitalizations spanning the next 20 years.

After I got out of the hospital, my problems continued. I went to visit Dale, who was then in New York City. I was walking around the streets of Harlem late one night and the police picked me up; I wound up at Bellevue Hospital, where they put me on high doses of medication. When I got out, I went to visit my sister, who doesn't believe in medical treatment. She believes in alternative care, so she took me to her chiropractor who took me off my medication "cold turkey" and put me on kelp instead. I went through withdrawal from stopping my medication. It was horrendous; the physical symptoms were really bad.

At that time, one of the biggest problems was isolation. People didn't know a lot. I couldn't talk to anyone about mental illness. My mother was frustrated; she didn't know where she could go for help, and she couldn't talk to any family members or friends about it because nobody was willing to talk to her.

I went to live with my mother, and for eight months I lay on her couch thinking about nothing but all the mistakes I had made in my life. It felt like there was a two-ton car on top of me and I didn't have the strength to lift it off my chest. I was paralyzed on the couch. I didn't have the energy to move.

Mom insisted that I go for a short walk with her every day. If she hadn't insisted I go with her, I never would have left the couch. Those short, ten-minute walks were very hard on me. I talked with only one friend once a week, and we would just chit-chat. She had no idea what my lifestyle was like and I wouldn't tell her. I didn't know that I could do anything else; I just didn't think I could do anything.

At that time, I was not involved at all in the community mental health (CMH) system; I didn't even know there was such a thing as CMH. I hardly knew anyone with mental illness. My education about mental illness consisted of the book *One Flew over the Cuckoo's Nest,* which was really bad news. I felt all alone, and I believed there were a lot of really bad things wrong with me.

After eight months of lying around, my mom said she was taking me to a therapist. It had never occurred to me that there might be some treatment for this. Because I had never been in therapy before and had never been educated about selecting a therapist I ended up with a therapist who was not well versed in mental illness.

With my therapist's encouragement I started doing more. I would bake bread once a week. That was a big deal! Then I started doing volunteer work one day a week, then two days a week. Eventually, I started working part-time 20 hours a week. My therapist encouraged me to do these things. I then began to deal with my issues, concerns, and goals.

Eventually, I went back to school. I went to Oakland University because I could commute there and still live at my mom's house. I took one class, then two. I even started working on a novel under a Michigan Council for the Arts grant about the six months I spent in a mental hospital. Over time, I got my degree and started working in communications, and I started making more and better friends.

When I had gone a period of time without hospitalization, I started to ask myself if I really had to be on medication for the rest of my life. So I talked to my therapist, my family, coworkers, and my friends. We decided I would try to go off my medications on a trial basis. Within two weeks, I was in a state mental hospital. My doctor there believed that I wasn't manic but schizophrenic, and she tried a different medication on me. My mother and my therapist would try to talk to her, but she wouldn't even see them. They wanted to encourage her to put me on lithium. Not only did she refuse to change my medications, she wouldn't even give them the time of day. She put me on a variety of other medications, and I was just wiped out. She kept this up for five-and-a-half months before she finally put me on lithium. Within two weeks, I was out of there.

Believe me, a state hospital is no place to go for a five-and-a-half-month vacation. I was left feeling powerless. At the time, I tried to sign myself out voluntarily, but they initiated quick proceedings to involuntarily commit me. I was very angry, but I'm glad now that they were able to prevent me from leaving. My involuntary commitment was beneficial, though I didn't have the insight to realize it at the time. I just wish I had received appropriate treatment.

This hospitalization made me feel powerless; it felt like they stripped me of my soul. I was put in seclusion 18 times—talk about powerlessness. I was on a ward of 30 women, and we had three seclusion rooms. The seclusion rooms were always full. I was not a danger to myself or others when they put me in seclusion, I swear to God. I know I needed to be in the hospital but not under the treatment they gave me.

It is ironic that, if you go to a hospital for physical care, you have your own phone and your own room. But if you are in a state hospital for mental illness, you get one phone for 30 women, in the hallway, with no privacy. We had to line up for a chance to use the phone.

One experience during that hospitalization was especially memorable. I was very close to my twin brother, and I was on the phone with him. One of the attendants said to hang up, that it was time to sleep. I put up a finger to signal to him to give me just one minute and I would say good-bye. Before I knew it, two attendants had forced my arms behind my back and dragged me to the seclusion room, leaving the telephone receiver dangling. I was yelling, "Dale, Dale, Dale," and I couldn't even say good-bye to him. They put me in seclusion overnight. I could only think, "Oh, no, Dale's going to really worry about what happened to me!" I was worried about my brother, didn't know why they put me in there, didn't know what I had to do to get out or even when I would get out. All I could do was take four steps one way, then two steps another way. The room smelled of urine really strongly. There was only a plastic bed to lie on and a really high window to look out. Because of my condition, I was experiencing an altered sense of time, so it seemed like I was there for a million years. It was a terrible experience.

Sometimes they threw people in there and told them to calm down as they closed the door. What a joke! Who would calm down? Yeah, right; as if those rooms would calm anyone down. They called this treatment; to help people with calming down. They had to be kidding. One time I felt so powerless and frustrated, I began head banging in the seclusion room. I was sent to intensive care for ten days. I did enough damage to my eyes that there was no white in them; they were completely red for weeks, and I didn't know if I would ever see the whites of my eyes again. Later, I received intensive treatment for this closed head injury.

Back then, there was no multidisciplinary treatment at the state hospital. I remember my social worker telling me to read the Bible and it would treat me. That's all he ever said to me. That was my social work treatment at the state hospital. Not extraordinarily effective. As I was being discharged from the hospital, my social worker said, "Donna, face the facts; you're only going to be a store clerk a few months out of every year, and as you get older you're going to have more and more hospitalizations." That was my mental illness "education."

They used to have workshops for us back then. They consisted of reading the front page of the paper and making belts and ashtrays—I didn't even smoke. I remember a funny story about that. A group of us were talking and, somehow, we got on the subject of Vincent van Gogh. Someone said, "Gee, isn't it a shame there weren't hospitals like the hospitals we have today back in van Gogh's time?" Someone else in the group said, "Yeah, just think of all those ashtrays and leather belts he missed out on."

Not all my hospitalizations have been like my state hospital experience. There are a lot of good psychiatric hospitals around. I have been to at least three. They provide a lot more freedom, a lot more respect, and better treatment. They provide therapy, though I must admit it is sometimes hard for therapy to be effective when people are functioning at a really low level. Cognitive theory and therapy are wonderful tools. It is hard to teach people much when they are hospitalized for only a couple of weeks, but cognitive therapy has been wonderful for me. I do think that hospitals educate people about their mental illness better than in the past. Yet they need to make more for people to do on weekends so they don't regress.

From 1972 to 1992, I had about 40 hospitalizations, but I have turned things around. I have had no hospitalization in the last five years. A number of things have helped me turn things around. One was electroconvulsive therapy (ECT). It was a last-resort treatment after a suicide attempt. I had taken a hundred aspirin, but they pumped my stomach. I also tried to kill myself when I was on MAO inhibitors (an antidepressant). I ate the foods that are prohibited with MAO inhibitors: wine, cheese, and chocolate. I did other things, too. I was really trying to kill myself, and nothing was working. I had given up hope and everyone else, with the exception of my therapist, had given up hope. I had finally found a good therapist. I became able to overcome traumatic times and negative thoughts, feelings, and actions. I created new, positive beliefs by releasing my distress through a form of cognitive therapy. The therapy was instrumental in my development of the quality of life of my choice.

Without the combination of therapy and ECT, I would probably be dead. At a minimum, I certainly wouldn't have the quality of life I have now. ECT alone would not have done the job, but ECT and therapy were really quite wonderful.

A third intervention was also extremely important. It was a simple intervention but was very difficult to get. When I was discharged from the hospital after having ECT, I was a CMH client. I requested that someone from CMH call me every morning and every evening to remind me to take my medications every day. These reminder calls were extremely valuable.

The fourth reason for my success is that I have learned to recognize and know my individual symptoms. I am celebrating my five-year anniversary, but that doesn't mean I haven't had manic and psychotic symptoms over the last five years; I have. However, I now recognize them immediately and I take appropriate action. I go to a nonstimulating environment. I go to my home; it's my own personal retreat. Then I call up my therapist and let him know. I call him every day until I get better. I make sure I get plenty of sleep, plenty of food, and do my best not to think about any psychological issues. With an understanding with my psychiatrist, I increase my thorazine. In three to four days, I'm back to stability. Those four things—ECT, therapy, medication reminder calls, and self-awareness and self-care—are the reasons why I am celebrating my five-year anniversary without hospitalization.

Earlier I mentioned my reminder calls. I want to talk more about these. The calls were my idea, but the CMH professionals made it really difficult to get this service. They kept asking me to prove that I needed this assistance. At one point they wanted to give me an IQ test; another time they wanted to give me a memory test. It was after being diagnosed with severe attention deficit disorder without hyperactivity that I understood why I don't remember to take my meds. I can be in the bathroom and think, "I've got to remember to take my meds," but two minutes later I haven't taken my meds and have forgotten that I need to take them.

When I think about what I had to go through to get those medication reminder calls, it just infuriates me. I'm a pretty assertive person and, in fact, I was on the CMH board at the time. Yet they said I was trying to be "taken care of." That's like saying somebody with a physical disability is asking to be taken care of if they need a wheelchair. No, a wheelchair is a tool or instrument that enables them to have an independent life. A wheelchair is what they need to take care of themselves and move on in life. My medication calls were my tool and were extremely cost effective—two one-minute phone calls a day compared to two months of hospitalization. It makes me wonder: if getting those calls was that difficult for me, what is it like for other consumers when they ask for the help they know they need?

Not being able to work was very hard on me. I come from a hardworking family. My grandmother told us, "do for others, do for others." We were trained to do for others, so it was painful for me when I was not able to work. I felt just terrible about myself. Though my family and friends kept saying, "Donna, don't work right now; it's not time," I felt like I ought to be working. Financially, I didn't need to work because I got social security disability and was able to squeak by. At different times I got little jobs. But by listening to myself I knew when it was time, and that's when I went back to work. I must say employment isn't the be-all and end-all of things; recovery is the most important and comes before employment. People must allow time to recover before becoming employed. Had I been rushed into employment before I recovered, I would not be doing as well as I'm doing now. I tell others with mental illness, "Don't feel guilty if you're not working yet. Know that you must do what is best for you. You can't help somebody else if you're not taking care of yourself."

The reaction of others is one of the most difficult parts of mental illness. When things get bad, people really shy away. I understand that now more than I did in the past because I have a family member with mental illness who doesn't want to go public with it, so I see it from that perspective now. In a lot of ways, the way we are treated is worse than the symptoms themselves. We're avoided, we're abandoned and treated in very inhumane ways; I think worse than an alley cat or dog should be treated.

With depression, one of the symptoms is poverty of thought; if you have poverty of thought, you're going to have poverty of communication, and if you have poverty of communication, you don't make such a good friend. It seems that when people are most needy and can't do it alone, others usually aren't willing to reach out to them. Maybe it's because they feel helpless.

I think it's very important for family and friends to know that they may be helping out more than they realize when things seem bad. Family members and friends may not realize how helpful they are because they don't know what's going on with the individual. They don't see the person's internal thoughts and realizations or understand the importance of their bond with the person. I can't think of anything more important than a family member or friend helping someone stay alive; and sometimes being there is helping them stay alive. There is hope. I've been there. I've gone through years of doing nothing but getting up in the morning and going to bed at night, but I made it through all that.

It's important for people to know that people with mental illness want to contribute and we want to work. People just don't seem to know that, and it's a shame. When someone is not allowed to contribute, they are being denied their humanity and spirituality. They are being denied their self-worth. Sometimes mental illness is like drowning in the ocean. We have to concentrate on getting safely to the beach. But once we survive, please let us help. We want to help. I think it would be great if we had psychoeducation workshops for families and individuals and professionals all together; we need to see everyone else's perspective. We have a seemingly impossible mission, and we can accomplish it only if we all work together.

I have gone from people hanging up on me, avoiding me, and abandoning me to getting paid really well just so people can hear what I have to say. It is very rewarding. What I am doing now is really exciting. I'm involved in policy making. I have my own business and do lots of public speaking. I love giving talks; I love engaging the audience. I'll give a talk, and all these people will come up to me afterward and tell me how much they got out of it.

Twenty years with almost 40 hospitalizations contrasted to 30 speeches in one year. I like the 30 speeches part better; it's just such a wonderful feeling. I have also developed successful recovery materials and ongoing workshops for consumers. I've written six nationally published articles, and another is going to be published soon. I am helping others avoid the kind of pain that I went through. I am helping family members avoid the pain that my family went through. It is extremely rewarding.

When I was in high school, I was known as an activist and took on many causes, but I can't think of a better cause for me to advance than helping people understand mental illness. I believe I have a talent in writing, and I use it for the most important cause I can imagine.

I am better off now than I would have been if I had never had mental illness. One of the reasons is all the therapy that I've had. Therapy has made a monumental difference in my life. It's made me know myself and helped me be myself. In my work, all I have to do is be myself. One of the best rewards in my life is that my mother now feels it was worth it to go through all of the pain that she went through. She knows that every person I help is someone she has helped because I wouldn't be here without her.

In offering advice, one thing I would suggest to professionals working in hospitals is to let friends and family members know that visits mean a great deal to your patients. One of the things that my friends have done is visit me in pairs. I couldn't always communicate that well when I was doing poorly, but when people came to the hospital in pairs, they could talk to each other and I could benefit from their discussions. Suggest that people visit in pairs so they can keep the conversation rolling and provide company for the individual. Those visits are very helpful and prevent isolation.

Professionals need to view us as adults, not children. Don't be condescending; expect the person to be a mature person. Sometimes, and in some ways, communications may need to be very basic in the sense of telling the person, "You need to do this, this, and this." But just because you may need to help people in very basic ways doesn't mean that you should treat them like children. Professionals need to know that even when an adult's behavior is childlike, the person is not a child. The person can make some decisions and should be treated as an adult.

I think that teaching people about person-centered planning is important— letting individuals decide what their goals and dreams are and helping them go for it. Imagine what we could do if the system believed in us. What if we didn't have to fight the system? What if the system helped us? What levels would we soar to? A social worker told me I would require more and more hospitalizations as I got older and would not be employable. Fortunately, others believed in me. I now have my master's degree in social work from the University of Michigan and have worked as a psychiatric social worker in both state and private hospitals and have my own business. Instead of having more and more hospitalizations, I had fewer and fewer.

The system has to believe in us. This includes professionals in health and mental health systems. I'm talking about doctors, social workers, nurses, personal care attendants, and other professionals. I was lucky. I had a therapist who believed in me. If it hadn't been for him, I wouldn't have gotten my MSW degree. If it hadn't been for him, who knows, maybe I would be dead. During my worst times, he was there fighting for me, and he never gave up hope on me.

I think hope is a really major issue. Professionals must instill a sense of hope in people and their families. Always give the individual logical, concrete examples of why they should be hopeful. When I speak to groups of consumers, I ask them, "In your suicidal days, were you able to hang on because you had one, just one person who believed in you?" I also ask, "How many of you have come farther in your recovery than you thought possible because someone, just one person had hope for you?" When I ask just those two questions, almost all the hands in the audience go up. They tell me they got through their suicidal times because someone had hope for them. The best advice I can give professionals is to encourage people. Provide a sense of hope. You may be saving someone's life. You may be making a lifelong difference to an individual.

Mental health consumers must be involved in decision making. To improve treatment, we need consumer input. I wrote a book on policy making and in it I have 36 opportunities for policy making for consumers, including how to apply policy-making strategies. People think that people with mental illness can't contribute, but we can. I will never forget the first state-level community mental health meeting I attended. I was at the Michigan Association of Community Health Boards conference, where board members and directors voted on an amendment for the mental health code revisions that would include consumer representation in policy making. I was appalled. We had a 45-minute debate on whether or not consumers should be on the board. These were board members and directors talking. The amendment to include consumers squeaked by with a vote of 54 to 48. I sat there for 45 minutes and listened as these board members came up to the microphone, one at a time, saying things like, "Consumers are not competent to sit on the board." There is fear and anger and hesitation and discrimination about mental illness. Such attitudes demonstrate the very reason why we need consumers on the board; because if those policy makers and professionals don't know what's possible, if they don't know how much we can recover, and if they don't know our perspective, there is no way they are going to come up with the best policies on our behalf.

◆   ◆   ◆

Discussion Questions

1. What are some of the specific types of discrimination experienced by persons with psychiatric disabilities and their family members?

2. Describe the impact of social stigma for persons with psychiatric disabilities.

3. What are some specific characteristics of psychotic reactions?

4. Describe the characteristics of the three main types of psychiatric disabilities. What are the similarities? What are the differences?

5. Discuss the possible roles of consumers and family members in the planning and implementation of mental health services.

6. What language and terms would be "disability sensitive" when working with this population?

7. In relation to psychiatric disabilities, what would constitute reasonable accommodations within a work situation? Within a family?

Suggested Readings

American Psychiatric Association. (1994). *Diagnostic and statistical manual of mental disorders* (4th ed.). Washington, DC: APA.

Brzuzy, S. (1997). Deconstructing disability: The impact of definition. *Journal of Poverty, 1*(1), 81–91.

Chamberlin, J. (1995). Rehabilitating ourselves: The psychiatric survivor movement. *International Journal of Mental Health, 24*(1), 39–46.

Deegan, P. (1992). The independent living movement and people with psychiatric disabilities: Taking back control over our own lives. *Psychosocial Rehabilitation Journal, 15*(3), 3–19.

Duke, P., and Hochman, G. (1992). *A brilliant madness: Living with manic depressive illness.* New York: Bantam Books.

Jamison, K. R. (1995). *The unquiet mind.* New York: Random House.

Johnson, D. (1990). Schizophrenia as a brain disease: Implications for psychologists and families. *American Psychologist, 44*(3), 553–555.

Kirk, S. A., and Einbinder, S. D. (1994). *Controversial issues in mental health.* Boston: Allyn & Bacon.

Lefley, H. P. (1996). *Family caregiving in mental illness.* Thousand Oaks, CA: Sage.

Marsh, D. T., and Dickens, R. M. (1997). *Troubled journey: Coming to terms with the mental illness of a sibling or parent.* New York: Jeremy P. Tarcher/Putnam.

Spaniol, L., Gagne, C., and Koehler, M. (1997). *Psychological and social aspects of psychiatric disability.* Boston: Center for Psychiatric Rehabilitation, Boston University.

Torrey, E. F. (1995). *Surviving schizophrenia.* New York: HarperCollins.

Wasow, M. (1995). *The skipping stone: Ripple effects of mental illness in the family.* Palo Alto, CA: Science and Behavior Books.

References

American Psychiatric Association. (1994). *Diagnostic and statistical manual of mental disorders* (4th ed.). Washington, DC: Author.

Anderson, C., Reiss, D. J., and Hogarty, G. (1986). *Schizophrenia and the family: A practitioner's guide to psychoeducation and management.* New York: Guilford Press.

Barker, P. R., Manderscheid, R. W., Hendershot, G. E., Jack, S. S., Schoenborn, C. A., and Goldstrom, I. (1992). Serious mental illness and disability in the adult household population: United States, 1989. In R. W. Manderscheid and M. A. Sonnenschein (Eds.), *Mental health, United States, 1992* (pp. 255–261). DHHS Publication No. SMA 92–1942. Washington, DC: U.S. Government Printing Office.

Biegel, D. E., Sales, E., and Schulz, R. (1991). *Family caregiving in chronic illness.* Newbury Park, CA: Sage.

Brown, K., and Fellin, P. (1988). Practice models for serving the homeless mentally ill in community shelter programs. In J. Bowkers (Ed.), *Services for the chronically mentally ill: New approaches for mental health professionals* (Vol. 1). Washington, DC: Council on Social Work Education.

Brzuzy, S. (1997). Deconstructing disability: The impact of definition. *Journal of Poverty, 1*(1), 81–91.

Carling, P. J. (1995). *Return to community: Building support systems for people with psychiatric disabilities.* New York: Guilford Press.

Castanuela, M. H. (1994). Have mental health professionals abandoned the chronically mentally ill? Yes. In S. A. Kirk and S. D. Einbinder (Eds.), *Controversial issues in mental health* (pp. 265–270, 278–279). Boston: Allyn & Bacon.

Chamberlin, J. (1995). Rehabilitating ourselves: The psychiatric survivor movement. *International Journal of Mental Health, 24*(1), 39–46.

Deegan, P. (1992). The independent living movement and people with psychiatric disabilities: Taking back control over our own lives. *Psychosocial Rehabilitation Journal, 15*(3), 3–19.

Deegan, P. E. (1997). Recovery: The lived experience of rehabilitation. In L. Spaniol, C. Gagne, and M. Koehler (Eds.), *Psychological and social aspects of psychiatric disability* (pp. 92–98). Boston: Center for Psychiatric Rehabilitation, Boston University.

Duke, P., and Hochman, G. (1992). *A brilliant madness: Living with manic depressive illness.* New York: Bantam Books.

Fellin, P. (1996). *Mental health and mental illness: Policies, programs, and services.* Itasca, IL: F. E. Peacock.

Fink, P. J., and Tasman, A. (1992). *Stigma and mental illness.* Washington, DC: American Psychiatric Press.

Francell, E. G. (1994). What mental illness needs: Public education and a new name. *Hospital and Community Psychiatry, 45*(5), 409.

Frank, E., and Kupfer, D. J. (1993). Depression as a mental illness. In M. Nagler (Ed.), *Perspectives on disability* (pp. 379–384). Palo Alto, CA: Health Markets Research.

Frese, F. (1997). Twelve aspects of coping for persons with serious and persistent mental illness. In L. Spaniol, C. Gagne, and M. Koehler (Eds.), *Psychological and social aspects of psychiatric disability.* Boston: Center for Psychiatric Rehabilitation, Boston University.

Hatfield, A. B. (1990). *Family education in mental illness.* New York: Guilford Press.

Hatfield, A. B. (1994). The family's role in caregiving and service delivery. In H. P. Lefley and M. Wasow (Eds.), *Helping families cope with mental illness* (pp. 65–77). Newark, NJ: Gordon Breach Publishing Group.

Hatfield, A. B., and Lefley, H. P. (1993). *Surviving mental illness.* New York: Guilford Press.

Jamison, K. R. (1993). *Touched with fire: Manic depressive illness and the artistic temperament.* New York: Free Press.

Jamison, K. R. (1995). *The unquiet mind.* New York: Random House.

Johnson, D. (1990). Schizophrenia as a brain disease: Implications for psychologists and families. *American Psychologist, 44*(3), 553–555.

Kopfstein, R. (1997). Becoming disability sensitive. Presented at the Disability Symposium, Annual Program Meeting of the Council on Social Work Education, Chicago, IL.

Kurtz, L. F. (1988). Mutual aid for affective disorders: The manic depressive and depressive association. *American Journal of Orthopsychiatry, 58,* 152–155.

Kurtz, L. F. (1997). *Self-help and support groups: A handbook for practitioners.* Thousand Oaks, CA: Sage.

Kurtz, L., and Chambron, A. (1987). A comparison of self-help groups for mental health. *Health and Social Work, 12,* 275–283.

Leete, E. (1997). How I perceive and manage my illness. In L. Spaniol, C. Gagne, and M. Koehler (Eds.), *Psychological and social aspects of psychiatric disability* (pp. 99–103). Boston: Center for Psychiatric Rehabilitation, Boston University.

Lefley, H. P. (1987). Aging parents as caregivers of mentally ill children: An emerging social problem. *Hospital & Community Psychiatry, 38,* 1063–1070.

Lefley, H. P. (1996). *Family caregiving in mental illness* (Family Caregiver Applications No. 7). Thousand Oaks, CA: Sage.

Lefley, H. P., and Wasow, M. (1994). *Helping families cope with mental illness.* Newark, NJ: Gordon Breach Publishing Group.

Mackelprang, R. W, and Salsgiver, R. O. (1996). People with disabilities and social work: Historical and contemporary issues. *Social Work, 41*(1), 7–14.

Mancuso, L. L. (1994). Reasonable accommodation for workers with psychiatric disabilities. In W. Anthony and L. Spaniol (Eds.), *Readings in psychiatric rehabilitation.* Boston: Center for Psychiatric Rehabilitation, Boston University.

Manning, S. S. (1998). Empowerment in mental health programs: Listening to the voices. In L. M. Gutierrez, R. J. Parsons, and E. O. Cox (Eds.), *Empowerment in social work practice: A sourcebook.* Pacific Grove, CA: Brooks/Cole.

Marsh, D. (1992). *Families and mental illness: New directions in professional practice.* New York: Praeger.

Mowbray, C., Wellwood, R., and Chamberlain, P. (1988). Project stay: A consumer-run support service. *Psychosocial Rehabilitation Journal, 12*(1), 33–42.

Nagler, M. (1993). The disabled: The acquisition of power. In M. Nagler (Ed.), *Perspectives on disability* (pp. 33–36). Palo Alto, CA: Health Markets Research.

National Alliance for the Mentally Ill. (1997). *Depression to rise worldwide, says WHO* [www.nami. org].

National Institute of Mental Health. (1989). Bipolar disorder/manic depressive illness. Alcohol, Drug Abuse, and Mental Health Administration, DHHS Publication No. ADM 89-1609. Washington, DC: U.S. Government Printing Office.

National Institute of Mental Health. (1990). Clinical training in serious mental illness. DHHS Publication No. ADM 90-1679. Washington, DC: U.S. Government Printing Office.

Orrin, D. (1997). Past the struggles of mental illness, toward the development of quality lives. In L. Spaniol, C. Gagne, and M. Roehler (Eds.), *Psychological and social aspects of psychiatric disability* (pp. 138–144). Boston: Center for Psychiatric Rehabilitation, Boston University.

Powell, T. (1990). *Working with self-help.* Washington, DC: National Association of Social Workers.

Rolland, J. S. (1994). *Families, illness, and disability.* New York: Basic Books.

Rubin, A., and Johnson, P. J. (1984). Direct practice interests of entering MSW students. *Journal of Education for Social Work, 20,* 5–16.

Segal, S. P., Silverman, C., and Temkin, T. (1993). Empowerment and self-help agency practice for people with mental disabilities. *Social Work, 38*(3), 705–712.

Solomon, P. (1994). Families' views of service delivery. In H. P. Lefley and M. Wasow (Eds.), *Helping families cope with mental illness.* Newark, NJ: Gordon Breach Publishing Group.

Solomon, P., and Marcenko, M. O. (1992). Families of adults with severe mental illness: Their satisfaction with inpatient and outpatient treatment. *Psychosocial Rehabilitation Journal, 16*(1), 121–134.

Spaniol, L., Zipple, A. M., and Lockwood, D. (1992). The role of the family in psychiatric rehabilitation. *Schizophrenia Bulletin, 18*(3), 341–357.

Stainsby, J. (1997). Schizophrenia: Some issues. In L. Spaniol, C. Gagne, and M. Koehler (Eds.), *Psychological and social aspects of psychiatric disability* (pp. 108–111). Boston: Center for Psychiatric Rehabilitation, Boston University.

Styron, W. (1990). *Darkness visible: A memoir of madness.* New York: Random House.

Tessler, R. C., Gamache, G., and Fisher, G. A. (1991). Patterns of contact of patients' families and mental health professionals and attitudes toward professionals. *Hospital and Community Psychiatry, 42*(9), 929–935.

Wasow, M. (1995). *The skipping stone: Ripple effects of mental illness on the family.* Palo Alto, CA: Science and Behavior Books.

Watkins, T. R., and Callicutt, J. W. (1997). Self-help and advocacy groups in mental health. In T. R. Watkins and J. W. Callicutt (Eds.), *Mental health: Policy and practice today* (pp. 146–162). Thousand Oaks, CA: Sage.

Wedenoja, M. (1991). Mothers are not to blame: Confronting cultural bias in the area of serious mental illness. In N. Hooyman, M. Bricker-Jenkins, and N. Gottlieb (Eds.), *Feminist social work practice in clinical settings* (pp. 179–196). Newbury Park, CA: Sage.

Wedenoja, M., and Brown, K. S. (1996). Shifting paradigms regarding psychiatric disability: Integrating psychosocial rehabilitation, empowerment, and disability advocacy. Presented at the Progressive Social Work Symposium, Annual Program Meeting of the Council on Social Work Education, San Diego, CA.

Wedenoja, M., and Neal, D. (1995). Family caregiving in the area of psychiatric disability: A collaborative research project for the mutual benefit of social work practice and education. Presented at the Social Work and Disabilities Conference, New York, NY.

Weingarten, R. (1997). How I've managed my mental illness. In L. Spaniol, C. Gagne, and M. Koehler (Eds.), *Psychological and social aspects of psychiatric disability* (pp. 123–129). Boston: Center for Psychiatric Rehabilitation, Boston University.

Werrbach, G. B., and DePoy, E. (1993). Social work students' interests in working with persons with serious mental illness. *Journal of Social Work Education, 29*(2), 200–211.

Wilson, W. H. (1997). Neuroscientific research in mental health. In T. R. Watkins and J. W. Callicutt (Eds.), *Mental health: Policy and practice today* (pp. 89–106). Thousand Oaks, CA: Sage.

Chapter 10

PERSONS WITH COGNITIVE DISABILITIES

I was in the coma for a couple of weeks, and, waking up, I didn't know my mother. My mother had come to visit me, but I didn't know who she was. I did recognize my father. My parents were divorced and had been living apart for many years, but when I was first waking up I didn't understand that. I didn't understand any-thing. When I was taken out of intensive care in a wheelchair it started to register with me, "Wow, something's happened here." I didn't believe anything had happened until I got out of bed and started using the wheelchair. Then it all started coming together.

—Kevin Shirey, IL counselor, Center for Independent Living, Fresno, California

Student Learning Objectives:

1. To understand issues around defining the various cognitive disabilities.

2. To understand the many varieties of cognitive disabilities.

3. To have a very basic knowledge of the major cognitive disabilities likely to be experienced by clients and consumers.

4. To understand the social consequences of having a cognitive disability.

5. To understand the issues concerning the recent questioning of learning disabilities and attention deficit hyperactivity disorder.

◆ GENERAL DEFINITIONS

Bruyere (1994) defines cognitive disabilities as disabilities that impact the ability to comprehend what the individual sees and hears. Included in cognitive disabilities are impairments that affect the ability to gain information from social cues and what is commonly called "body language." Individuals with cognitive disabilities may have difficulty in learning new things, generalizing from specifics, and using language for expression in both oral and written form. Sigler and Mackelprang (1993) observe that persons with cognitive disabilities can be impulsive, reacting to situations without fully considering consequences. In addition, persons with cogni-tive disabilities can have difficulty belonging to groups or finding social acceptance. Cognitive disabilities include learning disabilities, intellectual disabilities, traumatic brain injury, autism, and Down syndrome. Since we have previously looked at intellectual disabilities, autism, and Down syndrome, this chapter concentrates on people who have learning disabilities, people who have attention deficit hyperactivity disorder, and people who have traumatic brain injuries.

◆ Learning Disabilities

Definitions

Simpson and Umbach (1989) offer the federal definition of learning disability, which defines it as an impairment that impacts one or more of the physiological processes involved in understanding and using either spoken or written language. These impairments may manifest themselves in difficulties with listening, thinking, speaking, writing, spelling, and/or doing mathematical calculations. The federal definition encompasses perceptual disabilities, brain injury, minimal brain dysfunction, dyslexia, and developmental aphasia. It excludes learning problems linked to visual, hearing, or motor disabilities and learning problems related to mental retardation, emotional disabilities, or environmental, cultural, or economic disadvantage.

Oliver, Cole, and Hollingsworth (1991) discuss a definition constructed by the National Joint Committee for Learning Disabilities (NJCLD), which brings the condition further into focus:

> *Learning disability is a generic term that refers to a heterogeneous group of disorders manifested by significant difficulties in the acquisition and use of listening, speaking, reading, writing, reasoning, or mathematical abilities. These disorders are intrinsic to the individual and presumed to be due to central nervous system dysfunction. Even though a learning disability may occur concomitantly with other handicapping conditions (e.g., sensory impairment, mental retardation, social and emotional disturbance) or environmental influences (e.g., cultural differences, insufficient/inappropriate instruction, psychogenic factors), it is not the direct result of those conditions or influences.* (p. 427)

The two key elements of this definition presume that learning disabilities are the result of a neurological impairment and that they are not a manifestation of another disorder.

As with other disabilities, there are several problems in defining learning disabilities. First, the causes of learning disabilities often remain an enigma. Case histories as well as neurological testing commonly fail to find an exact etiology. Second, there are no specifically designated physical and/or behavioral manifestations of learning disabilities. Some individuals with learning disabilities may exhibit impairments or behaviors that are totally different from others designated as having a learning disability. Third, no single impairment or base combination of impairments manifests itself in an individual with a learning disability. There are many combinations of learning abilities and performance levels that differ from one person to the next (Simpson and Umbach, 1989). These ambiguities in characteristics and evaluation support the mythology that learning disabilities are not real; that individuals with learning disabilities "aren't trying hard enough" or are just "dumb." We will return to these issues later.

Characteristics

Coles (1987) explains that the first real differentiation of learning disabilities was made by James Hinshelwood, an ophthalmologist living at the turn of the 20th century in Glasgow, Scotland. Researching what was then called congenital word blindness, he found evidence that some schoolchildren had difficulties reading even though they had good mental abilities. Hinshelwood concluded that the etiology of this condition was in the brain because he found similar dysfunctional reading abilities in adults with brain lesions. He believed that the problem was confined to the area of the brain dealing with visual memory of words and letters. Hinshelwood sought effective ways of teaching children with this condition. Today, research indicates that the cause is not so concrete. Although there is evidence that some learning disabilities have neurological roots, with others there is no apparent brain dysfunction.

There is some agreement, however, on the characteristics that encompass learning disabilities. Cruickshank (1990) discusses ten identifying characteristics of persons with learning disabilities. The first of these is that persons with learning disabilities have difficulty *discriminating* fine differences in auditory, visual, and/or tactual input. For example, persons with learning disabilities exhibiting this characteristic may have difficulty feeling the difference between the sizes of different objects or telling the difference in texture:

> *John, ever since he was in elementary school, has had trouble telling the difference between denominations of money. He has difficulty telling the difference between a dime and a quarter. At the same time, he gets twenty-dollar bills confused with fives and ones.*

They may have difficulty hearing the difference between two similarly sounding words:

> *Susan is having real difficulties at her first social work position. She has trouble following the instructions of her supervisor. Words like "call" and "saw" sound the same to her. In reading and writing reports, she tends to misuse words like "two," "too," and "to."*

The second characteristic of persons with learning disabilities discussed by Cruickshank concerns *memory*. Persons with learning disabilities have a decreased ability to retain and recall discriminating sounds and forms both in the short term and the long term. These individuals can learn and manipulate concepts but sometimes have difficulty with the specifics that support the concepts:

> *Richard has been very successful in his academic career. He graduated with a bachelor of science degree in education with honors. He did very well in classes dealing with concepts such as intellectual history and philosophy. He did adequately in courses involving math through the use of reasonable accommodation in the form of a calculator. Richard understood most math concepts but had trouble recalling the multiplication tables. As long as he could use a calculator, he did well. Now he is facing the State Teaching Credential Test, which prohibits the use of any calculators during the math portion of the exam.*

The third characteristic of persons with learning disabilities is difficulty in *sequencing.* Related to the characteristic of limited recall, persons with learning disabilities generally have difficulty remembering the correct sequence necessary to complete a task:

> *Joe was an expert automobile diagnostician. He could merely listen to an engine and pretty much tell what was going on. When he hooked it up to the electronic diagnostic machine, the findings were always corroborated. Yet Joe was having problems on the job. He could diagnose the problem better than any mechanic in the dealership, but it took him three times the "book time" to replace parts and make repairs. He had difficulty remembering the sequence of removing old parts and replacing them. He had to constantly refer to the repair manual even to do simple jobs.*

A fourth characteristic that persons with learning disabilities frequently experience is difficulty distinguishing between *figure-background* relationships. These can be visual, auditory, or tactual in nature. This difficulty has ramifications not only in school performance but in the world of work in terms of reading and listening to directions and training:

> *Joyce's boss asked her to go to a conference on establishing a computer network within a company with links to the broader Internet. The conference was held in a busy hotel downtown, and the only separation between conference rooms was a thin moveable wall. In the next room, part of the presentation involved relatively loud music. No one in her room seemed to be annoyed or distracted, but Joyce found it impossible to focus on what the instructor was saying. Joyce was worried because she was going to take the lead in setting up her company's network and she needed this information.*

Persons with learning disabilities also have difficulties with *time and space orientation.* They have difficulty answering the question, "Where am I in time and space?" This fifth characteristic has tremendous ramifications in terms of performance and self-esteem. In school and in work, these individuals have difficulty with time deadlines and restrictions. They have problems in maneuvering geographically within cities, buildings, and offices.

A sixth characteristic of persons who have learning disabilities involves difficulty in bringing *closure* either to a concept or a physical form:

> *Alicia, when asked by her teacher to draw a circle, would always come up with something that looked like the letter U. When she tried to tell a joke to her classmates, she always left out the punchline.*

A seventh characteristic put forth by Cruickshank of persons who have learning disabilities is difficulty in integrating input from two or more senses; that is, *integrating intersensory information.* An individual whose learning disability encompasses this characteristic will have difficulty coordinating a task that has, for example, a listening component, a visual component, and a motor skills component:

> *José was having difficulty in math class. The teacher had students copy a problem from the board. Then the class was supposed to work the problem and give a verbal*

response. José could not make sense out of what the teacher was saying and writing. He was terrified that she would call on him to show his work.

An eighth characteristic, related to sequencing, is difficulty *relating perception to motor function*. Persons with learning disabilities may have difficulty judging the energy requirements of performing a specific task, which can lead to taking on projects well beyond their capabilities to complete. It can mean that a person with a cognitive disability will jump into a motor-related task without considering how to go about completing the task:

> *Bill was always eager on Saturday morning to get out in the yard and get some work done. Usually by the late morning, the front and back yards were in chaos. Bill had mowed half the front yard but had failed to finish. He had gotten involved in trimming the shrubs but did not complete this. Before doing so, he became immersed into fixing a sprinkler head and in the process decided to dig a trench to put in a new sprinkler line. At 11:30 A.M., his wife went to get him for an important phone call, but Bill was nowhere to be found. He had left for the local hardware store to find a part to fix the garden fence.*

The ninth characteristic discussed by Cruickshank involves *dissociation*. Persons with cognitive disabilities may have difficulty viewing specifics in relationship to the whole. This may be either visual or conceptual or both. Persons with learning disabilities may have difficulty with pegboard designs or other designs related to tasks, like tying shoelaces. This characteristic may manifest itself in the inability to see the importance of a concept or in missing the concept by focusing on the parts ("not seeing the forest for the trees").

The tenth characteristic of persons with learning disabilities brought forth by Cruickshank is that of *attention disturbances*. This characteristic shows up as an inability to avoid reacting to stimuli from the environment. Although related to learning disabilities, this condition is currently associated with a separate disorder known as attention deficit hyperactivity disorder (Brown, 1994), which will be discussed next.

◆ Attention Deficit Hyperactivity Disorder

According to Clark (1996), 4% of children in the United States exhibit attention deficit hyperactivity disorder (ADHD). It is more common in boys than girls and tends to be diagnosed most often in preadolescent children. ADHD's etiology appears to be genetic in nature; it is most likely linked to several different genes with mixed dominant features. Research also indicates that ADHD is linked genetically to families, and usually one or more parent has the condition. In large families of three or more children, it is not uncommon to find more than one child with ADHD. Recent studies have linked possible locations in the brain from which some of the unique behaviors of persons with ADHD originate.

Zentall (1993) outlines several characteristics of students with ADHD in an educational environment, which also manifest themselves in other environments such as work. What has been traditionally defined as attention deficit is more like a bias toward certain kinds of stimuli with inattention to other kinds of stimuli. Students with ADHD generally move their attention to things that are novel, such as "new" colors or sounds, a change in size, or sudden movement. This characteristic can result in several problems. In first learning a task, the person with ADHD does not focus on stimuli that are neutral, bland, detailed, or part of an overall task. Therefore, the person with ADHD may fail to learn vital information:

> *Tommy couldn't wait to start taking gym. He had always liked sports, particularly basketball. Today the teacher was going to have them start playing. When Tommy got in class, the teacher began the class by explaining the game, how it should be played, and the rules of playing. Tommy was bored and very fidgety. He had difficulty concentrating on what the teacher was saying. There was a game going on the other side of the gymnasium with lots of noise and excitement. When his teacher divided the class into teams to start the game, Tommy was lost. He didn't remember the rules and was removed from the game on the first play for inappropriately touching another student in trying to get the ball away from him.*

In the performance part of learning, a second characteristic may be a failure to sustain attention. Persons with ADHD find it difficult to continue attending to stimuli when the novelty wears off. This results in increased error in long-term performance. Zentall found that persons with ADHD have difficulty sustaining attention, particularly in repeated tasks. When information is repeated, there appear to be more behavioral problems, such as increased activity and impulsivity, which makes it extremely difficult to develop rote skills.

Impulsivity is a third characteristic outlined by Zentall that limits achievement in most environments. The inability to withhold verbal or behavioral responses produces many problems. It means that the person with ADHD does not consider the full array of data before making a decision—a skill that is crucial to problem solving. Impulsivity results in difficulty for persons with ADHD to plan, which requires developing priorities based upon consideration of a wide spectrum of information. Impulsivity makes reading and following directions difficult:

> *Kirk loved to build models of fighter planes. But his love mostly resulted in frustration and anger. When he got a new model, he would jump right into building it without reading the directions. The end result never matched what was on the box and usually ended up in the waste can after about 15 minutes of a flurry of activity.*

Impulsivity also makes it more difficult to obtain help because of distractions or delays in educational and work environments. Because teachers and supervisors may be dealing with large numbers of students and workers, they are not likely to pick up on individual problems. This results in the person with ADHD not completing tasks correctly.

Impulsiveness has social consequences as well. Sigler and Mackelprang (1993) demonstrate that impulsivity impacts social judgment and appropriate social behavior. Persons with ADHD who exhibit impulsivity in inappropriate social situations can be subject to social isolation and employment vulnerability:

> *David had been working at a local fast-food restaurant for two months successfully. He was doing very well, and both his immediate supervisor and his coworkers liked him. Occasionally, he exhibited an eccentric sense of humor, but nobody really took much notice. One day, the supervisor asked David to join her and a couple of other workers for lunch at the restaurant when the noon crunch was over. They were talking and eating when suddenly David grabbed his throat, held his breath, and fell on the floor. The supervisor thought he was choking and proceeded to do the Heimlich maneuver when David started laughing, saying that it was a joke. His supervisor and coworkers were enraged.*

David's impulsivity damaged his social belonging with his coworkers and placed grave questions in his supervisor's mind about his maturity and ability to be successful at the restaurant.

◆ TRAUMATIC BRAIN INJURY

More than half a million Americans are hospitalized each year from traumatic head injuries. The National Head Injury Foundation concludes that traumatic brain injury (TBI) of children and young adults is the leading killer and cause of disability in the United States. Approximately 20% of those injured experience lifelong physical, mental, and emotional changes. Even mild TBI may result in long-term changes. However, mild TBI often goes unrecognized because its manifestations are often subtle.

Mild TBI—with or without loss of consciousness—can produce an array of sequelae, including memory loss of events occurring shortly before the injury (retrograde amnesia) and memory difficulties relative to events following the injury (posttraumatic amnesia). People with mild TBI can experience diminished reasoning abilities and reduced frustration tolerance, sometimes long term. A condition called postconcussion syndrome can occur, in which people may experience changes in cognition and personality after a relatively mild brain injury. Symptoms of postconcussion syndrome often ameliorate within weeks or months of injury.

There are two main types of TBI. Closed TBIs typically result from accidents in which the head strikes, or is struck by, an object with no penetration of the skull. Common causes of closed TBI are motor vehicle accidents, wherein the head strikes, or is struck by, an object such as pavement or a windshield and the brain shakes within and scrapes along the inside of the skull. Open TBIs occur when an object, such as a bullet, penetrates the skull and enters the brain. Other brain injuries, such as those caused by insufficient oxygen, poisoning, or infection, can cause changes similar to those that occur with closed TBI. Open TBI usually results in localized injury, whereas closed TBI tends to produce diffuse damage to more than one area of the brain. Damage can occur as a result of direct impact, increased cranial pressure, bruising, blood loss, scraping of the brain along the inside of the skull, oxygen deprivation, and other factors.

The manifestations of TBI vary widely and depend primarily on the specific areas of the brain that are affected and the severity of injury to these sites. When TBI occurs, function is usually lost immediately or within a few hours (as with slow bleeding or slowly increasing pressure in the brain). Severe damage can produce coma or even death. After initial crisis and stabilization, spontaneous recovery of function can occur for two years or more. Recovery is rarely immediate. For example, situations in which people suddenly awaken from a coma (as shown frequently on television) are extremely rare. As they recover from severe TBI, people generally go through phases of recovery in which arousal, memory, reasoning, judgment, and impulse control gradually improve. Lifelong improvement can occur with sufficient supports.

The brain stem, frontal, and temporal lobes are particularly prone to traumatic injury more than other parts of the brain because they are adjacent to hard bony structures. The brain stem, located at the base of the brain, is also susceptible to damage from cranial pressure as a result of brain swelling. It is involved primarily in primitive life functions, including arousal and nervous system regulation of other organs. It acts as a switchboard, routing messages to and from the body and higher brain centers. Injury to this area can cause coma or even death if basic life functions such as respiration and cardiovascular function are compromised. The temporal lobes are located at the anterolateral aspects of the brain. They are involved in memory and language. Damage to the temporal lobes can result in behavioral changes as well as language impairment and sensory loss to the face and extremities. The frontal lobes occupy the anterior portion of the cranium. Because of their large size and their position, the frontal lobes are especially susceptible when TBI occurs. They are involved in important cognitive functions such as abstract reasoning, judgment, and voluntary muscle control. Injury to this area usually results in behavioral changes associated with decreased judgment, reduced anger control, and increased impulsiveness (Tierney, McPhee, and Papadakis, 1994).

Cognitive changes are common with TBI. These changes can impact language and communication, information processing, memory, and perceptual skills. Both receptive aphasia (an inability to understand language) and expressive aphasia (an inability to express language) may result. When perception, memory, and higher reasoning are affected, people experience difficulty with reading, writing, or reasoning such as is required in doing math (Winnick, 1995). People must often develop new compensatory cognitive skills and coping strategies.

Physical changes can affect ambulation, balance and coordination, general motor skills, strength, and endurance. Psychological changes are also encountered and can impact mood, life perspective, emotions, and the senses (Alexander, 1996).

Finally, it is important to note that some people experience disabilities as a result of TBIs sustained over time that may not be identified as such. People who have experienced long-term domestic violence can encounter subtle but progressive effects of TBI. This is especially true for young children who have been subjected to shaking, whereby their brains are shaken within their skulls.

◆ PSYCHOSOCIAL CONSEQUENCES OF COGNITIVE DISABILITIES

Kronick (1981) focused on the social development of persons with learning disabilities (LD). Although she found solutions to the social problems of persons with cognitive disabilities through intervention with the individual, her findings bring insight into the pyschosocial consequences that cognitive disabilities bring to people. Most of the overt characteristics associated with a cognitive disability bring about a lower status within the major systems of social living. Within the family, if learning and academic achievement are the pillars of family culture, there is danger that a positive self-concept will not develop; at best, there may be doubts of self-worth by the family member with a cognitive disability. As the child or adolescent compares himself or herself to parents and brothers and sisters, the discrepancy may reinforce a negative self-concept. And if the disability is dealt with poorly by punishment, ridicule, discomfort, shame, or secrecy, the family member with the cognitive disability may feel guilt or shame or inadequacy:

> *Roger's family consisted of his mom and dad and his older brother Ray. Roger's father was a pharmacist who owned and ran a drugstore in the area of the city where mostly Italian and Irish folks lived. Roger's mother taught science at the local high school. Roger's brother just graduated from college and had been accepted into Harvard medical school. Roger had been diagnosed with a learning disability in junior high school. Although he scored well on IQ tests, he did poorly in school. He was about to graduate but with barely a C average.*

> *Roger's parents were basically ashamed of him. They never mentioned the "younger son" to friends. They always talked about Ray. When someone would ask about Roger, a frown would appear on his mother's face, and his father simply did not reply. Roger knew he was "damaged goods." Even though people at school said he was really intelligent, Roger knew that he was a failure. On report card days, he would stay in his room, telling his parents he was sick. Roger wished he had never been born.*

Within the family, Roger's intelligence and other strengths were never acknowledged. As a result, Roger's poor image of himself and his low self-esteem resulted in severe depression and withdrawal.

The educational environment presents many potential psychosocial perils to the student with a cognitive disability. The skills involved with reading, writing, math, listening, working independently and within a group, presenting, and critical thinking are in fact the essence of the educational process. A disability that critically impacts the acquisition of these skills can make the student with a cognitive disability susceptible to scorn, ridicule, social isolation, and low status. Lack of academic achievement as well as behavioral characteristics of impulsivity and attention bias can stigmatize people with LD in the eyes of both teachers and fellow students. If the student with a cognitive disability "is unable to function in the same academic and behavioral fashion as his fellow students" (Kronick, 1981, p. 61), students and teachers can fail to recognize and reinforce the person's unique learning styles and positive behaviors. Our educational establishment's emphasis on a narrow definition of productivity and success results in a world that can be hostile to a person with a cognitive disability:

> *A child might be affable, intelligent, creative, humorous, and cooperative yet become discouraged and depressed over his academic or athletic limitations. If he is unable to limit his feelings of failure to the situation in which he has failed, relate the failure to a component of the situation, and find compensatory ways of handling or avoiding the difficult component, then his depression and anxiety will result in disorganization and hence successive failure in other areas of functioning. Eventually he will feel that he has lost so much ground that he becomes overwhelmed and immobilized by his lack of success.* (Kronick, 1981, p. 76)

In light of Kronick's observations, it is not surprising that Naylor, Staskowski, Kenney, and King (1994) found a strong connection between the psychiatric condition of school refusal and cognitive disability. (School refusal is the failure to attend school, despite the physical ability to do so, because of anxiety or depression.)

Dunham, Koller, and McIntosh (1996) discuss difficulties encountered by persons with cognitive disabilities in higher education. Because of issues of low self-esteem, students with cognitive disabilities tend not to be self-advocates in an environment where accommodation is minimal. Because the disability may not manifest itself in overt physical characteristics, students must continually "prove" they have a disability. Faculty and staff may be reluctant to provide reasonable accommodation and may even display hostility toward students with learning disabilities. Lack of academic accommodation may negatively affect student's ability to graduate. In addition, students in college with cognitive disabilities find social acceptance neither with nondisabled nor disabled students, thus adding to the social isolation.

Dunham, Koller, and McIntosh also explore the ramifications of persons with cognitive disabilities (specifically LD) in the work arena. Persons with cognitive disabilities have a harder time finding and keeping jobs than persons without. Generally, persons with cognitive disabilities who find work have jobs with lower pay and lower status than those without. These are usually unskilled, entry-level positions. Typically, persons with cognitive disabilities are underemployed, and many remain at home with their families of origin.

On the job, workers with cognitive disabilities encounter difficulties in understanding instructions in technical manuals, in writing summaries of completed work, and in getting along with fellow workers and supervisors. The "pity" side of ableism also shows up in the work environment, where supervisors give untruthful positive assessments of the work of persons with cognitive disabilities, often resulting in the eventual failure of the worker:

> *Karen graduated from a nationally known university with a master's degree in rehabilitation counseling. She has a fairly severe learning disability brought about by a head injury sustained in a motorcycle accident when she was 19. Now almost 30, she had made her way through the halls of academia with the help of the disabled student*

services in both the colleges she attended. In addition, most of her professors provided reasonable accommodation in testing and paper writing.

She had been hired by a local junior college to be a member of its mental health center, providing mental health counseling to students, staff, and faculty. Karen loved working with her clients. She was adept at helping them understand their strengths and facilitating them in finding their way out of circumstances causing them pain. Unfortunately, she had great difficulty doing her paperwork. Afraid to declare herself a "person with a disability" and request reasonable accommodation, she stayed late into the evening and spent her lunch break trying to catch up with the paperwork.

Because she spent extra time working, she failed to socialize with the rest of the staff. Fellow workers thought that she was stuck up and trying to look good with her supervisor. Her supervisor, John, was concerned about the poor quality of her paperwork and also by the fact that none of the staff liked Karen. He would overhear people joking about her constantly working. John felt uncomfortable approaching Karen about any of these issues. In fact, every time John had to deal with Karen, he felt angry because she had come with such great references and her performance in college really looked good. During her first sixth-month evaluation, he basically said she was doing well. After a year, however, because of many mistakes in treatment notes and the unreadability of assessments, Karen was let go.

Bruyere (1994) emphasizes that direct and honest communication between the supervisor and the worker with a cognitive disability is crucial in the completion of the task at hand and to a sense of well-being for the worker.

◆ THE CURRENT ATTACK

There is a growing body of literature that questions whether or not certain cognitive disabilities really are disabilities. This is particularly the case with ADHD and LD. Smelter, Rasch, Fleming, Nazos, and Baranowski (1996) question the existence of attention deficit hyperactivity disorder. They argue that there is no agreed-upon etiology and no specific test for the disorder. They believe that the explanation of this behavior in medical model terms is an attempt by some professionals, politicians, and parents to excuse antisocial and inappropriate behavior. According to Smelter and colleagues (1996), the "creation" of ADHD alleviates the guilt of both parents and professionals for a job poorly done and serves as a way to avoid punitive action by the schools and the courts. It also results in a number of negative consequences for children so labeled and for the schools they attend. A diagnosis of ADHD gives children a license to misbehave with little or no consequence to themselves and without regard for the future ramifications to society:

> *Doing a "bad" thing implies responsibility and guilt, as well as the need for some punitive action on the part of one's social peers. But having a "dysfunction" carries no such social stigma; instead, it evokes sympathy, feelings of compassion, and a genuine desire to help the transgressor.* (p. 430)

Smelter and associates also conclude that a diagnosis of ADHD lowers both parent and teacher expectations for achievement and that children with ADHD conform to its limitations. Schools cannot afford to make the necessary accommodations for cases of ADHD diagnosis. These accommodations mean additional services provided to persons with a condition that has a wide spectrum of characteristics. In addition, the extra attention required for children diagnosed with ADHD puts extensive burdens on classroom teachers.

Finlan (1994) puts forth similar arguments around LD:

> *There is no such thing as a learning disability. You may think LD exists since more than two million schoolchildren have currently been identified with this federally legislated disability, but LD does not exist any more than there are witches in Salem, monsters in Loch Ness, or abominable snowmen in the Himalayas.* (p. 1)

Finlan bases this absolute conclusion on the following. First, the definition of LD is vague and ambiguous. No one has behaviorally defined any component of the definition. Second, the testing process for LD is value biased, and the results are inconclusive. In addition, the tests do not adequately predict school performance with or without special supports and accommodation. Third, the existence of LD is rooted not in science but in politics. Through the efforts of middle-class parents, banded together as a special interest, their children slid under the protective blanket of disability. Finlan stated, "LD, by getting itself included as a handicap, benefited from a major political force, and on the basis of legislation brought about by political activism, LD theory became law without evidence" (p. 24).

As in Smelter's arguments about a diagnosis of ADHD, Finlan argues that a diagnosis of LD has negative consequences for the child and the schools. First and perhaps most important, a diagnosis of LD puts the problem on the individual, the child. It blames the victim. Blaming the victim relieves parents and schools of the responsibility for the problem. Once relieved, changing the family structure or the educational structure becomes next to impossible because the problem really resides with the child. The educational structure need not examine the graded system or the pedagogy of reading or math. It can create a special auxiliary system for the child with the learning disability and basically leave the rest of the system intact. Second, as a product of the medical model, a diagnosis of LD makes the child pathological, abnormal. Labeling children as having LD limits them and establishes lowered performance expectations. Finlan states: "Lowered expectations brought about by labels applied by experts damn these children to lives as second-class citizens as soon as the adults in their lives buy into the labels" (p. 60). Labels become self-fulfilling prophecies.

These viewpoints are important to our discussion of cognitive disabilities and disability in general. Their primary importance centers on revealing the other side of ableism. Ableism assumes the superiority of the person who is nondisabled and views persons with disabilities who have different physical and mental characteristics as somehow inferior. Along with this assumption is a low expectation of the level of performance and responsibility of persons with disabilities. By assigning a person the label of ADHD or LD, we in this culture relegate them to a lower status with little or no expectation that they "reach for the stars."

On the other hand, some significant amount of caution must be applied to the preceding views. First, *do ADHD and LD exist?* Just because a condition covers a wide range of behavioral characteristics that are three-dimensional and dynamic rather than linear does not mean that the condition doesn't exist. Similarly, our inability to fully understand the etiology of a condition does not negate its existence. Various new techniques in brain scans have led the National Institute of Mental Health to suggest that there are specific regions of the brain where these conditions find their origin. The efficacy of a combination of medical and psychological testing is beginning to pinpoint causes resulting in effective treatment (Clark, 1996). The fact that political action has spawned investigation does not negate the legitimacy of the findings. In the course of the history of the United States, many health-related problems and solutions were brought to the surface by political action. This was particularly true in the area of stopping the spread of infectious diseases such as measles and polio. The same can be said about cognitive disabilities.

Second, *who benefits from a diagnosis of ADHD or LD and who does not?* Effective treatment centers on a combination of medications, counseling, and restructuring the environment both at home and at school (Clark, 1996). Adults with cognitive disabilities gain self-direction through new techniques of case management (Eiel, 1994). Most important, when the cause of a painful condition can be found and, based upon its origin, a plan can be developed to eliminate the pain, it removes a sense of guilt and shame from the person experiencing the condition:

> *Dr. Frederick's 12-year-old boy Sam was diagnosed with both a learning disability and ADHD. His condition manifested itself in the inability to use a pencil to write and difficulty in integrating input from two or more senses. The results were that he was doing poorly in his work at school and his hyperactivity was disrupting the rest of the class. Even though Dr. Frederick, at his own expense, had Sam tested, the school district refused to accept the diagnosis, and the school's psychologist said that Sam was "normal."*

> *As the year moved forward, Sam was becoming progressively worse. Although Sam was taking medication, he still was not doing well at school. Each day he would come home depressed, go up to his room, and shut the door. Sam believed that his behavior in school was because he was "bad." At times, Sam thought he would be better off dead.*

> *At Sam's next individualized educational program meeting, Dr. Frederick was emphatic about the need for certain changes in Sam's school program, including Sam's movement for half a day into a special resource room. On threat of legal action, the school complied with Dr. Frederick's demands. Sam's new teacher was himself diagnosed as having a learning disability. Sam no longer disrupts the classroom. He uses a computer to write and is doing A– work in his "regular" English class. Even more important, Sam is no longer depressed and never thinks about killing himself.*

Parents do not seek this diagnosis for their sons or daughters to escape responsibility or to gain services that allow them to maintain their status quo. They seek an answer to help their children. In most cases, the diagnosis of ADHD or LD means changing family routine, with curtailing the use of the television, establishing a quiet time, and so on (Clark, 1996). It may also mean seeking family counseling and examining how the members relate to one another.

Accommodation of cognitive disabilities within the school structure is expensive. School administrators are finding it more and more difficult to maintain traditional programs, not to mention providing auxiliary services for students with disabilities. Schools do not benefit economically in the short run by having students diagnosed with ADHD or LD. In the long run, if changes within "special" programs can be generalized to the total system, then, in fact, they do benefit (Zentall, 1993).

◆ SUMMARY

Cognitive disabilities are ones that impact the ability to comprehend what the individual sees and hears. Included in cognitive disabilities are impairments that affect the ability to gain information from social cues. Individuals with cognitive disabilities may have difficulty in learning new things, generalizing from specifics, and using language for expression in both oral and written form.

Characteristics of persons with learning disabilities include difficulty discriminating fine differences in auditory, visual, and/or tactual input; decreased ability to retain and recall discriminating sounds and forms both in the short term and the long term; difficulty ordering the correct sequences necessary to complete tasks; difficulty distinguishing between figure-background relationships; difficulties with time and space orientation; difficulty bringing closure to either a concept or a physical form and in integrating intersensory information; difficulties relating perception to motor function; difficulty judging the energy requirements of performing a specific task; difficulty viewing specifics in relationship to the whole; and inability to avoid reacting to stimuli from the environment.

Characteristics of students with ADHD include a bias toward certain kinds of stimuli in the educational environment, with inattention to other kinds. Students with ADHD generally move their attention to things that are novel and find it difficult to continue attending once the novelty has worn off. This results in increased error in long-term performance. Impulsivity is another characteristic that limits achievement in many environments.

More than half a million Americans are hospitalized each year from traumatic head injuries. Approximately 20% of those injured experience lifelong physical, mental, and emotional changes. Physical changes can affect ambulation, balance and coordination, motor skills, strength, and endurance. Cognitive changes can impact language and communication, information processing, memory, and perceptual skills.

Most of the overt characteristics associated with a cognitive disability bring about a lower status within the major systems of social living. Within the family, if learning and academic achievement are the pillars of family culture, there is danger that a positive self-concept will not develop or doubts of self-worth will be experienced by the family member with a cognitive disability. The educational environment offers the student with a cognitive disability many potential psychosocial perils. The skills involved with reading, writing, math, listening, working independently and within a group, presenting, and critical thinking are in fact the essence of the educational process. A disability that critically impacts the acquisition of these skills opens the student with a cognitive disability to scorn, ridicule, social isolation, and low status. On the job, workers with cognitive disabilities encounter difficulties in understanding instructions in technical manuals, writing summaries of completed work, and in getting along with fellow workers and supervisors.

There is a growing body of literature that questions whether or not certain cognitive disabilities really are disabilities. This is particularly the case with ADHD and LD. Although these voices raise some important issues, ADHD and LD are real disabilities with positive ramifications upon discovery for the person with these conditions.

◆ ◆ ◆   *Personal Narrative: Kevin Shirey*   ◆ ◆ ◆

Kevin Shirey is a 41-year-old social work student and independent living counselor.

My primary disability is an acquired traumatic brain injury that I received in April 1986 when I was 30 years old. I also have an alcohol problem that is in remission. Before I became disabled, I used to feel sorry for disabled people. I would feel sorry for them and do what I could to avoid them.

I remember the day I became head injured. I had just finished up a 12-pack of beer that I had on the back of my motorcycle. I had also just hit up on some drugs, and I went for a ride in the mountains. A truck came at me; it surely seemed like it was in my lane. I wound up trying to avoid the truck, not wanting to go underneath it, so I drove off the side of a hill. I tried to get my bike back up to the road, but the rear wheel hit a root hole and I spun out. Being on the side of a cliff, I was powerless so my bike and I fell. I hit a tree, and that put me into a coma.

I was in the coma for a couple of weeks, and, waking up, I didn't know my mother. My mother had come to visit me, but I didn't know who she was. I did recognize my father. My parents were divorced and had been living apart for many years, but when I was first waking up I didn't understand that. I didn't understand anything. When I was taken out of intensive care in a wheelchair it started to register with me, "Wow, something's happened here." I didn't believe anything had happened until I got out of bed and started using the wheelchair. Then it all started coming together.

Mom was the loving type of mom after the accident. Dad was always a distant type of a person, but after my accident he was really assertive. He talked to the doctors at the hospital, and he actually gave up some work to come into town for me.

He applied for social security, SSI, and MediCal for me. He did that while I was in the coma. It surprised me he had done that for me.

When I got out of rehabilitation, I tried to go back to my old job. They were still honoring my insurance, but they were going out of business. So I didn't have a job to go back to. I looked for other jobs, but I couldn't get any. Some of my friends, my drinking buddies, made fun of my disability. They would say, "Ha, ha, you'll be back." But it didn't look like I would, and I became locked into depression.

Eventually, I went to the independent living center and met the people there. Sharon was an IL counselor. Her specialty was chemical dependency–type clients. She started talking to me about school possibilities, so I went back to school. I had social security disability, so I didn't have to go back to work right away. I also needed a place to live, and she directed me to some halfway houses. One accepted me, so I lived there for some time. I was really happy with the IL experience.

I got into recovery for my alcoholism. My Alcoholics Anonymous meetings are really important to me. AA has been one of my main supports. I also went to some brain injury support group meetings. They referred me to a psychologist who did an evaluation on me and pretty much told me that I should get some mental health counseling. I went to mental health services, but they just wanted to put me onto drugs. I figured that I'm an alcoholic so I can't be doing these drugs, and that's all mental health wanted to do with me. So I totally quit them.

Sharon at the independent living center really helped a lot. She helped me get into recovery. At Fresno City College, Chuck was the adapted PE instructor. He's good at it, really good. I took a lot of gym classes with Chuck. Also, Richard, who was the director of the independent living center and used a wheelchair, was a role model. It was explained to me that he had multiple sclerosis, which is a constant deterioration process that people go through. I saw that he was in charge of the independent living center, and I knew that he had the education. I didn't believe I could ever get an education, but he helped give me hope. I thought if he could do it, maybe I could try.

Right now I'm a student in a bachelor's program in social work. I'm doing an internship at an independent living center. I make it a point to be there for people with disabilities. Though I like to consider myself pretty much recovered cognitively, I'm still disabled and I can be a better peer counselor with people because of that. The people I work with are people just like me. I appreciate them because they've gone through the things that I went through. Also, because of my chemical dependency, I am in a fellowship with others like me. I know I can't have even one sip of a drink. None of us can. We understand each other.

My past is like a lead weight holding me back. It's real; I have to deal with it. I have to be able to explain things in my past from before my head injury. I've been in prison in three different states, in jail in five states. I've already had my third felony, so the next time I offend I go away for good.

I really appreciate Sharon. She helped me accept the alcoholism tag. She helped me find a house, a place to live where I wasn't left to drink. It got me living with people who were sober and got me sober. Then she pushed for me to go to college. She explained to me how to use my MediCal card, which I didn't know how to use. I appreciate her for getting involved. She was important to me. I hope that other students and professionals, whether they are disabled or not, will participate *with* their clients. They need to guide them and to help them.

Disabled people have got to go through so much red tape to be able to get things done. People in society need to understand that. We need to have the opportunity to function in our homes and in society. Society's views of people with disabilities have affected me; that is why those of us with disabilities need each other and need programs to help us deal with these problems.

Discussion Questions

1. What are some of the major issues in defining learning disabilities?

2. Explain the various characteristics of learning disabilities. Which do you think may have the most social impact?

3. Explain the various characteristics of ADHD. What factors make success in the educational system difficult for persons with ADHD? How would a person with ADHD be accommodated in the workplace?

4. What issues might need to be addressed in working with a person with TBI?

5. Discuss the psychosocial consequences for persons with cognitive disabilities in the family, in school, and at work.

6. Discuss the issues concerning the current questions about LD and ADHD diagnosis for children. What is the relationship between these issues and the problems related to defining these disabilities?

Suggested Readings

Coles, G. (1987). *The learning mystique: A critical look at "learning disabilities."* New York: Pantheon Books.

Cruickshank, W. M. (1990). Definition: A major issue in the field of learning disabilities. In M. Nagler (Ed.), *Perspectives on disability* (pp. 389–406). Palo Alto, CA: Health Markets Research.

Finlan, T. G. (1994). *Learning disability: The imaginary disease.* Westport, CT: Bergin & Garvey.

References

Alexander, R. (1996). *The traumatically brain injured and the law* [consumerlawpage.com/article/brain/shtml].

Brown, D. S. (1994). *Working effectively with people who have learning disabilities and attention deficit hyperactivity disorder.* Ithaca, NY: Program on Employment and Disability, New York School of Industrial and Labor Relations, Cornell University.

Bruyere, S. M. (1994). *Working effectively with persons who have cognitive disabilities.* Ithaca, NY: Program on Employment and Disability, New York School of Industrial and Labor Relations, Cornell University.

Clark, C. G. (1996). *Understanding and coping with ADHD* [AXI Internet]. (postmaster@axi.net).

Coles, G. (1987). *The learning mystique: A critical look at "learning disabilities."* New York: Pantheon Books.

Cruickshank, W. M. (1990). Definition: A major issue in the field of learning disabilities. In M. Nagler (Ed.), *Perspectives on disability* (pp. 389–406). Palo Alto, CA: Health Markets Research.

Dunham, M. D., Koller, J. R., and McIntosh, D. E. (1996). A preliminary comparison of successful and nonsuccessful closure types among adults with specific learning disabilities in the vocational rehabilitation system. *The Journal of Rehabilitation, 26*(1), 42–48.

Eiel, C. (1994). Managing the learning disabled client. *Behavioral Health Management, 14*(5), 42–44.

Finlan, T. G. (1994). *Learning disability: The imaginary disease.* Westport, CT: Bergin & Garvey.

Kronick, D. (1981). *Social development of learning disabled persons.* San Francisco: Jossey-Bass.

Naylor, M. W., Staskowski, M., Kenney, M. C., and King, C. A. (1994). Language disorders and learning disabilities in school-refusing adolescents. *Journal of the American Academy of Child and Adolescent Psychiatry, 33*(9), 1331–1338.

Oliver, J. M., Cole, N. H., and Hollingsworth, H. (1991). Learning disabilities as functions of familial learning problems. *Exceptional Children, 57*(5), 427–441.

Sigler, G., and Mackelprang, R. W. (1993). Cognitive impairment: Psychosocial and sexual implication and strategies for social work intervention. In R. W. Mackelprang and D. Valentine (Eds.), *Sexuality and disabilities: A guide for human service practitioners* (pp. 89–106). New York: Haworth Press.

Simpson, R. G., and Umbach, B. T. (1989). Identifying and providing vocational services for adults with specific learning disabilities. *The Journal of Rehabilitation, 55*(3), 49–56.

Smelter, R. W., Rasch, B. W., Fleming, J., Nazos, P., and Baranowski, S. (1996). Is attention deficit disorder becoming a desired diagnosis? *Phi Delta Kappan, 77*(6), 429–433.

Tierney, L. M. Jr., McPhee, S. J., and Papadakis, M. A. (Eds.). (1994). *Current medical diagnosis and treatment.* Norwalk, CT: Appleton & Lange.

Winnick, J. P. (1995). *Adapted physical education and sport* (2nd ed.). Champaign, IL: Human Kinetics.

Zentall, S. S. (1993). Research on the educational implications of attention deficit hyperactive disorder. *Exceptional Children, 60*(2), 143–154.

Part Three

HUMAN SERVICE
PRACTICE FRAMEWORK

In the United States, human services for persons with disabilities have traditionally centered around the medical model. In the medical model, the assessment process directs practitioners to diagnose the characteristics of persons with disabilities against the context of "normalcy." The elements of the person that are not "within normal limits" are defined as "dysfunctional." Practitioners have created intervention plans for persons with disabilities geared to fixing their "broken" or "dysfunctional" parts. They have applied a combination of medical, psychological, and training interventions to make persons with disabilities as "normal" or as nondisabled as possible. Essentially, this approach expects practitioners to focus on the individual as the source of the problem. Although appropriate for immediate medical concerns, this perspective in human service practice is very limiting and often reinforces the social oppression experienced by persons with disabilities because it takes away their control.

The following chapters propose alternate practice perspectives to the medical model. We discuss assessment and how assessment guides professional relationships. We discuss models of practice and how practitioners work at micro, meso, and macro levels of intervention. We then provide a guide for professional practice based on respect and focusing on strengths.

In Chapter 11, we discuss the assessment process from a strengths perspective. When the human service professional helps individuals examine their needs, the professional helps in assessing strengths as well as limitations. This assessment looks not only at the individual but also at the social and economic environment of the person with a disability.

Chapter 12 explores a variety of practice models that could be utilized in the process of facilitating the empowerment of a person with a disability. Like the assessment process, the method of intervention must address change not only in the individual but in the individual's social environment.

Finally, Chapter 13 looks at a practice model that we have synthesized from other empowerment models. We address in detail four primary roles that human service professionals play in working with persons with disabilities: counselor, teacher, broker, and political advocate. Using the principles articulated in this chapter, practitioners can develop relationships that promote dignity and self-determination and that maximize people's quality of life.

Chapter 11

ASSESSMENT IN
HUMAN SERVICE PRACTICE

I remember this bullheaded psychologist who gave me a small-print IQ test and told my mother that I was retarded. What he had really tested was my ability to read small print. Even my mother knew that his diagnosis was not correct. After all, why would someone give me a small-print test when they knew I couldn't read small print very well? Because I was very determined, my mother told the school officials, "You'll have to fight with her. She wants to go here." So this bullheaded psychologist then said to my mother, "Well, we'll let her go here so she can learn about failure." So my mother says, "Yeah, OK." She only had an eighth-grade education, but she understood intuitively that I was brighter than they gave me credit for.

—Brenda Premo, Director, California Department of Rehabilitation, Sacramento, California

Student Learning Objectives:

1. To understand the limitations of assessment models coming from a pathological/dysfunctional frame of reference.

2. To develop an understanding of the social model of assessment with its origins in strengths-based practice and the independent living movement.

3. To understand the various layers of the social model of assessment, including the biological, psychological/emotional, social, and cultural.

4. To understand the various systems that need to be taken into account in the assessment process.

A routine and critical component of human service practice is assessment. Assessment occurs at all system levels, from the individual and personal to the institutional and societal. Hepworth, Rooney, and Larsen (1997) state

Assessment is the basis for contracting, goal setting, and intervention planning. Indeed, the effectiveness of selected interventions, and ultimately the case outcome, depend in large measure upon the accuracy of assessment. (p. 194)

Effective assessments are multidimensional and purposeful. Assessments of individuals and families can be divided into three components: information and history, impressions and evaluations, and plans. The first component focuses on people's histories, background information, and current situations and problems that bring them into contact with practitioners.

This information can be referred to as the *social history* portion of the assessment. Several elements are relevant to this section, and are outlined here. *Identifying information* includes demographic information such as age, gender, ethnicity, onset and type of disability, and living conditions. It also includes the reasons consumers are using professional services. *Family background* can include information about the person's family of origin, current relationships with family and significant others, and about living situations: past, present, and anticipated. *Social history* can include information on a person's educational and work history, friends and relationships, cultural information, places of residence, substance use history, and legal involvement. Since persons with disabilities are especially susceptible to financial problems, the history should include information on *financial status*. This includes income, expenses and financial obligations as well as insurance, medical coverage, and medical needs. The person's *psychosocial situation* may also be important to discuss, and may include the person's cognitive and emotional status. Sexuality concerns may be addressed. Information about the person's history with mental health professionals and the mental health system may be relevant. Family reactions and supports should be considered. Information on the person's relationships within the community may be gathered. Strengths in judgment and planning are also relevant to the person's psychosocial situation. Genograms and ecomaps can be valuable in developing comprehensive histories. The information gathered in the social history component of an evaluation will vary greatly depending on the circumstances of each person.

In the second, *evaluation* or *impressions,* section of psychosocial assessments, the human service practitioner and consumer consider the meaning of the information gathered in the social history. For example, a person who has had strong family relationships is likely to be able to rely on family for continued support. The evaluation section should include information about people's strengths, and their realized and potential capabilities as well as their needs and limitations. It can consider consumers' social supports and their ability to impact people and organizations in their lives. The level and adequacy of personal and environmental resources also can be evaluated.

The final, or *plan,* section of psychosocial evaluations arises directly from the evaluation section. Plans should be explicit and goal directed. In the plan, the consumer and professional determine desired outputs and outcomes. Outputs may include services that professionals may provide (e.g., counseling, advocacy, referrals), and actions in which consumers may engage. Outcomes focus on the results the consumer and practitioner wish to achieve in their work together. Attention to micro, meso, and macro elements of people's lives are critical elements in effective plans.

Five questions, which provide a framework for assessment activities, can be asked in developing human service assessments. First, What is the reason for the assessment? This helps the practitioner evaluate people's needs and their reasons for engaging in a relationship with a human service agency. Second, What is the scope of the assessment? Scope is determined by a variety of factors, including people's needs, agency mandates, and social conditions. For example, the reasons for and scope of an employment assessment in a vocational rehabilitation agency differ from an assessment performed during the course of family therapy. A third question is, Who receives the information and knowledge gained as a result of the assessment? In an individual and family therapy agency, assessment information is usually kept within the confines of the practitioner and family relationship. However, if family therapy is taking place within a medical and/or psychiatric facility, the same information is, generally, more widely disseminated to other professionals and to third parties. A fourth question is, What are the sources of knowledge needed to engage in the assessment? This will determine how information is obtained. Some assessments utilize only one source of information, whereas others utilize multiple sources. Court-ordered assessments for substance abuse offenses may utilize numerous informants as well as court records. On the other hand, assessments for participation in an educational group may rely exclusively on an individual interview. Fifth, What will the assessment be used for? For example, if assessments are being paid for by a third party, especially in managed care settings, a clinical (pathology-based) diagnosed assessment is often necessary to obtain funding (Strom, 1992). Medical and psychiatric settings require pathology-based diagnoses. In contrast, assessments performed in independent living centers focus on consumer definitions of needs and problems.

◆ Pathology and Assessment

Human service professionals working with persons with disabilities will invariably be required to engage in assessments. Traditional assessment models have focused on the presence or absence of pathology (Schuler and Perez, 1991). There are several reasons for this emphasis. Persons seeking professional help have done so to receive assistance in treating or solving problems. For example, people see physicians to treat or cure illness. Professional training and sanctioning centers on pathology have driven models of practice. Medical specialties (e.g., neurosurgery, cardiology, rheumatology) have heavily concentrated on treating pathological conditions with relatively little emphasis on preventive and health-maintaining specialties (e.g., family practice). Similarly, mental health training has primarily focused not on maintaining mental health but on treating mental illness. The focus on pathology has been driven, in great measure, by financial interests. Funding has been institutionally based in places such as hospitals and nursing homes, and service providers have been paid only after diagnosing and treating pathology.

Certainly, the focus on pathology is essential in many situations (Blotzer and Ruth, 1995). A person taken to an emergency room with multiple injuries from an automobile accident requires immediate treatment for injuries sustained. A person experiencing an acute psychotic episode is in need of protection and treatment.

However, this exclusive focus on pathology is inadequate in the long term. This is especially true in human services. By attending primarily to problems, assessments can fail to account for individual strengths. A deficiency focus can lead to devaluing and, in some cases, dehumanizing people (Cowger, 1994). For example, in reviewing old patient hospital records, one of the authors repeatedly found the notation "FLK" in the records of children with mental retardation. Upon investigating the meaning, he found that FLK was an acronym for "funny-looking kid" used routinely to refer to patients with mental retardation. FLK was originally used as a type of medical shorthand, because children with intellectual disabilities can have atypical facial and body features. However, the term FLK devalues the people it supposedly describes.

The individual pathology focus also fails to recognize the complexity of experiences and relationships (Salsgiver, 1996). This is illustrated in the case of a Native American patient hospitalized with an acute spinal cord injury in a rehabilitation center. Nurses and therapists became increasingly frustrated with his lateness for therapy and his nonparticipation in the general milieu of the center. They attributed his behaviors to denial, resistance, and noncompliance. They failed to realize that he had been raised in a remote community on a reservation. He was overwhelmed, not just with his spinal cord injury, but by his surroundings. The rehabilitation center employed far more people than lived in his community. He had never owned a watch, yet they expected him to follow a tight schedule. He was a "night" person, yet he was expected to begin his day at 7:00 A.M. There were also language and cultural barriers. However, the staff focused only on "fixing" his behavior so they could provide the therapies they determined he needed. A more holistic assessment would have led professionals to assess ways they could change their expectations of him and modify the environment in such a way to better meet his needs while ensuring that he receive the medical and physical attention he needed. For example, times for breakfast and therapies could have been modified to meet the demands of his lifestyle. The staff could have taken the time to get to know the patient and learn about his culture.

◆ Models of Assessment

The last 20 years have seen several different models of assessment proposed for persons with disabilities. For example, Trieschmann (1980) compared two models of service delivery for persons with spinal cord injuries—the medical model and the learning model. Trieschmann pointed out that "in the medical model, the behavioral equation for rehabilitation success consists of: $B = F(O \times p)$. Behavior (B) is a function of treatments to the organic variables (O) unless hindered by underlying personality problems." (p. 24).

In the medical model, the primary assessment targets are organic, physical, and medical problems. Psychosocial emphasis is on personality problems and their amelioration. Personality is assessed in the context of the obstacles it creates for the treating professionals. Strengths are not assessed—only the absence of pathology.

The unit of assessment is the individual, problems reside within the individual, and treatment plans center on fixing the individual. Professionals assume responsibility for assessment and treatment. This model may be appropriate in crisis situations, such as during a medical or mental health emergency, but it has limited benefit in the long term.

Trieschmann contrasted the medical model with the learning model, where "the behavioral equation for rehabilitation success is: $B = F(P \times O \times E)$. Behavior (B) is a function of the person (P) the organism (O) and the environment (E)" (p. 26). In Trieschmann's learning model, "person" variables include personality style, coping mechanisms, and internal or external locus of control. Organic variables include age, health, and severity of disability. Environmental variables include family support, finances, and public policies. Assessment broadens to include psychological and environmental well-being. Individuals are still the focus, but assessment is used to help professionals determine how to educate patients and clients to function better. Assessments are performed to identify knowledge and skills clients need to function as independently as possible. Control still resides primarily in professionals, who act as educators. The learning model attends to internal strengths and social variables. It may be appropriate in the initial stages of disabilities when persons with disabilities and their families are in need of knowledge and skill development. However, it is inadequate in the long run because the perception of problems and needs as well as the control of services still rests with professionals.

Condeluci (1995) discusses another model of professional assessment—the economic paradigm. From this perspective, problems lie in the person's inability to earn a living. Professional assessment focuses on problems people have that prevent them from being productive. Condeluci states

> *Today, in the human service world that surrounds disability, a battery of tests and surveys attempts to identify and predict the economic potential of its clients. These tests look at aptitude, interests, skills, education, and deficits. It is mostly the deficits, however, that cast a shadow on the plan that is set up for the individual.* (p. 72)

Condeluci observes that people with certain types of disabilities are likely to be stereotyped and that the experts "push people with certain disabilities toward job areas thought to be best with disability groups" (p. 74). For example, people with intellectual disabilities are often pushed into custodial, dishwashing, and busperson jobs, whereas those with brain injuries are classically pushed into repetitive work. Assessment tools and interventions such as aptitude tests can be valuable aids in the quest for economic self-sufficiency. However, this model is similar to other models in that it focuses primarily on the individual's deficits and possible interventions to overcome problems.

The approach that best meets the needs of persons with disabilities takes a social rather than individual approach to disability. Hahn (1991) labels this approach the "minority group model" and states that social stigma is the major problem facing persons with disabilities, which is best *addressed through civil rights rather than social services. The minority model group model also alters the view of the disabled person as defected or deficient . . . . (The) call for improvements in social services is a step in the right direction, but it should be expanded to include civil rights as the major focus for improving the lives of the disabled.* (p. 17)

Condeluci (1995) labels this approach an "interdependence paradigm." He contends that interdependence focuses on individual capabilities rather than deficits. Problems reside in systems rather than individuals, and actions are tailored to create environmental supports and consumer empowerment.

There are several elements in approaching assessment from a social perspective. A critical component of the independent living approach (Mackelprang and Salsgiver, 1996) is that individuals identify their own needs. The minority group model, the interdependence paradigm, and the independent living approaches all have many similarities. For ease of use, we call our approach to assessment the social model.

In the social model of assessment, traditional medical model roles are reversed. Persons with disabilities take on the expert role while professionals act as consultants. Rather than professionals making decisions based on client information and feedback, consumers identify needs and problems and enlist the help of professionals to meet their needs. Professionals may not always agree with the individual's perceptions, but this approach assumes that people with disabilities have the ability to recognize their individual realities (Condeluci, 1995). Unlike other approaches, the social model does not assume that professional perceptions are superior to those of "clients" or "patients." Rather, it assumes that the consumers of professional services understand their own lives. People's perceptions are their realities, and the social model acknowledges this.

In the social model, a critical element of assessment is the environment. For example, people who use wheelchairs for mobility face problems, not because they are "confined" to wheelchairs but because of physical barriers that limit their access to full societal participation. The fact that "persons with disabilities tend to make up a disproportionate share of residents at the lower end of the economic scale" (Bryan, 1996, p. 17) has much to do with social policies and institutions that make it extremely difficult for them to be economically self-sufficient. Assessment emphasizes the availability and limitations of social and community resources and ways to enhance deficits.

The social model emphasizes people's strengths and potential. Strengths encompass the knowledge and skills that an individual possesses (Saleebey, 1996). Potential refers to the potential abilities that people can develop with sufficient resources. Persons with disabilities can identify their own strengths; sometimes professionals can help them identify strengths they may not perceive that they possess. With consumer direction, professionals can also consult to help people develop their potential. This can be illustrated in the case of a young couple, both with neuromuscular disabilities, who requested assistance from one of the authors. This couple, both in their early twenties, had met and fallen in love in the nursing home in which they resided. Their medical records, which focused on their physical limitations, clearly justified their continued stay in the facility. Initially, they came into contact with one of the authors because of their desire to get out of the nursing home for occasional recreation. With increased community exposure, they began to realize that others with similar capabilities were not forced to live with parents or in nursing homes with others directing their lives. Encouraged to identify their strengths, they began to believe that they could marry and have a sexual relationship if they chose. Both began to realize that their need for physical assistance in ADLs did not mean they had to give up control over how, what, where, and by whom assistance was provided. Eventually, they each developed their potential and identified their strengths to the point that they left the nursing home to live in their own apartments with attendant care assistance. Their relationship evolved platonically; however, they maintained their friendship and began to see themselves as sexual beings. Along the road to independent living, each person began to assess and develop strengths, eschewing traditional, pathology-based models of assessment and treatment.

The social model acknowledges that people have disabilities but contends that they are not defined by their disabilities (Fine and Asch, 1988). For example, people with psychiatric disabilities also have many other traits, interests, and capabilities. Labeling a person as "schizophrenic" defines the individual. However, saying that a person lives with schizophrenia acknowledges that the person has other qualities and traits. Defining the person and the person's disability as synonymous is a natural outgrowth of traditional models that focus on problems and ways to fix problems. By contrast, the social model views the disability as one aspect of people's existence.

The social model of disability emphasizes the importance of institutionalized oppression and devaluation to which people with disabilities have been subjected. Szymanski and Trueba (1994) offer the observation that

> *the difficulties faced by persons with disabilities are not the result of functional impairments related to the disability, but rather are the result of a castification process embedded in societal institutions for rehabilitation and education that are enforced by well-meaning professionals.* (p. 12)

The "castification" that Szymanski and Trueba refer to is pervasive throughout societal institutions, even those that have been developed to serve persons with disabilities. Traditionally, long-term dependence on Medicaid has been assessed as a functional individual problem. Social model assessment acknowledges a problem in societal institutions wherein people are forced to choose between low-paying jobs and hazard losing health coverage or being financially dependent so they can maintain access to health care. Another example of this castification occurs in vocational rehabilitation agencies where pressure to employ people quickly and with limited resources induces counselors to find the easiest sources of employment (e.g., dishwashing, custodial work) and to exclude people with severe disabilities from these caseloads by labeling them as unemployable. In employing a social model, societal rather than individual assessment and intervention is the focus.

The social model of assessment acknowledges that consumers control their resources. Condeluci (1995) contends that "people must be deemed capable to be in control of their lives, and only challenged if family, support people, and advocates are convinced, beyond a shadow of a doubt that they are not" (pp. 102–103). Most professional approaches assume that people with disabilities must prove they are capable before others relinquish control. Unfortunately, those who are to relinquish control often have conflicts of interest in that their loss of control also means loss of their role and, possibly, their usefulness. For example, the nursing home in which the previously cited couple resided had significant disincentives to discharge them—the most important of which was the loss of tens of thousands of dollars in annual revenue.

In the social model, consumers determine how and to whom resources are expended. For example, persons with intellectual disabilities in a supported living situation can determine the help they need with finances, but they may use social workers and independent living specialists as consultants to assist them in managing their affairs. Rather than a home health agency employing attendants on their behalf, individuals with physical disabilities who need physical assistance handle their own financial concerns and employee decisions.

A major philosophical difference in using a social model to assess people with disabilities is that assessment begins with the assumption that persons with disabilities are competent and have the right and responsibility to control their lives and to manage the professionals who enter their lives (DeJong, 1979). By contrast, other assessments begin with the assumption that professional assessment is needed to help fix individuals' problems. The terminology used is an example of this contrast in assumptions. In the social model, independent living specialists consult with clients, who direct the interventions. In a traditional model, case managers assess and manage cases (i.e., clients, students, or patients). The locus of control resides with the person with the disability in the social model and with the case manager in the traditional model.

Both traditional and social models recognize that there are situations when people are not able to function independently. Traditional models, however, are inclined to impose professional control over individuals to fix their pathology. The social model, on the other hand, considers the need for assistance to be a part of human existence for all people. No one person is completely independent in today's society. DeJong (1979), in tracing the philosophic roots of the independent living movement, states that the IL movement "has steered away from destructive individualism. It has encouraged community support and mutual responsibility. The emphasis on self-help and self-reliance has a communal as well as an individual component" (p. 50). People without disabilities use the expertise of others in everything from buying automobiles to purchasing groceries. Likewise, people with disabilities rely on others. People with severe intellectual disabilities may need assistance managing their money or using transportation. People with hearing disabilities require TTYs to talk on the phone. Reliance on others, or what Condeluci (1995) calls "interdependence," is a reality for everyone in society. Problems arise, therefore, because of limited or absent resources, and needs are met by empowering people and creating adequate supports. Assessment strives to find solutions rather than to fix problems.

◆ ## THE SCOPE OF ASSESSMENT

Effective assessments are contextual; that is, the context in which the assessment occurs determines the nature and extent of the assessment (Miley, O'Melia, and DuBois, 1995). Human service assessments can be considered to involve two overlapping constructs. In the broadest context, assessments of individuals and groups performed by human service workers encompass biological, psychological/emotional, social, and cultural dimensions. In addition, assessment involves the micro, meso, macro continuum, which accounts for structural and systemic influences on individuals and systems.

According to Rosenthal (1989), a comprehensive, holistic individual and family assessment includes the biological, psychological/emotional, and social domains. Fee (1994) adds to this the importance of the cultural domain in assessment. Each of these four areas is interrelated to the others. Each of the domains influences people, and people have control and influence on each of the domains.

The biological domain encompasses all of the body's systems. However, biological functioning does not define people. For example, people with spinal cord injuries have paraplegia or quadriplegia—they are not defined as paraplegics or quadriplegics. People with intellectual disabilities are not retarded.

The social model assesses biological functioning in the holistic context. Human service workers need to rely on persons with disabilities to identify their levels of biological functioning and the meaning of that functioning in their lives. The focus is on their strengths and capabilities. This can be illustrated using an example of a person with T-12 paraplegia. Traditional assessment focuses on paralysis and lack of sensation in the lower extremities and the genitals, lack of bowel and bladder functioning, sexual dysfunction, and wheelchair confinement. From this assessment, treatments are developed that are intended to make people closer to normal. Long leg braces for walking are often prescribed that are rarely used. Psychosocial interventions are developed that focus on helping people deal with their losses. In contrast, a strengths-oriented assessment focuses on capabilities. The practitioner seeks the meaning of paraplegia to the individual. Rather than viewing the person as confined to a wheelchair, the professional perceives the person as using a wheelchair for mobility. Sexual function is seen as different but not as inherently dysfunctional. The gamut of emotional responses are jointly evaluated, focusing on building strengths, not just fixing pathology.

Human service workers most often are responsible for an evaluation of the psychological and emotional functioning of clients. To justify involvement and to receive reimbursement for services, a DSM-IV diagnosis may be required. If so, assessment is, by necessity, pathology based. In playing the reimbursement game, human service professionals may learn to engage in labeling an individual with an innocuous diagnosis, such as an anxiety or adjustment disorder (Saleebey, 1996). By contrast, the social model recognizes that individuals have problems, but assessments focus on strengths. Human service professionals work to identify strengths and capabilities as consultants to the individuals they serve. They emphasize supporting consumers' capacities rather than fixing their problems. Workers rely on those with whom they work to identify their own needs. The individual's perceptions, rather than the professional's expectations, are paramount. The difference in the traditional and social approaches was repeatedly illustrated to one of the authors in his work with persons with neurological disabilities. The following example was typical:

> *Late one afternoon I received a call from a nurse and a resident physician to consult on the case of 30-year-old "Bill," who had paraplegia resulting from a fall. Bill was well known to me and had been doing very well during inpatient rehabilitation for his spinal cord injury. I had met with Bill, his wife, and their young children on a number of occasions in the month he had been hospitalized. However, the nurse and physician were very upset because Bill was nearing discharge and he had "not dealt emotionally with his paraplegia." When I asked them what they saw as the problem, they told me Bill was "in denial." I asked how they reached that conclusion. They replied, "He has never been depressed and is too pleasant all the time." "Sounds good to me," I responded. "Yes, but he needs to begin to deal with his disability," they stressed. I replied that in repeated conversations with Bill and his family, they felt they were coping with things well. I saw nothing to indicate anything different.*

> *I expressed concern that their expectations of Bill placed him in a no-win situation. If Bill didn't become depressed, he was in denial. Bill could become psychologically healthy only by pervasively experiencing emotional states they considered pathological (e.g., depression, anger, anxiety). They assumed the lack of pathology meant pathology, and they would be satisfied that he was healthy only by being depressed. Their latent expectations could even produce unnecessary difficulties.*

In the months following this incident, Bill and his wife sought the author out on a number of occasions. In one instance, they asked for help finding social support from others with spinal cord injuries. On another occasion, they sought sexual education and counseling. Assessment and counseling was provided in the context of change rather than dysfunction.

Although an acute disability such as paraplegia can be traumatic and produce a range of emotional responses, we reject the idea that disabilities automatically cause psychological/emotional problems. A social model recognizes the tremendous resources people possess in dealing with life's experiences. Individual coping problems are often a result of others' reactions to and expectations of disability.

Human service workers are cautioned to listen to each person's personal perceptions of the emotional impact of his or her disability rather than assuming people will react in preconceived ways. This concept is illustrated in a study of persons with long-term spinal cord injuries by Mackelprang and Hepworth (1987). Two of their findings ran counter to extant beliefs of professionals. First, it was widely assumed that the higher the spinal cord injury, the lower the level of adjustment people would experience. Instead, their study found that those with the lower levels of injury (lumbar and sacral) had lower levels of adjustment than people with thoracic and low cervical injuries. Second, people with spinal cord injuries reported less emotional distress overall than was expected. This study supports the notion that people's perceptions of their disabilities are the most critical factor in psychological assessment. To assume that persons with disabilities are at greater need for professionals to determine their emotional status is an ableist notion.

Cowger (1994) offers twelve principles of assessment, all of which underlie the need for the human service practitioner to seek the perception of the person with whom they are working. First of all, the individual's understanding of the facts and issues is of foremost importance. Second, the human service practitioner must believe in the credibility and ability of the person. Third, look for what the person wants. Do not bring into the assessment process preconceived notions and bias. Fourth, move the assessment toward an emphasis on personal and environmental strengths. Fifth, look for strengths on a multidimensional level—address individual, family, and community strengths. Sixth, use language that the person understands and relates to. The use of professional jargon should be avoided. Seventh, make the assessment process a combined effort; this should be easy if you believe in the person. Eighth, and much related to the preceding principle, reach a mutual agreement on the assessment. Ninth, do not "blame the victim." In working with persons with disabilities, it is easy to make their "laziness" or their "dependency" the cause of the problem that needs to be addressed. Tenth, avoid cause-and-effect analysis in assessment. Humans are far too complex for the human service practitioner to figure out the "cause." Eleventh, "assess; do not diagnose" (p. 267). Diagnosis assumes pathology and dysfunction. Last, see difference and uniqueness as strengths. This is particularly the case when the cultural domain is addressed as it intersects with disability.

Rounds, Weil, and Bishop (1994) address the need for a multicultural perspective in dealing with families of children with disabilities. Within assessment and practice, several elements must be applied in maintaining the cultural domain. Cultural diversity must not only be recognized but valued. Different ethnic cultures deal with disability in different ways. In most cases, these differences need to be accounted for and put within the perspective of strengths. Culture affects when and how certain individuals or families seek assistance; it impacts how individuals participate in the human service framework. Practitioners must also be aware of their own cultural perspective and how that impacts the assessment process. The human service practitioner must recognize and understand the different levels of culture and how they interact. Fee (1994) points out the myriad of cultural levels within human service delivery systems for persons with disabilities. There is the ethnic culture of the individual and his or her family, the culture of the human service practitioner, the culture of the human service system, and the culture of disability. All of these cultures play into the process of assessment.

Imperative in a social model assessment process is the ethnographic interviewing technique. Originally utilized by anthropologists in obtaining objective information about various ethnic cultures, this technique has been expanded into an interviewing process that can help human service practitioners understand the world view from any cultural perspective. Green (1982) defines an ethnographic interview as one used to determine a description of the problem of the person the practitioner is working with from that person's world view. The person with whom the practitioner is working becomes the teacher, guiding the practitioner into an understanding of his or her world. The ethnographic interviewing process assumes that language becomes the bridge to understanding the various cultures that are a part of the service provision. Words may have meanings that are understood only within a certain cultural context, even though the word may be used outside that culture. The human service practitioner must explore these words to get an understanding of the person's life view. An example from disability culture is the term *crip*. "Cripple" has a certain meaning to mainstream culture. If a person without a disability refers to someone with a disability as "crip," it would be construed as pejorative. Within disability culture, however, when the term is used between persons with disabilities, it is one of kinship and belonging. Persons with disabilities may use the term in referring to themselves or to each other. But the term *super-crip* is one of disdain for a person with a disability. It means someone who is trying to prove that he or she is not disabled. To be called a *super-crip* by another person with a disability is not a good thing. Without this inside knowledge, the human service practitioner is at a loss to really understand the world of disability. But in order to find these pieces of information, the practitioner must ask within an ethnographic perspective (Green, 1982).

In the social component of assessment, it is important to recognize the many societal elements impacting persons with disabilities (Norlin and Chess, 1997). It can be helpful to make assessments on the micro, meso, and macro levels. The flow of energy in support systems is also important—the social model recognizes that not only are people impacted by their environments, but they impact their environments as well. The independent living movement is built around the concept of people impacting their environments. On the macro level, Herling (1996) states that

> only the systematic and intentional building of local organizations owned by, and dedicated to the empowerment of people with disabilities will change the societal structures that perpetuate injustice. [The] primary goal is to organize [people] with disabilities and empower them to take an active role in shaping their lives and circumstances. (p. 26)

Therefore, a systematic evaluation of the impact—both realized and potential—of people to influence their environments is crucial. This can be facilitated through a personal-professional collaboration.

Micro-level support systems are usually reciprocal; that is, relationships are dependent on the commitment and actions of both parties. It is also critical to determine the nature of social supports (Crewe and Zola, 1983) and the levels of support, including both physical and emotional supports. For example, some people may provide much physical support, such as personal attendant care or assistance with shopping. Others may provide no physical care but may provide emotional support. In addition to the strength of the support, conflict should also be assessed. Sometimes, strong support comes at a high price when conflict is present; therefore, people should be encouraged to assess the benefits and costs of their social supports. The type of relationship is also important. For example, the connection people have with professionals who provide services is usually temporary and is much different than that of family and friends.

Meso-level assessment is also important. Effective meso assessment is concerned with the impact of social systems on people's lives and the impact people can have on those systems. Meso assessment should encompass neighborhoods, health care organizations, churches, schools, social agencies, and businesses in which people may be employed. It is critical that the influences of these systems are addressed in assessment. For example, Brown (1996) chronicles the low income and employment levels of persons with disabilities, which traditionally have been attributed to people with disabilities being less capable than persons without disabilities. However, it is clear that people with disabilities have been denied opportunities and subjected to much discrimination in employment. Assessment of the meso domain must include the social meso opportunities and obstacles people face rather than focusing primarily on the individual. It is also important to assess the individual's ability to impact meso systems. For example, people now have recourse against organizations such as schools and businesses that practice discrimination. When institutional discrimination occurs, meso assessment will identify the sources of and factors contributing to discrimination and the resources to combat it. Initially, the individual with a disability may be the primary beneficiary; however, meso assessment can have further-reaching consequences as institutional ableism and societal barriers are identified that impact others as well. This is illustrated in the following example of a student seeking a degree in education.

> *Javier, a 35-year-old Latino/Hispanic male with a visual disability seeking a B.S. degree in education, filed an action with the ADA compliance committee of his university for discrimination he experienced in student teaching. He had been removed from his internship without warning. Reasons given for his termination were lateness in showing up for work, poorly prepared lesson plans, nonattendance of school functions, and failure to control students in class.*

Initially, Javier sought support to deal with his personal failure through a local organization for persons with visual disabilities. As the independent living specialist discussed Javier's situation, they jointly assessed a number of institutional procedural problems that hindered Javier's experience. First, Javier had requested that the school accommodate his disability by finding a site near his home. Instead, he was placed in a school several miles from his home that had no public transportation access. As a result, he was dependent on others for transportation, which was inconsistent, and extracurricular activities were impossible to attend. Second, his mentor teacher's style of mentoring was hands off; little attempt was made to orient Javier geographically. Finally, when students took advantage of Javier's visual disability, the teacher did not consult with Javier to develop strategies to better control the class. Instead, the teacher stated that these were problems caused by Javier's visual disability, which limited his ability to teach effectively.

In spite of these practices, Javier initially internalized his dismissal as being caused by his inadequacies. By exploring meso-level factors, Javier began to recognize the environmental conditions that contributed to his problems. He was also able to identify areas in which he needed to grow to become an effective teacher. However, he began to reject the notion that the problems resided exclusively within himself. As a result, he filed a successful complaint against the education department of his university because it failed to reasonably accommodate his disability. Had his counselor focused only on emotional adjustment, his problems would have been assessed as coming from a lack of personal adjustment rather than factoring in the school environment.

Macro-level assessment evaluates the impact of social structures and institutions on people's lives. A macro assessment for persons with disabilities starts with an acknowledgment of power differences and social conditions that disempower them and make them vulnerable to abuse and devaluation (Sobsey, 1994). For example, in assessing employment of a person with a health-related disability, it may be essential to evaluate the impact of health policies and practices, vocational agencies, and business. This can be illustrated in the following case of a person with a psychiatric disability.

Erica was a 27-year-old woman diagnosed with schizophrenia who approached a vocational rehabilitation agency for help in finding work. Since age 20, Erica had been in and out of psychiatric institutions. She had a high school diploma but few skills to make her employable. She had begun taking Clozaril six months earlier with very positive results. Hallucinations and delusions had subsided and her isolation decreased dramatically. She became more social and desired to seek employment. Unfortunately, the social barriers were formidable. Erica was supported by SSI and received Medicaid, which paid for her Clozaril. Since she was "unskilled" and had a psychiatric history, she could only find employment in low-paying jobs that had no benefits. If she took a job at this level, she would lose her SSI and Medicaid coverage. The costs of medication and ongoing mental health treatment made the price of employment prohibitive. When Erica sought vocational rehabilitation, she was informed that they could find her a lower-paying job but could not afford to provide her with the education she desired to obtain adequate employment.

A micro-level evaluation of Erica would focus on her psychiatric illness as the cause of her unemployment. A macro-level evaluation, however, uncovers the institutional barriers to self-sufficiency. This assessment clarifies the lack of resources to obtain goals. The federal/state Medicaid system makes it nearly impossible for some persons to work and live because working renders them ineligible for needed health and mental health coverage. The SSI system allows people to work for a short time, but ineligibility can be a significant deterrent. State and federal funding of vocational rehabilitation agencies leads to the exclusion of people from essential services.

Whereas individuals and small groups can have a relatively strong impact on micro and meso systems, it generally takes a collective effort to change macro systems. Assessments of the environment by groups of people can lead to collective action and social change that is impossible for individuals alone. Passage of laws such as the Americans with Disabilities Act is an example of collective action. The movement of persons with intellectual disabilities out of institutions and into the community is another example of policies and institutional change brought about by grassroots efforts and the collective voices of advocates.

◆ SUMMARY

Human service professionals working with persons with disabilities will invariably be required to engage in assessments. Traditional assessment models have focused on the presence or absence of pathology. Certainly, the focus on pathology is essential in many situations. However, exclusive focus on pathology has had negative consequences in long-term involvement. This is especially true in human services. By attending primarily to problems, assessments can fail to account for individual strengths. A deficiency focus can lead to devaluing and, in some cases, dehumanizing people. The individual pathology focus also fails to recognize the complexity of experiences and relationships.

The approach that best meets the needs of persons with disabilities takes a social rather than individual approach to disability. There are several elements in approaching assessment from a social perspective. A critical component of the independent living approach is that individuals identify their own needs. In the social model, a critical element of assessment is the environment. The social model emphasizes people's strengths and potential. It acknowledges that people have disabilities but contends that they are not defined by their disabilities. The social model of disability emphasizes the importance of institutionalized oppression and devaluation to which people with disabilities have been subjected. It also acknowledges that consumers control their resources—they determine how and to whom resources are expended.

Effective assessments are contextual; that is, the context in which the assessment occurs determines the nature and extent of the assessment. Human service assessments can be considered to involve two overlapping constructs. In the broadest context, assessments of individuals and groups performed by human service workers encompass biological, psychological/emotional, social, and cultural dimensions. In addition, assessment involves the micro, meso, macro continuum, which accounts for structural and systemic influences on individuals and systems.

◆   ◆   ◆

Discussion Questions

1. What are some of the issues around a medical model of assessment? What are the advantages and disadvantages to using it in working with persons with disabilities?

2. Explain the individual components of a social model of assessment. How could you use it if you are working in a health facility that may require a pathologically based assessment model?

3. Relate the micro, meso, and macro components of the social model of assessment to Cowger's statement: "Assessment that focuses on deficits provides obstacles to clients exercising personal and social power and reinforces those social structures that generate and regulate the unequal power relationships that victimize clients" (1994, p. 264).

4. Compare the following two assessments:

    a. Mr. Anderson is an African American male, age 19, with an average IQ, who was severely injured in a motorcycle accident. Mr. Anderson never completed high school. His injury has resulted in partial paralysis of both his arms and legs. He has limited hand movement. Mr. Anderson suffers chronic depression for which he takes medication.

       Mr. Anderson is severely limited in his mobility. He is confined to a wheelchair and totally dependent on attendants or family members to prepare his food, bathe him, attend to his bowel program, and so on. His family was uncooperative in his rehabilitation. They missed appointments. They did not follow through on suggestions to make the apartment more accessible. Mr. Anderson appears to have limited ambition toward education or employment. He rarely gets out in the community other than in his immediate neighborhood. He does not take advantage of community resources made available to him.

    b. Mr. Anderson is a 19-year-old African American male with partial paralysis from a motorcycle accident who lives with his mother and his younger brother in a housing project. Several of his relatives live in the same project, and they stop in frequently to visit. His family is very close. They agreed that he will stay with them rather than be institutionalized or live on his own. Mr. Anderson has trained his family to provide his attendant care under his supervision. Attendants from a local agency also provide personal care. With assistive devices, he is able to feed himself and transfer between bed and wheelchair. His emotional status has improved significantly since he began using antidepressants.

Mr. Anderson gets along well in the neighborhood using a wheelchair for community mobility. The apartment building is wheelchair accessible, however, he lacks financial resources to make his bathroom completely accessible. He uses a portable commode chair to make do. He visits other family members frequently. He gets out into the neighborhood quite often, and various store owners "watch out" for him.

Mr. Anderson visits the local Radio Shack where Ralph Henderson, the owner, takes time to show him how to use a computer on display. Mr. Anderson is giving Ralph $10 a week toward the purchase of a computer. Mr. Anderson has talked about obtaining a GED, and is thinking about going to computer school to learn programming.

What assumptions are being made in the first assessment? What are the assumptions in the second assessment? What things are left out of the first assessment? What components are missing in the second assessment? Which assessment more accurately reflects the perceptions of the person in question?

Suggested Readings

Blotzer, M. A., and Ruth, R. (1995). On sitting with uncertainty: Treatment considerations for persons with disabilities. In M. A. Blotzer and R. Ruth (Eds.), *Sometimes you just want to feel like a human being: Case studies of empowering psychotherapy with people with disabilities* (pp. 15–24). Baltimore: Paul H. Brookes.

Brown, W. V. (1996). *In search of freedom: How people with disabilities have been disenfranchised from the mainstream of American society.* Springfield, IL: Charles C Thomas.

Cowger, C. D. (1994). Assessing client strengths: Clinical assessment for client empowerment. *Social Work, 39*(3), 262–268.

Szymanski, E. M., and Trueba, H. T. (1994). Castification of people with disabilities: Potential disempowering aspects of classification in disability services. *The Journal of Rehabilitation, 60*(3), 12(9).

References

Blotzer, M. A., and Ruth, R. (1995). On sitting with uncertainty: Treatment considerations for persons with disabilities. In M. A. Blotzer and R. Ruth (Eds.), *Sometimes you just want to feel like a human being: Case studies of empowering psychotherapy with people with disabilities* (pp. 15–24). Baltimore: Paul H. Brookes.

Brown, W. V. (1996). *In search of freedom: How people with disabilities have been disenfranchised from the mainstream of American society.* Springfield, IL: Charles C Thomas.

Condeluci, A. (1995). *Interdependence: The route to community* (2nd ed.). Winter Park, FL: GR Press.

Cowger, C. D. (1994). Assessing client strengths: Clinical assessment for client empowerment. *Social Work, 39*(3), 262–268.

Crewe, N. M., and Zola, I. K. (1983). *Independent living and physically disabled people: Developing, implementing, and evaluating self-help rehabilitation programs.* San Francisco: Jossey-Bass.

DeJong, G. (1979). *The movement for independent living: Origins, ideology, and implications for disability research.* East Lansing: Michigan State University, Center for International Rehabilitation.

Fee, F. A. (1994). An introduction to multicultural issues in spinal cord injury rehabilitation. *VSCI Psychosocial Process, 7*(3), 104–107.

Fine, M., and Asch, A. (1988). Disability beyond stigma: Social interaction, discrimination, and activism. In M. Nagler (Ed.), *Perspectives in disability* (pp. 61–74). Palo Alto, CA: Health Markets Research.

Green, J. W. (1982). *Cultural awareness in the human services.* Englewood Cliffs, NJ: Prentice Hall.

Hahn, H. (1991). Alternate views of empowerment: Social services and civil rights. (Editorial). *The Journal of Rehabilitation, 57*(4), 17(3).

Hepworth, D. H., Rooney, R. H., and Larsen, J. (1997). *Direct social work practice: Theory and Skills* (5th ed.). Pacific Grove, CA: Brooks/Cole.

Herling, D. (1996). Keeping promises: Coalition of Montanans concerned with disabilities. *The Rural Exchange, 9*(2), 26–28.

Mackelprang, R. W, and Hepworth, D. H. (1987). Ecological factors in the rehabilitation of people with severe spinal cord injuries. *Social Work in Health Care, 13,* 23–38.

Mackelprang, R. W, and Salsgiver, R. O. (1996). People with disabilities and social work: Historical and contemporary issues. *Social Work, 41*(1), 7–14.

Miley, K. K., O'Melia, M., and DuBois, B. L. (1995). *Generalist social work practice: An empowering approach*. Boston: Allyn & Bacon.

Norlin, J. M. and Chess, W. A. (1997). *Human behavior and the social environment: Social systems theory* (3rd ed.). Boston: Allyn & Bacon.

Rosenthal, M. (1989). Psychosocial evaluation of physically disabled persons. In B. W. Heller, L. M. Flohr, and L. S. Zegans (Eds.), *Psychosocial interventions with physically disabled persons.* New Brunswick, NJ: Rutgers University Press.

Rounds, K. A., Weil, M., and Bishop, K. K. (1994). Practice with culturally diverse families of young children with disabilities. *Families in Society: The Journal of Contemporary Human Services, 38,* 3–13.

Saleebey, D. (1996). The strengths perspective in social work practice: Extensions and cautions. *Social Work, 41*(3), 296–305.

Salsgiver, R. O. (1996). Perspectives on families with children with disabilities. *SCI Psychosocial Process, 9*(1), 18–23.

Schuler, A. L., and Perez, L. (1991). Assessment: Current concerns and future directions. In L.H. Myer, C. A. Peck, and L. Brown (Eds.), *Critical issues in the lives of people with severe disabilities* (pp. 101–106). Baltimore: Paul H. Brookes.

Sobsey, D. (1994). *Violence and abuse in the lives of people with disabilities: The end of silent acceptance?* Baltimore: Paul H. Brooks.

Strom, K. (1992). Reimbursement demands and treatment decisions: A growing dilemma for social workers. *Social Work, 37*(5), 398–403.

Szymanski, E. M., and Trueba, H. T. (1994). Castification of people with disabilities: Potential disempowering aspects of classification in disability services. *The Journal of Rehabilitation, 60*(3), 12(9).

Trieschmann, R. B. (1980). *Spinal cord injuries: Psychosocial, social, and vocational adjustment.* New York: Pergamon.

Chapter 12

MODELS OF PROFESSIONAL PRACTICE

I had a real role model here at the Center for Independent Living—my supervisor, a licensed clinical social worker. Since that time, there has never been a doubt in my mind that I am a person with a disability. It is so much a part of who I am today. It feels liberating. I swore to myself I would never hide anything about my disability.

—Abby Kovalsky, LCSW, disabilities project coordinator, Jewish Family and Children's Services, San Francisco, California

Student Learning Objectives:

1. To understand that most traditional models of practice stem from an individual pathological perspective. Many of these models see the individual in need as dysfunctional; broken; pathological; impaired. The role of the professional is to make the individual as perfect as possible; to cure them.

2. To understand that some contemporary models, including strengths-based practice, case management, the independent living model, and empowerment, allow for looking at disability from a societal perspective and seeking intervention not only with the individual but with agencies and communities.

3. To understand that effective practice models view the disability community as a source of change and power.

◆ MODELS OF PRACTICE IN HUMAN SERVICE PROVISION

There are numerous models of practice in the human service field. Among the more noted and fundamental models of practice with individuals and families are psychoanalysis, gestalt, cognitive, behavioral, existential, problem solving, task centered, crisis, ego psychology, client centered, transactional, psychosocial, life model approach, and casework (Turner, 1986). Some of the more recent models include case management, generalist, and advanced generalist approaches, empowerment, strengths-based approach, and brief intervention (Johnson, 1995). Some contemporary professional practice models approach intervention not just with individuals and families but at the systems level as well. This includes intervention to change and solve problems in agencies and organizations, neighborhoods, and communities (Neugeboren, 1991).

Most traditional models of practice stem from an individual pathological perspective. These models see individuals and families in need as dysfunctional or impaired. Traditional approaches have proven valuable for large numbers of people. They have helped people overcome problems, develop strengths, and enhance their lives. We acknowledge the importance of these models in individual and family practice. However, traditional models do not account for the devaluation and oppression experienced by persons with disabilities as a group. As a rule, society views disability as a problem and people with disabilities as innately deficient. Therefore, the individual repair focus of traditional therapies can reinforce ableism and classism by failing to recognize the environment as a primary locus of problems for persons with disabilities. Traditional models focus on helping individuals cope with or overcome problems associated with their disabilities rather than emphasizing the social devaluation and institutional ableism associated with being a person with a disability.

The professional emphasis on making the individual as perfect as possible originally stemmed from the Enlightenment movement in European history (Mackelprang and Salsgiver, 1996; Rhodes, 1993). Later versions of this perspective have accounted for the environment as a factor in people's problems; however, they have stressed helping individuals cope with the environment rather than changing the environment to meet people's needs. Traditional models view people with disabilities in the role of "patient" or "client." Physicians, counselors, social workers, therapists, rehabilitation workers, and other professionals apply their expertise and knowledge to the patient or client in order to "cure" the affliction or abnormality. The patient or client, in turn, is expected to play a passive role in responding to the expertise and knowledge of the professional (Tower, 1994). Environmental intervention is contemplated only as a means of helping the individual cope, and it is rarely attempted as a way of changing a dysfunctional system (Mackelprang, 1986).

More recent models of practice offer alternative approaches and are particularly applicable to persons with disabilities. We discuss four current approaches. The first two, the strengths and empowerment approaches, provide conceptual frameworks that focus on potential and capabilities. The third, case management, is a widely used professional modality that acknowledges the need for community and personal involvement. Finally, the independent living model, which was developed and nurtured within the disability community, is built on a foundation of self-determination and civil rights for persons with disabilities.

The Strengths Approach

It is critical that human service professionals see people with disabilities as people before they see their disabilities. It has been far too common and easy for human service practitioners to view people from a deficit, pathology-based perspective (Cowger, 1994; Hepworth, Rooney, and Larsen, 1997), especially persons with disabilities. By contrast, when approaching people from a strengths perspective (Saleebey, 1992), human service practitioners focus on capabilities, capacities, and opportunities rather than limitations. Just as important, as Cowger (1994) suggests, practitioners begin to

> *nourish, encourage, assist, enable, support, stimulate, and unleash the strengths within people; to illuminate the strengths available to people in their own environment; and to promote equity and justice at all levels of society.* (p. 246)

The strengths view of practice also

> *comes from an awareness that U.S. culture and helping professionals are saturated with psychosocial approaches based on individual, family, and community pathology, deficits, problems, abnormality, victimization, and disorder. A conglomeration of businesses, professions, institutions, and individuals—from medicine to the pharmaceutical industry, from the insurance industry to the media—assure the nation that everyone has a storehouse of vulnerabilities.* (Saleebey, 1996, p. 296)

Practitioners using the strengths perspective focus on the capabilities and potential of individuals with whom they work. In addition, rather than concentrating exclusively on the individual, they attend to the environment. They acknowledge the influence of communities, social structures, and institutions. Practice transcends efforts to help individuals improve their lives and becomes political as "its thrust is the development of client power and the equitable distribution of societal resources" (Cowger, 1994, p. 264). For example, in dealing with the lack of housing, practitioners using the strengths perspective could intervene in several areas. They might assist people with personal problems such as isolation and depression that individuals who cannot obtain housing might experience. They could also work to help them obtain accessible and affordable housing. In addition, they could work within the community to increase the availability of such housing and to influence social policy. Finally, they might work with persons with disabilities individually and collectively to empower them to influence the community and change public policy.

Human service practitioners employing a strengths approach work to help clients nurture and generate their individual strengths and to control their lives. In conjunction with consumers with disabilities, they work to make communities respond equitably to all people. They acknowledge societal structures and economic forces and work to promote social policies and structures that are based on principles of social justice. Practice then becomes a consumer-driven partnership that encompasses micro, meso, and macro levels of intervention.

Empowerment

The empowerment approach has grown in popularity in recent years. Empowerment seeks to facilitate people in taking control over their lives. It shares many components of the strengths perspective. Gutiérrez (1990) defines this practice model as *a process of increasing personal, interpersonal, or political power so that individuals can take action to improve their life situations. Empowerment theory and practice have roots in community organization methods, adult education techniques, feminist theory, and political psychology.* (p. 142)

Miley, O'Melia, and DuBois (1995) view the empowerment intervention model as focusing on three areas: the client's strengths, the resources that exist in the client's neighborhood and community, and a vision that solutions are possible. The outcome of empowerment is the client's increased control over the social and organizational environment (Cohen, 1994; Emener, 1991).

Solomon (1976) outlines the roles of a human service provider in the empowerment process. A key role is that of *resource consultant*. The practitioner must be able to link clients with resources in their neighborhoods or communities. At times, these resources may be national in scope. Of course, for the practitioner, this means having knowledge of the array of available resources in the community. The resource consultant fosters independence, not dependency, by actively involving the client in the process of finding and utilizing resources:

It involves linking clients to resources in a manner that enhances their self-esteem as well as their problem-solving capacities. The consultant's knowledge of the resource systems and expertise in using these systems are placed at the disposal of the client and his participation in the process from identification to location to utilization is intensive. (Solomon, 1976, p. 347)

The human service provider also acts as a *sensitizer*. This role of the practitioner helps the client discover past or present life situations that may hinder self-fulfillment and empowerment. It is within this role that the practitioner helps the client perceive stereotypes and societal barriers, which, on a personal level, reinforce self-doubt and in some cases self-hatred. Solomon sees the practitioner's role of *teacher/trainer* as crucial in the empowering process. This role focuses specifically on helping the client master tasks related to solving problems of social living. Last, Solomon describes one of the most important roles of the practitioner: *placing the client in the role of service provider*. This results in two things:

It provides an opportunity for the client to step out of the supplicant role of one who seeks advice into the more favored position of helper or one who provides service. (p. 354)

It also allows the person receiving the help from the client to gain wisdom and insight from someone who has been through it; someone who has experienced the problem and situation firsthand. In the independent living model, this is known as peer counseling.

Gutiérrez (1990) outlines additional empowerment techniques. For one, the practitioner accepts the client's perceptions of problems and needs. In doing this, the practitioner is acknowledging the client's competence and the individual's right to self-determination and personal control. In addition, the practitioner needs to assess existing strengths and help the client build new ones. The practitioner should also help facilitate a power assessment with the client on both the personal and neighborhood/community levels: What are the conditions resulting in powerlessness? What sources of power exist for the client? Further, the practitioner needs to advocate for the client in getting needed services and resources. Practitioners do not empower clients; people empower themselves. Professionals can be tools to help people identify, nurture, and develop internal competencies and external resources for self-empowerment.

Case Management

In the last two decades, human service practice has evolved to the point where case management is a preeminent method of providing human services. Case management is similar to the old casework model of practice in social work (Moore, 1990); however, case management emphasizes professional involvement with systems that impact clients rather than focusing primarily on micro system interventions. Rothman (1991) presents this succinct definition of case management:

> *Case management incorporates two broad functions: (1) providing individualized advice, counseling, and therapy to clients in the community and (2) linking clients to needed services and supports in community agencies and informal helping networks. Case management, in professional terms, is both micro and macro in nature. It entails both individual practice and community practice in integrated form. (pp. 520–521)*

In addition, case management assumes long-term care management with a coordination of a wide range of services from the community.

In utilizing case management techniques with persons with severe disabilities, the case manager does an assessment and seeks the required services for the individual. These may include housing, health and mental health care, socialization, day activities/recreation, and education. After the necessary services have been obtained, the case manager continually monitors each case to assure that the services are maintained. Case managers must be extremely knowledgeable about the groups they serve. They work in numerous settings, including group homes, long-term care facilities, acute care settings, and foster care environments (Netting, 1992). They utilize various roles such as counselor, advocate, educator, and mediator on behalf of their clients or patients (Mackelprang and Salsgiver, 1996). A strength of the case management approach is the attention given to multiple system levels. In addition, professionals assume a variety of roles and functions in response to client or patient needs.

Case management, however, has significant limitations. In this approach, professionals are the experts on whom clients or "cases" rely for services. Case managers, not clients, maintain control over decisions. In addition, current case management has evolved in an era of cutbacks and cost containment. Quality and access to care have been limited to reduce costs. Therefore, case managers have been forced to reduce services and limit client eligibility. The limitations of case management are due, in part, to the fact that case management is practiced primarily under the auspices of agencies and institutions that adopt mainstream perceptions of people with disabilities. Therefore, case managers are often in roles that perpetuate professional control and "case" dependence.

The Independent Living Model

Though case management is an extant model of professional practice, a more progressive model of involvement is the independent living model of practice, where, in effect, consumers manage their own cases—their own lives. Whereas case management's roots are deeply imbedded in professional practice, the independent living (IL) model is derived from the minority perspective and the social model of viewing disability. The minority perspective assumes that people with disabilities are minorities and have been denied opportunities that nondisabled persons take for granted. The social model assumes that the greatest obstacles facing persons with disabilities are devaluation, lack of opportunity, and oppression (DeJong, 1979).

This perspective differs from traditional approaches to disability that begin with the assumption that individual deficiencies are the primary causes for people seeking services (DeLoach, Wilkins, and Walker, 1983). In defining problems, the IL model first looks to the social and environmental deficiencies in which a person with a disability lives (Zola, 1983). This contrasts sharply with professional models that assume problems arise primarily from within individuals. IL suggests that problems reside primarily within nonadaptive and hostile environments. Pity, lack of physical access, and limited opportunities have been the primary problems facing people with mobility disabilities, not their need to use wheelchairs for mobility. The primary problems for people with intellectual disabilities have been institutions that segregate and limit their opportunities, not their personal limitations. Fear, segregation, and stereotyping have been the primary constraints for persons with psychiatric disabilities. Lack of opportunity, not lack of capability, has been the primary problem for persons with disabilities as a group.

Traditional models view people with disabilities in roles such as patients and clients. The independent living model views persons with disabilities as individuals, citizens, and/or consumers. The roles of professionals under the IL model are also different. They may be considered experts in their fields; however, that expertise does not translate into control over people's lives (White, Gutierrez, and Seekins, 1996). Instead, they act as consultants and assistants. Their roles are akin to financial investment consultants who educate and sell investment packages to consumers. However, decisions rest with consumers who decide whether or not they act on the advice of their consultants (Zola, 1983). In the independent living model, consumers may rely on physicians, social workers, and others for advice in a similar manner.

In the IL model, consumers are responsible for their own decisions about their lives. They may utilize the services of professionals such as physicians, social workers, nurses, vocational counselors, and others. However, professionals rely on the individual's direction rather than ordering or prescribing *for* the patient or client.

A new role is also critical to the independent living model. Peer or independent living counselors are key participants in this model. IL counselors work with consumers, as do other professionals. However, IL counselors have disabilities themselves and are committed to individual self-determination and control. Mackelprang and Salsgiver (1996) provide the following example of the contrast in approaches:

> *Sharon is a 32-year-old woman who received social work case management services after an automobile accident in which she experienced a spinal cord injury resulting in quadriplegia. During Sharon's hospitalization, her social worker provided case management services, facilitating the procurement of Medicaid, ordering medical equipment such as a wheelchair, procuring the services of a home health agency for home nursing visits, arranging for vocational rehabilitation services, and working with Sharon's family to prepare for her discharge from the hospital. Similar case management services were provided for six months following discharge; the social worker generally informed Sharon of the services she would be providing, and Sharon also made requests for services.*

> *Six months after discharge from the hospital, Sharon became involved with a local independent living center for peer counseling and independent living training. When she had trouble with Medicaid, she asked the IL counselor to intervene on her behalf. Similarly, she asked the IL counselor to procure a commode chair. Rather than meet her requests as the social worker had done, the IL counselor taught Sharon to self-advocate with Medicaid and guided her through the process of ordering medical equipment so she could do so in the future. In addition, the counselor informed Sharon how she could gain access to a program in which she could hire and direct her attendants rather than having nurses and aides assigned to her. Sharon developed the knowledge and skills to direct her own personal care, including hiring, firing, and money management, essentially reclaiming control over her life. (p. 12)*

In the preceding example, Sharon's social worker, acting in the role of case manager, thought the best way to help Sharon was to provide services. In contrast, the IL counselor sought to help Sharon develop skills and recognize her ability to control the systems affecting her life. The IL counselor assumed Sharon was capable of independence. Sharon needed physical attendant care; however, she learned to independently direct her care, to access systems, and to self-advocate. Though Sharon needed the social worker's help initially following her injury, she was capable of taking control of her life once the crisis of her spinal cord injury was over.

In the IL model, all helping professionals, including IL counselors, are expected to function within the parameters set by the individual consumer, who retains ultimate control (Tower, 1994). Just as financial consultants must leave decisions to individuals, IL proposes that individuals retain control over treatments, physical and psychosocial therapies, and other decisions. In multidisciplinary/ interdisciplinary teamwork, the head of the team is the individual. Professionals may consult, recommend, and suggest, but self-determination is paramount. Human service workers are often needed to help people make decisions by educating, counseling, and helping obtain resources; however, this is done under the control and direction of the consumers.

In the IL model, the expectations for persons with disabilities differ greatly from other practice models. First, people with disabilities are perceived as competent. Traditional models of practice assume they need others, usually professionals, to take control and make decisions, essentially assuming people with disabilities are incompetent. The IL model presupposes that people with disabilities are fully functioning human beings (Zola, 1983). Traditional models treat people with disabilities as being "worthy poor," receiving services and financial sustenance from a sympathetic society. The IL model expects society to remove barriers that deny full participation to persons with disabilities; at the same time, it places higher expectations on people with disabilities by assuming they are capable of functioning in and contributing to society. Rather than gratefully accepting society's generosity, IL sees persons with disabilities as part of the larger society. Their disabilities make them different from persons without disabilities; however, the commonality of their humanity is far more important. Thus, persons with intellectual disabilities are able to live in society, and to participate and function with persons with and without disabilities. Persons with blindness, given reasonable accommodation are able to function in the same roles as persons who see. Conversely, there is a societal expectation that barriers will be removed and opportunities for full participation will be provided.

Persons with disabilities may need to rely on professionals to make decisions at times. A person with a spinal cord injury who has a urinary tract infection may need to rely on a physician to direct care and prescribe an appropriate antibiotic. However, the physician is still responsible to fully inform and obtain consent from the person for treatment. Likewise, a family seeking counseling needs to rely on the counselor or therapist to employ an approach that meets the needs of the family. Yet the provider is responsible to reach mutually acceptable agreements about the expectations of therapy.

IL also recognizes that people with disabilities, like all persons, are sometimes unable to make decisions in specific situations. For example, some people with intellectual disabilities may be unable to understand how to manage complex financial affairs and may need help in managing their personal finances. Some people with depression may have times in which depression immobilizes them and they need help from others to manage their affairs. The IL model of intervention recognizes these circumstances. However, it begins with the assumption that people with disabilities are capable (Tower, 1994). The burden of proof lies in determining when people may need help rather than in proving people do not need others to direct their lives.

To achieve the overall goal of independence for persons with disabilities, IL intervention focuses on five objectives (McAweeney, Farchheimer, and Tate, 1996):

1. providing consumers with information about local, regional, and national resources and establishing ways the consumer can access these resources and services
2. facilitating attendant care for persons who need it
3. offering peer counseling
4. working with individuals to obtain affordable and accessible housing
5. teaching personal and political advocacy

The IL model requires that the practitioner be knowledgeable about local, regional, and national resources. The practitioner must teach the consumer about resources that are available and about how to access them (Saxton, 1983). For example, the IL model requires practitioners to be knowledgeable about local attendant care services and to teach consumers how to access these services and how to hire, fire, and manage attendants (DeJong and Wenker, 1983). The IL model assumes that counseling for persons with disabilities is provided by persons with disabilities. Counselors who are not persons with disabilities need to be aware of peer counselors in the local community and any peer support groups that may exist (Saxton, 1983). The IL model also requires practitioners to be knowledgeable about local accessible housing and services that can make existing housing accessible (Wiggins, 1983). In addition, it requires human service practitioners to be advocates on three levels. First, a key role is to teach persons with disabilities to be self-advocates in getting the services and resources they need. Second, practitioners need to teach persons with disabilities how to be politically active. Third, the IL model expects human service practitioners themselves to become involved in advocating for increased services and accessibility (Tower, 1994). Finally, the IL model recognizes that, like any minority group, the strength of the disability community must ultimately come from within. Human service practitioners and other professionals without disabilities can provide services and be valued allies; however, persons with disabilities must take control over their own collective destiny.

◆ SUMMARY

There are numerous models of practice in the human service field. Most traditional models of practice stem from an individual pathological perspective. In traditional models, the individual is viewed as dysfunctional; broken; pathological; impaired. The role of the professional in these models is to make the individual as perfect as possible. Traditional models view people with disabilities in the roles of "patient" or "client." Physicians, counselors, social workers, therapists, rehabilitation workers, and other professionals apply their expertise and knowledge to the patient or client in order to "cure" the affliction or abnormality. The patient or client plays a passive role in responding to the expertise and knowledge of the professional.

Recent models offer alternative approaches and are particularly applicable to persons with disabilities. These include the strengths–based and empowerment approaches as well as case management and independent living models.

Practitioners using the strengths perspective focus on the capabilities and potential of individuals with whom they work. In addition, rather than concentrating exclusively on the individual, they attend to the environment. They attend to the environment. They acknowledge the influence of communities, social structures, and institutions.

The empowerment intervention model focuses on three areas: the client's strengths, the resources that exist in the client's neighborhood and community, and a vision that solutions are possible as well as the nature of these solutions. The outcome of empowerment is client control over the social and organizational environment. The practitioner in this model has four roles: resource consultant, sensitizer, teacher/trainer, and facilitator of the client as service provider. Additional empowerment techniques include accepting the client's perception of the problem, assessing and increasing client strengths, assessing the limits and potential sources of power related to the client, and advocating for the client.

Case management emphasizes professional involvement with systems that impact clients rather than focusing primarily on micro system interventions. The case manager, after assessment, seeks the required services for the individual. These may include housing, health and mental health care, socialization, day activities/recreation, and education. After the necessary services have been obtained, the case manager continually monitors each case to assure that the services are maintained. Case managers must be extremely knowledgeable about the various target groups being serviced.

Within the framework of the independent living model of practice, consumers manage their own cases—their own lives. IL suggests that problems reside primarily within nonadaptive and hostile environments. Lack of opportunity, not lack of capability, is the primary problem for persons with disabilities as a group. The IL model is consumer driven, with individual and political advocacy at its core. It recognizes that persons with disabilities are involved in a human rights struggle.

In conclusion, we encourage human service practitioners to adopt a strengths-based perspective. Professionals will find competence and potential only when they actively seek them in people. We applaud the political component in empowerment-based practice. Only by looking past the individual will we see the institutional and societal barriers that devalue people and limit their opportunities. Case management has much potential, especially with its focus on multiple systems levels and professional roles. As a current practice model, we find that the consumer-driven IL approach has utilized many of the best concepts of the three professionally derived approaches to practice with persons with disabilities.

◆　◆　◆

Discussion Questions

1. What are the similarities among the four models of practice presented in this chapter? What are the differences?

2. What elements of the strengths-based model particularly apply to persons with disabilities?

3. What elements of the case management model particularly apply to persons with disabilities?

4. Using the four models presented in this chapter, formulate a model of intervention that you could use with persons with disabilities.

Suggested Readings

DeJong, G. (1979). *The movement for independent living: Origins, ideology, and implications for disability research*. East Lansing: Michigan State University, Center for International Rehabilitation.

Mackelprang, R. W, and Salsgiver, R. O. (1996). People with disabilities and social work: Historical and contemporary issues. *Social Work, 41*(1), 7–14.

Saleebey, D. (Ed.) (1992). *The strengths perspective in social work practice*. New York: Longman.

Solomon, B. B. (1976). *Black empowerment: Social work in oppressed communities*. New York: Columbia University Press.

Tower, K. D. (1994). Consumer-centered social work practice: Restoring client self-determination. *Social Work, 41*(1), 191–196.

References

Cohen, M. B. (1994). Overcoming obstacles to forming empowerment groups: A consumer advisory board of homeless clients. *Social Work, 39*(6), 742–749.

Cowger, C. D. (1994). Assessing client strengths: Clinical assessment for client empowerment. *Social Work, 39*(3), 262–269.

DeJong, G. (1979). *The movement for independent living: Origins, ideology, and implications for disability research*. East Lansing: Michigan State University, Center for International Rehabilitation.

DeJong, G., and Wenker, T. (1983). Attendant care. In N. M. Crewe and I. K. Zola (Eds.), *Independent living for physically disabled people* (pp. 157–170). San Francisco: Jossey-Bass.

DeLoach, C. P., Wilkins, R. D., and Walker, G. W. (1983). *Independent living: Philosophy, process, and services*. Baltimore: University Park Press.

Emener, W. G. (1991). An empowerment philosophy for rehabilitation in the 20th century. *The Journal of Rehabilitation, 57*(4), 7–13.

Gutiérrez, L. M. (1990). Working with women of color: An empowerment perspective. *Social Work, 35*(2), 149–153.

Hepworth, D. H., Rooney, R. H., and Larsen, J. (1997). *Direct social work practice: Theory and skills* (5th ed.). Pacific Grove, CA: Brooks/Cole.

Johnson, H. W. (1995). *The social services: An introduction*. Itasca, IL: F. E. Peacock.

Mackelprang, R. W (1986). *Social and emotional adjustment following spinal cord injury*. Unpublished doctoral dissertation. Salt Lake City: University of Utah.

Mackelprang, R. W, and Salsgiver, R. O. (1996). People with disabilities and social work: Historical and contemporary issues. *Social Work, 41*(1), 7–14.

McAweeney, M. J., Farchheimer, M., and Tate, D. B. (1996). Identifying the unmet independent living needs of persons with spinal cord injury. *The Journal of Rehabilitation, 62*(3), 29–35.

Miley, K. K., O'Melia, M., and DuBois, B. L. (1995). *Generalist social work practice: An empowering approach*. Boston: Allyn & Bacon.

Moore, S. T. (1990). A social work practice model of case management: The case management grid. *Social Work, 35*(5), 444–448.

Netting, F. E. (1992). Case management: Service or symptom. *Social Work, 37*(2), 160–164.

Neugenboren, B. (1991). *Organization, policy, and practice in the human services*. Binghamton, NY: Haworth Press.

Rhodes, R. (1993). Mental retardation and sexual expression: An historical perspective. In R.W Mackelprang and D.Valentine (Eds.), *Sexuality and disabilities: A guide for human service practitioners* (pp. 1–27). Binghamton, NY: Haworth Press.

Rothman, J. (1991). A model of case management: Toward empirically based practice. *Social Work, 36*(4), 520–522.

Saleebey, D. (Ed.) (1992). *The strengths perspective in social work practice.* New York: Longman.

Saleebey, D. (1996). The strengths perspective in social work practice: Extensions and cautions. *Social Work, 41*(3), 296–305.

Saxton, M. (1983). Peer counseling. In N. M. Crewe and I. K. Zola (Eds.), *Independent living for physically disabled people* (pp. 171–186). San Francisco: Jossey-Bass.

Solomon, B. B. (1976). *Black empowerment: Social work in oppressed communities.* New York: Columbia University Press.

Tower, K. D. (1994). Consumer-centered social work practice: Restoring client self-determination. *Social Work, 41*(1), 191–196.

Turner, F. S. (Ed.). (1986). *Social work treatment: Interlocking theoretical approaches.* New York: Free Press.

White, G.W., Gutierrez, R.T., and Seekins,T. (1996). Preventing and managing secondary conditions: A proposed role for independent living centers. *The Journal of Rehabilitation, 62*(3), 14–22.

Wiggins, S. F. (1983). Specialized housing. In N. M. Crewe and I. K. Zola (Eds.), *Independent living for physically disabled people* (pp. 219–244). San Francisco: Jossey-Bass.

Zola, I. K. (1983). Developing new self-images and interdependence. In N. M. Crewe and I. K. Zola (Eds.), *Independent living for physically disabled people* (pp. 49–50). San Francisco: Jossey-Bass.

Chapter 13

GUIDELINES FOR PRACTICE WITH PERSONS WITH DISABILITIES

If you [professionals] don't believe that disabled people can achieve, get out of the way. They [the professionals] need to learn as much as they can to help assure that disabled people are given the tools we need in order to move ahead in our lives. Professionals who work with kids need to give their parents positive images of their children's abilities and possibilities. They should not limit people's thinking; they should help expand people's horizons. They need to understand the implications of discrimination and bias in order to allow people to remedy those problems. They need to be part of the solution, not part of the problem.

—Judy Heumann, Assistant Secretary for the Office of Special Education and Rehabilitation Services, Washington, D.C.

Student Learning Objective:

To develop intervention skills with persons with disabilities based upon a strengths perspective, self-management, independent living, and empowerment.

◆ BASIC ASSUMPTIONS AND PRINCIPLES

Six principles guide our approach to working with persons with disabilities. First, we assume that people are capable or *potentially* capable (Cowger, 1994; Saleebey, 1992; DeJong, 1979; Zola, 1983; Tower, 1994; Gutiérrez, 1990; Solomon, 1976). If people currently lack insight, knowledge, and skills, professionals are responsible to help them become insightful, knowledgeable, and skillful. As an example, professionals may need to help people with intellectual disabilities develop knowledge and skills to manage financial matters to the greatest extent of their capability. It is the human service professional's responsibility to facilitate the mobilization of resources to help people achieve their greatest potential. When people lack the ability for the whole, we assume they are capable of parts of the whole. For example, persons with intellectual disabilities may not be able to handle all their financial matters but should manage the elements they are capable of handling. Similarly, people with quadriplegia may be physically unable to dress themselves; however, they are capable of directing who, how, and when attendant care is provided.

We should constantly evaluate people's capabilities and potential. As people develop, their capabilities grow. New capabilities should continually be assessed, nurtured, and maximized. When determining capability, we adopt the minority view and work to reject the imposition of the dominant society's views of capability on persons with disabilities (Zola, 1983). As an illustration of the minority view, one of the authors spent several years of his childhood and adolescence in an institution because the dominant culture determined he needed to be made as physically "normal" as possible. The majority decided that institutionalization, multiple surgeries, and removal from his family and community were necessary for him to adequately function and fit into society. Dominant cultural and professional values led professionals to make decisions that were inhumane and dehumanizing to a child. Like others with disabilities, the author needed adequate resources, advocates who valued persons with disabilities, and role models with disabilities. Instead, he was institutionalized, isolated, and ostracized from society. (His story is illustrated in the "Case Examples" section at the end of the chapter.)

Second, we reject traditional methods of practice that assume that the problem with disability lies with the person and that individuals with disabilities must change or "be fixed" before they can function adequately in society (DeJong, 1979; Zola, 1983; Emener, 1991; Hahn, 1991; Blotzer and Ruth, 1995). We reject the pathological interpretation of disability, along with its baggage that disability requires grief and mourning, "equating disability to death" (Salsgiver, 1996, p. 18).

Third, we believe that any model of practice applied to working with persons with disabilities must assume that disability is a social construct and that a primary emphasis on intervention must be political in nature (DeJong, 1979; Zola, 1983; Tower, 1994; Fine and Asch, 1988). As a whole, persons with disabilities constitute a minority group that has suffered oppression just as people of color, women, gays and lesbians, and older persons have suffered oppression (Mackelprang and Salsgiver, 1996). The solutions to problems faced by persons with disabilities rest primarily on access to society's benefits and rewards. Environmental, attitudinal, and policy barriers to participation must be eliminated.

Fourth, we believe there is a disability history and culture. Even though different people may have different disabilities, they have more in common than they have differences. Because of the shared experience of oppression, containment, and isolation, it is imperative that anyone working with persons with disabilities be knowledgeable of the history of oppression toward this group. In addition, they need to be aware of political figures, advocates, and conveyors of disability culture and how they have contributed to the fight for disability respect and rights. Further, practitioners need to be highly knowledgeable about political advocacy. They must be willing to help consumers themselves to become politically involved (Tower, 1994).

Fifth, although persons with disabilities have experienced oppression, we strongly believe that there is joy to be found in disability. Models of practice applied to working with persons with disabilities must view *disability as different and not necessarily dysfunctional. They will view a child with a disability as one more panel of color which makes up the glorious tapestry of human existence.* (Salsgiver, 1996, p. 23)

Indeed, we believe that disability is beautiful and that most people with disabilities are actually happy with themselves and their lives (Hahn, 1993).

Sixth, we believe that persons with disabilities have, *without question*, the right to control their lives (DeJong, 1979). This means that the consumer controls the professional's involvement. This means that the professional brings expertise to the consumer to be rejected or accepted, or rejected in part or accepted in part (DeJong, 1979; Zola, 1983; Hahn, 1991). Consumers have the right to walk or roll away from services they believe are not in their best interests. The natural place for persons with disabilities, even if professionals disagree with their choices, is in control of their own lives, living independently from custodial environments, with the same rights and opportunities as persons without disabilities.

◆   # Integrating a Positive Disability Identity

In addition to the preceding principles of practice, we believe human service practitioners must also be aware of the need for persons with disabilities to develop healthy self-identities. This changes the focus of human service practice from repairing individuals to helping people integrate a healthy self-identity in a society that accepts and values them, disability and all. This process has many similarities to the process of positive identity development for sexual minorities (Chan, 1989; Coleman, 1982; Troiden, 1993). As with sexual minorities, persons with disabilities may experience a "coming out" process as they integrate disability into their self-images. In our experience, positive disability identity develops differently in different people; there are no stages people must experience to reach an ultimate positive disability identity. However, human service practitioners may identify processes that are commonly experienced. The processes listed here are based on the work of Onken (Onken and Mackelprang, 1997), who applied them to persons with disabilities and to sexual minorities. They can aid professionals in identifying consumer experiences.

Preawareness conformity is characterized by an unquestioning acceptance of societal stereotypes and oppression. The person is unaware of alternate, positive views of disability and attributes problems to personal deficits. *Contact* occurs when an individual is exposed to challenges to ableist views of disability. The individual may be oblivious to the personal implications of ableist oppression but may begin to feel different by virtue of having a disability. With *denial* or *avoidance,* the person rejects the implications of ableism and oppression. Some may acknowledge the implications for others but deny being personally affected; some attempt to "pass" as nondisabled; some distance themselves from others with disabilities and reject membership in this marginalized population. *Comparison* is a state in which the person begins to develop an awareness of the reasons behind feelings of difference. The individual develops a heightened sense of not fully belonging in ableist society and begins to recognize the disadvantages and disempowerment of having a disability in an ableist society. As a result of increased awareness, the person may begin to feel *confusion* and *dissonance.* There can be a growing sense of personal isolation and lack of group identity. There may be an acknowledgment of being a member of the disability community but a hesitance or refusal to claim membership. There may be a feeling of, "I'm not like them," or, "I don't want to be around them." Feelings of isolation can lead to *tolerance,* in which the person begins to acknowledge membership in the disability community. The individual may seek out others with disabilities to increase socialization and avoid isolation and may experience a heightened sense of alienation in an ableist society. *Connection* occurs as an individual increases an identity in the individual's family or community of choice, the community of persons with disabilities. Disability is seen in a positive light. Respect for others with disabilities grows and a positive disability identity is enhanced. *Immersion* and *resistance* occurs for some people. In this state, individuals may react in the extreme by rejecting and retreating from an ableist society into nearly exclusive contact with others with disabilities. Persons involved in the deaf separatist movement (as well as the lesbian separatist movement for sexual minorities) provide examples of this. Some find permanent happiness in this state. *Acceptance* and *pride* are related to immersion and resistance, but reactions are less "extreme." An individual may begin to actively challenge ableist practices and beliefs; a sense of disability pride develops. An example of this is manifested in adopting labels (e.g., "cripple," "gimp"), which have commonly been used to demean, with pride. *Introspection* and *synthesis* occur when an individual balances personal and community disability identity with past identities, memberships, and relationships. There is a renewed appreciation for diversity and multicultural society. An individual continues to acknowledge the societal implications of living with a disability but may feel less anger and stridence.

> *The person seeks to be competent in disabled-nondisabled (and/or sexual minority-sexual majority) interactions, including ongoing self-assessment, attention to the dynamics of difference, and expansion of knowledge, resources, and adaptations in order to better connect with people regardless of difference. The person is comfortable in challenging and in developing allies in challenging ableist (and/or heterosexist) practices and beliefs and corresponding oppression.* (Onken and Mackelprang, 1997, pp. 25–26)

◆ Human Service Practice Roles

The six pillars outlined previously, combined with a disability-affirming approach, guide our practice with persons with disabilities. They provide a foundation of empowerment with a strengths orientation that takes into account the systems in which persons live. Given these pillars, effective human service practitioners must function at three systems levels: micro, meso, and macro. We believe that effective clinical or direct practice must also involve intervening at the institutional and societal levels. Similarly, administrators and community practitioners must make decisions in the interests and with the input of individuals with disabilities.

In this section, we outline the four major functions of human service practitioners working with persons with disabilities: counselor, teacher, broker, and political activist or advocate. The functions of counselor and teacher are manifested primarily at the micro and meso levels. The function of broker spans micro, meso, and macro levels. The functions of political activist or advocate play out primarily in the meso and macro arenas. Within each function, practitioners may carry out a variety of roles. Functions may overlap with each other; however, to be comprehensive, we discuss them as discrete entities. All of these functions are based on a consumer-driven, independent living approach.

The Human Service Practitioner as Counselor

The function of counselor is multifaceted and goes well beyond the traditional role of clinical psychotherapist. We see a critical component of the counseling function for human service practitioners working with persons with disabilities as Solomon's role of sensitizer (1976), in which practitioners sensitize consumers to the oppression that persons with disabilities experience and how oppression can impact sense of self, self-esteem, and the ability to gain personal and political power. Sometimes awareness of oppression lies buried and prevents people from developing the self-concept necessary for success defined in their terms. Sometimes the denial that allows persons with disabilities to survive and mature (Wright, 1960) also can become a hindrance when attitudinal, social, and environmental factors later begin to destroy the "reality" found in the denial. The counseling role of the human service practitioner allows an understanding of that process and helps persons with disabilities understand themselves in a positive light with a disability identity (Blotzer and Ruth, 1995; Sullivan and Scanlan, 1990). Therefore, an understanding of the impact of oppression on persons with disabilities is crucial to the counseling role of human service practitioners.

Wright (1960) makes the following statement concerning people with physical disabilities that can be applied to all persons with disabilities:

> *Physical limitations per se may produce suffering and frustrations, but the limitations imposed by the evaluative attitudes toward physique cut far deeper and spread far wider; they affect the person's feelings about himself as a whole. One of man's basic strivings is for acceptance by the group, for being important in the lives of others, and for having others count positively in his life. As long as physical disability is linked with shame and inferiority, realistic acceptance of one's position and one's self is precluded. (p.14)*

The role of counselor requires the exploration of this domain. Sometimes counselors and consumers must explore the personal effects of this negativity and stereotyping. It may be especially difficult when people explore the effects of these perceptions on how their family members, loved ones, and others have perceived and treated them. For example, persons with physical disabilities whose parents subjected them to futile surgeries and other painful procedures as advised by health care providers may harbor a multitude of feelings. They may acknowledge their parents' love but harbor resentment toward them for unnecessary pain. They may struggle to form a positive disability identity. They may also need help in reestablishing and redefining relationships with family and friends. In these instances, a practitioner acting in the role of *therapist* with an understanding of disability is important.

When disabilities are acquired later in life, counselors can help consumers in a number of ways. They can provide therapy to help individuals and loved ones cope with the adjustment and personal loss many experience. Just as important, they can help them understand ableist societal attitudes and help them develop new perspectives on disabilities. Oftentimes, *peer counselors* can fill this valuable role by exposing individuals to competent, adjusted persons with disabilities who can guide them in dealing with devaluation and stereotyping.

There are a variety of other counseling roles that human service practitioners can fill. *Group counselors* can facilitate groups of persons with disabilities in coming together to share personal experiences and life stories. Interaction and sharing help develop disability identity and culture. *Resource counseling* is a role in which practitioners help counsel and teach consumers about community resources and how to utilize them. *Family counselors* can help consumers and their loved ones understand and cope with the vicissitudes of life.

The primary function of disability counseling is to help individuals cope and function with life within their social environments and society. Counselors can facilitate the coming out process discussed earlier in the chapter. It is critical that counseling be consumer driven and that it focus on people's strengths and potential. Counseling is provided in the context of helping people understand the ableist society in which they live and how to use their strengths to overcome oppression and reject devaluation.

The Human Service Practitioner as Teacher/Consultant

A second major function in human service practice encompasses the role of teacher/consultant. The human service practitioner teaches the consumer only about those areas about which the consumer seeks to learn. In other words, the teacher is a consultant rather than an educational director. Teaching by the human service practitioner covers three basic areas: 1) personal techniques for dealing with the results of oppression, 2) self-management and self-advocacy, and 3) political advocacy. The first two areas are similar to the counseling function. However, we place them separately because of the strong social and community emphasis involved in teaching about these areas.

Teaching and learning about oppression helps people eschew dependency that creates nonassertiveness and passivity (Sussman, 1977). Passive, conforming behavior results in social isolation (Orr, Thein, and Aronson, 1995) and the inability to function successfully in employment and in the political process. The first step in helping overcome dependency and passivity is to teach the person about the societal forces imposing negative stereotypes, about incorporating disability into the definition of self, and about developing assertiveness (Joiner, Lovett, and Goodwin, 1989). Smith's classic model of assertiveness training (1975) is still relevant for practice today. It involves teaching about the dynamics of guilt and shame and developing assertive verbal and behavioral skills. Assertiveness also involves self-disclosure and individual persistence in getting needs met.

The next step in teaching and consulting involves helping people modify their expectations and acknowledge and demand their rights. For example, individuals can be helped to develop personal assertiveness in a job interview by recognizing their strengths and asserting their needs. In addition, a potential employee can convey the expectation that an employer make reasonable accommodations in the workplace. Expectations of accommodation expand to the community as individuals begin to expect accessible communities as a basic human right and as a societal responsibility.

The second area of teaching lies with self-management and self-advocacy. Rather than acting as a case manager, we see the role of the human service practitioner as teaching personal management skills to persons with disabilities so that they can manage their lives themselves. Based upon the IL model of practice, areas of teaching in self-management and advocacy include peer education and support, transportation, attendant care, accessible housing, and personal advocacy.

As discussed previously, the sharing of the disabled experience is crucial in the lives of persons with disabilities. There are some experiences that can only be understood by another person with a disability. Consumers can derive great benefit from contact with peer counselors, role models, and others with disabilities. Human service practitioners must first have knowledge of neighborhood and community resources offering peer support and of disability advocacy groups. They may need to show persons with disabilities how to link with services in person, by phone, and/or electronically. Practitioners may need to make referrals and pave the way so that persons with disabilities can begin to involve themselves in the disability community.

Self-advocacy may also entail teaching a person with a disability to use public transportation. If public transportation is not available, the human service practitioner may have to help arrange alternative transportation, but the consumer must be fully involved with this process (Cole, 1983). When accessible transportation is problematic, the human service professional may need to teach the consumer how to begin the political process of pressuring local government and government transit agencies to develop accessible transportation (Bowe, 1983).

Self-advocacy is also critical in other areas. Some consumers with disabilities need attendant care. They may need to be taught how to access attendants through independent living centers, local government agencies, or private means (DeJong and Wenker, 1983). In addition, consumers may request training in how to manage personal attendants. Attendant management training includes interviewing, hiring, training, and firing attendants. Human service practitioners must be knowledgeable about management issues and techniques in order to teach them to consumers. Consumers may need education to avoid problems such as physical abuse and the development of romantic relationships. Boundary maintenance strategies between employee and employer can help prevent these problems.

Another important area in which many persons with disabilities request training is the acquisition of accessible housing. In most places in the country, wheelchair-accessible housing is at a premium. This means that persons with disabilities may need to modify existing housing or seek out accessible housing. The human service professional may need to be aware of or have access to existing accessible housing options. In addition, the human service practitioner may be able to help the consumer access private contractors who provide modification services (Wiggins, 1983). Just as with the issue of transportation, it may be necessary for the human service professional to help the consumer advocate for the addition of accessible housing and the enforcement of existing codes and laws requiring wheelchair accessibility by both public housing entities and private builders.

Another component of self-management is personal advocacy, which involves teaching consumers techniques for asserting and acquiring the things they need or desire. Becoming a self-advocate begins with an understanding of the impact of oppression and lack of opportunity. Then consumers need to develop assertiveness skills, as discussed earlier, and to work within the agency or organization providing the services to achieve their goals. At times, self-advocacy involves going outside existing social agencies and institutions. For example, consumers may seek legal solutions or redress to force institutions to meet their needs.

In our model, the final teaching role for the human service professional centers on political advocacy. The passage of most of the legislation discussed in Chapter 3 was facilitated by the political efforts of persons with disabilities. Shapiro (1993) chronicles the movements controlled and directed by persons with a variety of disabilities, which resulted in a range of historic legislation including the Rehabilitation Act of 1973 and the Americans with Disabilities Act of 1990.

This process begins by the practitioner being knowledgeable of these various political undertakings and communicating the importance of political activity to the consumer (Tower, 1994). The next step involves helping the consumer access the local groups involved with political advocacy around disabilities. There are hundreds of these groups across the country, many accessible by the Internet. Many are connected with the hundreds of independent living centers across the United States. Practitioners can teach consumers about the political decision-making process and how to connect with local, state, and national political representatives. They can provide consumers with lists of the politicians who represent them and can help consumers access them. Strategies ranging from cooperation to co-optation to confrontation can also be taught. Consumers can be taught skills such as how to testify before legislative bodies, interview with the media, and participate in political demonstrations. Tower (1994) states

> *Consumers need good role models if they are to become more autonomous. In direct practice social workers can demonstrate good advocacy skills, teach strategies for effective communication, and coach clients through the maze of policies and procedures. They can commiserate about the inequities and absurdities that are ubiquitous to the human services. Meanwhile, they can encourage their clients to take purposeful action to improve their condition through self-advocacy and organization with peers.* (p. 195)

In teaching self-advocacy, human service professionals should not be directive. However, by developing political knowledge and skills and passing them along to consumers, human service practitioners can facilitate consumer empowerment.

The Human Service Practitioner as Broker

Human service practitioners may be called upon to act as social brokers. Brokers identify and help consumers gain access to resources. It is important for human service practitioners to involve consumers in the brokering process as much as possible and to help consumers develop brokering and self-advocacy skills. Effective brokering requires the human service practitioner to know which agencies within the community provide the services that the person with a disability may need. Next, brokering may require practitioners to know how to utilize agency personnel and policies effectively. For example, there may be a certain administrator or supervisor in an agency or a particularly conscientious worker with whom the human service practitioner can broker to access services. Finally, brokering requires practitioners to pass on their knowledge of how to access resources to consumers and to help them develop personal brokering skills. They can teach consumers how to make phone calls, write letters, and participate in meetings with bureaucrats. Consumers may also need to learn how to connect the services of various agencies and how to organize others with disabilities. Practitioners can strategize, advise, and support consumers (Tower, 1994) as they begin to broker for themselves.

Brokering (and facilitating self-advocacy) requires work on the micro, meso, and macro levels as practitioners assess situations and intervene with individuals as they come in contact with larger systems and communities. Interventions at these levels require helpers to also assess community strengths and limitations. Direct service practitioners must consider the impact that meso and macro systems have on people and how people can impact these systems. Together with consumers, they can plan and implement strategies to enhance the responsiveness of larger systems.

Meso- and macro-level practitioners also act as social brokers in working to help communities become more responsive to needs. They may act as *consultants* to help individuals and groups of people with disabilities learn how to impact communities. Because professionals often hold status and power, they may fill the role of *advocates* in working to facilitate positive community environments. *Community developers* and *social planners* can broker disability-friendly environments, as can *policy developers* within agencies and organizations. The role of *mediator* can also be valuable in connecting people and organizations as well as in interceding between organizations.

Human service professionals who work at all systems levels on behalf of persons with disabilities should remember that their ultimate goal is to help people self-advocate by realizing their own personal potential and by using their skills. The various roles used should be directed at helping persons take control. We can use our expertise to help people examine their problems and needs. We can advocate for adequate resources and accessible communities. Ultimately, however, it is persons with disabilities who offer the strongest voice and direct the struggle for self-determination.

The Human Service Professional as Political Advocate

Our model stresses that human service professionals work at the meso and macro levels for political change around issues relating to persons with disabilities. Traditionally, however, there have been conflicts of interest between professions and communities of disability. For example, large institutions have been used for centuries to house persons with intellectual and psychiatric disabilities. As these facilities, which rely on the medical model of treatment, close down, human service jobs, including nursing, social work, and medical jobs, are lost, and human service professionals are forced to find different roles. Practitioners may need to acknowledge that political advocacy on behalf of persons with disabilities can have negative effects on their traditional professional roles. We believe, however, that there is a place for the human service professions if we are proactive in working with persons with disabilities to carve out niches that focus on their strengths and their empowerment. Human service professions can join forces with consumer-directed organizations and movements. Collaboration between professional organizations and these groups increases trust and understanding and fosters consumer-professional interdependence (Condeluci, 1996). The convergence of diverse groups of persons with and without disabilities led to the passage of the Americans with Disabilities Act. The creation of federally funded centers for independent living occurred as people with disabilities advocated for themselves and professionals and policy makers listened and acted. As the human service professions begin to welcome increased numbers of persons with disabilities as colleagues and peers, we will be increasingly equipped to act in the roles of advocates, brokers, community planners, and policy developers.

This means that human service professionals must be taught political skills by human service educators (Tower, 1994). It means that human service professionals must become involved with local, state, and national elections by volunteering time and money. And it means that human service professionals must access politicians to support policies and programs that empower and promote the independence of persons with disabilities.

◆   Case Examples

We include several case examples here to illustrate and identify major points made throughout this chapter and to help readers apply the principles used in the text.

The Author

An understanding of the impact of oppression on persons with disabilities is crucial to the counseling role of human service practitioners. The life experience of one of the authors, Richard Salsgiver, reflects the impact of devaluation and oppression. He was born with cerebral palsy, institutionalized between the ages of 6 and 12, and received a master's degree in social work and a doctorate of arts in history as an adult. He moved to California in 1984 at the age of 38. As you read his story, identify the impact that the dominant view of disability has had on his life. Take into account the decisions made about him as a child, his self-perceptions, and the process of coming out with a disability to himself and others. In addition, identify the role a counselor played in this process.

> *I came to California in 1984 after being a successful mental health worker in a private psychiatric/school facility in western Pennsylvania. My first job in California was that of a social worker at the Golden Gate Regional Center in San Francisco. The first day on the job I met a person, herself a person with a disability, who would become a lifelong friend. When I referred to myself over lunch as "handicapped," she jumped down my throat. She informed me that the correct term was "person with a disability." I replied that it didn't really matter what I called myself. She replied that it did. She proceeded to tell me about the independent living movement, a story (which I didn't realize at the time) that would change my whole life.*

> *In Pennsylvania, my friends and professional colleagues rarely acknowledged my disability. I never perceived myself as a person with a disability. I remember catching a glimpse in a store window of myself walking with my crutches, and being taken aback that this was not really me. I negated my need for accommodation. I bought a three-story house that sat on a bank with stairs leading up to the entrance. It had no garage. Even though it was hell getting to it in the winter, I never let my disability enter into the decision to purchase the house.*

> *At my work, issues of accessibility were not even an afterthought. I remember going to a social work conference where I slipped and fell on the ice. The injury to my hip was so severe that I could get into my car only with great difficulty. I pulled myself in and drove home, however; I could hardly get into the house. The next day I took two students to the local community college to meet with the admissions counselor; I refused to acknowledge the pain in my hip or the fact that I could hardly walk with my crutches. I had to prove that "I was not like the rest of them." This incident is representative of my attitude at the time, supported by my friends and colleagues, that I was not really "handicapped."*

In California, things began to change. I quickly became immersed in the independent living movement. I took a management position at the Center for Independent Living in Belmont, California. There I became involved not only in the practice of independent living but in politics and political advocacy on all levels. In 1986, I moved into the executive directorship of the California Association of the Physically Handicapped (now the Center for Independent Living) in Fresno, California. Here I was truly engulfed in disability. The majority of my staff were persons with disabilities. The members of my board of directors were persons with disabilities. The professionals on the state and national levels I worked with were mostly persons with disabilities. I began to feel resentment and anger and I didn't know why. I began to hate to come to work and to hate dealing with my staff and board. My hatred and anger turned into depression, and I sought help. One of my staff members told me about a local social worker in private practice she had met at a party, who seemed really good. I called him. Fortunately, the therapist understood disability and the oppression around disability. He opened up points of understanding that had been hidden in me for years. We explored the years of institutionalization and society's stereotypes of persons with disabilities. We explored the impact of the stereotypes on my family and how that influenced their treatment of me. This knowledge helped me understand my anger toward and resentment of my colleagues and other persons with disabilities. That knowledge allowed me to embrace myself as a person with a disability as a positive self-loved being. It allowed me to embrace other people with disabilities as truly beautiful and whole.

In the years since I started integrating my disability into my concept of self, I have witnessed others as they have struggled with the shame and internalized ableism and sought to embrace themselves, disability and all. I have seen persons with disabilities acting as mentors helping others integrate disability into their definition of who they are. One tremendous source of personal strength is my tie to an international disability community that is just beginning the long journey of changing how society perceives us. This community has fostered a collective disability pride and identity.

Robert and Lisa

The following is the case example of Robert and Lisa (pseudonyms), two young nursing home residents with quadriplegia from neuromuscular disabilities who were able to leave the nursing home and begin living in the community. Their case, which was mentioned briefly in Chapter 11, provides readers an opportunity to assess human service practices. Contrast the impact of the social model and the medical model approaches used to identify their problems and apply intervention strategies. Had a traditional model of intervention been employed, what strategies would likely have been used to help Robert and Lisa? What was the impact of self-determination and community resources in their lives? What systems and system levels were targets for professional intervention? Identify professional functions and roles utilized. In what areas of personal advocacy and self-management did Robert and Lisa participate? Identify community resources employed to enhance their lives. Describe the relationship and power balances between professionals and consumers.

Robert and Lisa were residents of a large nursing home with a unit devoted to young residents (under 60 years of age). Robert had come to the nursing home to leave his small community and live in an urban area. Lisa left her parents' home because she wanted to "break away" and live "on my own." When they met in the nursing home, they fell in love. They wanted to room together, but the nursing home staff, with the strong concurrence of Robert's and Lisa's families, refused.

A social work consultant was brought in by the nursing home with the consent of Robert and Lisa. Nursing home staff members were concerned that Robert and Lisa were not ready for a sexual relationship, emphasizing their physical limitations. They also identified Robert as "borderline mentally retarded" and as being depressed. Lisa was diagnosed with depression and as lacking social skills. Robert and Lisa were upset that the nursing home did not allow them freedom and self-determination.

The social worker was initially sought to provide counseling for the couple. Individual and couples counseling was provided; however, it was clear that meso-level interventions were needed. Robert and Lisa both strongly expressed desires to live in the community and become more autonomous.

At the meso level, the social worker began acting as a mediator between the couple and the nursing home so that Robert and Lisa could spend more time together in their courtship. The social worker helped the couple articulate their needs. They were able to reach agreements about dating outside the facility and to alter schedules and activities inside the facility. The facility had to expend more resources to meet their demands.

Robert's "borderline" diagnosis had been used to withhold decision-making authority from him. He now wanted to challenge this pattern. The nursing home's corporate office used this diagnosis to stop the couple from rooming together because of concerns about liability if they became sexually active. The social worker acted as a broker by helping Robert contact a legal center that provided services to persons with disabilities. They helped Robert assert his right to self-determination by having him judged "competent" to handle his own affairs. The nursing home was then allowed/forced to deal with Robert exclusively rather than relying on the wishes of Robert's parents, which sometimes conflicted with Robert's desires. This opened the door for Robert and Lisa to room together.

Robert's and Lisa's case forced the nursing home to reassess its practices relative to unmarried persons rooming together. The social worker was instrumental as a policy developer in helping the facility develop policies that would allow for greater self-determination of its residents.

The role of community developer was critical for the social worker. Robert, Lisa, and others in similar situations were catalysts to creating noninstitutional community living situations for persons with disabilities. With the involvement of several consumers, professionals, and agencies, community living resources were developed to allow people with physical disabilities to live outside institutions. Robert, Lisa, and others were anxious to let people know they were in nursing homes, not by choice or need, but because there were no resources for them to live outside nursing homes. The social worker acted as an educator to help them make their stories known and to self-advocate. Mona, a woman with a spinal cord injury, went public with a news story to chronicle her plight of being forced to live in a nursing home. She demonstrated that she could live in an apartment with attendant care, at much less cost to the state than living in the nursing home. Robert and Lisa attended a city council meeting to ask them to set aside public housing for people with needs similar to theirs. The social worker who worked with Robert and Lisa, along with other human service workers, acted as a consultant to help them determine effective strategies, but consumers were responsible. At the request of consumers, human service workers acted as advocates to help with increasing access to housing, transportation, and community-independent living services.

Eventually, Robert and Lisa located housing outside the nursing home. The community housing authority provided subsidized accessible housing and the state social services agency provided funding for personal care attendants. Lisa (and Mona) moved into individual apartments. Robert moved to a residence with three roommates with disabilities. He continued to consult a human service professional for financial planning help but controlled his personal affairs. By the time they moved out, Robert and Lisa's relationship had developed platonically, and they remained friends.

Theron Sloan

The following case of Theron Sloan (pseudonym) is an additional example of multiple professional roles in direct service provision. Identify the roles of the direct practitioner. What was the power balance between Theron and the practitioner? What are the strengths and weaknesses of the approach used by the clinician on a systems level? What are the advantages and disadvantages of this approach for nondisabled family members of persons with disabilities? What were the circumstances in order for other professionals to be used as resources? How were Theron's relationships with other professionals influenced?

Theron Sloan was a 27-year-old male with a disability from a closed head injury sustained in a motorcycle accident that occurred six months prior to his seeking help from a social worker. As a result of his head injury, Theron had left-sided weakness and was on medication for seizures. He also had short-term memory problems and would "lose control" emotionally under stress. He had worked, prior to his disability, as an accountant. His primary reason for seeking counseling was for help with depression.

The social worker began individual counseling and worked with Theron on issues of self-esteem and reclaiming control over his life. He also began to educate Theron on strategies to help him compensate for his memory difficulties, such as keeping a log of activities and writing down his plans and activities at the beginning of each day.

Early in the relationship, the social worker realized Theron was having marital difficulties and suggested that Theron consider marriage counseling. When Theron declined, however, the social worker respected his wishes and did not push for marriage counseling even though he knew marital problems were an ongoing stress. Although the social worker was not employed in an independent living center, he used an IL approach, reasoning that Theron was capable of deciding on interventions that were in his best interests.

During counseling, Theron revealed that he had been having difficulty with his physician, who he felt was unresponsive to his needs. He was frustrated because he wanted to work again but was unable to return to his previous employment. In addition, he felt socially isolated from others. The social worker could have acted as a case manager by arranging for various services. Using an independent living counselor approach, however, he began planning with Theron to address his problems. Theron wrote out a list of his frustrations with his physician; he and the social worker then role-played talking with his physician about the concerns on the list. The social worker identified a vocational rehabilitation counselor with whom Theron could work. Theron called the counselor from the social worker's office, using the social worker as support. The social worker also gave Theron the names of key people in the head injury community who could act as resources. In these activities, the social worker used the roles of consultant and broker.

Theron maintained his relationship with the social worker for a period of several months. At one point, Theron disclosed that he and his wife were having sexual problems and requested help. The social worker, acting as a marital therapist, provided help for the couple's sexual problems. The social worker also referred Theron to a physician to evaluate the effects of physical problems and/or medications on sexual functioning.

A. Bruce Benet

In reviewing the case of A. Bruce Benet (pseudonym), identify elements of self-advocacy and personal empowerment. Discuss the impact of defining Bruce's personal problems in their social context. What was the value of a peer counselor in this scenario?

A. Bruce Benet had developed a malignant tumor at the base of his spine, which, when removed, left him paralyzed from the waist down. He was released from a local rehabilitation hospital and referred to a peer counselor at the local independent living center.

Bruce exhibited long periods of depression with occasional outbursts of anger. At his first session, he was an hour late for his appointment. The lift on the local transit bus broke halfway into the process of loading Bruce and his wheelchair. The driver told him that all the lifts on the buses were in poor repair but the county refused to allocate money to fix them. Upon arriving at the independent living center, he was furious. He told the peer counselor (after he waited for another hour because of the counselor's next appointment) what had happened. The peer counselor suggested that he involve himself in the local transit advisory meeting where citizens could give input into transit issues. The peer counselor provided Bruce with the place and time of the next meeting. When Bruce expressed his intent to attend, the peer counselor told Bruce to let him know at the next session what had happened.

At the next session, Bruce was like a different person. He was neither angry nor depressed but intense. Attending the meeting was a singular event for Bruce. He told the counselor that at the meeting there were two other wheelchair riders angry about the same thing—lifts on public buses that didn't work. The county representative blew off their statements, saying that there was simply no money to fix the buses. After the meeting, Bruce got together with the other two concerned citizens at the local "watering hole." They decided to form a political action group to force the county to put more resources into its accessibility of public transit.

The peer counselor, a wheelchair user himself, listened intently. He offered to come to the next meeting of the "group" to discuss different political strategies that might work. He also referred Bruce to a friend of his who worked for one of the county supervisors interested in public transit. This gave Bruce access to the formal decision-making system. As Bruce began to self-advocate, he not only started to feel better about himself, but he was making a contribution to the larger disability community. He began to apply his understanding that his problems extended beyond himself to the social system and societal institutions.

◆ SUMMARY

Six principles guide our approach to working with persons with disabilities. First, we assume that people are capable or potentially capable. Second, we reject traditional methods of practice that assume that the problem with disability lies with the person and that individuals with disabilities must change or "be fixed" before they can function adequately in society. Third, we believe that any model of practice applied to working with persons with disabilities must assume that disability is a social construct and that the primary emphasis on intervention must be political in nature. Fourth, we believe in an identity and culture of disability. Fifth, although persons with disabilities have experienced oppression, we strongly believe that there is joy to be found in disability. Sixth, we believe that persons with disabilities are without question the ones in control of their lives. This means that the consumer controls the professional.

These six principles become the pillars of our practice model. This model rests upon these pillars and upon principles of strengths–based practice and empowerment. Further, we adopt a social model of disability with a consumer-driven model of practice. Our practice model proposes four fundamental functions for the human service practitioner working with persons with disabilities: counselor, teacher, broker, and political activist or advocate. Several roles are involved within these functions. The functions of counselor and teacher are used basically on the micro and meso levels. Brokers function at all three levels, whereas the role of political activist or advocate plays out in the meso and macro arenas.

◆   ◆   ◆

Discussion Question

Apply the model of practice presented in this chapter to the following scenario: You are a rehabilitation social worker at a major midwestern rehabilitation hospital in the United States. You have been presented the following case:

> *Anthony Mares is a 43-year-old male with blindness as a result of a progressive degenerative eye condition. Married, with three children (ages 15, 13, and 6), Anthony worked for 20 years, until recently, as an auto mechanic. His wife, Patty, age 41, has worked as a homemaker. She has also worked part-time as a billing clerk out of her home. The Mares are buying a home in a small community that is 25 miles from the city in which your hospital is located. Anthony is depressed over his recent loss of sight. He exhibits a depressed affect and displays anger to hospital staff; his wife states he is "rejecting" her. You have been referred to the case because he is caus-ing trouble for staff and because he needs help with discharge from the hospital, due to occur in three days.*

How would you assess Anthony and his family using a strengths perspective? Compare how you would view working with Anthony from a traditional and from a social model of intervention. What are the functions and roles you might use in working with Anthony? Discuss strategies you might use to help Anthony with empowerment. Discuss how a case manager would handle this case and compare this to an independent living counselor.

Suggested Readings

Blotzer, M. A., and Ruth, R. (1995). *Sometimes you just want to feel like a human being: Case studies of empowering psychotherapy with people with disabilities.* Baltimore: Paul H. Brookes.

Hahn, H. (1993). Can disability be beautiful? In M. Nagler (Ed.), *Perspectives in disability* (2nd ed.) (pp. 213–216). Palo Alto, CA: Health Markets Research.

Tower, K. D. (1994). Consumer-centered social work practice: Restoring client self-determination. *Social Work, 41*(1), 191–196.

Wright, B. (1960). *Physical disability—a psychological approach.* New York: Harper & Row.

References

Blotzer, M. A., and Ruth, R. (1995). *Sometimes you just want to feel like a human being: Case studies of empowering psychotherapy with people with disabilities.* Baltimore: Paul H. Brookes.

Bowe, F. (1983). Accessible transportation. In N. M. Crewe and I. K. Zola (Eds.), *Independent living for physically disabled people* (pp. 205–218). San Francisco: Jossey-Bass.

Chan, V. C. (1989). Issues of identity development among Asian–American lesbians and gay men. *Journal of Counseling & Development, 68*, 16–20.

Cole, J. A. (1983). Skills training. In N.M. Crewe and I.K. Zola (Eds.), *Independent living for physically disabled people* (pp. 187–204). San Francisco: Jossey-Bass.

Coleman, E. (1982). Developmental stages of the coming out process. *Journal of Homosexuality, 7*(2/3), 31–43.

Condeluci, A. (1996). *Interdependence: The route to community* (2nd ed.). Winter Park, FL: GR Press.

Cowger, C. D. (1994). Assessing client strengths: Clinical assessment for client empowerment. *Social Work, 39*(3), 262–269.

DeJong, G. (1979). *The movement for independent living: Origins, ideology, and implications for disability research.* East Lansing: Michigan State University, Center for International Rehabilitation.

DeJong, G., and Wenker, T. (1983). Attendant care. In N. M. Crewe and I. K. Zola (Eds.), *Independent living for physically disabled people* (pp. 157–170). San Francisco: Jossey-Bass.

Emener, W. G. (1991). An empowerment philosophy for rehabilitation in the 20th century. *The Journal of Rehabilitation, 57*(4), 7–13.

Fine, M., and Asch, A. (1988). Disability beyond stigma: Social interaction, discrimination, and activism. *Journal of Social Issues, 44*(1), 3–21.

Gutiérrez, L. M. (1990). Working with women of color: An empowerment perspective. *Social Work, 35*(2), 149–153.

Hahn, H. (1993). Can disability be beautiful? In M. Nagler (Ed.), *Perspectives in disability* (2nd ed.) (pp. 213–216). Palo Alto, CA: Health Markets Research.

Hahn, H. (1991). Alternative views on empowerment: Social services and civil rights. *The Journal of Rehabilitation, 57*(4), 17–20.

Hepworth, D. H., Rooney, R. H., and Larsen, J. (1997). *Direct social work practice: Theory and skills* (5th ed.). Pacific Grove, CA: Brooks/Cole.

Joiner, J. G., Lovett, P. S., and Goodwin, L. K. (1989). Positive assertion and acceptance among persons with disabilities. *The Journal of Rehabilitation, 55*(3), 22–30.

Mackelprang, R. W, and Salsgiver, R. O. (1996). People with disabilities and social work: Historical and contemporary issues. *Social Work, 41*(1), 7–14.

Onken, S. J., and Mackelprang, R. W (1997). Building on shared experiences: Teaching disability and sexual minority content and practice. Presented at the Annual Program Meeting, Council on Social Work Education, Chicago, IL.

Orr, E., Thein, R. D., and Aronson, E. (1995). Orthopedic disability, conformity, and social support. *The Journal of Psychology, 129*(2), 203–220.

Saleebey, D. (Ed.) (1992). *The strengths perspective in social work practice.* New York: Longman.

Salsgiver, R. O. (1996). Perspectives on families with children with disabilities. *SCI Psychosocial Process, 9*(1), 18–23.

Shapiro, J. P. (1993). *No pity: People with disabilities, forging a new civil rights movement.* New York: Times Books.

Smith, M. J. (1975). *When I say no I feel guilty: How to cope using skills of systemic therapy.* New York: Dial Press.

Solomon, B. B. (1976). *Black empowerment: Social work in oppressed communities.* New York: Columbia University Press.

Sullivan, P. M., and Scanlan, J. M. (1990). Psychotherapy with handicapped sexually abused children. *Developmental Disabilities, 18*(2), 21–24.

Sussman, M. B. (1977). Dependent disabled and dependent poor: Similarity of conceptual issues and research needs. In S. Tubbins (Ed.), *Social and psychological aspects of disability* (pp. 247–249). Baltimore: University Park Press.

Tower, K. D. (1994). Consumer-centered social work practice: Restoring client self-determination. *Social Work, 41*(1), 191–196.

Troiden, R. R. (1993). The formation of homosexual identities. In L. D. Garnets and D. C. Kimmel (Eds.), *Psychosocial perspectives on lesbian & gay male experiences* (pp. 191–217). New York: Columbia University Press.

Wiggins, S. F. (1983). Specialized housing. In N. M. Crewe and I. K. Zola (Eds.), *Independent living for physically disabled people* (pp. 219–244). San Francisco: Jossey-Bass.

Wright, B. (1960). *Physical disability—a psychological approach.* New York: Harper & Row.

Zola, I. K. (1983). Developing new self-images and interdependence. In N. M. Crewe and I. K. Zola (Eds.), *Independent living for physically disabled people* (pp. 49–59). San Francisco: Jossey-Bass.

INDEX

TO THE OWNER OF THIS BOOK:

We hope that you have found *Disability: A Diversity Model Approach in Human Service Practice* useful. So that this book can be improved in a future edition, would you take the time to complete this sheet and return it? Thank you.

School and address: ─────────────────────────────────

Department: ──────────────────────────────────────

Instructor's name: ──────────────────────────────────

1. What I like most about this book is: ──────────────────────

──

──

2. What I like least about this book is: ─────────────────────

──

──

3. My general reaction to this book is: ──────────────────────

──

4. The name of the course in which I used this book is: ───────────

──

5. Were all of the chapters of the book assigned for you to read? ──────────

   If not, which ones weren't? ─────────────────────────

6. In the space below, or on a separate sheet of paper, please write specific suggestions for improving this book and anything else you'd care to share about your experience in using the book.

──

──

──

──

──

Optional:

Your name: _____ Date: _____

May Brooks/Cole quote you, either in promotion for *Disability: A Diversity Model Approach in Human Service Practice* or in future publishing ventures?

Yes: _____ No: _____

Sincerely,

Romel W Mackelprang
Richard O. Salsgiver

FOLD HERE

FOLD HERE